This English edition is a translation of the original Spanish edition *De la mano de Joaquín Rodrigo*, published by the Fundación Banco Exterior in 1986.

Cover art from the Brambilla collection *Views of the Royal Sites*, Library of the Royal Palace, Madrid. Courtesy of the Patrimonio Nacional de España.

HAND IN HAND WITH JOAQUIN RODRIGO: MY LIFE AT THE MAESTRO'S SIDE

HAND IN HAND WITH JOAQUIN RODRIGO: MY LIFE AT THE MAESTRO'S SIDE

by

VICTORIA KAMHI DE RODRIGO

Translation

by

ELLEN WILKERSON

Prologue

by

PEDRO ROCAMORA

LATIN AMERICAN LITERARY REVIEW PRESS
SERIES: DISCOVERIES
PITTSBURGH, PENNSYLVANIA

YVETTE E. MILLER, EDITOR

1992

The Latin American Literary Review Press publishes Latin American creative writing under the series title *Discoveries*, and critical works under the series title *Explorations*.

Library of Congress Cataloging-in-Publication Data

Kamhi de Rodrigo, Victoria.
[De la mano de Joaquín Rodrigo. English]
Hand in hand with Joaquín Rodrigo: my life at the maestro's side / by Victorira Kamhi de Rodrigo ; translated by Ellen Wilkerson ; prologue by Pedro Rocamora.
p. cm. -- (Discoveries)
Translation of: De la mano de Joaquín Rodrigo.
Includes index.
ISBN 0-935480-51-X
1. Rodrigo, Joaquín. 2. Kamhi de Rodrigo, Victoria.
3. Composers--Spain--Biography. 4. Pianists--Spain--Biography.
I. Title. II. Series.
ML410.R6318K313 1992
780'.92'2--dc20 91-22154
[B] CIP
MN

Cover design by Ewa Kamienska

Hand in Hand with Joaquín Rodrigo: My Life at the Maestro's Side may be ordered directly from the publisher:

Latin American Literary Review Press
2300 Palmer Street, Pittsburgh, PA 15218
Tel (412) 351-1477 Fax (412) 351-6831

TABLE OF CONTENTS

Prologue

This is a book of memories written by a delightful feminine pen. Victoria Kamhi was born in Turkey. She recalls from her childhood a background of almost legendary scenes: Constantinople, the Golden Horn in the background—silhouettes of mosques, their white minarets gilded by the setting sun. Echoes of ancient Byzantium, footprints of the past. Victoria Kamhi has seen the courts of the Turkish Sultans passing in parade along the banks of the Bosporus, whose waters change from green to blue or silver with the changing light of day. She has lived in an ancient world of religious sacrifices, caravans to Mecca, prayers in the Synagogue. Her childhood is an interplay of Greek and Byzantine sounds. Everything that surrounds her increases her exceptional sensitivity. The atmosphere of beauty in which she lives sharpens the call of Art. And Victoria devotes herself to the vocation of music.

Far away, across the continent of Europe, in a small town of the Spanish Levant, there is a boy who, when barely beginning to live—at only three years of age—must learn to live without sight. His name is Joaquín Rodrigo.

Is there a fate which can bring two lives together? The poets say that the surest thing is chance. And perhaps it is true that what the world sees as impossible in the end, becomes the most likely.

For these lives met. Paris. The *Preludio al gallo mañanero*. The Théâtre des Champs-Elysées. *Cinco Piezas Infantiles*. It was as if a mysterious force had bound two destinies together.

For more than half a century Victoria Kamhi has led one of the most distinguished musicians of our time by the hand. She has been a light confronting darkness and sorrow. And at the same time, an inspiration for the creation she has encouraged by her faith in the ultimate result of hard work, a faith she has maintained among the ashes of hopelessness and doubt.

In the music of Joaquín Rodrigo the memory of things dreamed of is reborn, the remembrance of things he scarcely knew, lost in a reliquary of colors. Within that innermost sanctuary—the interior garden of a Mystic—the maestro finds his arpeggios of light.

That is why Joaquín Rodrigo always speaks with a smile, smiling at life. Perhaps he smiles that others will not be saddened for him, or that they will feel that he is happy in his shadowy labyrinth. He is happy, as are all artists. For great creators find the most joy in living. And Rodrigo has the enjoyment of his music, his supreme illuminating grace.

Joaquín Rodrigo's luminous thought is the secret of his art. Inventor of a beauty in which painting and poetry are merged, he presents Spanish music to us while trying to hide his enormous sensitivity behind an appearance of childlike shyness. One might think that the maestro has continued definitively—to smile now and forever—that same smile with which, in infancy, he contemplated the blue horizon, and the flowering countryside of his Levantine homeland. He has traveled the world since then. But he has been spared the knowledge of the dirty, wrong side of things, the sadness of our cities, blackened by time, from whose streets one can no longer see the sky. In this the composer is fortunate. For he still has, alive in his heart, what the rest of us have lost. In our desire to see and dominate everything, we have made of our life a somber winter, and of the earth, a world without stars.

Joaquín Rodrigo walks in the radiance of his music. It is a music without dramatic effects or bitterness. It contains a message that is pure and deep, lyric and delicate. He gives us what he has not received. He does not seek to arouse our anguish or our tension. His concertos, his poems and his songs tell us that not everything in this moonless forest through which we wander, is lost. Instead of our own darkness, he offers us a miracle: the sonorous uniqueness of his work. And he offers it in such a way that the flashes of insight from his music may give us courage and save us from life's bitterness.

This is the man who Victoria Kamhi has evoked with her descriptive words. But through this book the readers perceives not only the events of two lives, but an impressionistic sketch of an entire epoch.

The reader begins to walk through the author's historic time, and is captured by the story. The purely quotidian details become a novelistic enchantment. The narrative is lineal, as befits the biographical genre, but personal circumstance has sown this woman's life with drama. She is reflected in her memories just as light that plays along the surface of a lake can suggest the profound nostalgia of its depths.

Victoria Kamhi turns her gaze to the past and tells us her human experience. With each stroke of the pen she defines a figure, sketches a nuance—pages written between memory and forgetfulness. The memories are shadows that permit one to reconstruct a past sometimes tinged with melancholy. The literary accent becomes almost lyrical. And a powerfully communicative emotion seems to tremble in the written confession. Here there is no room for an indifferent reader. Something attractive and fascinating is the secret of this book, written totally without artifice. Its style is natural and simple.

In Victoria Kamhi's purpose the autobiographical form is expanded and amplified. She does not aspire to be the sole object of contemplation. What she wants is for her personality to be integrated with that of the singular personality with whom she has shared her years as a woman in love. That is the reason for the transference which occurs regarding the biographical protagonist. What begins by telling, step by step, the peripateia of her life, will end up exalting—with ineffable tenderness—the image of the man who has been for her, Maestro, friend, husband and companion.

By the end of the book the reader realizes that Joaquín Rodrigo and Victoria Kamhi have set an admirable example of work done with enthusiasm and, at the same time, with abnegation. Neither of them sought triumph or riches.

They know that the luxury of the artist is inspiration.

Pedro Rocamora

Playing a XIX Century "Pleyel" at the Palace of Aranjuez, 1990.
(Photograph courtesy of the "Patrimonio Nacional" of the
Spanish government).

PART I

To send light
into the depths of the human heart
is the profession of the artist.

Robert Schumann

Chapter I

A Happy Childhood

At the beginning of this century Besiktas was still a suburb of Constantinople, situated on the European coast of the Bosporus, about three kilometers from the old bridge over the Golden Horn. In ancient times its name had been *Diplokyon*, which means "Double Columns." History tells us that the *Fatih*, Mohammed the Conqueror, disembarked on the Byzantine coast, probably between Besiktas and Dolma Bahcé, where the palace of the Sultans of Turkey was later built. To the east of Besiktas once stood the ancient palace of Ciragan, but only its ruins remain.

The palace of Dolma Bahcé was built in the year 1858 by the Sultan Abdul Mescid, who entrusted the work to the architect Balian. Previously, the Sultans had lived in Topkapi palace, whose fabulous treasures attract visitors from the entire world. Topkapi was built soon after the taking of Constantinople in 1462. As for Dolma Bahcé, it is a magnificent building of Oriental style, surrounded by marvelous gardens.

Adjacent to the great reception hall, with its air of pomp and luxury, are several apartments with frescoes by famous painters. Here were lodged the composers, Liszt and Donizetti, and other outstanding musicians, who gave brilliant concerts.

All the last sultans of Turkey lived at Dolma Bahcé, except the Sultan Abdul Hamid—"the red Sultan"—who retired to the palace of Yildiz.

Mustafa Kemal Ataturk also lived in Dolma Bahcé until the end of his life, dying there in 1938.

Besiktas was famous for its magnificent climate and for its health-giving waters, flowing from many natural springs in the area.

The great boulevard between Dolma Bahcé, Yildiz and Ciragan was very imposing in the times of the sultans. It had been designed by the architect Garnier, the same man who drew the plans for the Paris Opera.

The beautiful trees, wide-spreading, tall and leafy, which shaded the luxurious palaces along the way, are still there. And along the boulevard, every Friday, passed the court of the sultan, when he would go, before all the people, to pray at the mosque on the day of *Selamlik*. It was a fabulous sight, engraved forever in my memory, since I saw it so often with the impressionable eyes of a little girl.

Along the main street of Besiktas, not very far from the palace of Dolma Bahcé, stood the three houses of the Kamhi family, connected by a wide terrace on the upper floor. My grandparents lived in the middle house, with my parents on one side, and Uncle Vitali and his family on the other.

My grandfather, Rafael Kamhi, had launched his career at the age of eleven. An orphan, he had gone to work as a messenger boy in an uncle's business establishment. He worked eleven or twelve hours a day there, supporting his slightly older sister, Kadun. Soon he was able to establish his own business, a drug store, and he married. He had nine children: seven sons, with whom he founded the firm Rafael Kamhi and Sons, and two daughters.

My father, Isaac, was the fifth son. Because he demonstrated a great aptitude for study, he was sent to Marseille, where he received a degree from the Business School.

During a trip to Vienna he met my mother, Sofia Arditti, who was then twenty years old. She was slim and blonde, with blue eyes and fair skin. She had a Nordic type beauty, while my father, with his curly black hair and great dark eyes, looked very oriental. They were a most attractive couple and dressed with great elegance.

Mamá had studied the piano and she sang very well. They were both devotees of music. They had only two daughters. I was the elder, two-and-a-half years older than my sister Mathilde.

Our houses in Besiktas were built on the *yali* [coast], just a few yards from the Bosporus. From the dining room window I used to watch its waters, changing from blue to green or silver according to the weather or the time of day.

Innumerable ships, some of considerable tonnage, made their way through the strait, transporting merchandise to the Black Sea ports: to Bulgaria, or Russia or Rumania. But we also saw a multitude of small steamers called "mouches," crowded with passengers, which ferried back and forth between the European and the Asiatic river banks.

For me, these steamers were fascinating. On board, ambulant vendors offered every kind of treat: crusty, twisted rolls covered with sesame seeds called *semit,* a kind of cookie called *pandespaña* [Spanish bread], cookies called *curabies*, caramels, hazelnuts, toasted chick-peas, soft drinks.

Sometimes we traveled on a steamer to Kavak, the last little village on the European bank, and there I would stare at the imposing cliffs that stood at the entrance to the Black Sea, whose waters were usually turbulent.

In winter, thick fog drifted over the cold water, wrapping everything in an immense white curtain. Then one could see only a few pale lights gleaming through the mist, like phantom ships slipping silently through the choppy waves.

The lugubrious sound of their horns filled the air day and night; the sound gave me cold chills.

But with spring came a total change of atmosphere.

Both banks of the strait were covered with an exuberant burst of bloom: white marguerites, blue and red anemones, lilacs and jasmine. The Judas tree clothed itself in a rose-colored shawl. The restaurants and cafeterias of Bebek and Terapia opened their doors, and all was bustle and gaiety.

At the time I was born, my grandfather was regarded as one of the most important businessmen of the Balkans. He had founded the finest drug business in the country, with several factories scattered through the Peninsula. My father often used to travel to Anatolia to check on the different branches, which operated perfectly in competent hands. My grandfather's office was in the headquarters building, Kamhi Han, in old Istanbul. When my father took me there with him, I would marvel at the enormous sacks of spices from all parts of the globe. What attracted me most were the little white shells that were used as a sort of pendant on horses, to protect them from "the evil eye." They were inlaid with little beads of blue crystal that frightened away the evil spirits. My grandfather would give me a handful of anything that pleased me, smiling kindly at my happiness.

Riches and honors had not corrupted my grandfather's noble soul. His modesty was as great as his generosity and his talent. With his long gray beard and his simple clothing, he recalled the patriarchs of ancient times. He ate frugally, spoke little and left his home only to go to his work. He inspired a profound respect in us children, tinged with a little fear, and when we committed some mischief, a threat to tell it to grandfather was enough to make us obedient. In spite of that, I don't remember ever having seen him angry with me.

As he was very religious, all the liturgical holy days were celebrated in his house in the traditional manner. He gave large sums of money to hospitals and synagogues, and alms to the poor, who often knocked at the door. He supported his sister, Aunt Kadun, and her husband, as well as his two old friends, "Cibi Zahar," and "Avram el Preto," who were his inseparable companions until the end of his life.

My grandmother was his second wife; her name was Vida. I remember her as a woman of medium height, a little chubby. Her hair was gray, and she always wore it very carefully arranged. She dressed simply, but on the feast days she would wear gowns of costly silk. When she left the house, a sable cape imported from Russia covered her shoulders.

I was her favorite grandchild, and whenever I went to see her—at least once a day—she would give me a sweet or a toy. Until I was seven I was never far from her, and when my parents moved to the flat in Perá, I was grief-stricken.

Like all children, I loved to spend time in the kitchen. My grandparents' kitchen was spacious, and as busy as a beehive, with four or five servants coming and going, laughing and humming. Overseeing all of this was the cook, "tía Lunachi" a stout, energetic women, and a true master of her trade. Her specialty was puff-pastry, and I remember that on holy days and Saturdays the dining room table would nearly collapse from the weight of the *borekas*, and pepper pastries, the *bulemas*, and all the other delicacies typical of Oriental cooking.

It was tía Lunachi who saved my life when I was nine months old. One night when all the family had gathered in my grandparents' living room, several people expressed the desire to see the baby, who was beginning to be "cute." My nurse, a young girl named Perla, gave me a chicken neck to play with, and carelessly let me put it in my mouth. I swallowed a sharp piece of bone, which lodged in my throat. I began to choke before the terrified eyes of everyone present, all of them incapable of giving me aid. My mother, seeing my face turn purple and my eyes roll back, became hysterical. Screaming loudly, she hit a window pane with such force that it shattered, and she cut a vein. She carried the scar all her life.

At that time there were no telephones, so servants were quickly sent to find a doctor, with scant hope that he would arrive in time. It was then that tía Lunachi, attracted by the uproar, came flying up from the kitchen. "Give me the child," she ordered. Laying me across her knees, she put her fingers down my throat and removed the bone with an air of triumph. The general happiness was indescribable, and tía Lunachi received much praise for her accomplishment, in addition to a handsome gift from my father.

As for the unfortunate nursemaid, who was dismissed on the spot, she visited us at our home in Paris many years later. She was returning from Chile where, after her marriage, she had made a fortune founding a chain of department stores similar to "Galeries Lafayette." She offered us her full hospitality.

I made my first trip abroad at the age of nine months, when my parents took me on a voyage to Varna, the picturesque Bulgarian city on the banks of the Black Sea, to visit my Aunt Beya, older sister of my mother, and Uncle Bito. My maternal grandmother, Mazal Arditti, upon the death of her husband, had retired to Rustchuk—a Bulgarian city on the banks of the Danube. The marriage had been a happy one, and they had had twelve children, nine of whom survived. My grandmother was light-hearted and witty, and we loved to spend summer vacations at her house, a chalet surrounded by an enormous garden full of flowers and fruit trees. I remember the old almond tree with its twisted trunk, the plums loaded with juicy fruit, and the tree full of sweet jujubes which I gathered every morning. There my sister and I joined our little cousins and other children of the neighborhood to run and play. Those were happy days which I will always remember.

My mother told me that I began to walk very early, at nine months, and that when I began to run, I looked like a wound-up doll. I also started to talk early, and by the time I was four, I spoke several languages. This was not unusual among the children of Constantinople, then a very cosmopolitan city. I spoke Turkish, Spanish, French, German and modern Greek, which I learned at primary school, the *mestra.*

Sometimes, while playing alone, I would hide under the dining room table. The heavy table cover almost reached the floor. I spent long hours there, in the company of a kitten, or cuddling my favorite doll. That was my refuge, an escape from the noisy, common world.

My love of plants and animals manifested itself very early. Mamá tells of a strange thing that happened when I was only three, and which reminds me of tales from *The Thousand And One Nights.*

It was a lovely spring day, and I had gone out to walk with my nurse. The best place to stretch one's legs a little was along Pasa Mahalé, the principal street of Besiktas, whose sidewalk was wide enough for two people. It had rained earlier, and small white and yellow flowers were pushing up from the humid earth. Attracted by the humble marguerites and ranunculus, I let go of my nurse's hand and knelt down to gather them. I had composed quite a bouquet, but I wanted more flowers, and I wandered off a little way to continue looking for them.

Suddenly a beautiful carriage came down the street towards us, drawn by two spirited Arabian horses and followed by two black eunuchs on horseback. In the carriage were two women from the harem of Dolma Bahcé palace; perhaps they were princesses, for they wore silk gowns of vivid colors, and their faces were covered by the white veil which was the privilege of women of high rank. When they noticed the baby girl—so tiny—who was eagerly searching for flowers along the sidewalk, they ordered the coachman to stop. A little window was opened far enough for them to toss out a magnificent bouquet of roses and jasmine that fell at my feet. They gave me a friendly wave and smile, and then the carriage continued rapidly on its way. The exciting news spread quickly through the district, and the neighbors dropped by to admire the gift from the harem princesses and to congratulate the entire family.

And what can I say about my passion for cats and dogs, for birds and other animals? Once, one of my father's friends gave me two little rabbits, which two men delivered in a large cage to place in the garden. Speechless with happiness, I brought them lettuce leaves and acacia, which they ate from my hands. I cared for them during the whole summer, and it was a terrible disappointment when I had to leave them.

Another time, my grandfather gave me a white lamb that followed me when I went for a walk. They had gilded his horns and from them hung a string of blue beads to frighten away the evil spirits. But I had to give him up too, most unwillingly, when he grew to be a large aggressive ram.

The *Surré-emini*

One of the most vivid of my childhood memories is of the feast of *surré-emini*.

Every year this ceremony took place in the middle of the month of *Shaban*, the eighth lunar month, with great pomp and splendor. It was an important occasion for the Palace as well as for the people, for on that day it was the Sultan of Turkey's custom to send rich gifts to the sacred cities of Mecca and Medina. A train of many camels was loaded with bags (*surrées*) and heavy sacks to be transported across the desert.

Furthermore, each "true believer" was permitted to contribute to the offering with a few coins or some gift, however modest. These were collected by the *Evkaf* (a religious institution) in leather bags which bore on one side the name of the donors, and on the other, those of the recipients.

Those who were unable to make the pilgrimage in person could be represented by another person who would pray for them at the *Kaaba*, the sacred stone.

On the day of departure, the ministers of the Sultan and the officials for the Sacred Cities met at the park of Dolma Bahcé Palace. When the Sultan appeared at a window of the Palace, a camel would be led out and loaded with the royal gifts for the Emir of Mecca.

Then began the religious ceremony, with prayers and the sacrifice of lambs. Finally, the caravan set out, to the sound of drums. At the head of the retinue rode an officer in elaborate uniform, followed by all the dignitaries, and then the hundreds of pilgrims who were taking part in the *Haj* [the Pilgrimage to Mecca which guarantees eternal life.]

Soldiers and police surrounded the group on all sides, for in years past the caravans had often been attacked by bandits, who stripped them of everything. This custom of an armed escort had been preserved and was now traditional.

I never left the window while the motley, noisy caravan was passing in front of our house, watching, enraptured, every detail of the phantasmagorical spectacle until the last *Haji*, or pilgrim, had disappeared.

In our house in Besiktas three young sisters worked as servants. The oldest, Vida, was an excellent cook, and I adored her. Many a night I fell asleep in her bed, listening to her tales.

The housemaid, Caló, was happy, bubbling with high spirits and very witty. She had a great talent for comedy, and everyone laughed with her. When she went out she was very stylish, and I remember that in winter she always carried her rabbit fur muff.

The third, Dudú, had more education, and was an ideal nanny for my sister and me. We had also, one or another German governess, but, generally speaking, they were never people we were very fond of. The three sisters left our house when they married. Dudú was with us for twenty years, and followed us to Paris, because she didn't want to be separated from us. She had more than one suitor, and finally married a modest, loyal, hard-working young man. They had two darling little girls whom we often saw at the house. During the Nazi terror, the whole family was deported, and we never knew what happened to them. It was a real tragedy for us, for Dudú had been like a second mother to my sister and me.

When I entered the German School, at the age of seven, I was a very small child with olive skin and sparking gray-green eyes—one a little darker than the other. I had chestnut hair, quite long, which I wore in two braids gathered into a loop at the nape of my neck.

I was blessed with an excellent memory, so that I only needed to read a lesson once in order to learn it, and I was second in the class. The professor, Herr Merganthaler, was fond of me, and I remember that on one occasion he invited me to his house to celebrate Christmas. There were forty pupils in the class, half girls and half boys. I made friends with two of the German children, Marie and Lorenz. Lorenz was the best looking of the class—his blonde hair, in ringlets, came almost to his shoulders—but he won no stars for intelligence; his answers aroused derisive laughter, which used to make me mad.

I was never good in the gymnasium classes, except when there were races. Then I was always first at the goal; with my slim little legs I flew like an arrow.

Mamá says that when I was only three and a half years old, I sat down at the piano and played a song I had heard from my nanny, accompanying the melody very correctly with the left hand. It was a tune from a musical comedy, *La Gran Vía* by Federico Chueca, then very popular in Constantinople, whose refrain implored: "I want to see the light." Everyone was dumbfounded at the accomplishment, and it was soon the talk of the neighborhood.

Childhood photo of Victoria and her sister Matilde.

Soon after this, a travelling Italian opera company came to the city, and my parents took me to all the performances, so that at a very early age I became familiar with the music of *Aida*, *La Traviata*, *Il Trovatore* and *Mignon*. I could play the famous arias with no mistakes, and soon I was considered a child prodigy along the whole street of Pasa Mahalé.

One day my cousin Luisa, who was going on fifteen and was already an excellent pianist, called to me while I was playing with my friends in the garden, "Come here, Totty, I'm going to play a very lovely piece and you will have to play it afterwards. Sit by me, and watch my fingers."

And I, somewhat offended, answered, "I don't have to see, I hear." The "piece" was the Andante from Beethoven's *Fifth Symphony*.

When I was five the nuns of the School of Our Lady of Zion taught me a little solfeggio, and at seven I began to study piano with an Italian teacher.

That year we moved to the new flat in the Perá section, an area that was more like a modern city. My grandfather had just constructed a building in the very center; it was across from the Perá Palace, the most luxurious hotel in Constantinople, host to many famous visitors, among them Sarah Bernhardt and Agatha Christie. To one side stood the United States Embassy and the Hotel Kroecker, and facing our windows, the French Club. In the distance one could see the Golden Horn with its mosques and innumerable white minarets.

We used to spend summer vacations with my grandparents, who liked to gather the various families around them. At first they rented a large Turkish-style house in Büyük Deré [Big River] on the banks of the Bosporus. Later they rented a chalet on the island of Prinkipo; today it is called Büyük Ada [Big Island]. Finally they bought large property there, including an old house which my father modernized. It was a very large chalet, three or four stories high, and big enough to house almost the entire Kamhi family. There I spent the happiest vacations of my life. I still dream of them.

My Aunt María often came, bringing two of her sons, Emilio and Isaac, who were more or less my age. They were my favorite cousins, and in those days we were inseparable. We played and ran all through the gardens, which were enormous—more than two acres of land. And during the summer, Uncle Vitali came often.

I loved my Uncle Vitali and admired him enormously, and I thought him very handsome. Decidedly oriental in appearance, he was tall and slim. Mamá used to say that "Uncle Vitali's teeth are like pearls." He dressed with sober elegance and had what the French call "charme." He had a keen intelligence, and was a cultured man, a patron of the arts. He held positions of great responsibility, among them that of senator. I was his favorite niece.

When my sister and I were very young, he often invited us to his home for lunch—those meals were truly feasts—and afterward would give us tickets to go to the circus with our governess.

I remember once, on New Year's Eve, walking along the main street of Perá, we paused in front of the Bon Marché window, where there was a marvelous display of toys. What attracted my attention was a blonde doll, dressed in pink, seated on a swing. I was crazy about her; I couldn't take my eyes away from her.

A little later, when we went home, to my surprised delight I found the wonderful doll in my room—a gift from Uncle Vitali. For my sister there was another, a baby doll, lying in a little white cradle.

I still have another of his gifts: an album of Grieg's complete works for the piano, in the deluxe edition.

For the house in Prinkipo, my father had hired a Greek gardener, a master of his trade, and provided him with the finest plants: rose bushes ordered from France, jasmine of intoxicating fragrance, carnations, fuchsias, orchids. In the orchard there were all sorts of fruit trees: pears, cherries, apples, apricots and peaches, which provided exquisite fruit.

Next to the pond there was an ancient fig tree. It was tall and leafy, and often lunch was served under the shady branches. It bore black figs, very large, and sweeter than honey. Rifaat, the young assistant gardener, would climb to the top to bring down a basketful. And those figs were the very best dessert for young and old alike!

Years later I learned that this marvelous old fig tree had withered and died on the very day of grandfather's death. A mere coincidence?

The mulberries were another delight for me, both the black ones and the white. At the end of the orchard grew three lovely mulberry trees, and to please me, my grandfather's dear old friend, Cibi Zahar, would climb to the highest branches and shake them hard, even though he was then more than seventy years old. How he loved to watch me run around picking up the fallen berries to stuff them in my mouth!

Prinkipo, or the Island of the Princes, was the largest among the islands of the archipelago of the Sea of Marmara. I believe that it was so called because it was the place of exile of the emperors and princes of Byzantium, who ended their days in the Monastery of St. George, built on the highest peak of a mountain which dominates the sea. It was difficult to reach, for the path which led to the ancient ruins was narrow and steep. Visitors used to make the ascent to the site by riding sure-footed burros. It was an impressive place with an unforgettable panoramic view.

We often used to go to the most picturesque picnic spots of the pine covered island: Cristos, San Nicolás, Yurguli, Greek names from the Byzantium epoch.

In the mornings we would all go to the Maritime Club, to swim and sun bathe. The sea was like a mirror; in this bay there were never waves. The water was crystal clear, transparent, and the fine sand underfoot was like a soft rug. We were almost always alone—ten to fifteen people at the most—for at that time the avalanche of tourists which now invades the island had not yet discovered it. "A family gathering" is a privilege which nowadays is rapidly becoming an impossibility.

I was ten years old when I was presented to the great Hungarian pianist, Geza Heguey, who had been a pupil of Franz Liszt. My parents had attended his recitals and were his fervent admirers. Heguey took a lively interest in me, and for several months he gave me private lessons. He had the acumen to make me study classic works very soon, such as Beethoven's *Variations* and the easy *Sonatas* by Mozart. In order to spur me on, he assured me that within a year or two I would be able to give a public concert, dressed like the young Mozart, with pantaloons and a white wig, a vision which filled me with joy. I studied eagerly and made rapid progress.

Summer came and my parents had to make a trip to Vienna, where my mother was to undergo surgery. They took me with them, while my sister remained with the governess in my grandparents' house. After the operation, the doctors recommended that Mamá pass her convalescence on the Semmering, a spa surrounded by pine forests and snowy peaks, situated in the mountains south of Vienna at an altitude of more than 3,000 feet. We stayed at the Hotel Panhans, a veritable palace, where the cream of Viennese society used to meet.

I spent most of my day in the woodland park, filled with deer and roebuck which approached me tamely. The blue bells of the campanulas and gentians were beginning to appear among the ferns, along with pink cyclamen. Every day I returned with bouquets of flowers for Mamá, filling her room with the woodland fragrance.

I was very happy in this alpine nature-land, so new for me, and grieved to think that our return journey was approaching.

That year the first cold days came early, and it began to snow in mid-September. But at the Hotel Panhans, seated in comfortable chairs around a lighted fireplace, we would have tea with my parents' friends, who made up a companionable group.

I remember a man who would come to join us. Of a "certain age," his unusual appearance attracted attention. His hair was almost completely white, and his thick, long moustaches made him look like a seal. He always wore the typical Tyrolean dress, with knee-length trousers and a hat, adorned with a capercaillie feather. The others never called him by name, but always "Herr Dichter," for he was a poet, well-known in the literary circles of Vienna. I noticed that people made fun of him a bit, considering him a rare bird, which grieved me, since from the first day I had liked him very much.

"He's crazy," some said. And "he runs after all the young girls," said others. Nevertheless when the "Dichter" arrived with his long cape, holding his pipe between his teeth, everyone gathered around him, happy to see him and to listen to his tales and his jokes.

Some years later, visiting the Colonial Exposition in Paris in 1930 with Mamá, we both stood a long time in front of the Austrian pavilion which was one of the most highly praised, with a replica of the temple of Angkor. Engraved in the imposing gray mass, with its somber outlines, were the names of the great men of Austria: Mozart, Schubert, Haydn, Grillparzer, Bruckner, Johann Strauss, and also there was the name of Peter Altenberg, an inspired modern poet, author of delightful books, word paintings full of tenderness and sensitivity. I had read his *Stories of Life*, *Premonition*, *How I See It*, *Semmering, 1912*.

"Ah," exclaimed Mamá. "Do you remember him?"

"No," I replied, astonished, "Have I met him?"

"Naturally," she answered, laughing, "He is that old "Herr Dichter" who was with us in the Hotel Panhans. A little after that, Papá and I left you in the boarding school in Vienna and returned to Constantinople."

Of course I remembered that singular man, his expression, so full of tenderness, his delicate hands that stroked my hair. Would he perhaps have immortalized me in one of his poems, where he placed innocent, vivacious children on a pedestal? And here you have what I discovered, with profound emotion, in his book, *Semmering, 1912*.

Lied

Was nützt des Herbstes braune Symphonie?
Ich bin zu krank.
Sonst sah ich alles mit dem Blick der Liebe,
Dem Blicke einer namenlosen Zärtlichkeit,
Ich wusste wie die Buche sich verfärbt im
Frühem Froste
Und wie ihre Röte allmählich erbräunt.
Die Amsel raschelte im dürren laub, die
Schwarze Schnecke zog über die Wege.
Du Sagtest mir, holdestes Kind, du müsstest

nun in ein Institut, für 2, 3 Jahre...
Ja, es ist Herbst geworden, und ich bin
zu krank.

Peter Altenberg

Song

To what purpose the dark symphony of autumn?
I am too sick.
Before, I saw everything with eyes of love,
The gaze of an ineffable tenderness.
I knew how the beech tree lost its colors
When the frosts came.
And how its scarlet tints would turn to brown.
The blackbird rustling in the dry leaves.
The black snail sliding over the paths.
And you, my loveliest little one, told me
That you must enter a boarding school
For two or three years.
Yes, Autumn has come, and I —
I am too sick.

Just before the return trip, Mamá had taken me to the clinic of an orthopaedist recommended by "Uncle Doctor," her brother, who diagnosed a slight deviation of the spinal column. As this had to be corrected with exercise and massage, my uncle advised her that I should register at a boarding school in Vienna. Losing no time, Mamá, totally alarmed, enrolled me in the Institut Szanto, where she had studied as a girl, and of which she had fond memories.

With real terror I saw the moment of the separation draw nearer. My father could not conceal his own distress.

Every morning, when I got out of bed, I would see his reddened eyes, and his face would be so sad that it touched my heart. On the other hand, Mamá had no doubts. Her brother, "Uncle Doctor," had completely convinced her that if drastic measures were not taken, I could become deformed.

And so they both went home, leaving me in a place where I would miss everything that I had had in the family home, and above all, love.

Chapter II

My Studies

It did not take me long to adapt to the austere life of the Szanto Institut. The boarders were wakened at seven in the morning, and a half-hour later breakfast was served, consisting of a cup of malt coffee with milk and a roll.

We were in class three or four hours, and at one went down to the dining room, where lunch was a cream soup and a small serving of beef with vegetables. We had to buy our own dessert from the fruit vendor, who came up every afternoon with a great basket of oranges, apples, or some other fruit.

Four times a week, elderly Frau Koblinger came at three in the afternoon to accompany me to the gymnasium. We always walked, even if it was raining or snowing. On returning, I had a snack of coffee with milk and a pastry, and then I had to prepare assignments for class. Twice a week we had to write to our families.

Supper was very frugal: on Mondays they served a dish of rice with milk, on Tuesdays, a cheese sandwich, Wednesdays, cottage fried potatoes with Augsburger sausage, on Thursdays, two pairs of Vienna sausages with mustard, Friday brought rice with meat, Saturday, Emmenthaler cheese and a glass of beer, and Sunday, potato salad with cold cuts.

I enjoyed going to class and soon became a favorite of all the professors, perhaps because I was the most exotic student.

I finished the fourth grade with 'excellent' in all subjects, and the young professor, Fräulein Klein, congratulated me in public with an affectionate embrace. Consequently I was allowed to skip the fifth grade and enter the sixth, where I had wonderfully congenial classmates, almost all Viennese or Hungarian, although some were Bulgarian or Serbian. I was the spoiled child, upon whom everyone heaped attention. I remember one very attractive day pupil, named Lilly, who would bring me a little gift every day, either a little doll, a bag of caramels, or a little book of stories. The boarders shared with me the delicatessen packages they received from their families: delicious cakes, white bread, sausages, bonbons.

I went out every Sunday and holiday, for my three aunts took turns coming to get me, and I got along stupendously in their houses. I went to the movies or the theatre with my little cousins, or else to the Wurstlprater. When the weather was good, we would make excursions, generally to the Kobenzl, to the Kahlenberg or to the Kriau.

Summer came and I was very happy to see my parents and my sister again. However, Mathilde and I would spend this vacation at the boarding school, because our parents went to the Spas at Bohemia, Marienbad, and Franzensbad, to take the waters. Several Bulgarian students and two or three Serbians also remained, and together we were totally bored in the little town of Weidling, on the outskirts of Vienna, which had no attractions to offer.

In September came another separation: my family returned to Constantinople, and I found myself in the Institut for one more year.

Despite my pleas, I was not enrolled at the Conservatory of Music, because our Headmistress, Fräulein Ella, said that she saw no need, since "the best professors in Vienna" taught in her school. She advised me to take classes with Fräulein Müller, an excellent teacher.

When I first saw Fräulein Müller, I was a little shocked: with her long nose, her sunken little eyes, and her mustachioed mouth, she looked like a witch from the fairy tales of the Brothers Grimm. Furthermore she used to talk to herself and burst out laughing during the lesson, which could not fail to startle me.

But I soon realized that she was a kind person, and I became very fond of her. Under her direction I would have progressed rapidly if I had been allowed more practice. Barely an hour a day was too little time.

That year I experienced my first sorrow, the loss of a loved one. My paternal grandmother, who was suffering from cancer, had been brought to Vienna for an operation by a famous surgeon. A few days after her arrival, she died in the Sanatorium, and was mourned by everyone.

The winter was very harsh that year, and I caught a terrible cold, to which the professors attributed no importance, until my attacks of coughing alarmed the students' parents, who got involved. Then I was taken to the office of the famous internist, Dr. Schlesinger, who diagnosed an acute bronchial catarrh, and ordered a treatment on the basis of compresses of cold water, called "Priesnitz." It was extremely uncomfortable. Nevertheless, I did not improve. My nervous system began to deteriorate and I became acutely sensitive. When my parents arrived in June, I was so weak and emaciated that they were frightened and decided to take me with them to Constantinople, since I needed other care.

I left Vienna, and likewise my friends and teachers, with real sadness. Once more I would have to interrupt my studies, and change my surroundings.

In any event, we had to return home, for world war had broken out, some days earlier, and the country was in full mobilization.

When I arrived in Constantinople, I was not the same child who had set out for Austria two years earlier: happy, sociable, witty, sure of herself. I had become gloomy, wistful and diffident. I had lost touch with my old friends and did not find anyone to strike up a new friendship with. Mathilde had her own group, but they didn't accept me in their midst, so that every day I felt more alone, more misunderstood. The French School had closed its doors for political reasons, and therefore Mamá had to engage a private tutor, who came every morning. She, a very German woman, had a French surname, which always seemed odd to us.

Fräulein Morand was an affable old maid, cheerful and energetic, although she appeared to be more than seventy years old, with white hair and a face furrowed with deep wrinkles.

I studied several subjects with her, and she seemed happy with my progress. Once, as the subject of a composition, she gave me "Constantinople, my Native City." At first, the subject seemed easy, and from day to day I put off doing the work. But by the day before it was due, I was really worried. How would I be able to come up with something acceptable on the subject in so little time? And how could I tell of its splendid history, its unique monuments, its marvelous landscapes? An extensive book would have to be written to include it all, and perhaps more than one.

Then I had a sudden inspiration. Why not write a poem, more precisely a hymn, to the immortal city of Byzantium? Inexplicably, I felt capable of doing it, and with no further ado, began to work on it. The next day I was able to hand over to Fräulein Morand a hymn of several stanzas, which she read attentively.

"Did you write this?" she asked, in amazement.

"Yes," I answered, a little uneasy.

"And no one helped you?"

"Of course not, Fräulein Morant."

"This is incredible," she exclaimed, and rushed off to find my mother.

"If I am not mistaken, your daughter has the talent to be a famous poet," she declared, showing it to Mamá.

Mamá smiled, half-skeptical, half-flattered. In truth, this prediction didn't fill her with enthusiasm. What she wanted for me, as for my sister, was a bourgeois marriage with a "good match," like her own, a tranquil life without problems or preoccupations.

A year later, cured of my bronchitis, I again enrolled in the German School, where I found a very different atmosphere than at the Lycée Français. And I also lacked the great consolation of music. In spite of my pleading, I could not return to Professor Heguey's classes, because Mamá's friends had convinced her that Professor Radeglia, who was very much in vogue at the time, was a better teacher. With him, I began to study Beethoven's Sonatas and the works of Chopin. There is no doubt that he was an excellent musician, but his lessons weren't stimulating, and I made very little progress during that year.

In that period Constantinople was a capital of outstanding brilliance. Although the war had impoverished many families, despite the fact that wages were low and one saw need and distress in many areas, such as Balaat, Hasköy and in old Istanbul, part of the population was swimming in opulence. The "new rich," whose ostentation surpassed all limits, organized magnificent fêtes; and balls, banquets, and productions of the theater and opera went on every day. A group of enthusiasts staged the opera, *Der Evangelimann*, by Julius Bittner, with the famous singer Schmedes, from the Vienna Opera, which had enormous success. Later they produced the ballet, *Die Puppenfee*. They asked me to play the piano accompaniment for the rehearsals, which was very flattering.

My parents were friends of several prominent Levantine families: the Corpis, the Saverios, the Hubers, the Maleas, and they led a very active social life. My inseparable friends were María Rosa Corpi and Iva Radeglia, of whom I cherish wonderful memories.

In the summer of 1915, although the world war continued with all its horrors, my parents decided to spend their vacation in Austria. Mamá, who was suffering from liver problems, had great faith in the mineral waters of Karlsbad—where indeed she would be cured—and my father felt obliged to make an escape to Marienbad to leave his superfluous pounds there. How enthusiastically we boarded the Orient-Express that hot day of July first!

A group of family and friends had gathered at the station to see us off, with flowers for Mamá and sweetmeats for the children. The porters carried on a gigantic basket of food, enough to feed us for several days. This journey was begun under the most favorable auspices. Nevertheless, it would be a voyage of no return; through a series of unhappy circumstances, we would never again see our house in Perá, where we had passed the happiest days of our lives.

The vacations in Karlsbad and later in Marienbad were pleasant and restful. In Karlsbad, my father rented luxurious accommodations at the Villa Humboldt, surrounded by a large garden, and furnished with a grand piano I could use to practice.

The owner, Frau von Koch, was a kind and distinguished person. Short in stature and a little chubby, she had white hair and a youthful face. Her grand-daughter, Gerda, a very pretty little girl, was my sister's age, and quickly became her inseparable friend. She told her, among other things, that her grandfather, who had died, had been a famous doctor, and that her grandmother had been a world-renowned opera singer.

One day Frau von Koch asked me if I could accompany her in some songs at the piano. She put before me the *Lieder* of Schubert and Schumann and some of Wagner's scores, which I played without mistakes.

"You play very well, child," she said, smiling, "if you keep on like this, you will go far."

"But you, Ma'am, you have a marvelous voice," I exclaimed. "Where did you sing?"

"I performed often in the Bayreuth festivals and I was the first to sing "Kundry" in *Parsifal*. My professional name was Materna."

I was astonished. To think that I had had the privilege of collaborating with one of the most famous Wagnerian sopranos! I was bursting with pride, and this event of my childhood would remain forever in my memory.

The autumn came, and I thought that we would soon return to Constantinople. But it was not to be. My grandfather had died after a very brief illness—on the day of the funeral all the business establishments of the district had closed in tribute—and it had been decided that my father would represent the Rafael Kamhi and Sons firm in Vienna. Mathilde and I would continue our studies in a school there.

Before enrolling me, Mamá, who always was concerned about her family's health, took me to one of the most prestigious internists in Austria, Doctor Mannaberg. I remember him well, with his gray beard and his dark, penetrating eyes.

"There is nothing wrong with you," he told me paternally, "but you are too small and you weigh too little for your age. Don't forget that thin women are no longer in vogue; you will be more popular with a few more pounds."

And he recommended that I spend a few weeks at the Breitenstein Sanatorium, near the Semmering and highly recommended for people who were convalescent, anemic or undernourished. The location was ideal: pine groves and waterfalls surrounded it. The air was pure and the silence total. The ambience could not have been better: there were artists, writers, members of the old aristocracy, like the attractive Countess Z., who had a lovely voice, and whom I accompanied at the piano in the ballads of Loewe and the *Lieder* of Schumann.

A young student, whose name was Karl Popper, used to come on week-ends. He was devoted to music, and we had long conversations. I enjoyed our times together very much, and today I wonder if that youth wasn't the man who would one day acquire world fame as "the great philosopher of science."

I stayed at Breitenstein two months, and when Mamá came to pick me up, she hardly recognized me. I looked marvelous, and had gained twelve pounds!

The physician at the Sanatorium, a great music-lover, whom I had asked for advice, recommended a Polish pianist as maestro to me. He was Georg von Lalewicz, a Professor of the Royal Academy of Music, who was renowned as a teacher and concert pianist.

I was enrolled in the Grammar School of Waehring, where my sister was already a student. The Headmaster, Dr. Bloch, was a cultured man, and his sister, Irma Leuchter, head of the boarding school, was very musical. One of her sons, Erwin, played the violoncello, and we often performed duets. Years later I would see Erwin again in Buenos Aires, where he had achieved fame as a musicologist.

I entered the fifth class, and immediately realized that I was very much behind the rest in mathematics and Latin, because I had missed the first trimester. On the other hand, I was very comfortable with French, literature, history and natural science. I made friends with all my classmates, all very congenial and affectionate. On the other hand I could not get close to the boarding students, most of them Hungarians, who were already beginning to be conceited and flirtatious. I was very different from all of them, and thought only of my studies and my music. How to get to Professor Lalewicz? This was my sole preoccupation.

That year, my sister and I went to spend Easter vacation with our parents, who had rented a furnished flat in St. Stephen's Platz. The weather was rainy and I had spent the whole morning bored, with nothing to do. After lunch I complained again of being without a piano instructor, and unable to practice seriously. This time Mamá's patience was exhausted.

"Put on your coat, we are going right this minute to Professor Lalewicz's house," she ordered.

"But—this is not possible," I protested. "I'm not prepared. I haven't been near a piano in—I don't know how long."

"That doesn't matter, the professor will realize right away if you have talent, and in that case he will accept you as a pupil."

I had no alternative but to obey, and shortly thereafter we entered the flat on Favoritenstrasse, which truly looked like the home of an artist to me. Later I learned that the Maestro's wife, Antka, was an eminent painter and decorator. I inspected the music room attentively; it was very spacious, with two grand pianos, a Petroff and a Bösendorfer. The walls were draped with great garlands of laurel, tied with red silk ribbons. The marble hands of Chopin and of the Maestro himself were displayed in vitrines. On a pedestal was a bust of Annette Essipoff, the famous Russian pianist, who had been Lalewicz's teacher.

The professor received us very courteously. At that time he was forty-two years old, tall and slim, with abundant reddish hair and a little moustache.

"What will you play, Fräulein?" he asked, gesturing toward the Petroff piano. The only thing that I had at my finger tips was Chopin's *Polonaise in C Sharp Minor*. The first part I did well enough, but when I came to the arpeggios, I panicked, and stopped suddenly, pretending a lapse of memory. I was at the point of rising from the bench, when the Maestro placed a score on the lectern. I remember that it was a page of Bach, not at all easy.

"I want to see what sort of reader you are," he said, seating himself beside me.

Later, he went to the Bösendorfer, and played several chords, asking me which key they were. He seemed satisfied with my answers. At last, Mamá, who had not intervened until then, dared to ask, "What do you think, Maestro? How does she sound?"

"Now, far from perfect," he replied drily. "She is very lax. But I am going to admit her as a pupil because she has potential."

And, directing himself to me, "How many hours a day do you plan to practice?"

"One hour," I answered with aplomb.

"Fräulein," he replied, "if you do not promise to practice a minimum of three hours, I cannot accept you."

Completely confused, I promised him, and I kept my word to the letter.

The two years that followed were very profitable for me, and I have the fondest memory of them, in spite of privations, hunger and cold. I knew that I had found my path—the piano—and I was determined to travel it to the end.

The new plan of study let me make rapid progress: three to four hours of practice daily, usually in the afternoon, one lesson a week with the Maestro and one with his assistant, Professor Fifi Grün, who corrected my technique.

The first works that I prepared for the lessons were Bach's *English Suites*, the *Sonata in F Major, Op. 10*, of Beethoven, and Rheinhold's *Impromptu*. Besides these, there were large doses of Czerny and Pischna. The Maestro demanded that everything be played from memory, including the practice.

He was very pleased with me, assuring me that he might soon be able to present me to the public in Vienna. By then I had begun to do chamber music with a young violinist—the one who later on would create the Amadeus Quartet—and I was delighted to play the Concertos of Bach and the Sonatas of Mozart, Schubert and Beethoven with him.

To be able to dedicate myself exclusively to the piano, I had to leave the Grammar School, with its studies of Latin and Greek, and obtain the bachelor's degree two years sooner. I was therefore enrolled in the Lyceum Luithlen, where I entered the sixth class. There I found among my classmates, Luise Perner—who would become my closest friend—and Franzi Hegenbarth, daughter of the great sculptor, and grand-daughter of the famous composer, Karl Goldmark (author of the operas *The Queen of Sheba* and *Merlin*, among others.)

During those months I had to neglect music a bit, for I had to prepare for the Baccalaureate exams. I had the best grades in literature, French, history and natural sciences, but not in mathematics and physics. However, I was unanimously awarded the longed-for diploma, which permitted me to devote myself entirely to the piano.

At that time Vienna was perhaps the musical center of the world. The Philharmonic Orchestra gave magnificent concerts under the direction of illustrious conductors, among them Richard Strauss, Franz Schalk, Felix Weingartner. We never missed a single one, my family and I.

Several times a week we attended recitals of famous artists, like the pianists Emil Sauer, Moritz Rosenthal, Alfred Grünfeld—the best interpreter of Schubert,—Lalewicz and Eugen d'Albert; and of violinists like Bronislaw Hubermann, Erica Morini, Yeno Hübay and Franz von Veczey. We often heard the magnificent Rosé Quartet in works of Beethoven, Brahms and Schubert.

For several years my parents had a subscription box for the "Hofoper," so that I soon became familiar with the operas of Mozart, Wagner, Verdi, Puccini, Leoncavallo, Flotow, Goldmark, etc. We went to see *Fidelio* more than once; it was one of my favorite operas. The singers were always first class, but I was most enthusiastic about Leo Slezak, Alfred Piccaver and Mayr, as well as the divas, Selma Kurz, Lotte Lehmann, Lotte Schöne, Elizabeth Schumann and María

Jeritza. I was enchanted, too, by the ballerina Grete Wiesenthal, whose performances always attracted an enormous audience.

That was a unique time and place, which would leave its impression on me for the rest of my life.

We spent the summer in Marienbad, in the company of family and friends, and I renewed my acquaintance with my cousin Rifaat, who was now twenty-two years old. He was very popular with the young Viennese girls, since he was elegant—his oriental features had earned him the nickname "Mufti" a Moslem priest—and had won several prizes in modern dance competition. I felt very flattered to stroll with him through the Kurpark, wearing a suit with a jacket and high-heeled shoes. I was trying to conquer my complexes, for I found in myself many physical defects: I was very small and not well-developed. My nose, which was relatively large, made my profile ugly, according to some, but according to others, it gave it character. I had olive skin and pale lips. Only my eyes were worth compliments; they were large, gray-green, typically oriental. And my hair was also nice, very fine and curly, and fell to my waist. Still, I was tremendously timid, and extremely uncomfortable in the company of strangers. Boys of my own age inspired a real panic in me, and when one of them singled me out with his attention, I was incapable of making a casual reply as all my friends did.

When we returned to Vienna, I resumed my studies with the Maestro. Now I had more time at my disposal, and could devote up to five hours every day to the piano, with more difficult works, like the Etudes of Chopin, the Sonatas of Beethoven and Schubert, and the works of Liszt, Liadow and Arensky. My technique had improved greatly, and this filled me with happiness.

At the end of the winter of 1918 my parents decided to move with us to Switzerland, mainly for reasons of health. The situation in Vienna was much worse, due to the war. Every day food was becoming more scarce, and the lack of fuel was a serious problem. And besides, my parents needed a change of atmosphere and wanted to join the members of the family who were in that lovely country, a true peaceful refuge.

I said goodbye to Maestro Lalewicz with real grief, and he too was regretful, although we both thought that the separation would be a short one.

The journey to Zurich was very uncomfortable. The trains were in dreadful condition; there were only third class cars, with no glass in the windows. The panes had been replaced by wooden boards, and blasts of cold air entered through the cracks. There were few passengers, and in our compartment there was only an Austrian officer, a convalescent, who spoke with nostalgia of his wife and children. I remember the sad expression in his eyes and his hesitant smile when he spoke to my sister and me.

In spite of the hard, uncushioned benches, I went to sleep, my head on the back rest. Later, half-awakened, I felt myself being lifted up. Two strong arms laid me on one of the benches, covering me up to my neck. It was the Austrian officer, who had given me his seat and stretched himself out on the floor, wrapped in his military cape.

When we arrived in Zurich, it seemed a paradise: the fine white flour croissants, the foaming milk, the fragrant coffee and the lumps of sugar of our first breakfast tasted heavenly. Our aunts and cousins overwhelmed us with delicacies, and the chocolate, marzipan, delicious cookies, in addition to the succulent meals at the Hotel Dolder, filled us with euphoria.

Spring floated in the air, and the woods and meadows of the surrounding countryside were thick with violets, primulas and anemones.

With my cousin Emilio—a student at the University of Zurich—I made frequent trips to the countryside and to the surrounding mountains, and sometimes we went down to the city to take the little steamer which circled in the lake. We would get off at some little village for lunch, and return to the Dolder tired, but enchanted with life. I remember that our conversations speculated on Einstein's theory of relativity, which was creating a sensation in Zurich, and would soon revolutionize the whole world of science.

Some weeks later we went to Lucerne, where we stayed at the Hotel Beau Séjour, next to the beautiful lake, where we completely forgot that the world was shaken by an atrocious war and that humanity was lashed by hunger, cold and misery. During the summer my father gave us a magnificent trip through Switzerland. I was particularly enthusiastic over Bern, with its zoological garden, and the Oberland; Thun, with its romantic lake; Grindlwald, with its snow-capped mountains. In September we went to Lausanne, where Mathilde and I entered Brilliantmont College. In the *Ecole Ménagère* I learned all the things an accomplished housewife should know. Furthermore, I took courses in child care and in nursing. At the same time, we had the possibility of some spiritual enrichment, for we attended the best concerts, the theatre, lectures, etc.

Among my classmates was Renée, the daughter of Baron Pierre de Coubertin, founder of the Olympic games. She was an intelligent, lovely girl. There were also two sisters-in-law of Mustafa Kemal Ataturk and a daughter of the Bulgarian Minister Tufekchief. During the Christmas vacation we went with the Head Mistress, Lili Heubi, to Château d'Oex, to practice skiing and other winter sports, but there I was only a spectator, for I was never good at sports, and neither was my sister. The only difficulty I found in this college was the impossibility of continuing my piano studies. Later I learned that there was a great pianist in Lausanne, Professor Blanchet. Nevertheless, I dreamed of returning to Vienna to continue with Lalewicz.

In the spring of that year my parents decided to make a visit to Paris, simply as tourists, and to take me with them. My father was in his element, and the three of us enjoyed our stay in the "City of Light" enormously. For a month, Papá showed us every corner worthy of interest, and had us visit the Museums, the Churches, the parks and the gardens. He took us to Versailles, to Saint Cloud, to Saint-Germain, and also to the most famous restaurants and cabarets. To finish the day's work, we would go to the Grand Opera, or perhaps to the Opera-Comique or to some theater on the Boulevards. Several times we attended marvelous concerts, the most impressive of which was by the pianist Busoni. To cap it all off, my parents bought me elegant dresses, shoes, hats, and beautiful handbags, all of which filled the timid schoolgirl from Lausanne with happiness.

When summer came, my parents left for Constantinople in order to gather the household furnishings, for we were to move definitively to Paris, where Papá had been named head of the branch of Rafael Kamhi and Sons. How I awaited that moment! Life in Paris would be so fabulous!

At the end of August my parents returned, bringing with them all the furniture, paintings, clothing and tableware. Mathilde and I made the trip to join them at Montreux, where the train stopped for a few minutes. How surprised we were to see our beloved Dudú there in the compartment of the Orient Express. She had left her family to follow us to France. Our happiness was immense!

We spent the first days in the Hotel des Deux-Mondes, on the Avenue de l'Opéra, and then Papá rented a very luxurious furnished flat, next to the Parc Monceau. We were not alone for long, for my maternal grandmother came to spend a few months with us, as did Aunt María with her daughter Luisa, who had just become engaged to Sami Davico, a very nice and intelligent young man. In their honor there was one festivity after another: receptions and dinner parties, as well as excursions to the most popular spots in the vicinity of Paris.

But now we needed to find an unfurnished apartment to rent, and to install our own furnishings.

By chance, my parents heard of a flat on the rue de Passy, the property of a Russian prince, who wanted to sell it. When Mamá saw it, she was amazed. It was very spacious, and the arrangement of the rooms was perfect for us.

As for the furnishings, they were truly princely: the large drawing room—in beautiful taste—was by Aubusson, and the dining room suite had been made by the house of Krieger, one of the finest French furniture makers.

The three bedrooms were very elegant. I had a room of my own, which was both bedroom and sitting room, where I could retire to read and write. The Pleyel grand piano, on which I practiced several hours a day, was placed in the drawing room. Besides this, there was another room, which Mamá had made into a "Turkish room," full of oriental rugs, which were even hung on the walls.

I will never forget the magnificent chandeliers, especially the one in the dining room, nor the sconces, nor the wall clock, nor the glass display cases, which Papá, a great collector, filled with works of art.

It was an ideal flat, universally admired, where we lived almost twelve years.

Mamá had engaged a Czech cook, who each day presented us with a different specialty. Her repertory was inexhaustible.

The moment had come to think about renewing my piano studies, lapsed for so long. Someone had recommended Professor Philipp, a famous teacher at the National Conservatory, who also taught at the Ecole Normale. Once again Mamá accompanied me when I presented myself at his house. After listening to me a while, the Maestro said that, while I had a great deal of talent, I was not advanced enough for his class, and he suggested that I take classes with one of his assistants, who would prepare me for his class the following year. I left disappointed, but began to earnestly practice the works he had given me.

Several days later I went to take my first lesson from Madame Chauvet, a stout, middle-aged woman, who began to pitilessly criticize Professor Lalewicz's method, praising to the skies the old method: arms and wrists rigid, and fingers round like "little hammers." I went home heartsick, wondering where I would find the strength to study with that sergeant. My sister met me, very excited, and full of news.

"Guess who's in Paris to give a concert! You'll never guess, so I'll tell you! It's Professor Lalewicz! I've seen the posters announcing his concert for this week!"

I almost fainted. The Maestro was in Paris! How was it possible! My father quickly bought four tickets, and we were able to hear the great pianist again in an eclectic program.

But, oh! how he had changed in these years! He was thin and wasted-looking, his hair was gray and he seemed much older than his 48 or 49 years. After the concert we went to congratulate him, and his surprise at seeing all of us in Paris was enormous. After throwing his arms around me, he told me that he was thinking of settling permanently in Paris, where he had already found some of his old pupils.

At his little flat in Auteuil, my lessons with the Maestro seemed even more interesting than in Vienna. Sometimes he would come to give me the lesson at home and would stay for supper or for tea. A Hungarian student of his, Eugen Bures, always accompanied him. He was already an excellent pianist. As for the maestro's wife, Antka, she remained in Poland. They had lost all their fortune because of monetary inflation, and he, not wishing to renounce his Polish citizenship, had lost his position as professor at the Vienna Conservatory. He had to begin anew, not an easy thing at his age and with his prestige. However, he was very encouraged and determined to adjust himself to his new life in Paris. I was in seventh heaven, and set out to study earnestly, according to the hereditary method of the Russian Essipoff School, improved and modernized by Lalewicz.

The winter of 1920 was very harsh, and I developed an acute bronchitis which left me very weak. Since my aunt and uncle from Manchester had rented a flat in Nice, they invited me to spend time with them to recover my health. I have a very happy memory of the carnival, so gay and amusing, as well as of the battle of flowers, in which I took part with my cousin Irene, who was my age. Our float, "la Chaumière," on which twenty girls rode, won a prize, and we had a fine time tossing flowers and receiving them from the sailors, who followed us, laughing and shouting compliments.

I returned to Paris at the beginning of spring and took up my classes again with great enthusiasm. I felt stronger than ever, and nothing could distract me from my music. But one day—it was the last of May—the Maestro spoke at the end of the lesson:

"Dear friend, I must give you some bad news. We will have to separate soon, for I have been offered a chair at the Buenos Aires Conservatory. Here in Paris, it is difficult to establish oneself, above all for an artist of my age and my category. In the New World, the competition is not as great, and it will be easier for me to make my way. My wife has already found a position in the Polish Consulate, and I plan to leave with her this summer."

Listening to him, I felt a profound sorrow, and I bowed my head to hide my tears. Once more bad luck pursued me. And once more I saw my dream of a career as a concert pianist being frustrated.

"Don't be upset," said the Maestro, clearly touched, "I am going to recommend a magnificent professor, who is also a great concert pianist. She is teaching now in the Schola Cantorum. After the vacation go to see her and tell her that I sent you. Her name is Blanca Selva."

A few days later, the Maestro and his wife left for Buenos Aires, where he did indeed make a place for himself. He achieved great prestige as Professor of the Conservatory, where he trained a whole generation of Spanish-American pianists, some of them famous, like Lia Cimaglia, Eugenio Bures, Haydée Giordano, Pia Sebastiani, Haydée Loustounau and others.

In 1920 after our vacation in La Bourboule, I began to prepare for my examination for admission to the Schola Cantorum. I was disappointed to learn that Blanca Selva had resigned her chair, in order to devote herself more to concerts. But I soon recovered from the new setback, for I realized that there would be other fine professors in the Schola.

The day arrived, and I set out with light footsteps toward the ancient building on the Rue St. Jacques, where I found other young candidates already gathered.

Presiding over the jury was the famous composer Vincent d'Indy, whom I had never seen before. He was tall and stout, with completely white hair, and his wide moustache and curly beard gave him a typically Gallic appearance. With a friendly smile, he invited me to sit down at the piano, and I played with considerable aplomb, controlling my nervousness. I was so pleased with my performance that, once outside the Salon, I began to dance, finishing with a few pirouettes and leaps, to the amazement of the other students and their respective mothers. At the end, I was called to d'Indy's office where he told me that I had been admitted to the advanced course, Mademoiselle Duranton's class. All that remained was to pass the examination in solfeggio, which was obligatory and which would take place a week later.

During the interval I studied tirelessly with a professor recommended by the Conservatory. My chances of passing were scant indeed, for I had never studied advanced solfeggio, and it was a matter of reading, at first sight, works written with frequent changes, in eight keys. Of course, it was not an easy test, and, as could be expected, I failed it.

Nevertheless, this wasn't a complete failure, because I was accepted immediately for the elementary course, which I refused to enter, as I thought it would be a waste of time. This was a mistake on my part, one of the professors later told me, because the most difficult step was to enter the Schola. Once accepted, if my grades had been good, I would have automatically passed to the advanced course and to Mademoiselle Duranton's class. But I didn't know that at the time.

The stay in Salzburg with Mamá and my sister was a magnificent diversion. As all the hotels and pensions were crowded, we had lodgings in a secularized convent near the Salzach River. I will never forget the performances of *Faust*, and *Jedermann* and *The Great Theatre of the World*, produced by the genial Max Reinhardt, nor the excursions to Mirabell, Moenchsberg and Kapuzinerberg. The forests were full of cyclamen, anemones and gentians, and it was a pleasure to lose oneself there.

Later we spent several weeks in Bad Gastein. There too, the hotels and pensions were filled to capacity, and everywhere we were told that every room was reserved until the end of the season. Then, at the eleventh hour, when we had lost all hope of finding lodging, I saw a chalet surrounded by a shady garden, with the sign "Villa Victoria," and I went in. I was greatly surprised when the owner told me, with a friendly smile, that she had two nice rooms available, and that we could move in that very day.

Later I learned that she had confused me with the famous Viennese violinist, Erica Morini, to whom I bore a striking resemblance.

When we returned to Paris I was more perplexed than ever. I had studied for several months with a professor recommended by a friend of ours, but the lessons were not stimulating and my progress, that year, was negligible.

I finally consulted my sister's violin teacher, Maestro Andolfi, who suggested that I study with Professor Lazare Lévy, who held the chair at the Conservatory. He was an excellent teacher and a great concert pianist.

Some weeks later, well prepared, I presented myself before the Maestro, who, after hearing me play an étude of Chopin, admitted me as a student.

His lessons were immensely interesting, and I studied with him for five years, until I received my diploma as a music teacher, awarded by the Paris Conservatory.

Our first years in the rue de Passy were, perhaps, the happiest of our family life. My father had an important position as head of Rafael Kamhi and Sons, and we viewed the world through rose-colored glasses. Our social life was busy, and we had guests almost daily for lunch or tea or dinner. Mamá was a perfect housekeeper, and had a special gift as a hostess, making everyone feel at ease in her home.

We frequently went to the Opera, to the Comédie Française and to the theatres of the Boulevards. We had a box for lectures by famous writers and artists, and we attended symphony concerts and the recital of the Salles Pleyel, Gaveau, etc.

Because I wanted to get involved in some sort of social work, I went to the "Nouvelle Etoile des Petits Enfants de France" [The New Star of the Children of France] a charitable institution which included several centers of infant and child care, dispensaries, children's dining rooms, etc. Its President at that time was Madame Veil-Picard, who showed me every kindness. An immensely wealthy woman, she was very attractive and elegant. She dedicated herself body and soul to charitable work, personally dealing with the little ones whose mothers brought them to the clinics, and treating them very affectionately.

I was accepted at once as an aide in a dispensary at the Porte d'Italie, but I had to commit myself to take a course as interne in the Maternity Center at Porchefontaine (near Versailles) to acquire the title of childcare worker.

In spite of opposition from my father, who could find no reason whatsoever for my new "caprice," I presented myself there one day in June, accompanied by faithful Dudú. And, dressed in a white uniform, head covered in a starched cap, I took possession of little Josette, eight months old, with the responsibility to bathe her, dress her, feed her and take her for a walk along with twelve or fifteen other students, all volunteers from the French upper-middle class. Each one of us had to care for a baby no more than one year old. The training course lasted twelve days, and at the end we were tested by a jury, consisting of Madame Veil-Picard, a pediatrician and the head nurse. I received the highest grade—an outstanding—and Dudú, who came to pick me up, heard many praises of my "devotion" and my talent for childcare.

From that time I spent two mornings a week with the children of poor families who were brought to the dispensary in the Porte d'Italie. I had to prepare food, bathe the little ones and, if necessary, treat them. For several months I carried out this work happily and enthusiastically, until the catastrophe fell upon my family which would radically change my life.

Chapter III

My Life Changes

It was at the end of February of that same year that my father and I both felt a sort of premonition of what was going to happen. I remember that I was on a platform of the Metro, waiting for a train, when I was seized suddenly with a feeling of impending disaster—the idea that our lives couldn't continue as they were—that something fearful would soon happen.

That same night, my father, who was a supersensitive man, began to moan and cry out in terror in his sleep. Mamá, alarmed, woke him, shaking him by the arm.

"What's the matter? Are you sick?"

He opened his eyes and sat up, trembling: "I was dreaming that my father was here, beside me, insisting that I go to look after my brother, Vitali, who is in great danger. This really disturbs me. What can I do? He is in Istanbul and I am here!"

"You've had a nightmare, and it's probably due to indigestion. I will tell Germaine to make our suppers lighter. Don't worry about your brother. At this time of night he is perfectly safe."

The next day, after lunch, my father left as usual to go to the office. I was sitting in the little "Turkish room," leafing through a magazine, when the telephone rang.

Mamá answered it, and I understood that the call was from one of her cousins. He must have been giving her truly hair-raising news, to judge by the frightened exclamations I overheard.

"It's not possible! And Vitali? How is he now? It's horrible, horrible! How can I tell my husband?"

A moment later, Mamá came into the room, her face covered with tears, and collapsed in a chair.

"What has happened, Mamá?" I cried, running to her.

She sat for a few moments, unable to speak. Finally, she answered, still sobbing.

"My cousin said that the Kamhi firm has just declared bankruptcy in Russia, and that the entire fortune is lost, many millions of pounds. Your Uncle Vitali, who handled all the business, shot himself when he got the news. He's in a critical condition. Oh, God! What will become of us! And what will happen to you, my poor babies!" she added in despair.

A little later Mathilde returned from the Sorbonne and, learning of the tragedy, cried with us. As for Papá, surprisingly, he showed great fortitude, trying to calm us with encouraging words. We will never forget that fateful day; we knew that everything would soon change for us.

Until then our lives had been like a fairy tale, but struggle for existence was to begin, something utterly unknown in our family. Poverty with dignity is a difficult apprenticeship, and more difficult if one must adjust oneself overnight. Suddenly, with no preparation whatever, Mathilde and I had ceased to be "wealthy heiresses," envied by everyone, and had become instead, "young ladies in reduced circumstances." Mamá knew it; that is why she wept so bitterly.

The next day my parents left for Turkey, hoping to find their brother still alive. The only close friend of the Brothers Kamhi who came to see them off was the ex-Minister, B. Pacha, who presented Mamá with a beautiful bouquet of flowers.

For the first time Mathilde and I were alone in the house, with dear Dudú and the cook, Germaine. No one came to see us except our cousin Rifaat, a student in political science, who brought us the latest news and the daily papers, which carried detailed accounts of the sad event.

Uncle Vitali lingered three days before he died, mourned by everyone. He enjoyed great prestige in the whole country, not only as the head of one of the most important business enterprises, but also because he had held high political positions.

Widowed soon after his first marriage, and at that time already forty-five years of age, he had married his young sister-in-law, who was twenty years his junior. Adela, an attractive blonde, gave him one son. A few years later, she also died, a victim of typhus. It was all very tragic.

After the funeral in Istanbul, my parents, completely shattered, returned to Paris. They faced a great deal of work in reorganizing and adapting themselves to the new situation. We let the cook go, and Papá rented out most of his spacious office, retaining only a small room, where he worked during the mornings with his secretary.

Gone were the evenings at the theater, the concerts, the parties. Silence and sadness took possession of our home, now avoided by those who had besieged it so happily only a few months earlier.

I could find no better consolation than my music. I practiced tirelessly, and soon I acquired a clear and powerful tone and a precise technique. Lazare Lévy, when he learned that we were going through a difficult time, wrote me an affectionate note, offering to give me free lessons. When I went to thank him, completely confused and asked him how I could possibly repay him, he answered, smiling, "By studying."

Summer came, and despite all the difficulties, Mamá refused to deny us a good vacation. While Mathilde went with her friends to a spa in vogue at the time, Mamá and I headed for the beach at Pornichet, in Brittany. There, Mademoiselle Blanche, the ex-director of the Lycée Français in Istanbul had rented a chalet, where she entertained some friends during the summer. The atmosphere was that of a family gathering, and I found all the guests congenial.

I would get up very early to go to the beach, deserted at that hour, and dive into the cold water, staying a long time in the sea. I swam well enough, but what I liked most was to "float," letting myself be rocked by the waves. When the noisy crowd of bathers began to invade the beach, I returned to the pension, where Mamá would be anxiously waiting for me.

I used to take long walks through the dunes, almost always alone. Once Mademoiselle Blanche said to me:

"Do you know the path along the edge of the cliffs? Along there lay the salt marshes that produce great quantities of salt, the town's main resource. The view is lovely, and besides, that's where the marsh flower grows, *la fleur des marais*. It's a color between rose and lavender, and it never wilts. If you go, be sure to bring home a bouquet."

This was very tempting for me, and the same day I set out on an expedition. The path was narrow, always clinging to the shore. No one passed me along the way, and there was not a sign of the coveted flower; only a few mountain pinks, beginning to appear among the scant grass. It was getting late, the sun had set and a fresh breeze was beginning to blow.

"I'll have to go back," I thought, "It's not safe to keep on looking; it will soon be dark."

But some mysterious impulse urged me on further. Suddenly, I saw a dark object directly in front of me. "A dog? or a hare?," I thought, approaching it cautiously. To my amazement, it proved to be a big bouquet of lavender-pink flowers, tied with a ribbon, and propped against a stone. They were the flowers I wanted, without a doubt! But who on earth, I wondered, had left that lovely bouquet? A mystery—! Another surprise awaited me there: several abandoned vine stalks, loaded with bunches of ripe grapes, with which I filled my bag. And then, with the miraculous bouquet in my arms, I set out for home.

However, the vacation at Pornichet did not really agree with me, and I returned to Paris with my health impaired, perhaps because I had swum too much, but more probably because the stress of our situation had affected my nerves. I was overcome with complete exhaustion. It was as if I carried an enormous weight on my shoulders, which threatened to crush me. I was unable to concentrate on any work, and I spent most of the day lying in bed, unable to read or to sleep. I couldn't sit down at the piano to play the fugues of Bach or the études of Chopin, as I had been doing every single day.

It hurt me to see my parents completely isolated in the great, cold indifferent city of Paris. Only three years had passed since our arrival, when everyone smiled at us, and everyone opened their arms to us. What a change!

The difficult winter of 1924 passed, and spring came. In August I went with Mathilde and loyal Dudú to the little town of Port Lesney in the Jura, where friends had recommended a quiet hotel, beside a trout stream. The price was within our reach, and we were able to spend some very pleasant days there with good friends. Excursions were the order of the day, and in the evenings, after dinner, there was a little informal dancing, much enjoyed by the young guests. The owner of the hotel would come out of the kitchen and take off his apron to ask the ladies to dance, demonstrating that his skill was as great on the dance floor as in the kitchen!

I returned to Paris in better spirits, with the desire to do something: to study, to work, to earn a little money. That winter I enrolled in the school of Jacques Dalcroze, whose method, "rhythmics," I knew from my stay in Geneva. I had been greatly impressed by his students' performances, especially their interpretations of Bach's fugues. In Paris, I found the classes very interesting, and when Dalcroze came to test us, at the end of the course, I did not do badly.

A little earlier, I had become friendly with a very talented young Rumanian pianist of my own age. He was also a student of Lazare Lévy, and was introduced to us by some of Mamá's cousins. Soon Alexander Demetriad became our family's best friend. Once or twice a week he came for supper, and would stay for hours afterward, playing the piano and asking for my opinions and advice. I, too, would play the works I was preparing for my lessons, and his praise always encouraged me.

"Vicky plays like a butterfly," he used to say to me.

We had a fraternal affection, and it never occurred to me that he could ever be a suitor.

I did have a romance with a distant relative of ours whom everyone called "Jackito." We were childhood friends, and he came often to the house. In spite of the fact that he was ten years older, we were very congenial, because music enchanted him, and he enjoyed listening to me enormously. I found him very attractive, with his abundant blond hair and clear blue eyes.

Victoria Kamhi in her early twenties, 1925.

When he asked for my hand I was nineteen, but my parents put him off because his economic situation was not sound.

Some years later my father would write from Istanbul that Jackito had not forgotten me, and that he planned to come to Paris soon to marry me. Papá added that first he would have to surmount some "difficulties." It was easy to guess that the reference was to his stepmother, who did not view favorably his marriage to a young girl with no dowry.

Jackito was unable to overcome the "difficulties," and for a long time I heard nothing of him.

Nevertheless, fate did not separate us completely, and we were to meet again several times and in several places: in Paris, Buenos Aires, Istanbul. Jackito attended Joaquín's lectures and the opening nights of his works, and he admired Joaquín profoundly. I knew that his affection for me not only continued, but that his feelings also included my husband.

During this time, my sister Mathilde was studying Philosophy and Letters at the Sorbonne. She was very popular, and had several suitors of substance, for she was most attractive. But she had the misfortune to fall in love with an adventurer—a fortune hunter. The engagement lasted a very short time, since, on learning that the dowry would be scant, he vanished like smoke, leaving my sister completely crushed. It was one more example of the curse of gold, of which all our family was victim. Nevertheless, Mathilde overcame the trauma, passed a brilliant examination for a Masters degree in Letters, and made a place for herself in the literary life of Paris.

After a short vacation with my parents at the spa in Vittel, I returned to Paris, where I devoted myself completely to the piano.

In the fall of 1926, Mamá had a serious accident. Tripping over a rolled-up rug, she fell against a bronze figure, and broke her arm in several places. The famous surgeon, Dr. Capette, set it and treated it during the whole winter. Those were unfortunate days, but happily, Mamá was able to recover completely.

When she began to improve, I accepted an invitation from my aunt, Ester Canetti, to visit her in Vienna. At first I was disappointed, for after an absence of four years, everything seemed different, the city and the people. Only my friend Luise was the same. And she was always ready to go for a walk or to plan excursions to nearby places. One day we visited the magnificent park of Lainz, ancient property of the Empress Elizabeth, whose restless soul found some serenity in its peaceful woodland, filled with roebuck, fallow deer and all the Alpine fauna.

Another day my aunt invited my cousin, Elias Canetti, to have lunch with us. Much later, he would win the Nobel prize for Literature. I remember that we had a very pleasant time with him.

When I returned to Paris, I felt completely disoriented, not knowing to what purpose I should devote myself. The music lessons were my only distraction. But—was that enough for a girl of my age?

Several months passed, gray and monotonous. The atmosphere at the Rue de Passy became increasingly depressing, for we saw no relief anywhere. And that is why I accepted the invitation from my aunt and uncle in Bucharest, who urged me insistently to visit them. A few weeks spent in a new environment would serve as a distraction, I thought. Surely I would return stronger and more cheerful.

In spite of my father, who worried every time I went out of the house, I boarded the Orient-Express on a cold day in January and, thirty-six hours later, I disembarked on the snow-covered platform of the railroad station of the capital of Rumania. My aunt and uncle had come to meet me, and gave me a warm welcome.

Uncle Maurice was the youngest of the nine Arditti brothers, and he was Mamá's favorite. He was a jovial, good-looking man, very impulsive and somewhat slipshod. He was the terror of his six children, between four and fourteen years of age.

Aunt Celine, a young Rumanian, fairly pretty and sophisticated, had placed him on a pedestal, and whatever he said was received as gospel.

That same day I went with them to a wedding celebrated according to the orthodox rite, which I had never seen before.

"To arrive on a wedding day is a good omen," my uncle declared emphatically. "Soon it will be your turn. You'll see!"

The following Sunday in Uncle Maurice's home there was a grand banquet, attended by some fifty persons, family and friends elegantly attired. An orchestra played Rumanian folk music continuously, alternating the lively dances with nostalgic melodies.

The Rhine wine and French champagne flowed freely, accompanying trays of fresh caviar from the Danube, roast lamb, and mountains of sweets and fruits.

The future bridegroom exchanged toasts with his fellow guests, laughing noisily with a swaggering air. He was tall and robust and had the profile of a Greek god, but fine lines furrowed his temples and there was some gray in his dark hair.

At his side, his fiancée, very tiny and dark, wore an absent expression, and never opened her lips nor tasted a bite. Yes, I was the bride-to-be.

When the guests had risen from the table, I noticed that my other uncle, Uncle Leon, who was very fond of me, drew the future bridegroom aside to say to him quietly, "Careful! Treat her well, for my little niece is a pearl!"

Some days passed, and little by little I realized just who my Uncle Maurice had chosen to be my husband. The son of a German mother and a Rumanian father, he was, in physical appearance, just as I have described: a successful combination. Morally, he was not. A womanizer, gambler and heavy drinker, he disliked work. Furthermore, it terrified me to realize that music bored him beyond words. He couldn't imagine that I spent hours at the piano, or that I liked to attend concerts and recitals, listening to Rubinstein, Rachmaninoff or Pablo Casals. We were at opposite poles in everything.

Nevertheless, the family began preparations for my wedding, which would be celebrated with great pomp at the beginning of March, according to my Uncle's wishes.

Mamá, who had arrived with Mathilde to attend the ceremony, could not imagine that her own brother could cause me unhappiness, and every time that I confided my fears to her, she reproached me with sharp words for my lack of confidence. As for my grandmother, a kind, sensible woman, she took great pains to cheer me up: "Do you think your uncle wants to do you harm?" she repeated again and again. "He knows that Hugo is a good man, with experience in life, and that you will be happy with him. Be confident. Believe me."

Now there were only a few days until that alien wedding. They had brought me the white silk gown with the veil and the crown of orange blossoms, which I contemplated, almost with horror.

One afternoon, to entertain me, someone brought a gypsy woman who was passing on the street into the dining room. I remember that she was a woman of middle age, with dark skin and eyes as black as jet. She examined the dregs of the Turkish coffee which we had just finished, and when my turn came, she looked at me fixedly, "You will marry," she said.

"Certainly."

"Your husband will be very famous."

I burst out laughing, "And what else?"

"Also he will be very rich."

"You're mistaken."

"I swear it."

"And will he be tall or short?"

"Of medium height."

"You're wrong. And how about his hair, what color will it be?"

"It is chestnut brown."

"And his eyes?"

"....This I don't see clearly."

"And what will his name be?"

"Something like Jo, perhaps José."

"You are mistaken, good woman."

Now angry, she cried out, "I swear that what I say is true. And furthermore, I see you seated on a *minder* [Turkish for sofa] with many honors. You will have many servants, and the people will kiss your hand. I swear it!"

One morning, unexpectedly, we received an urgent telegram from my father, announcing his arrival. I saw the heavens open! When he saw the pallor of my face, and the reddened eyes that looked at him in anguish, he understood everything. That very night, while the rest of the family was at the movies, he managed to have a showdown with Hugo, explaining our economic situation. Hugo, in turn, did not deny that what interested him most about this marriage was the dowry the family had promised him.

For some moments my father and I looked at each other in silence. Finally, Papá made his pronouncement:

"In that case, my daughter is not for you."

I threw myself into his arms, my heart overflowing with gratitude. When I turned my head, that man, who never should have crossed my path, had already left.

Two days later, my parents, Mathilde and I began the return journey. To distract me from this nightmare, my father suggested that we spend a few days in Venice, where we diligently visited churches, museums and palaces. We enjoyed gondola rides, and made excursions to the Lido, deserted at that time of the year, and to Murano, where we visited the factories famous for glass and costume jewelry, acquiring artistic necklaces and bracelets. The short vacation agreed with me, and little by little the "Rumanian adventure" was erased from my memory.

The first days in Paris were not very pleasant, for my untimely return had caused a veritable uproar. The house was full of friends who sympathized with me and all but offered me their condolences. Many approved of my decision, but others criticized my behavior. The gossip lasted a few weeks, but with time people forgot about it and everything returned to normal.

The only friend who didn't withdraw from us was Alexander, who appeared at the house almost every day to entertain us with his conversations sprinkled with jokes and with his renditions of Bach, Chopin and Debussy.

During the intermission of a concert by Paderewski I came upon Maestro Lazare Lévy. He seemed so truly glad to see me that I expressed my desire to resume our classes.

"Come when you like, you know that I am always glad to see you," he answered.

The long interval had not hurt me much, and with each lesson the maestro was more pleased with my progress. One day he advised me to take a state examination to acquire the title of teacher, which would authorize me to give private lessons. On his recommendation I went to see M. Schidenhelm, secretary of the Association des Prix de Piano du Conservatoire de Paris, which awarded these prestigious diplomas.

That year the prospects for a summer vacation were not very pleasing, because the unfortunate trip to Rumania had been an enormous expense for my parents. At the last minute it was decided that Mathilde would attend the summer course of the famous painter, Andre Lhôte, who had just discovered a very picturesque little village in the Rhone valley, a few kilometers from the Paris-Marseille-Rome highway. Mathilde had shown much talent for painting, and Lhôte was very interested in her. I was to accompany her to this little village, Mirmande, in the capacity of chaperon, which did not please me at all at first. But when I arrived and saw it, my disgust vanished completely, for the place was truly enchanting. Constructed in the shape of an amphitheatre on a hill surrounded by pine-covered mountains, it was a soft ochre color, with the true patina of the passing centuries. Many of the houses were in ruins, and those that remained standing had an age-old look, with grasses growing between the crevices.

The house acquired by Lhôte was an authentic medieval castle, with thick walls crowned by a tall tower. It was said that King Louis XIII had spent the night there on one of his journeys. And there Lhôte established his summer academy, where he held classes for painters who came from all over the world. Most were Americans, but there were also Germans, French and a few Australians. As a special favor, I was admitted to the group—the only pianist among so many painters! I could attend the classes and take part in the festivities in the town, which lasted until dawn.

Lhôte's wife, a woman of middle age, had great elegance and verve, although that did not keep him from running off with his secretary some time later, and eventually marrying her. Madame Lhôte took a great liking for me, and immediately found an ancient piano in the house of the parish priest, who invited me to practice there one or two hours a day, enough to prepare my next examination.

Mathilde and I enjoyed immensely the vacation in Mirmande, and when we returned to Paris, we were overflowing with health and optimism.

I had made friends with a few of Lhôte's pupils, whom I met from time to time in Montparnasse, either in the Café Dôme or in the Rotonde. Just like Montmartre, where the Bateau Lavior had welcomed so many future glories like Picasso, Modigliani, Braque and others, Montparnasse was, during those years, a nursery for artists of all nationalities who were struggling courageously to establish themselves.

One day a young painter from Baltimore introduced me to his friend Hans Hartung, and I spent quite a while with him, chatting about painting and music. Although I never saw him again, I learned through the press of his subsequent successes, and also of his vicissitudes. Fleeing from the Nazi inferno, he enlisted in the French Legion and fought against the German troops during the World War. In Metz, he lost a leg, and, when the war was over, he established himself in the Cote d'Azur, where he had a brilliant career, winning a place at the forefront of modern art.

I think that it was about that time that I first met Juana Mordó. We used to meet at a club where there were lively dances for young members. She was a very attractive girl who dressed tastefully.

I lost touch with her, and many years later, during the World War, we met again in Madrid. She came to see us at home and told us that she had lost her husband, and that she wanted to open a literary salon. She was clever and tactful, and soon began to gather together periodically the most distinguished of Madrid's intelligentsia. Joaquín and I were always invited and gladly attended those parties.

Years passed, and finally she told us that she had opened an art gallery in the center of Madrid. It quickly became enormously popular, and was known all over Europe.

Juana Mordó was one of the most intelligent women I have ever known. In addition, she had an infallible instinct for discovering budding talents, those who were destined to acquire, sooner or later, universal fame.

I never failed to visit all her exhibitions; they were truly lessons in art. Our long friendship lasted until she died at age 84, still very active.

Finally the day arrived, so anxiously awaited, for my piano examination. I remember that I was very confident, answering all the questions calmly, after having turned over to the jury my twelve biographies of famous composers. At the end, when I sat down at the piano to play the works on the program, I was so sure of myself that everything went very smoothly.

In the afternoon the candidates had to pass a dictated examination, extremely difficult, on the basis of chords. Here I became nervous, and I couldn't finish.

The following morning the applicants had to return to the Conservatory to hear the reading of the results. Monsieur Schidenhelm began with a brief speech, regretting that, of the seven candidates who had been examined, only one had passed with the grade "*assez bien*" [noteworthy]. Three had passed the written examination and would have to apply again for the oral, and the three others would have to present themselves again for the whole examination. My heart pounded, and I was overcome with anxiety at hearing these words. Surely, I was one of the three last ones and would have to begin again.

But Monsieur Schidenhelm had not finished, for he was going to read the names of all the candidates who presented themselves for the examination for the "Certificat d'aptitude a l'enseignement pianistique."

"Mademoiselle Victoria Kamhi passed with the grade '*assez bien.*"

I heard nothing more, so great was my emotion. When I went up to thank M. Schidenhelm, he congratulated me, saying that I almost achieved the '*mention bien*' [outstanding], but that I had lost two points because of the dictation.

I went home overwhelmed by happiness, which spread to my parents and Mathilde, who decided to give a little party that very night, inviting all our friends from the Lhôte Academy.

The house was filled, and more than one young man complimented me, not only on having passed the examination, but on my appearance and my elegant dress. I had never been happier, and I looked forward to a rosy future: students would flow in, I would give concerts endlessly, fame and money were assured! Now doors would open, thanks to this hard-earned diploma. Now, onward!

But days passed, and no student presented himself, nor was there any apparent interest regarding concerts from the agencies. "It was unbelievable!" Without losing hope, I stayed at home and continued to practice. I reviewed the works I had learned as if preparing to play them in a public concert: Haydn, Chopin, Ravel, not forgetting Schubert and Schumann. But no one heard me, except my dear father, who would doze off, after our frugal supper reclining in a big chair in the little Turkish room, rocked by the cadences of his favorite works.

Once again Alexander was the only friend who came to the house to keep us company and to divert us with his music and his jokes. And he encouraged me to keep on practicing as before.

I began to think seriously of looking for employment, so that I would not be a burden on my parents.

I read the ads in the papers, and it seemed to me that I had a good chance of finding something adequate, with a little luck. But I was very timid, and my somewhat childish appearance did not help me. Finally, I decided to reply to an advertisement seeking a governess who knew languages, with some knowledge of music.

I chose a skirt and jacket that were still in good condition, and wore the blue fox that my Aunt Adela had bought me in Berlin at my parents' request. She had bought it in a fine shop, paying the highest price. Thus attired, I could present myself in the Avenue Henri Martin, the most elegant part of Paris.

I knocked at the door of a palatial mansion and a uniformed maid answered. I was received by a very attractive woman of youthful appearance.

"Sit down, Mademoiselle," she said kindly. "I will tell you what this is about. I have a son and a daughter of school age, and I need a governess to be responsible for them in the afternoons. Besides French, what languages do you speak?"

"English, German and Spanish."

"Perfect. And now, tell me, could you review solfeggio with them and prepare them for their piano lessons?"

"Naturally, I'm a professional pianist, and a student of Professor Lazare Lévy."

"Stupendous, that's exactly what I need. The job is yours. What day would you be able to move into the house? We urgently need a resident governess."

"That won't be possible," I objected, "I live with my family, and I don't want to leave them."

"What a pity! You are exactly the person I need, because my husband and I often go out at night. I am so sorry."

"I am sorry, too," I answered, unable to repress a sigh.

The lady of the house accompanied me to the door, and I remember that she said to me, "Vous êtes trop bien pour nous" [You are too good for this.]

Some days later I found out that I had presented myself at the house of one of the most distinguished families of France. There was no luck.

Another day I noticed an ad by an English publishing house, looking for a secretary with knowledge of English and music.

At the reception desk a young, good-looking chap greeted me with a cheery "Hello."

He spoke French correctly, with a marked English accent.

"We edit light music for dancing. Could you play some of our things on the piano?"

"Why not!" I replied, and went to the upright piano, on which sheets of music were piled.

While I was playing the simple tunes, managing to give them the proper rhythm, the director watched me with visible admiration. "You play wonderfully," he exclaimed. "It's a pleasure to listen to you. But, I wonder if you know how to type and something of stenotypy?"

"Of course. I recently earned a diploma from the School of Stenotypy and I reached a hundred words a minute."

"Stupendous! Please bring your little machine, so that we can dictate a few words. When can you come back?"

"The day after tomorrow."

That same day I went to the school of Stenotypy to rent a machine, but they told me that a deposit was necessary. It was quite large, more than I could manage, and because I didn't want to trouble my father, I also lost that opportunity. It could have been a very interesting job for my future, according to my cousin, Jacques, a very clever lad, who, after joining the Philips record company as a "runner" had demonstrated such aptitude for the business that some years later he was named director of the firm.

It was 1928 and again winter had arrived, that long, raw Paris winter. Our spacious and luxurious flat on the Rue de Passy had become silent and lugubrious.

My brand new diploma had not brought me even one pupil. Lazare Lévy, whom I had gone to tell the happy news, had congratulated me warmly, adding that he was very busy and about to depart for a tour through Greece and Turkey. From the door he called to me, "Come see me at Christmas!" Crestfallen, I returned home.

How would I fill the time until Christmas? How would I manage to find pupils, lacking friendships and influence, without the backing of the Maestro? Devote myself to letters? Write poems as I had during the happy times in Vienna? Articles? But alas! I had lost all contact with the Viennese literary world, and no one there would remember me. Clearly there was nothing else to do but to wait.

My greatest comfort continued to be music. I never missed an important concert, and I also used every reduced-price ticket that I received from the agencies.

One night I went with my sister and her friend, Suzanne, to the opening concert of a young Polish pianist in the Salle Pleyel. The program was varied: Bach, Chopin, Beethoven, Ravel, Debussy. From the first notes I was spellbound by this singular artist: an astonishing technique, a rounded tone, a perfect style, emotion, he had everything. At the intermission, Mathilde and her friend wanted me to go home with them, for it was getting late.

"Impossible," I answered. "I don't want to miss a single note of this pianist. He is a genius!"

The next day, the Parisian press acclaimed Vladimir Horowitz, a twenty-four year old Polish pianist, as one of the great masters of the piano, predicting a brilliant international career for him. They were not mistaken.

Another night I attended the concert of Andrés Segovia, in the Salle Gaveau. It was the first time I had heard a classic guitar concert and what most impressed me was the Andalusian artist's tone, powerful, velvety, full of light and color. One well-known critic wrote: "There is more music in the little box of Andrés Segovia's guitar than in an entire orchestra."

With my family I attended the performance of the Ballets Russes and the Viennese Opera, the recital of La Argentina and Pavlova, etc.

I discussed them all with Alexander. He had by now given his first concert in Paris, and his artistic career had begun under the best auspices.

It was about this time that I met Dea Gombrich, a young Viennese violinist. She was very attractive: bright, gay and original. Her parents, great music lovers, had a predilection for Mozart, and that is why she was named Amadea.

We promptly became friends and began to play duets. We devoted several hours a week to the interpretation of Beethoven's sonatas. It was a pleasure to collaborate with her, for she was a formidable artist: a round, full tone, an amazing technique, great musicality; she had everything! She told me that Hermann Scherchen, the noted German orchestra conductor, was very interested in her, and that she had performed in his concerts on several occasions.

The manager of an agency offered us a contract for a concert tour through the casinos of popular spas during the summer season. But Dea advised me not to accept it, for it wasn't suitable for us.

When she departed for London, I was grief-stricken. I lost track of her for several years. Later, I learned that the director of the British Museum had fallen in love with her, and that they had married. I shall never forget my friend Dea....

Chapter IV

The *Preludio al Gallo Mañanero*

[The *Prelude to the Dawn Cockerel.* English glosses are provided for the convenience of non-Spanish-speaking readers.]

One day Alexander brought me a request from a fellow-student in Paul Dukas' class at the School of Music. His friend had sent a score to a conductor of the Wiesbaden Orchestra and, in spite of having requested its return several times, his letters, written in French and in Spanish, had produced no result. Would I not help by writing a letter in German to this gentleman?

"Why not! I'll write it right now," I replied, and a few minutes later I handed him the letter and thought no more of it.

But a few weeks later Alexander told me that his friend had at last received the score of *Cinco Piezas Infantiles* [*Five Children's Pieces*] and that he sent me his most profuse thanks.

"What is your friend's name?" I asked absentmindedly.

"He's a Valencian musician, and his name is Joaquín Rodrigo."

"I don't know how, but that name is familiar. But, of course, I have a piece of his in the house—it's magnificent—that I want to prepare for a performance."

"This may be difficult," observed Alexander, skeptically. "He is a very young man and not as well-known as Albéniz, Falla or Turina, although there's no doubt he has talent."

"I'm going to show you another opinion," I exclaimed.

And from the music cabinet I pulled out the July 31, 1928, issue of *Le Monde Musical*, in the supplement of which were published several pages of the *Preludio al Gallo Mañanero*, with an explanatory note which read thus: "With this fragment we give an example of the talent of this notable musician, a pupil of Paul Dukas at the Ecole Normale de Musique, who will soon prove himself the successor of Albéniz and of Manuel de Falla, although in his work the influence of folk melodies is not as great as in his illustrious compatriots."

This impressed me. "Listen, Alexander." I told him, "This young man has merit, and I want to meet him as soon as possible. Couldn't you ask him to come with you the next time you come to the house?"

Alexander agreed, and the two of us along with Mathilde planned a party, to which we also invited the young art students from the Lhôte Academy.

There were already a number of people in the drawing room when the Spanish musician made his entrance, on the arm of his faithful secretary, Rafael. A deep emotion shook me when he took my hand. I could only stammer a few words of welcome, and it seemed to me that my voice, a little childish, amused him. A bright smile lit his face, disclosing a row of very white teeth. What most attracted my attention was his broad forehead, framed by curly chestnut hair.

That night I didn't have to be coaxed when someone asked me to play a piece on the piano. I sat down immediately at my Pleyel and played for more than an hour, both classic and modern works. I felt no uneasiness, for the young composer clearly enjoyed my renditions: Haydn, Beethoven, Bach, Mendelssohn, Liszt and Fauré followed one another in an uninterrupted parade. The guests began to say good-night, for it was past midnight, but the two Spaniards gave no sign of weariness. By the time they took their leave, the metros and buses had stopped running.

"What a hike they will have to get home, and the night is so cold!" I thought compassionately.

The following morning I received a huge bouquet of flowers as a gift from Joaquín Rodrigo.

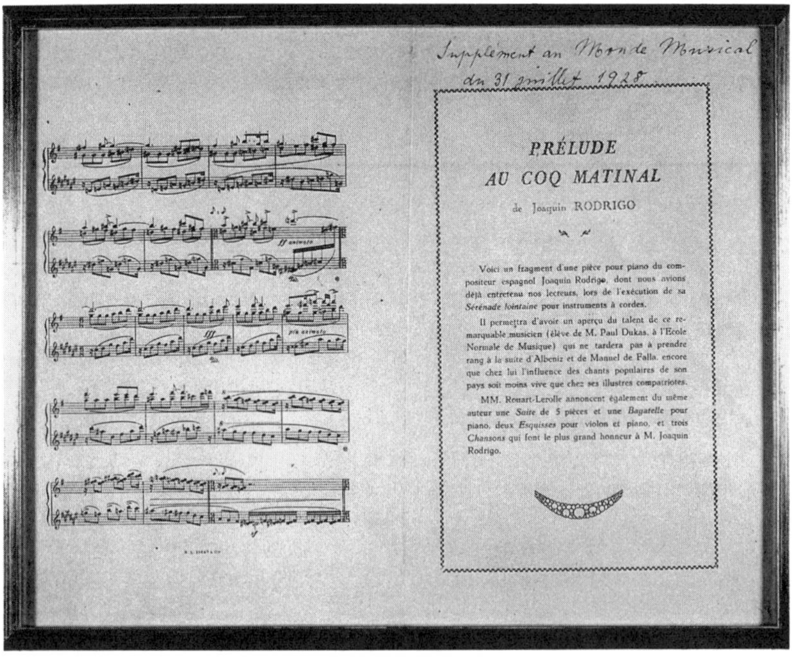

Fragment of the piece for piano, *Preludio al gallo mañanero*, 1928.

It was in March of that same year (1929) that I received two invitations to attend the première of his *Cinco Piezas Infantiles* [*Five Children's Pieces*] by the Straram Orchestra. I went to the concert with my friend, Marcelle.

The Théâtre des Champs Elysées was crowded with people, all the cream of the Parisian musical world. From my seat I watched the young composer, seated in a box, surrounded by friends. Once again I noticed the shape of his forehead. "It is the brow of a genius," I thought, and felt impressed.

With the first measures of the *Cinco Piezas Infantiles* I was seized by a profound emotion: I held my breath so as not to miss a note. It was the *Plegaria* [*Prayer*], pregnant with deep nostalgia, which most enraptured me. The audience's approval was unanimous, and the author was obliged to acknowledge their ovations several times from his box.

During the intermission, my friend and I went down to the dressing room, where we soon found him surrounded by admirers. I shyly approached and to my great astonishment, when he heard my voice he gave a half-turn, with both hands extended toward me. His face reflected his immense happiness as he thanked me for having attended the première.

"Will you let me see you home?" he asked, a little anxiously.

"No, indeed. I will go home with my friend. We live very near here. You mustn't trouble yourself."

He wanted to insist, but I didn't accept his offer; I didn't want to take him away from his admirers.

"Then let me dedicate this work to you, since you rescued it."

"I would be honored."

Later I asked him if I might not go to his house for the purpose of interpreting his works, which I was studying.

And as a matter of fact, some weeks later I went to the flat on the rue du Château d'Eau, where I played the *Bagatelle* and the *Berceuse de Printemps* [*Lullaby of Spring*]. The interpretations won the author's approval.

Shortly after this, Joaquín and I met at a concert and, as we were leaving the hall, he made a request: Why didn't we go to a Russian tea house which was very popular at the time? That was very tempting, and I accepted quickly. I remember it very clearly: a small dining room, very elegant and full of people. The young waitresses, wearing typical Russian clothing, served tea with all sorts of exquisite specialties, all accompanied by a background of folk music.

We had a wonderful time, but I did not suspect that the invitation had cost Joaquín a fortune—as he confessed to me much later—and that until the end of the month, he and his companion had to tighten their belts.

Rodrigo, nine months old.

Spring came with blue skies and radiant sunshine, bringing the urge to leave the city's asphalt, in quest of the green shade of the countryside, with the song of birds and the murmur of streams. And so we decided, Joaquín and I, to make an excursion to St. Cloud, accompanied by Raphael.

In those days, the historic park was not as crowded as today, and wild violets and anemones grew beneath the old trees. I remember that we spent a marvelous afternoon there, happy to be able to live in surroundings of peace and harmony.

Is there anything more beautiful than nature on a spring day?

During the long stroll through St. Cloud's forest, Joaquín talked about his childhood, his family and his studies.

He told me that he was born in the historic city of Sagunto, the 22nd of November (St. Cecilia's day) 1901.

His parents had ten children, six daughters and four sons. Joaquín was the youngest son. Two of his sisters died during childhood.

Joaquín was born in the family home, in the Plaza of the Glorieta. Just a few meters from his house stood the musical society, the *Lira Saguntina* [*Lyre of Sagunto*].

Many times, he would go to listen to the musicians during their rehearsals, and would stay with them for hours on end, absorbed, until the arrival of his father or an older brother made him return to reality.

His father, Vicente Rodrigo Peirats, merchant and landholder, was originally from Almenara, Castellón. Of robust build, he smoked a lot, and as a good vintner, he liked to drink, without overindulging.

He was a man of few words, but he knew how to make himself obeyed.

His mother, Juana Vidre Ribelles, was born in Cuartell de los Valles. She was of average height, with a pleasant, kindly face. Although she had no formal education, she was blessed with a refined spirit and was moved by art in all its forms.

I was saddened when Joaquín told me of the diphtheria epidemic that hit Sagunto when he was only three years old, and which caused the death of many children. It cost Joaquín most of his sight, although he could still see light and colors.

At the age of four, his parents took him to Barcelona, where Dr. Barraquer operated on his eyes, and was able to somewhat improve his vision.

Until he was ten his nurse, Rosalía Piedra, took care of him. She was a good woman, who remained in the house as cook until a very advanced age.

During summer vacations the family traveled to San Antonio de Requena, where they rented a spacious house. Joaquín's favorite pastime was to take long rides on his donkey through the meadows that surrounded the village.

At the age of fourteen he began to study harmony and composition with Professor Francisco Antich. He was already an excellent pianist, and also played the violin. His friendships with Enrique Gomá, and with the veteran Eduardo López Chavarri, who admitted him to his class, were born during that period.

Eventually his parents bought a summer home in Estivella, near Valencia.

In spite of many obstacles, Joaquín was able to matriculate at the Conservatory, then directed by Amancio Amorós.

At that point a period of misfortune and financial ruin began for the family.

Notwithstanding, Joaquín always had with him his young secretary, Rafael Ibáñez, an erstwhile employee of his father, whose duty was to read everything to him and to copy his music. Without formal knowledge, he nevertheless copied music admirably, better than a professional copyist!

Joaquín's first works were *La enamorada junto al pequeño surtidor* [*The Girl in Love Beside the Little Fountain*] with *Pequeña Ronda* [*A Little Night Serenade*] for violin and piano.

He soon saw one of his greatest aspirations fulfilled: the première of his work, *Juglares* [*Minstrels*] by the Valencia Symphony Orchestra, under the direction of Maestro Izquierdo. The work received very good critical reviews.

Encouraged by this success, the following year Joaquín entered the National Competition for Composition with his *Cinco Piezas Infantiles*, and won second prize. Soon after, the work had its première in Paris by the Straram Orchestra, with an enormous success, which I myself witnessed. I had been invited to that concert by the composer!

But let us go back. Faithful to the tradition established by Albéniz, Falla and Turina, Joaquín decided to undertake a journey to Paris to enroll in the Ecole Normale de Musique. In his valise he carried the *Zarabanda Lejana* [*Distant Sarabande*], the *Suite para Piano* [*Piano Suite*], *Cinco Piezas Infantiles* and the *Preludio al Gallo Mañanero*. There he studied composition in Paul Dukas's class for five years, becoming his favorite pupil. The great master said of him: "I have seen the arrival in Paris of Falla, Albéniz, Rodrigo. I'm not sure that this last is not the most gifted of the three." Joaquín tells many anecdotes about his Maestro, as well.

Joaquín Rodrigo posing with the Class of Music at the Ecole Normale de Musique of Paris. Professor Paul Dukas sits in front of Rodrigo, 1928.

He also speaks of Manuel de Falla, who became his great friend. One morning while Dukas was holding class, he was told that Falla was waiting for him downstairs. The Maestro made Joaquín go down with him, to introduce him to the composer of *El Amor Brujo*.

Falla came to Paris frequently, but the reason for this trip was that he had been made a member of the "Légion d'Honneur." The ceremony of investiture would take place in the Rothschild Palace, and a concert would be presented which, at first, was to be dedicated wholly to the music of Falla. He, nevertheless, wanted them to include renditions of the works of other Spanish musicians. As a result, the program included works by Turina, Halffter, Falla—who interpreted his concert for the clavicembolo—and by Joaquín, who played his Harpsichord Concerto—*Preludio al Gallo Mañanero* and the *Zarabanda Lejana*.

This concert's success was extraordinary. The cream of the French intelligentsia had filled the Rothschild Palace. Joaquín remembers the great opportunity that Falla offered him with gratitude, for it soon bore fruit.

As a matter of fact, Joaquín was soon able to publish his works in the Maison Eschig and the Maison Rouart & Lerolle. Now he was launched!

It was Papá's custom to eat lunch in a small restaurant near his office, in the Saint Lazare district. There he met a middle-aged Russian exile, manager of a theatrical agency. The Russian was a very kind, affable man, with a keen sense of humor, and they soon became friends.

One day Papá saw him arrive with a worried look on his face. "What's happened to you?" he asked, concerned.

"My secretary has just quit."

"But surely you can find another?"

"I'm afraid that it won't be easy. This girl knew languages and handled German perfectly. Would you know of anyone?"

"Of course! I know someone who is fluent in several languages: my own daughter."

"She's hired as of this minute," exclaimed Boronoff. "I'll give her a generous salary and hand her the keys to the office. I'll only need her in the afternoons."

The next day I went to the agency, where I was introduced to his partner, a young Catalán, good-humored and talkative, who was friendly and helpful. My attention was attracted by the numerous signed photographs in the large office: Nijinsky, Karsawina and other stars of Diaghilev's Ballets Russes.

My work was interesting and amusing. Through the office paraded vaudeville and circus performers, as well as singers and dancers of renown, like Vicente Escudero, whom I had applauded in his Paris recitals. When I asked for his autograph, he very gallantly signed a handsome photo for me. I still have it.

I had expected to continue with the agency. But Boronoff had another partner, a Polish woman, who was presumptuous and arrogant. She did not look kindly on my presence in the house, regarding me as a spoiled child. Every day she became more demanding, and managed to make my life impossible. My complaints were useless; I couldn't stand it.

Finally, tired of her insolences and annoyances, I had no choice but to resign this position, which had seemed so ideal. And Papá agreed with me, regretting it, as much as I did.

* * *

It was a soft, warm night in May. We had organized a small party at the flat in Passy for a few friends, because the following day I was going to Belgrade, to spend the vacation with my cousins, Luisa and Sami. Among the guests were Joaquín and Rafael.

Joaquín sat down beside me, and I noticed a profound sadness in his expression. When the time came to say good-bye, he asked if I would return soon.

"I don't know," I answered. "Perhaps never."

"What! It's impossible! If I never saw you again, I would die of grief!"

I began to laugh. "Don't take it so hard. In that case, I will come back, for sure."

"Truly?" he exclaimed, jubilant. "Then you will wait for me?"

"Yes, Joaquín," I answered firmly. "I will never leave you again."

As in a dream, I saw him bend over to kiss my hand.

Profoundly moved, I watched him walk away on the arm of his faithful esquire. A still, small voice told me that this could not be the end of our romance, and that some day we would meet again.

* * *

Austerlitz Station was an anthill of activity on that gray November afternoon. I looked impatiently toward the platform where I hoped to recognize my friend from Valencia. Almost six months had passed since we parted, and I had almost forgotten what he looked like. When the express from Hendaye arrived and the passengers began to get off, I carefully inspected each one who hurried toward the exit. What a long time he was taking! At last I saw him in the crowd. As always, he was on the arm of his faithful companion, who was looking to right and left. My heart stopped: instead of looking for me, he was looking into space, a worried look on his face. He had a feeling, a sense that I was very near him, but alas! he didn't see me. How could I have forgotten this detail? His letters, which I had received all during the summer, were like those of any other man in love, a little more melancholy, perhaps. But what grace, what tenderness, what wit in those lines! And now I found myself confronting the tremendous reality: the man who had filled my thoughts for so many months could never see me. Everything separated us, irreparably. And while his hands clasped mine and his warm voice caressed me, I gave into the saddest foreboding: I walked beside him, absorbed, without daring to look him in the face. He must have sensed my state of mind, for his face clouded little by little, and by the time I said good-bye to him, at the door of my house, he was pallid.

Little by little our relationship renewed itself. We would go to concerts together, and afterward, he and Rafael always took me home. And each time we discovered more community of interest: music, poetry, nature, the sea. We were in total agreement about everything, and I never remember having an argument with him.

Nevertheless, my father viewed our growing friendship with apprehension, and to avoid irritating him we had to conceal our meetings. And was he not right, my dear father? Where could this lead? Everything separated us, and the most difficult problem was Joaquín's lack of livelihood. He had no fortune of his own, nor any possibility of a position or of secure employment. Without a minimum income, how could we support a home or raise children? Man can not live on music alone. Therefore, the most sensible thing would be to break off the relationship. Mathilde, the only person who approved of this match, was very much criticized, even by her closest friends. For me, it was a situation with no way out.

A few weeks later, by pure chance, a friend of my sister's asked me if I would be interested in working in a children's home sponsored by the Rothschild Foundation. They had offered her a position at the center, but she was not attracted to that kind of work. I told her that it was exactly the kind of thing that interested me, and that I would appreciate very much her recommending me to the Baroness Rothschild, which she did immediately.

And so I set out eagerly one morning for the Rothschild Palace on rue Saint Florentin. My heart was beating rapidly as I went up the monumental stairs that led to the enormous salon. A very rigid butler indicated a chair, and while I marvelled at the Persian rugs which covered the floor, the antique porcelain jars and the paintings, all worthy of display in the Louvre, he walked from one side of the room to the other without taking his eyes off me.

I waited quite a while, until the lady of the house appeared. This was the Baroness Germaine herself, wife of Baron Edward Rothschild, President of the French Railways. Tall and slender, she wore a garnet velvet dress of refined elegance. Her face was beautiful, and she seemed very young, in spite of her white hair. She greeted me cordially and invited me to sit down beside her.

"They have told me, Mademoiselle, that you would like to work in one of my charitable institutions. Is that right?"

I replied that, in fact, I was very much interested in that kind of work, having spent quite some time in a dispensary, and that I had a diploma in childcare.

"Won't it be too tiring for you?" she asked. "You seem very fragile."

I assured her that I looked forward to the prospect of working in one of her charitable centers.

"Very well," replied the Baroness with a friendly smile. "We will accept you. But first you will have to take some courses at the School for Social Workers, and work as an assistant in several of the Foundation's Institutions. Naturally, the expenses will be borne by the Foundation, and you will receive a small monthly salary until you obtain a post as Director in one of our centers."

I said good-bye to the Baroness with a profound feeling of gratitude. My road was marked, my future secured.

Baron and Baroness Edward Rothschild were great lovers of music. Their daughter, Jacqueline, was an excellent pianist. She later married the famous cellist, Igor Piatigorski.

My admission to the Rothschild Foundation began a period of intensive work for me. I enrolled in the School for Social Workers, and attended classes every morning. Afterwards the students would visit different charitable centers and philanthropic institutions, such as homes for the elderly, hospitals, maternity centers, etc.

I remember that in one children's home, founded by Luise Kopp, there was an epidemic of mumps. A few days after that visit, I came down with the disease, with severe pain and high fever. It kept me in bed for more than a week.

In the afternoons we went to the Belleville Home, a day care center for children of working parents. Several monitors and I directed their games and took care of them until their parents came to pick them up.

My co-workers were almost all wonderful young women, and in that setting I was very content.

One day I received an invitation to attend a series of lectures on psychology and pedagogy. I was surprised to discover the name of Elsa von Koehler, my professor at the Lyceum Luithlen, in Vienna, on the list of speakers. She had been especially fond of me, and when I approached her after the lecture, she was very pleased to accept my praise.

"You have found your vocation," she exclaimed. "A few more months of study and you will be an excellent teacher and a brilliant lecturer, applauded everywhere."

"I don't believe it," I answered, in confusion. "I don't have the talent for it."

"Of course you do," she assured me. "What you lack is practice, but this is acquired with time. You won't have any problems, believe me."

The next day she had lunch at our home with my entire family, which gave us a chance to recall the happy days of the past.

"You must come to Vienna to visit our social institutions and study the new methods: pedagogical, psychological, psychotechnical, etc. These last few years an enormous project has been going on in

Austria, which could serve as a model for the whole world. Why don't you ask the Baroness Rothschild (and it is clear from all this how much I think of you) to grant you a scholarship for study which would redound to the benefit of her own institutions? Try to convince her, and once you are in Vienna, I will back you in every way I can."

Some days later I repeated Professor von Koehler's proposition to the Baroness's secretary, who promised to submit it to her at the first opportunity. Soon after, to my happy surprise, I received the news that my petition had been granted, and that at the beginning of summer I could leave for the Austrian capital with a scholarship from the Rothschild Foundation.

Professor Elsa von Koehler kept her word, and from the first days of my arrival, was my solicitous and efficient guide.

She handed me a complete list of influential people I should see. Prominent among them was the name of Paul Lazarsfeld, who was Director of the Psychotechnical Institute and also held a Chair at the University.

Encouraged by my history professor, Hildegard von Perckhammer —who was to die young, mourned by all her students—I went to see him at the University. I never regretted it, for his support was extremely helpful.

In the course of the six weeks spent in Vienna I visited all of the centers for social work: the specialized schools, the school for the retarded, several hospitals, maternity facilities, etc., all recently established, and true models for this genre. I visited the Center for Professional Orientation at City Hall several times, and also the center for pre-marital counseling. I toured the ultra-modern housing for workers, provided with all conveniences. I visited the Montessori School, which I thought was marvelous, and the famous *Mutterschule* (school for mothers), institutions which were attracting visitors from all the world. As Paul's guest I attended the courses of Karl and Charlotte Buehler, who were at the forefront of Vienna's modern psychology.

On Sundays I went out for excursions with my dear friend Luisl, and rediscovered the famous "Vienna Woods," going up to Kobenzl, Kahlenberg and Semmering, which brought back memories of our childhood. It was a beautiful and worthwhile trip, which left a profound impression.

A few days later I made a trip to the Palace on the rue Saint Florentin to hand over to the Baroness's secretary all of the notes and sketches, and the text which I had been able to amass during my interesting trip as student observer. Soon after I was told that the Baroness had read them all carefully, and was very pleased with my mission.

It was July and in Paris the heat was suffocating. I missed the Austrian forests and the flowering banks of the Danube, and only wanted to get away from the Parisian asphalt as soon as possible.

Several colleagues had told me of the vacation colonies which the Rothschild Foundation supported, and it occurred to me to apply for a position as monitor of the colony at St. Pol, a beach near Dunkirk. There I was entrusted with a group of thirty boys, between eight and twelve years old, little demons who were a constant harassment. They were mischievous, undisciplined and impertinent, and I didn't know how to make them obey me.

At night I took refuge in my little room, next to the boys' dormitory. I would hear their laughter and their scuffling without knowing how to intervene, knowing full well that they would pay me no attention whatever. And soon I realized that I was not of the stature to undertake a position of authority, not here nor elsewhere. At the same time, I felt a great desire to have a home of my own, to have children of my own to care for, to bring up and indulge. Nevertheless, I knew that this was not possible, and that I must keep on struggling along this thorny road which I had chosen, without looking back.

When I returned from St. Pol I took a few days of vacation at Mirmande, a real oasis, which I always left with regret.

My parents too, had become accustomed to country life, and spent long periods in the little village.

As always, Joaquín had celebrated Christmas of 1932 with his family, in Valencia.

He had written me that his parents were completely in favor of our marriage and that they would welcome me with open arms. He wanted to return soon to formally request my hand. His letters expressed a great euphoria, which I found contagious.

One day in February, Joaquín came to the house, full of hope.

I don't remember my parents' reaction, nor do I recall the exact words which were exchanged—I was so upset that day.

I only know that I saw an immense sadness in his face, and that all my courage drained away. I would never be able to leave my dear parents, to go far from them, into the unknown, in spite of all the vows of love and happiness.

Later, with my heart aching, I explained it to Joaquín, and he finally agreed with me. And so, resigned, we had to say good-bye once more, but this time it was to be good-bye forever.

My only consolation during that time was my social work at the Foundation.

One day the Baroness's secretary called me to her office to tell me that they had agreed to establish a social Club for young people in Belleville, and that I had been chosen to direct it, since I had all the requisite talents for the post. I could chat with young people, advise them, and play dance music. In short: liven everything up!

The new club would be open four times a week, from eight until eleven at night. I knew that there were more than twenty Metro stops between Passy—the station near my house—and Belleville, and that it would take me until after midnight to return home. Nevertheless, I accepted the offer.

At first all went well. My new job seemed interesting and even amusing, because it introduced me to another world. I was in contact with the youth of every social class, children of workers and of emigrants from Russia and central Europe, apprentices and University students.

I did everything possible to make them feel at home in their new Club, and to form a big family. I made sure that they heard good music, that they found interesting books and magazines there, and that they developed taste; and they rewarded me with their affection and devotion.

Naturally, more than one lad shyly courted me. I remember that a Polish student was determined to marry me as soon as he finished his studies at the University. Another Club member—this one more mature—declared that he was very sorry not to be a rich man, since that would have given him the right to ask for my hand.

I would almost always sit down at the piano to play a waltz or a one-step, and the young people would dance tirelessly until the Club closed its doors. But, all this activity was too much for me, and began to endanger my health. I never complained, but my father, who watched me with growing anxiety, clearly saw my pallor and my weariness. One day, he rebelled:

"Enough of this," he cried, beside himself. "I won't let you keep on like this! As if you were a soldier on manoeuvres! Don't forget that you were never very strong, and that your mother has looked after you as the apple of her eye! The best legacy we can leave our children is good health. If you don't slow down soon, you are going to have serious problems!"

My father was right, completely right. I wrote a letter to the Baroness, very sadly explaining the reasons that made it necessary for me to resign the position I had undertaken with such high hopes. My resignation was accepted, and once again I found myself facing the unknown, not knowing where to turn. I had lost my bearings completely.

Summer came, and again our family moved to Mirmande, now crowded with students from the Lhôte Academy.

I was completely dispirited, and found no comfort anywhere. Again misfortune had overcome the whole family: unable to maintain our way of life at the rue de Passy, my parents had been forced to leave that beautiful flat. The only shelter that remained was the humble little house in Mirmande. But where would we go when winter came? How would we live? Would it not have been better for me to continue working for the Rothschild Foundation as monitor, manager or whatever?

That summer Mathilde had accepted an invitation from a close friend of Papá's, who was at that time the French Consul in Barcelona. She took advantage of this visit to make a quick trip to Valencia to see Joaquín, who was spending the summer in a village near the city. When she came back to Mirmande she raved about everything she had seen there, with her painter's eye for color: the marvelous coloring of the sea, the green of the leafy orange groves, the whiteness of the typical houses of the villages, the friendliness of the people. Above all, she was moved by the reception given her by Joaquín's family, especially his mother, who had presented her with the fruits and delicacies of the country.

She said frankly that she had found Joaquín very unhappy. Apparently he was very much in love with me, and our break-up had caused him profound grief. He felt spiritually abandoned, without any sort of stimulus, had lost his desire to compose, and all the joy of living had left him.

Listening to her words, I felt shaken. Of course, I had not forgotten him, either; my thoughts were full of him. My tenderness was tinged with remorse: if he had stopped composing, if he was wasting his talent, I was the only one to blame. It was maddening!

But what comfort could I bring him? I was a thousand leagues from the little Valencian village where he had taken refuge. How could I make him understand that I was his best friend?

Chapter V

Love and Marriage

On a gray November day I had taken the train from Mirmande to the Spanish border. Mamá who was very worried, had come with me as far as Toulouse, saddened because I was going without my father's approval. In an effort not to increase her grief, I feigned happiness and optimism, but when the time came to say good-bye, I could not hold back my tears.

"Remember to call me if you are not happy with this," she said kissing me again and again. "You know that your parents' home will always be open to you."

In Barcelona Joaquín and his older brother, Paco, were waiting to welcome me to Spain. We were so overcome with emotion that we could scarcely say a word.

As we followed the highway to Valencia, I was lost in admiration of the picturesque little villages we passed through, and the exuberant vegetation—all so new to me.

It was autumn, but in Valencia I found blue skies and a radiant sun. At the spacious apartment on the Calle Sorní, the whole family was waiting for me: parents, brothers and sisters and many nieces and nephews, full of curiosity. They gave me a warm welcome, and did everything possible to make my stay pleasant. Of course, their lives seemed strange for me: the people, the customs, the activity. I was surprised to see so much luxury, such abundance, in the house of my future parents-in-law.

The meals were delicious, and there were mountains of nougat, marzipan and other sweets. But I saw no oranges anywhere, although we were in the house of a great Levantine landowner!

The feast days of Christmas and the New Year passed, celebrated with opulent banquets, "*paellas*" and informal receptions, all accompanied by the deafening noise of tambourines and "*zambombas*" [a rustic musical instrument of Spain.]

Immediately after the New Year preparations began for our wedding, set for January 19th, 1933. It was celebrated in the strictest intimacy, in accordance with our preference, since my family could not attend.

After the wedding banquet, Joaquín and I went for a long walk along the beach, where a cold wind whipped the shore. The following morning we set out for Madrid by automobile, accompanied by Rafael, who had sworn to stay with us as long as he lived.

Wedding day, Valencia, January 19, 1933.

The first months in Madrid passed tranquilly. We had rented a furnished apartment on "Castelló" street, and I remember that on the first night we had a tremendous fright, when the heavy chandelier in the living room fell from the ceiling, landing a few inches from the sofa where Joaquín and I were sitting after dinner.

We had hired a maid named Josefa, who did everything very satisfactorily, so that I had lots of free time. On sunny days, we made excursions to Aranjuez, Alcalá de Henares—how sick I was after eating tripe there, for the first time in my life!—to El Escorial and to Toledo.

We went to the Café almost every night, and had tickets to the symphony concerts, directed by Fernández Arbós and Pérez Casas. They welcomed us very cordially, as did the guitarist Regino Sainz de la Maza, and his attractive wife Josefina, daughter of the famous writer, Concha Espina.

At the time, Madrid was one of the most typical and welcoming of Europe's capitals. The dry, sunny climate was very healthful and the waters of Lozoya were a blessing. We found the city greatly to our liking, and hoped to be able to settle there some day.

Nevertheless, in spite of all his efforts Joaquín could not arrange for a single radio performance, nor any job with a fixed salary. After cooling his heels for several weeks at the Ministry of Public Education, he obtained an appointment as unpaid interim professor at the College for the Blind, a job he would never undertake.

For one day in April we received a telegram from Valencia, announcing that Joaquín's mother, who suffered from stomach ulcers, was critically ill, and that we should return immediately if we wanted to see her again. I had to quickly gather together all our clothes, the music and the books, with the help of Rafael and Josefa, in time for the night train. When we arrived in Valencia, we found my mother-in-law very weak from a heavy hemorrhage, but out of danger. She would live another nineteen years.

Nevertheless, we could not return to Madrid, for Paco, the older brother, told us that the family financial situation, which had been only fair during the winter, had become catastrophic, to the point that he had to leave his own apartment and move into his parents' house with his wife and their three daughters.

* * *

Summer arrived, and the entire family moved to Estivella. As it turned out, the "manorial home" was a big old house, right on the highway, with a tiny yard whose main feature was an ample henhouse, full of hens and chickens.

The place could not have been noisier, and the heat was truly asphyxiating.

Joaquín and I would get up very early in order to escape from the house in search of a little peace and quiet. We would climb up the hillside and sit, either in a vineyard or under an olive tree, where we would stay for long hours. The family meals were unavoidable, and we had to endure the clamor of the little nephews, as annoying to us as the flies and mosquitoes which pursued us relentlessly day and night.

Mathilde, who appeared unexpectedly for a short visit, was appalled by this situation, and promised me her help.

It was on the night before the return to Valencia that Joaquín's old nurse, Rosalía, who had been the family cook for many years, became gravely ill.

They called Don Damián, the village doctor, who diagnosed a severe gastronomic hemorrhage and declared that the patient should not be forced to travel to the capital. Someone would have to stay to care for her, and I was the person elected for the task.

When Joaquín and I found ourselves alone, with poor Rosalía prone in bed, I experienced a sense of relief. Without losing my head, I organized our new life, with the aid of Rafael and a kindly and skillful woman of the village. While she cared for the patient at night, I attended to her during the day. Don Damián, a good physician as well as an excellent person, paid us a daily visit and praised my talents as a nurse, assuring us that, with God's help, we would have the patient on her feet soon.

And actually, a few days later, she was able to eat a little and was permitted to move around in bed.

Meanwhile, our pantry was almost empty, and only a few little chickens remained in the henhouse. I refused to sacrifice them. Our savings had decreased lamentably, and I anxiously watched the specter of hunger approaching. Where would we get the money to feed four people? I went over the possibilities a thousand times, but came up with nothing.

Then one fine day, out of the blue, a car arrived, driven by Joaquín's brother, Pepe, who had had the brilliant idea of loading it with a mountain of food: fruits and vegetables from his garden, several hens, a sack of rice, and a load of firewood. All the food was freshly gathered from the farm he was working at Utiel, a nearby town. We all received it with gratitude, including Rosalía, who was by now able to walk around a bit in the yard.

Some neighbors had given me a puppy, only a few weeks old. He was a mixed breed puppy, very funny and clever. I named him Vartán, after our Armenian porter in Istanbul. One day we found, to our sorrow, that he had disappeared from the yard, where he had been playing with a ball. Some light-fingered passer-by had stolen him. However, several days later, when I opened the door to the street, there stood Vartán, panting. To come home, he had probably had to travel several miles under a blazing sun. When he saw us, he jumped all over us, mad with happiness. He was our best friend during our stay in Estivella.

A few days later Rafael asked me if I wanted to buy a chance on the next big lottery drawing. Mamá had just sent me a little money, so I told him to buy me two chances.

"I want the numbers to end with 5," I specified.

Rafael immediately went out to find the runner.

"There's one thing," he told him, "they must end in 5, eh!"

"And if they don't—?" replied the other man.

"They have to end in 5," ordered Rafael, half-turning away.

The next morning with joyous amazement I read in the newspaper that we had won a prize of 3500 pesetas, a fortune for us. It not only solved our economic problem for several weeks, but it let us redeem our piano, which had been attached in Valencia. That was the second miracle of the summer.

But matters would have to be cleared up in a very different manner. My parents, alarmed by the strange situation in which I found myself, decided to take a hand in the matter, and a few weeks before Christmas Mamá arrived in Estivella. Those were happy days for all of us. During this time Mamá tried to broach the subject with Joaquín's family, to try to convince them that we could not keep on living from hand to mouth. A young couple could not be expected to establish themselves without receiving some economic assistance. But it was all in vain. After several futile conversations, we decided that the best solution would be for us to separate for a while.

On the nineteenth of January, 1934, our first wedding anniversary, Joaquín and I said good-bye on the platform of the station in Valencia, promising eternal fidelity as we tearfully held each other in a long embrace.

On the train that took me to Paris with Mamá, profoundly saddened by the failure of my marriage, I could think only of what lay ahead of us, which did not seem very rosy.

I began to give free rein to my imagination: I fancied that fortune would come to us, to Joaquín and me, by way of the movies. We were the protagonists of a romantic film in which the whole story of our fantastic lives was retold. After having conquered all obstacles, we were reunited, proud and triumphant, heaped with honors and riches.

As a musical background I invented a melody—a sort of leitmotiv—that did not seem too bad to me.

And so, with smiling face, I presented myself to my dear father, who was impatiently awaiting our return. At first he seemed a little cool toward me, but that soon passed, and he welcomed me with affection, as always.

My parents had rented a very modest furnished apartment, on rue Daniel Stern, next to the metro station, which was a very noisy location. But it had a piano, so that I could find comfort in music. In this peaceful atmosphere, with the warmth of the family home, I soon began to recover from all the past hardships.

I received many nostalgic letters from Joaquín, which I answered, telling him everything I was doing and seeing, to amuse and encourage him: I urged him to be patient, assuring him that our ordeal would not last, and that we would soon be together again.

During those months of loneliness, Joaquín composed several songs, among them the *Cántico de la Esposa* [*The Bride's Song*] on the text of St. John of the Cross, his favorite work. Also, he composed the symphonic poem *Per La flor del Lliri Blau* [*The Blue Lily*], awarded a prize by Valencia's *Círculo de Bellas Artes*. It was an inspired work, which reflected his profound sadness and nostalgia.

Summer came, and Mamá, my sister and I moved to Mirmande to spend the summer in the little house that overlooked the Rhone valley. During the long hours I spent on the terrace, all my thoughts sought Joaquín, who was languishing far away from me. How tragic our fate was! To love one another so deeply and to have to live apart, although each of us was so necessary to the other. During those days my desolation was so great that I lost all hope for a better future.

It was a relief when we received a letter from Papá. His business affairs had improved and he wanted us to be with him. Right after our arrival, he gave me a railroad ticket for Madrid, for he saw that Joaquín was completely demoralized, and that it was my duty to go to him.

I was determined to join Joaquín, but I knew that our only salvation was the Conde de Cartagena scholarship which the *Academia de Bellas Artes* [*Academy of Fine Arts*] awarded every two years to musicians and painters. The last holder of the scholarship, the Valencian composer Moreno Gans, had already returned from Paris, and we needed to launch our campaign as soon as possible so that it would be awarded to Joaquín.

What happiness I felt when I saw Joaquín among the multitude of travellers in the North Station! He had arrived in Madrid that same day on a truck-load of soda water, and the pianist, Gonzalo Soriano, was with him. We had reserved a room in a pension on the Gran Vía, but there was no time to waste, for we had very little money, and the price of the room was beyond our means. As always, we trusted in Providence.

The next day we began the protocol visits. The academicians of the Music Section: Larregla, Arbós, Bordas, Pérez Casas, etc., received us with the greatest cordiality, promising us their vote. For the moment, everything was going well.

But one night, coming into a social gathering in the Café Molinero, we noticed that the group was talking confidentially among themselves, stopping short at our arrival. One of the members of the group came to meet us, and startled Joaquín with this statement.

"I must give you some bad news. The scholarship won't go to you!"

We were dumbfounded. "How is that?" stammered Joaquín, turning pale, "How do you know?"

"Your competitor, the violinist, F____, is the protegé of Maestro Arbós, who promises you his vote on another occasion. If you don't find someone with powerful influence, the scholarship will go to the violinist."

That night I could not close my eyes. I saw everything lost; a complete separation seemed inevitable. Joaquín's career would be cut short, his health compromised. Poverty and despair were all that the future held for us.

But before surrendering, we would fight back and try the impossible. After many misgivings, I thought to turn to the wife of Maestro Arbós, Berenjela. She was from Bordeaux, a distinguished and elegant woman whom we saw at concerts, and who had invited us to her home. I felt that she would understand me and would help, and without hesitation I wrote her a long letter, expounding our case and describing the agonizing situation in which we found ourselves.

Two days later, when I went with Joaquín to a symphony concert, "Ela" (as her friends called her) came to our box.

Your wife is a treasure," she said to Joaquín, embracing me fondly. And she went on to advise us that the best course would be to approach Manuel de Falla as soon as possible. He was then in Granada.

That very night Joaquín and I wrote a long letter to the famous musician, describing our dramatic situation and asking for his help. And it was not long before a telegram arrived, followed by an urgent letter to the Count of Romanones, director of the Academy of Fine Arts, insisting that he vote for Joaquín, and further, that he use all his influence on the rest of the Academicians. Finally, Falla promised to give his speech of acceptance on admission to the Academy, which had been delayed, as thanks for his help.

The Conde de Cartagena scholarship was awarded to Joaquín unanimously, and on the first of March, 1935, we undertook the journey to Paris, light-hearted and happy.

But after all that, Manuel de Falla did not present his admission speech at the Academy.

Part II

Chapter VI

Years of Struggle

My father had rented a furnished apartment on the rue Dupleix, and had set aside a small room for us where my beloved Pleyel grand piano occupied the place of honor. In that serene and familiar environment I began to forget all those dreadful days we had lived through.

Soon after our arrival in Paris we had to pay a courtesy visit to the Spanish Ambassador, Count Cárdenas, a very friendly person.

We were accompanied by the cultural attaché, Professor Aurelio Viñas, who introduced us to two young Valencian painters, Jenaro Lahuerta and Pedro de Valencia, also scholarship winners, who were destined for brilliant careers.

A close friendship would quickly be established between Aurelio Viñas and ourselves, a friendship which only his death—a tragic death—would end.

Inasmuch as Don Aurelio had invited me to attend the courses on Spanish literature at the Instituto Hispánico, I devoted a few hours a week to study. Joaquín, for his part, was composing assiduously, and in a short time finished his *Cuatro Danzas de España* [*Four Spanish Dances*] and several songs, among them *Coplas del Pastor Enamorado* [*Ballad of the Shepherd in Love*], which he dedicated to Don Aurelio.

We also met Maurice-Emmanuel, the History of Music professor at the National Conservatory, a most cordial and likeable man, who invited us to attend his classes. I recall that we studied the beginning of opera that year, from Monteverdi to Lully and Rameau.

We enrolled in the History of Music class taught by André Pirro at the Sorbonne. That year the lessons were devoted exclusively to the composer Orlando de Lassus, and the topic was somewhat arid for non-professionals. To me, they seemed extremely interesting, and it amazed me that there were only four of us in the class. We also attended a few classes by the great composer, Paul Dukas, at the Ecole Normale de Musique. Unfortunately, he was to die a few months later.

Summer was approaching, and we began to make plans to spend some time in Salzburg, a city that I had visited a few years earlier with my family.

At that time Mozart's native city was already regarded as the temple of music, but it had not yet been inundated by the flood of international tourism. Those who came were, for the most part, the moneyed melomanes of Austria, Germany and America, and also many professional musicians and students.

The performances of *Faust* and of the *Gran Teatro del Mundo*, staged by the genial Max Reinhardt, have become engraved in my memory, and I was enraptured by the operas, directed by Bruno Walter.

The whole atmosphere of this marvellous city was unique: its palaces, its churches, its welcoming cafés, and most of all, Mozart's birthplace.

Of course, it was venturesome on our part to think about a trip to Salzburg, for we had only the modest scholarship for study at our disposal, but as always, we trusted in Providence.

We expressed our desire to M. Mangeot, director of the Ecole Normale de Musique, which published *Le Monde Musical*, and had the happy surprise of seeing ourselves named by that publication as correspondents for the Summer Festivals. At the same time we were introduced to the Countess Peyrebère, a musicologist residing in Salzburg, affectionately called "Mozartmutter," (mother of Mozart) for having dedicated her life to the cult of "the divine Mozart." It was not difficult to persuade the director of the Valencian paper, *Las Provincias* to name us correspondents for the Festivals.

Everything was going very well. We bought two third-class tickets for the Paris-Salzburg train, departing the tenth of July, 1935.

Madame Peyrebère received us with maternal affection, and did everything possible to make our stay most pleasant. She introduced us to Barón Puton, Manager of the opera, to the Director of the Musical Festivals, and to other directors, who kindly provided us with tickets to all the operas, concerts and theatrical productions. That year the most famous orchestra conductors in the world were performing there: Toscanini, Bruno Walter and Weingartner; and, once more, Max Reinhardt presented *Faust*, *Jedermann* and *El Gran Teatro del Mundo*. Magnificent singers, like Ezio Pinza, Lotte Lehmann and Karl Mayr, filled us with enthusiasm.

Every day Joaquín and I made excursions to Hellbrun, the Moenchsberg or the Kapuzinerberg, for that summer there were almost no rainy days, a most unusual thing.

We enjoyed those unique weeks, happily settled in a private home in the suburbs, where the owner, Frau Prinz, prepared the typical dishes of the country for us, with delicious desserts.

We rented a piano, on which Joaquín composed his homage to Paul Dukas, commissioned by the *Musical Revue*.

Joaquín Rodrigo, Salzburg, 1935.

One day Frau Prinz, a fervent admirer of Joaquín—was it not she who prophesied that his works would certainly achieve universal fame?—invited us to go with her to the Moenschsberg to visit the famous convent, one of the oldest in Europe, founded by Saint Gertrude in the tenth century. The cloistered nuns there had expressed the desire to become acquainted with the works of "the young Spanish composer," and, concealed behind a heavy curtain, they listened to his pieces for the piano, and to the *Cántico de la Esposa.* When they learned that its text was from St. John of the Cross, one of the dear little nuns went to find the book of his verses in the German translation by Felix Braun, and I copied some of them. How surprised I was to find that the German version was identical to the original, and that the *Cántico de la Esposa* could be sung in German without changing a syllable or an accent! The Album of Songs, published some years later, features this same German translation, truly notable.

I devoted one or two hours a day to piano practice, and at night, when we stayed in, I would play works from my repertory for Joaquín and the owners of the house, Frau Prinz and Herr Karl, who were mad about music, like all good Austrians. And all of the neighbors would lean out of their windows so as not to miss a single note of the concert. In addition, we enjoyed the company of my good friend Luisl, who came from Vienna to share our vacation. The only bad memory I have of Salzburg is the sting of a poisonous insect, while I was lying in a hammock in our garden. During the performance of *Tristan and Isolde,* conducted by Bruno Walter, my right leg began to swell, and I felt intense pain. The Red Cross attendants had to get me out of the hall and take me home, where I stayed in bed for several days.

The final chapter of that memorable summer was a stay in our little house in Mirmande. Those were tranquil, untroubled days, spent in the little town where the farmers specialized in fruit, especially peaches and cherries, which were exported all over France.

The mayor, whom everyone called "père Caillet," overwhelmed us with kindness, and Joaquín and I would always return from his farm—a model farm—laden with garden produce and freshly laid eggs, and there was always a fine chicken from his yard. It was traditional in the town to offer visitors "*la goutte*" [a drop], which Madame Caillet would serve, accompanied by pastries which she had made herself. Her walnut liqueur was unforgettable, and I saved the recipe for many years.

One day, strolling through the pine grove planted many years earlier by the same "père Caillet," we discovered the "*cachette*" [the secret place] where the villagers harvested delicious milk mushrooms. What a banquet we prepared, broiling them on the grill!

We were so contented in this little village, far from the bustle of the capital, that we decided to prolong our stay until Christmas Eve.

My father had rented a comfortable flat in the district of Auteuil, in the rue Singer. There Joaquín composed several Spanish dances for the firm of Max Eschig, and the *Triptic de Mosén Cinto*. The Conde de Cartagena scholarship had been given to him for an additional year, thanks to Aurelio Viñas' intercession.

The winter months passed quickly, and we began to make plans for another vacation. Naturally, we thought of a trip for study, and we decided on Germany, which I had not yet seen.

My father had quite a significant sum of "frozen marks" there, derived from the sale of a building in the Ku-Damm, in downtown Berlin.

The Reich's laws were very strict, and it was extremely difficult to take marks out of Germany. Father's lawyer had been able to send him only a tenth of the money due him, which was a truly difficult situation.

On the other hand, he could spend the balance in Germany, investing it in clothing, books, furniture or any other needs. So it was not difficult to persuade Papá to spend his summer vacation with Mamá at a German spa, at the same time that we were there. A good rest after the noise and bustle of Paris would suit us all perfectly.

In the spring of 1936, a little before our departure for Germany, Aurelio Viñas proposed that Joaquín give a lecture at the Sorbonne. He chose the subject of the *vihuelistas* [The *vihuela* is a stringed instrument similar to the guitar, popular in the 16th and 17th Centuries.] Exactly four hundred years earlier, in 1536, *The Maestro*, by Luis Milan, had been published in Valencia. It was the first book on the *vihuela* to be published in Spain, and the lecture would mark the anniversary of its publication.

About the first of July, 1936, we set out with my parents for Baden-Baden, where we had two comfortable rooms in the Hotel Vier Jahreszeiten [Four Seasons], next to the park. What a happy feeling it was to see Mamá enjoying, at last, a few weeks of relaxation! The thermal baths agreed with her marvelously. As for Papá, he spent a number of afternoons in the Casino, where he amused himself risking a few marks at roulette. Later he would invite us to have a bite at one of the fine cafés, where the coffee with pastry was excellent, and where a good orchestra played. After supper, we would walk through the park, since the temperature was ideal during those summer days.

That year Baden-Baden was the most cosmopolitan city in Germany. During July the Olympic Games were taking place in Berlin, and were attracting athletes and tourists from all the world. Every manner of transportation had been organized to the capital of the Reich: trains, autobuses, etc. Seeing all this excitement, I was tempted to attend some of the competitions—but it was impossible to buy a ticket!

One day—July 18th—I announced that I was going to make a short trip on my own, and everyone agreed that it was a good idea.

Very early in the morning I took the train to the historic city of Heidelberg, of which Mamá had told me so much when I was a little girl. She had raved about it, and I had always wanted to visit it.

It was a day well-spent, for I could tour the most typical places, see the interesting Museum of Art and walk along the banks of the Neckar river, whose silvery waters glistened in the sunlight. Finally, I went to see the giant barrel, a humorous reminder of the romantic Germany of the student life—how different from the one I contemplated at that time.

When I returned to Baden-Baden—well after nightfall—my parents and Joaquín seemed very concerned about me.

"Whatever is the matter? Has anything happened?" I asked, completely alarmed.

"There is bad news from Spain," they told me. "Apparently, there's an uprising, but for now, the news is very confusing."

The next morning the local papers published alarming news from Madrid, Barcelona and Africa. The situation was disturbing, but we thought that it would soon be resolved somehow. Several days of waiting passed, and then my parents, having finished their treatment and feeling much improved, decided to enjoy a few weeks of quiet somewhere near Baden-Baden. They were advised to go to the picturesque little city of Freiburg, situated in the very heart of the Black Forest. My father quickly found a comfortable chalet there, with a piano, so that Joaquín and I could spend several hours a day practicing.

Meanwhile, the civil war was spreading throughout Spain, and there were no direct news reports. We received a communication from the San Fernando Academy of Fine Arts, informing us that all study scholarships had been canceled. We were stranded! Almost every day we met with the few Spaniards living in the city: a young doctor, who was also on scholarship; a general's daughter-in-law; a Catalán bartender, who would offer us a glass of wine in his tavern. We exchanged our impressions and heard the most diverse opinions. Everything was surrounded by uncertainty, and no one knew what to believe.

One afternoon the doctor announced his imminent departure for Madrid, where he had left his relatives and his fiancée.

Shortly afterward, the general's daughter-in-law took her leave. She wanted to offer her services to the Red Cross.

Infected by our friends' uneasiness, we, too, began to pack our bags, without knowing where to direct our footsteps.

It was then that I had a somewhat outlandish idea. Why didn't we look for work in Germany, in order to earn a few marks that would get us out of this predicament? We could give Spanish or music lessons, and we would have plenty of students. Joaquín agreed, and I immediately wrote to the director of the Institute for the Blind, explaining our situation.

Joaquín unexpectedly received an invitation to perform from the President of the Hispano-Swiss Society of Zurich, where a short time earlier he had given a lecture on the *vihuela*. I had performed the musical illustrations on the piano to accompany Joaquín's lecture. Señor Camacho was organizing a musical festival to benefit victims of the Spanish civil war, and he wanted Joaquín to interpret some of his works. That offer came like manna from Heaven!

It was a brilliant soirée in the Tonhalle, featuring famous artists, like the ballerina Joselito, accompanied by Joaquín at the piano. The auditorium was full, and the President of the Swiss Republic attended the performance.

We returned to Freiburg with a nice fee, but we spent it in a few days, and once again we were faced with a truly serious economic problem.

Meanwhile, my parents had bought their tickets to return to Paris. We had to let them go alone, although we were truly distressed and promised to join them as soon as possible. When we went to see them off at the little station in Freiburg, I could not have imagined that I was seeing my dear father for the last time. Soon afterwards he left for Istanbul to attend to business affairs. And there he ended his days, the victim of a heart attack, far from all his family. Poor Papá!

As for Joaquín and me, our lives would take another path. Just after our return from Zurich, we received a letter from the director of the Institute for the Blind, summoning us to his office. Somewhat anxiously, we presented ourselves at the austere building on the Karlstrasse, where we were received by a very tall man, of middle age. Large, dark glasses covered his eyes, and a gray beard fell to his chest. He was Herr Vanoli, a very cordial and sensitive person. When he had learned of our difficult situation, he offered Joaquín a room in the home for old men.

"As for your wife, I will look for lodgings for her on the outskirts of the city; and she can take the train every day to join you. This war can't last long, and I daresay that in three or four weeks you will be able to return to your country."

We had no recourse but to accept his generous offer, never suspecting that our 'brief' stay in Freiburg would be prolonged for another year and three months.

The Institute for the Blind consisted of several workshops in which men and women were employed, mainly in basketmaking and the manufacture of brushes. Many of them lived on the premises. In addition, there was a residence for the aged where about a dozen people lived companionably at that time.

The arrival of "the Spanish refugees" caused a real sensation in that tranquil household. We were given a comfortable room with a view of the garden, for Herr Vanoli had managed to arrange for me to stay with Joaquín.

The housekeeper, Fräulein Rosa, a stout, middle-aged woman, always with a smile on her lips, took us under her wing, trying to make us feel comfortable. Nevertheless, a profound sadness overcame me when we went into the dining room to share lunch with the old people, who walked in with uncertain steps to seat themselves at a long table.

"Today we have beef stew with cabbage and potatoes," announced Fräulein Rosa in stentorian tones.

I helped her served the food, but I couldn't eat a bite.

"Is there a little girl in here?" inquired a little old man whose gray beard covered half his face.

"Why, Grandpa," exclaimed Fräulein Rosa, "this is no little girl. This is the Spanish lady, and here is her husband, who is a famous Spanish composer."

Everyone burst out laughing, a lively conversation began, and very soon we realized that we would be living among friends.

We adapted with no difficulty to the life of the *Heim* [residence, or home]. There was a piano in the building, and Joaquín spent long hours practicing or composing, while I assisted with the domestic tasks. The pine groves were nearby, and in good weather, we would make an escape.

There were many birds, especially the cuckoo, a bird that nests in the Black Forest in such numbers that it led to the manufacture of the famous cuckoo clocks, known throughout the world.

We amused ourselves studying its peculiar song, which went from an interval of major second in the immature cuckoo to a perfect third in the adult bird. The song prompted me to write a poem, upon which Joaquín composed one of his most beautiful and moving songs, *La Canción del Cuclillo* [*The Song of the Cuckoo*].

Our favorite destination for excursions was the Schauinsland, a peak about 4,000 feet above sea level. The distance there from the center of the city was more than seven miles. To reach it one had to walk through thick pine forests, crossing streams and rushing waterfalls. In the spring the woods were thick with flowers, and coming up among the ferns were lilies-of-the-valley, whose fragrance was like a blessing.

We used to start out at dawn, with knapsacks on our shoulders, in order to be back before dark. The first time we got lost, after wandering off the path to pick flowers and mountain berries. There were no landmarks of any sort, and we began to walk in circles to the right and to the left, going over the same ground. There was not a human being to be seen, and even the silence was disquieting. It began to get dark, and we could scarcely take a step without tripping over underbrush. We were truly frightened by the prospect of spending the night on the mountain, without shelter and surrounded by beasts of prey and predatory birds. I couldn't hold back my tears, in spite of Joaquín's efforts to comfort me. At that point we suddenly heard the tinkling of cowbells in the distance. We seemed to grow wings as we clambered up the steep, brush-covered hillside. Finally, we reached the road, and in a few minutes we found ourselves, panting, in front of the Schauinsland café-restaurant, lighted from top to bottom. What a blessed relief! We rested there for a while, enjoying coffee and a pastry, and then made the descent in the cable car.

Another day we had a tragicomic adventure. As always, we were short of funds, and for our picnic we took only a few small rolls with sausage and two wrinkled apples. Halfway up the road we made a stop by a small spring to eat a roll with sausage. Just as Joaquín was lifting his to his mouth, a huge goat suddenly appeared from behind a pine tree and leaped for the roll, trying to snatch it away from him. I screamed in fright, but Joaquín, with lightning speed, grabbed the goat by the neck, ready to strangle her without mercy. At this, the beast turned loose her prize, and with a leap, disappeared into the bushes.

Twice, we came very close to being victims of mountain accidents. The first time we were walking along a narrow path, in the shade of tall trees still wet from a recent shower. The clouds had dispersed, and the sun shone brightly through the branches. Suddenly there was a thunderous noise, and an enormous boulder, loosened from high up on the mountain, came crashing down toward the valley. It passed within a meter of where we stood, paralyzed in horror. It was a miracle that we were spared on that occasion.

On another occasion—on a very hot day in July—we left the house at six in the morning, wearing our back-packs. Our goal, as always, was the peak of Schauinsland. We were still only half-way when a heavy rain storm came up. Very quickly the little stream became a turbulent torrent cutting our path. Although there was a wooden foot-bridge, it seemed too flimsy to bear our weight, and we thought that we could wade across, barefooted, with less risk. The water was knee-deep, but we reached the other bank safe and sound, and took refuge in a cave where we waited until the cloudburst had passed. We reached the peak with no problems, and could eat our frugal lunch and rest a few hours before undertaking the return trip. However, the next morning we were horrified to read in the Freiburg newspaper that on the day before a couple of young hikers, trying to cross the torrential river a little after us, were swept away by the raging waters, without being able to reach the other bank. Their lifeless bodies were recovered some hours later. It was a real tragedy that filled us with sorrow. Nevertheless, Joaquín and I didn't learn from experience, and we kept right on making Alpine excursions, which was our hobby in those days.

One day a lady, a devotee of music, presented herself at the Heim, asking to meet us. We saw before us a tiny woman, Frau Lessing, with white hair, who greeted us in French. She was a friend of the blind, to whom she dedicated a great part of her time, with readings, lessons and every kind of assistance. She invited us to lunch at one of the best pastry shops in town, and we soon became close friends of this great-hearted woman. She was a person of immense culture, and would bring me interesting books: *The Magic Mountain*, by Thomas Mann, and *Erasmus*, by Stefan Zweig and many more. These were banned in Germany at that time, and she suggested that I hide them among my clothes.

From time to time Frau Lessing travelled to Switzerland, where her son was living.

"Why are you so fond of Switzerland?" we asked her.

And lowering her voice, she answered, "Là-bas on peut parler." ["One can speak there."]

There she also met the younger daughter of Schumann. Of course the atmosphere in Germany was not pleasant, but in this province the Nazi persecution was less apparent, because the population was largely Catholic, and not very supportive of the regime.

"This cannot last," people thought. "These brutalities are unworthy of a civilized people."

This not only lasted, but it continued to get worse.

One afternoon, the Director of the Institute asked us to come down to his office on a very serious matter. We were dumbfounded to learn that there was an order of expulsion against us.

"I would be deeply disturbed if you should have to leave under these circumstances," Herr Vanoli told us, "but the orders are clear. You will have to leave the country within 24 hours, unless you exchange your passports for a document issued by the Government of Burgos, for our government does not recognize the Spanish Republic. To obtain said passport, you would have to leave as soon as possible for Berlin, where there is now a new consulate. You have tonight to think it over, and must give me your answer tomorrow."

That night neither Joaquín nor I closed an eye. For people as far removed from the political world as we were, it was a most difficult decision. My parents were far away and we had no one to whom we could turn for advice. And if we made a false step, we might compromise our entire future: poverty, exile and perhaps permanent separation, the end of our marriage, already so often threatened. I remember that all during the night the sound of the bell in the nearby cathedral seemed lugubrious and threatening.

When dawn came, I asked Joaquín, who waited anxiously for my decision, "Who was the French general who said: 'J'y suis; j'y reste'? [Here I am. Here I stay.] I think it was Mac-Mahon. Anyway, here we are safe, under the protection of the compassionate Director of the Heim. Here we stay."

And Joaquín agreed with me.

That same week we boarded the "*Kraft durch Freude*" train [Strength Through Joy] which would take us to the capital of the Reich. The journey was most uncomfortable, for we spent the whole night seated on the hard benches of the third-class car. No one could sleep, for most of the passengers devoted themselves to drinking beer and devouring enormous quantities of sausages while singing patriotic songs.

In Berlin we spent four days in a comfortable hotel. We visited Potsdam, the Zoo, and the hunters' exhibit, we dined in the Vaterland restaurant, of truly colossal dimensions, and naturally, we did not miss having a snack in the *Café Wien*, in the Ku-Damm, whose building had formerly been the property of my family.

With our brand-new passports in our possession, we returned to Freiburg, where our stay would be prolonged until January of 1938.

The months that we spent in the Black Forest were well-employed. We often went to the University, where we were introduced to the Director of the Library, a great Hispanist, who allowed us to take home all the books we liked. Spanish literature was well-represented; indeed, I would say that it occupied a place of honor, since books were included which were not found in other libraries.

We frequently went to concerts, and I particularly remember the concerts of the famous pianists Cortot and Claudio Arrau. We also attended a lecture of Padre Anglés. We received invitations to the Opera theater, where we heard a *Freischütz* and a *Traviata*, both very well-staged; and we also attended symphony concerts conducted by Konwitschny.

"Why don't you give a concert of your works for the piano?" I asked Joaquín one day.

My suggestion pleased him, and immediately we went to see the owner of the Ruckmich House, which was the only music hall and booking agency in the town. We were in luck, for the idea appealed to Frau Ruckmich, who, in a very few days, organized a concert, whose program included Spanish works from Cabezón to Rodrigo, going through Padre Soler, Granados, Albéniz, Falla and Turina.

For several weeks Joaquín spent six hours a day at the piano, practicing all these works.

The concert was a resounding success; we celebrated it in a beer garden, accompanied by many Hispanophile friends. The Ruckmich Hall had been filled with a knowledgeable and sensitive audience, and we had even earned a few marks!

The introduction had been made by Professor Merker, a fine and cultured man, who would die soon afterward in the Second World War.

During this time Joaquín finished his *Cuatro Piezas para Piano*: *Plegaria de la Infanta de Castilla*, *Fandango del Ventorrillo*, *Danza Valenciana* and *Caleseras* [Four Piano Pieces: 1. Prayer of the Princess of Castile; 2. Fandango of the Country Inn; 3. Valencian Dance; 4. Women riding in a carriage.]

As we were always short of money, we tried to give Spanish language classes. First we found a pupil who was about to travel to Argentina. Apparently he was extremely gifted, for only a few weeks after beginning his studies, he was able to read Cervantes' *Novelas Ejemplares* and translate them correctly. He was delighted with us, his teachers, and when Christmas came, presented us with a basket of delicious dates, a rare treat in those latitudes.

Then a young woman began to study with us. She was very intelligent and attractive, and of Baltic origin. Her family owned a large property near Kiel, and she invited me to spend the holidays with her there. I would have liked to accept that generous invitation—but how could I be away from Joaquín for Christmas? That student also left for South America, and we heard no more from her.

For two years we spent the Christmas holidays in the Heim, longing for home and family despite the overwhelming attentions of our friends. Among these were Frau Lessing and Beatriz, a girl who had been to Spain and spoke perfect Castilian Spanish. With them, we didn't feel that we were alone.

One day we received a letter from France which filled us with jubilation: the director of Radio Strasbourg was asking Joaquín to do a half-hour program, offering him a substantial fee in payment.

The trip was comfortable, since it was only half an hour by train, but we had to cross the border, which was somewhat risky at that time. In fact, on our arrival at Strasbourg the police subjected us to an interrogation, and we had to wait almost an hour before we were free.

Happily, we found a different atmosphere at the Radio studio. The director welcomed us cordially and invited Joaquín to perform his works with the microphone open. Joaquín played better than ever, and was warmly congratulated. Then, with the recently-earned fee in our pocket, we headed for a restaurant recommended by a traffic policeman.

The luncheon was marvellous: authentic Strasbourg foie gras, river trout and apple tart, all accented by an excellent wine. It was already getting dark when we started for the station. I clung to Joaquín's arm and both of us were loaded with packages, for we had picked up candies and clothing that Mamá had sent to the post office.

Suddenly I became aware of someone approaching me from behind. He whispered confidentially, "How about the concert on Radio Strasbourg?"

I turned my head and saw a huge man of somewhat sinister appearance who fixed me with his gaze.

"Ah," I exclaimed, flattered, "did you hear us?"

A few minutes later I realized that we had been watched since our arrival, as we were regarded as suspicious persons. My ingenuous exclamation must have reassured him, for he disappeared into the darkness like a ghost.

Summer arrived again and was very hot. There was an Olympic-size pool not far from the *Heim*, and we decided to go look it over. At the entrance the well-known little racist sign was displayed, which revolted us, as usual. We nearly went home, but the heat was stronger than our revulsion.

The swimming instructor was a young man, husky and very dark. His appearance was not at all Anglo-Saxon, but Mediterranean. We asked him to give us a few lessons, and for several weeks we went to the pool almost every day, which helped to break the monotony of life at the *Heim*. The instructor taught us the breast stroke, the crawl and the back stroke, and in very little time we made enough progress to be able to swim the length of the pool. I remember that he constantly kept an eye on Joaquín, turning the youngsters who came too close to him aside with one foot.

At the end, when I asked him what we owed him for the lessons, he announced, smiling, "I make no charge to Spanish refugees. It has been a pleasure for me."

The first cold weather came, and once again Christmas was approaching. The situation in Spain was still very uncertain, and we could not yet prepare to return there. But before the holidays I fell ill. I had become very sick after eating some *choucroute*, which must have been spoiled. The doctor at the *Heim*, prescribed fried eggs and pork chops, which didn't seem to be a logical treatment. I preferred to not eat at all, but every day I felt weaker. One Sunday, in order to get a breath of fresh air, we went out early to walk in the snowy woods. But soon I was overpowered by a feeling of exhaustion, and we had to knock at the door of some acquaintances. It was time for lunch, and the couple, suspecting that we expected an invitation, received us with a certain coolness. We left as rapidly as my depleted strength would permit and took refuge in a café, where we agreed that we should return to Paris. There we would find Mamá, who would take care of me as only she knew how to do. There was no need to discuss the matter any further. The separation from the Vanolis, whose hospitality we had enjoyed for so long saddened us. Our motherly friend Frau Lessing, and Beatriz and the friends at the *Heim* were also sorry to see us leave. But we could see no alternative.

A few days after New Year we arrived at the Gare du Nord, where Mamá, on seeing me so pale and thin, welcomed me with tears in her eyes. And as I embraced her emotionally, I felt sure that I would soon recover my health at her side. And I was right.

We rented a room in a very modest hotel in the rue Delambre, in the heart of Montparnasse, where Mamá and Mathilde were living. Papá was still in Turkey, trying to wind up his business so that he could finally rejoin us.

At the hotel Delambre days passed in monotonous procession.

Joaquín needed a piano to compose, and I had to accompany him to the house of a relative who had put an old out-of-tune piano at our disposal. She lived on the sixth floor, with no elevator, and that morning walk, in the raw cold of winter, cost me an enormous effort. At noon we gathered in Mamá's room, where she would prepare a plate of pasta or rice in a chafing dish. When we received a little money from

Papá, or when Joaquín earned a fee, we would go to a modest restaurant and order the cheapest meal. I did some typing for a well-known writer, which brought us a few francs.

It was our friend, Aurelio Viñas, who introduced us to the Spanish writer, Matilde Pomes, the translator of a number of literary texts. In her Left Bank salon she received many well-known personalities, such as Paul Valéry, Jean Cassou, Jean Camp, Federico Mompou, Aurelio Viñas and many others.

Knowing that Matilde had so many important connections, it occurred to Joaquín and me to ask her to introduce us to someone who might like to purchase antiques, for Papá had given me some very valuable pieces which, if we sold, would get us out of our difficulties for some time.

With Prussian punctuality we climbed the creaking stairs of an old house and pressed the doorbell full of hope. She opened the door herself and, with an amiable smile, said,

"Come in, come in! You'll forgive me for having forgotten completely that I had invited an old friend to dinner. You'll have to wait a little while. I assume that you have already eaten, no?"

Joaquín hastened to assure her that yes, indeed, we had had dinner at home. He was not lying, for we had just eaten the plate of white rice which was our supper every night, with half a banana for dessert.

Resigned to wait, we sat down in a corner of the room. Matilde's guest soon arrived.

I recall with complete clarity that memorable dinner, a real torture of Tantalus for a pair of refugees like us.

"My dear," said Matilde, smiling, "try some of these lovely slices of ham, it's just arrived from Perigord! How do you like it?"

"It's utterly delicious!" exclaimed the friend.

"Won't you have a little Burgundy?"

"Will you try some duck with orange sauce? It is at its best! Would you like some more? A pity that the only dessert is an apple tart, fruit and coffee!"

Joaquín and I were on hot coals, with a wild desire to escape, but we didn't dare move or say a word. Finally the banquet came to an end, and at that point Matilde took note of our presence.

"My dear Joaquín, I am so sorry that you haven't been able to join us, as I would have wanted. But don't you think that it is a little late now to talk business? I will just tell you that the other day I ran across a friend who owns a shop which sells antiques. He told me that he would be pleased to see something of yours. But I warn you that he doesn't pay much, because right now there is an enormous supply. We have so many refugees in France whom we must aid!"

Some years later, shortly after the World War, we met Matilde again in the home of Aurelio Viñas. Joaquín had already premièred the *Concierto de Aranjuez*, and was a famous musician in France. Matilde was blacklisted as a collaborator and had been removed from her chair at the University. It was sad to see her in that state. While we shared the potatoes and cabbage of the post-war period, I gave thanks to Almighty God for having let us get out of our difficulties, and because we no longer had to go hungry or endure indignities.

Nevertheless, our wartime penury would continue for some time to come.

Fortunately we came in contact with some generous people who knew how to find ways of helping us without wounding our pride. First among them were two eminent and perceptive musicians who took us under their wing: the composer, Emile Trépard, who entrusted me as copyist for his works. He frequently invited us for dinner in his home, and his wife, Isabelle, prepared exquisite dishes. I will always remember that veal roast accompanied by a Parisian salad, which was a delight, and a delicious apple tart.

The other musician was André Marchal, the famous organist of St. Gervais Church. We often were invited to his home. Marchal also introduced us to Gabriel Blanche, the architect who had become famous as the designer of the replica of the Angkor Temple for the colonial exposition of 1930.

His wife, Marie-Thèrése, was as lovely as a Sèvres figure, and her generosity was as great as her charm.

In the spring of this same year, the Blanches planned a lively party in their luxurious mansion on the Boulevard Flandrin. Joaquín gave a recital of his works for the piano, for which he received a nice fee.

In the home of André Marchal we met Count Miramon Fitz James, a relative of the Duke of Alba. He was a great man, a great lover of music and was enormously charming.

In his private home, located in the Bois de Boulogne, full of antique tapestries and works of art worthy of the Louvre, he hosted a brilliant soirée, attended by some two hundred guests, among them members of the old French aristocracy, musicians, painters and writers. There, too, Joaquín gave a concert of his works and was warmly applauded by all the guests. The fee for that performance, which the generous Count gave him at the end of the evening, funded us for quite a while. We stayed in contact with him for several years, and still keep his letters, which are full of affection.

Besides these, we would receive reinforcements from another source: a Spanish friend, the industrialist Rafael Attard, obtained an interesting engagement for Joaquín, and the fee was so sizable that it permitted him to have a suit made to measure. (And how he needed it!) We were invited more than once to the house of the Attards, a very nice couple, where we met their daughter, Fina, who would later achieve fame as a writer and composer under the name of Fina de Calderón.

Summer came, and we had begun to prepare to move to the little house in the Rhone Valley, with Mamá and Mathilde. But Joaquín received a letter from Spain, inviting him to take part in the summer courses of Santander, so we changed our plans.

At Santander we met several professors. The majority held chairs at the University of Madrid, and among them were renowned writers like Gerardo Diego, Luis Rosales, Luis Felipe Vivanco, Agustín de Foxá, Joaquín de Entrambasaguas. Also there was Eugenio d'Ors, whose courses were very popular. Those weeks, spent in so pleasant and healthful a spot, were a stroke of good luck.

Every morning, Joaquín and I would go down to the almost deserted beach of the Sardinero, to swim and sunbathe. The waves were very strong, and one had to be careful or one could be washed out to sea.

One day when we had left the house hurriedly, Joaquín forgot that our passport was in his jacket pocket. When he took the jacket off at the beach, everything fell out of the pocket, and the wind, blowing strongly, scattered our things along the beach. We both stood there horrified! It had been very difficult to obtain the passport, and without it we could not return to Paris. A few students and the nice secretary, Pilar Rodríguez, who often went to the beach with us, helped us to search the beach, with very little hope of finding anything. Suddenly we heard someone exclaim: "Here it is! Here's the passport!" It was Pilar who lifted it from the sand, and returned it to us intact with an air of triumph. Our happiness was indescribable, and this feat sealed our friendship, which still endures.

Before leaving Santander, a concert of Spanish music took place in the Athenaeum in which Joaquín and I participated, as did the singer, Josefina de Arámbarri, wife of the eminent orchestra conductor. The hall was completely filled and we three were given an ovation.

Chapter VII

The *Concierto de Aranjuez*

At the close of the summer courses in Santander, toward the end of August, we began the return trip to Paris. We had to stop overnight in San Sebastián, where we had arranged to meet the guitarist Regino Sáinz de la Maza, an old friend of Joaquín, and interpreter of one of his first works, the *Zarabanda lejana*. We were also meeting the Marqués de Bolarque, a great music-lover, who invited us to lunch at a restaurant on the Rompeolas in San Sebastián.

During the meal the conversation was largely about the guitar, as was natural.

"Why don't you write a concerto for guitar and orchestra?" asked Bolarque. "Regino would be willing to play it for you more than once."

"Of course," opined Regino enthusiastically, "I would introduce it in Madrid, and Jesús Arámbarri would come to conduct the orchestra."

"It's as good as done," declared Joaquín, euphoric, for he had finished off several glasses of fine wine. "I will write the concerto, and furthermore, I will dedicate it to you!"

It just so happened that on that day a political meeting took place in Munich that would postpone the World War for a year.

Right after our arrival in Paris we set about finding a small furnished apartment, for it was impossible to work in the tiny, noisy room at the Hotel Delambre, in the center of Montparnasse.

Once more it was our friend, Aurelio Viñas, who put us in touch with the Spanish professor, Amalia Carrasco. She had an extra room in her flat on the rue St. Jacques, a short distance from the Instituto Hispánico. She also let us have a tiny kitchen and a bathroom, and she put her piano at our disposal. Joaquín and I were thrilled, and we moved in immediately. The building was very old and utterly lacking in conveniences, but what did we care! We were happy to settle in, and the only thing we bought was a stove, at a bargain, for which we paid one hundred francs, and which would prove very useful.

Joaquín had completely forgotten the promise made to our friends in San Sebastián. He was preparing a small recital for Radio Paris, and orchestrating works on commission. One of them was the *Serenata de Don Juan*, on music by Albéniz, which was commissioned by the famous dancers Clotilde and Alexander Sakharoff, then at the peak of their career, whom we would meet several years later in Seville, where we would become inseparable friends.

I also want to mention some brilliant arrangements of Albéniz's *Sevilla*, and of the *Fire Dance* by Manuel de Falla, which Joaquín wrote for a Spanish orchestra, directed by Manolo Bel, which performed them in a café on the Champs Elysées.

I devoted myself to writing the scores that Joaquín dictated to me, and at the same time managed to type hundreds of pages for the writer Jean Camp, which meant one more addition to our funds. On the other hand, I had bad luck with the Radio. Even though I performed a complete program of *The Works of Rodrigo*, which I had carefully studied with the great pianist Amparo Iturbi, the management refused to give me any remuneration whatever. Their pretext was that I was the composer's wife!

I don't know who suggested to us that we write light music. If a two-step or a song caught on, either because it was launched by a popular singer or was danced by a star of the Folies-Bergère, it would make money, a lot of money!

Joaquín quickly set to work, while I looked for some romantic lyrics, even erotic ones, that might interest some famous performer.

This was how several songs were born, among others, *The Song of My Life*, based on some verses by Jean Camp, and *Chimères*, with my lyrics. Both works were published by the Max Eschig House, but I don't know whether they were played in Paris. On the other hand, I know they were performed in several Istanbul night clubs, thanks to my father. He acted as our unpaid agent and went in person to give the most popular performers there our musical scores. All of this yielded us no profit at all. It was a fiasco!

Winter came, and with it an intense cold. Our old stove burned night and day. And it was then that I felt symptoms that alarmed me. Our family doctor, while diagnosing my pregnancy, took great pains to reassure me, saying that it was a most propitious time for me to have a child, for my health was perfect. He opined, further, that the civil war would soon be over, which would permit us to return to Spain with a lovely baby.

A few days later we received some pleasant news: a group of French motion picture producers came to our house to ask Joaquín if he would be willing to compose the music for an important full-length movie on the life of Christopher Columbus and the discovery of America, to be directed by Abel Gance. Naturally, this production was accepted immediately, and as soon as the contract was signed, Joaquín began to write several numbers, among them *La Canción del Grumete*

[*The Cabin Boy's Song*], which would later be included in the repertory of every Spanish singer.

Jean Marietti, director of the Max Eschig House, had been kind enough to advance us the tidy sum of ten thousand francs, the balance to be paid on delivery of the score. This was Shangri-La for us; it would let us eat a good filet from time to time, and enjoy a cup of real coffee at breakfast, along with a freshly baked croissant!

And I began to buy a few maternity clothes for myself, since a friend had given me an exquisite layette for our future baby.

Unfortunately, black clouds were gathering on the horizon. The political situation became more threatening every day, and finally, the entire world shuddered at the dreadful news: Mussolini's troops had invaded Albania, and no one knew what would happen. A European war seemed imminent, and all business and commerce were paralyzed.

Because of this, the director of the Eschig House, which was scheduled to publish the film score about Christopher Columbus, notified Joaquín that the filming of the picture had been interrupted, and that, for the moment, he should not continue to work on the music. For us, this was a real catastrophe, and we had no idea how to get out of the impasse.

To top it all off, we were enduring a polar cold, 12 - 15 degrees below zero, and could only be comfortably warm next to our old stove. We went out as little as possible, and kindly Amalia did our shopping, while my heroic Mamá came from rue Delambre to bring us food and to help me in every way she could. I think that this was the hardest and most distressing period of our lives.

On Christmas Day we permitted ourselves the luxury of filling our old stove to the brim, and we hardly stepped away from it.

During the afternoon we had a visit from Aurelio Viñas, carrying a gigantic Christmas cake which he shared with us, accompanied by a steaming cup of coffee. This act of friendship filled us with emotion.

One morning Joaquín, to my great surprise, announced that he had already composed two movements of his concerto for the guitar: the second—which would attain such fame—and the third. Furthermore, he hoped to have the first ready very soon. This news filled me with pleasure and optimism.

But time passed, and there was no glimmer of change in our precarious financial situation.

Our social life, however, had not been interrupted, for at that time we had many friends in Paris. We received invitations, chiefly from musicians and musicologists, but also from writers and painters.

One place we visited frequently was the home of Roland-Manuel, composer and musicologist, a great Hispanophile, and author of several symphonies, and of ballets, such as *L'Ecran des Jeunes Filles* [*The Screen of the Maidens*], of a number of oratories, etc. He had heard Joaquín's *Cántico de la Esposa*, which he had praised enthusiastically, and about which he had written the following criticism: "A success of this order would suffice to classify its young author as one of today's outstanding composers."

Roland-Manuel was planning the creation of a ballet about the Spanish vihuelists, for which Joaquín was to write the music, with a plot by Roland-Manuel himself. However, this project never worked out.

I remember an evening at the home of Mademoiselle Duranton, piano professor at the Schola Cantorum, where we met the celebrated composer, Albert Roussel, author of the symphonic work, *Le festin de l'araignée* [*The Spider's Feast*].

We often went to the house of María Cid, the young Catalan singer, an excellent interpreter of Joaquín's songs. More than once Aurelio Viñas invited us to lunch in his flat on the Avenue de Suffren, crammed with books. The mother of Joaquín Nin-Culmell the young composer, was also there.

A very memorable supper took place in the elegant home of composer Joaquín Nin-Culmell, where he were served succulent dishes while he contented himself with a few raw radishes and turnips accompanied by some lettuce leaves with no dressing.

We dined more than once at the home of Federico Mompou, as well as at writer Jean Camp's home. Those are the visits I still remember.

On the other hand, in our modest little flat on the rue St. Jacques, we organized lively gatherings that had great success. One day we invited more than twenty people, among them the great pianist Ricardo Viñes—I had been his pupil for several months—, the guitarists Emilio Pujol and his wife Matilde, María Cid and her husband, composer Nin-Culmell. Naturally, Mamá and Amalia helped me to entertain our guests.

There were only two months left before our child was due to be born, and Joaquín and I were full of hope, for everything was going perfectly.

However, one morning I awoke with sharp pains, too weak to get out of the bed. Joaquín, in alarm, telephoned the obstetrician, who arrived very quickly. "It's a miscarriage," he said. "We'll have to get her to the clinic right away."

Several hours later a little girl was born lifeless at seven months of development, and I became very ill. I have never known the reason for this accident, but several friends have suggested that it might have been due to the shocks and disappointments I had suffered, and, above all, to an inadequate prenatal diet.

This misfortune left me completely weak for several days. Without Mamá and Amalia's efficient assistance, I don't know what we would have done.

While I was in the clinic, Amalia took care of Joaquín, trying to comfort him in his tremendous disappointment.

Later she would tell me how he would spend the long hours of the night at the old piano, unable to sleep and that she heard from her room a melody as full of sadness and longing that it truly gave her chills. This melody would become the "Adagio" of the *Concierto de Aranjuez.* He was playing it for the first time, wrapped in darkness. It was an evocation of the happy days of our honeymoon, when we walked in the park at Aranjuez, and at the same time, it was a love song. And for those reasons, the work would be entitled *Concierto de Aranjuez.*

How sad I was to return home with empty arms, and then to see the little pink and white cradle, empty and unused where it stood in the corner!

As a crowning blow, we had to sell my beloved Pleyel piano, a gift from my parents, to pay the clinic bills. Sorrow upon sorrow....

In the spring of 1939 better news began to come from Spain. In April, the civil war which had devastated the country for almost three years would at last come to an end.

At that time Joaquín received an affectionate letter from Manuel de Falla, offering him a chance to teach a class in the History of Music, either in the University of Seville, or in that of Granda—and this time with salary!

Moreover, once we arrived in San Sebastián, we learned that the Conde de Cartagena scholarship would be paid to him upon our return to Spain. And a few days later a letter arrived from the illustrious philologist, Antonio Tovar, offering him the position of Musical Advisor for the Radio Nacional de España. Joaquín was inclined to accept the latter post, because it would permit us to settle in Madrid.

We began to make preparations for the return to our country. But inasmuch as I was not yet fully recuperated, we decided to spend a few weeks first in the peaceful little house in Mirmande, where the rest and the fresh air would help my convalescence.

In mid-August, when Joaquín went to the Commissariat of Valence to renew our resident permit, the commissioner, a kindly man, told him that the political situation was very bad. He advised us to return to Spain immediately.

In a flash I packed our bags, and the next day Joaquín and I took the train for Hendaya.

I will never forget Mamá's weeping as we parted at the station. "What will become of me and your sister if war breaks out? Where will we go?"

"Don't be afraid, Mamá," I answered her, deeply moved. "We will come back to get you very soon, and you will stay with us in Madrid."

But eight long years, full of sadness and sorrow would pass before we would be able to return to France. My mother and sister endured a veritable Calvary, and did not recover from their suffering for many months. When, at last, I met my mother at the station in Paris, she had aged so much and was so emaciated that at first sight I could not recognize her.

The train was crowded with travellers, men, women and children, on whose faces one could read fear and exhaustion. Every seat was taken, so that we had to remain in the aisle with our two suitcases, which contained our entire wardrobe. We were packed like sardines. We were lucky to find two acquaintances in our car. One of them was the wife of the Uruguayan composer, Brocua, and the other, her travelling companion, had the kindness to give up her seat to us. The journey seemed interminable, for the heat was suffocating and the air almost unbreathable. But when the train reached the border, everyone got off, and we were alone until we reached the station at Hendaye. We went directly to the chalet of our friend, André Marchal, who was spending the summer there with his wife, his daughter and a few friends, all music lovers and a most congenial group.

They included us in their activities, and we shared many long walks along the beach, which at that time was almost deserted.

When we returned, Madame Marchal would serve us a succulent supper, and then André would play Bach, Cabezón and Brahms at the organ, ending with the famous improvisations which brought him worldwide celebrity.

This pleasant interlude divorced us from reality and made us forget the specter of world war that was threatening all around us. When we had to continue our journey, we said good-bye to those great friends with great regret.

World War II broke out two days after we crossed the Spanish border. The terrible news came to us at the home of Jesús Arámbarri, the Director of the Municipal Band of Bilbao. He and his wife, Josefina, an eminent harpist and singer, received us with fraternal kindness, as did their entire family, and we will never forget the two weeks spent in their home.

We left Bilbao somewhat apprehensively, for we knew that it would not be easy to find lodgings in Madrid.

Fortunately, Julio Osuna, a friend of Joaquín's, was about to move from his apartment on Rios Rosas street, and was able to persuade the landlord to let us rent the coveted flat. This was a special favor, since there were no unoccupied flats anywhere. Osuna sold us a double bed, a dining table and six chairs at a very low price, and also gave us some dishes and a few glasses. There were no conveniences. The elevator almost never worked—and we lived on the fifth floor! The only way to cook was at a coal stove, and when we managed, with great difficulty, to acquire a sack, we had to store it in the bedroom, for lack of space.

We settled in, by the grace of God, and thanks to the help of good friends, we never went hungry.

But our good luck would not last very long. One day Joaquín awoke with sharp pains in one eye and a very high fever. He had an abscess, and we had to call in an oculist. I don't remember the man's name; I only know that he was ignorant and very crude. After a superficial examination of the patient, he tried to calm me with the following words: "Nothing can be done here, and the worst that can happen to your husband is that he may be taken out for a *paseo*" (i.e. shot).

I almost fainted from fright, for we all knew the meaning of that sinister expression, which was current slang in Madrid at the time. I realized that Joaquín was very ill.

Pulling myself together, I later telephoned Regino Sáinz de la Maza, who hurriedly explained our situation to his mother-in-law, the writer Concha Espina. Full of compassion, she called her own oculist, Dr. Poyales. He lost no time in coming, and was very encouraging.

Thanks to his treatment, Joaquín was soon well enough to resume his work.

As I mentioned earlier, we arrived in Spain with only two suitcases, containing old clothes and some books and scores, among them the finished manuscript of the *Concierto de Aranjuez*.

Our economic situation was to improve appreciably within a few months. The Spanish National Organization for the Blind, called the ONCE for its initials in Spanish, had been established just after our arrival in Madrid. It was headed by Javier Tobar. Joaquín was named Chairman of Art and Publicity, a position he would fill until 1978.

The same year the Marqués de Lozoya, then Director General of Fine Arts, named Joaquín Interim Professor of Folklore at the Royal

Conservatory of Music, and in 1940, Jesús Ercilla, director of the newspaper, "Pueblo," appointed him music critic of that paper.

For once we could live in comfortable circumstances, without material worries. What a relief!

It was then when I knew, for the second time, that I was going to be a mother, that our dream would be fulfilled. At last! This was indeed joyous news for me, as well as for Joaquín.

At the same time, I felt somewhat worried, for I hadn't completely recovered my health. I was afraid that this time, too, my pregnancy might not end happily.

And indeed, during my seventh month I developed phlebitis, and Dr. Juan Harguindey, the eminent obstetrician so popular in Madrid, ordered absolute immobilization for me, with the affected leg fixed in an iron frame. My only food was broth and fruit juice.

In this *Matratzengruft*—mattress sepulchre, as the poet Heine once called it—I would remain about two months. It was a real punishment for me.

Several months previously we had moved from a shabby, noisy flat on Raimundo Fernández Villaverde street—where we had lived for some months after leaving the tiny place on Ríos Rosas street—to an apartment near the Retiro Park, on Villalar street, in the very center of Madrid. It was sunny and quiet—this was during 1940—and it had a large terrace where one could enjoy the fresh air.

Now we were not alone: we were surrounded by friends, who came and went in our home, and who telephoned us every night.

The great singer, Lola Rodríguez Aragón, merits special mention, for from the first day she was a close friend, as was all her family.

All our friends were expectantly looking forward with us to two important events: the opening performance of the *Concierto de Aranjuez*, which was imminent, and, a little later, the birth of the baby, so eagerly awaited.

Story of a Concerto

The *Concierto de Aranjuez* takes its title from the famous royal site fifty kilometers from Madrid, on the road to Andalusia, which was a particular favorite of the Bourbon kings. This concerto is a piece of pure music, with no program whatever. However, its author, by placing it in a given location, Aranjuez, had wanted to indicate a time: the end of the eighteenth century and the beginning of the nineteenth, the Courts of Carlos IV and Fernando VII, a subtly stylized atmosphere of *majas* and *toreros*, of Spanish sounds returning from America.

The guitar, with unprecedented audacity, is opposed to an entire orchestra composed of piccolo, flute, oboe, English horn, two clarinets, two bassoons, two French horns, two trumpets, and strings. The guitar is always the soloist, but the orchestral response is a true delight, transparent but sparkling, in constant scintillation.

The first movement, "Allegro con Spirito," is animated throughout with the same strength and rhythmic joy, without ever interrupting the stirring march of the two themes which form it.

The second, "Adagio," sets forth an elegiac dialogue between the guitar and the solo instruments: the English horn, bassoon, trumpet, etc., over a deep pulse, which maintains the entire sonorous structure of this movement.

The third movement, "Allegro Gentile," evokes a courtly dance, in which the combination of rhythm in two or three tempos as well as very light phrasing, maintain the lively tempo until the swift final pause.

The world première took place in Barcelona, November 9, 1940, with Regino Sáinz de la Maza and the Barcelona Philharmonic Orchestra, conducted by César Mendoza Lassalle.

Days before the opening Regino and Joaquín went to Barcelona together. I could not accompany them, since only a few weeks remained before the birth of the baby.

In the early hours before dawn, Regino, who was travelling with Joaquín in the same compartment of the sleeping car, woke him with these words: "I'm obsessed with an idea that won't let me sleep. What if tomorrow, in the rehearsal, the guitar can't be heard over the orchestra?"

As a result of this question, neither of the two slept for the rest of the night.

However, their fears proved groundless. The *Concierto* played exquisitely under the agile and incisive fingers of Regino, and the audience applauded the new work with enormous enthusiasm.

Days later, it opened in Bilbao with great success, and finally, there was the clamorous triumph in Madrid, under the direction of Jesús Arámbarri.

It received the highest praise from the critics, and soon after, in the famous tavern of Antonio Sánchez, poets, painters and *toreros* honored the author and the soloist at a supper. Much later that night, Joaquín was borne through the streets of old Madrid on the shoulders of the celebrants, to shouts of "Make way for Joaquín Rodrigo, author of the *Concierto de Aranjuez*!"

From the day of its première, the popularity of this work has grown and grown. One can state that there is no country where it has not been heard, nor any guitarist in the world who has not played it. Even small children recognize it. They sing it and dance to it.

It has been recorded numberless times on records and cassettes. Several fragments were requested for incorporation in textbooks for class work.

Often, Joaquín is asked his opinion of the jazz and pop versions. Although these are usually done without his authorization, he must admit that some of them are highly acceptable.

Recently Joaquín produced the version for harp in order to please Nicanor Zabaleta, who immediately recorded it, and distributed it widely.

For a long time the record of the *Concierto de Aranjuez* was the number one "best seller," and appeared among the twelve best works of universal musical literature.

Nevertheless, there was another side to the coin, as is usual. At the opening there were detractors who said to Joaquín,

"What a waste! Now Regino will play it two or three times. And then what? Concert guitarists are rare. Segovia lives abroad, and Regino is the only one in Spain at present. You should transcribe this concerto for piano. That's the only way it can be played more often. Then, little by little, the public will get to know it."

But these pessimists were poor prophets. The torch would be passed into Narciso Yepes' hands, after only ten years. When he played the work in the Théâtre des Champs Elysées in Paris, with the Spanish National Orchestra, directed by Argenta, it was the start of his long, triumphal international career.

The *Concierto de Aranjuez* was not published until 1949. Thanks to the Marqués de Bolarque, who provided the loan, the work was published in Spain. It was I who revised and corrected the score and the proofs for the publication, doing this kind of work for the first time.

The date of the copyright is 1957, and Joaquín is still the work's publisher.

Concierto de Aranjuez Anecdotes

There are many anecdotes about the concerto. I will limit myself to a few that are especially entertaining.

In a poll by Radio Paris in 1962, regarding the sale of records, a merchant in the little town of Romans (Drôme), owner of a record shop stated:

"The record we sell most is a Bach concerto, then one by Brahms, and the third is the *Concierto de Aranjuez*. But since many customers don't know how to pronounce the title and don't remember the author's name, they start to whistle it: 're-fa-la-la-la-la-la-etc,' and we hand it over right away."

* * *

In the French magazine *Musique Disque* of October 1962, a critic wrote, "...the Spanish composer Señor Aranjuez, the author of this recording...."

* * *

Returning from an excursion to Zaragoza in an automobile driven by our daughter Cecilia, the car's horn failed, and there was no way to make it sound. But when they arrived in Aranjuez, imagine father and daughter's surprise to note that it had spontaneously recovered and sounded stupendously.

* * *

On television they asked a little boy which era Maestro Rodrigo belonged to. "He is a great composer who lived in the eighteenth century," was the reply.

* * *

In 1967 the concerto was performed by Yepes and the Radio-Television Orchestra, directed by Igor Markevitch. A little before the concert, a high school student, about 14 years old, came to our door, asking to see the Maestro. He confessed that he did not much like his studies, but that he was a great admirer of the Maestro, and that he wanted to shake his hand. What he really regretted was that he hadn't been able to buy a ticket to the concert, for the entire theater had been sold out for a week.

* * *

One day, walking along the Castellana we met two lads about eight or ten years old. The more daring declared, "I like your *Concierto de Aranjuez* very much."

"What is his name?" I asked him, pointing to Joaquín.

"I don't know, but I like his music."

* * *

One day Joaquín went into a café and ordered a coffee at the bar. When he tried to pay for it, the waiter told him, "It's paid for, Don Joaquín, there is the patron who treated you."

Joaquín went to thank him, and his admirer replied, "It's nothing. It was an honor for me. I only ask one thing: Write us another *Concierto de Aranjuez*, but even better."

* * *

Across from our little house on the beach at Cullera there was a supermarket. One day a French couple came in asking for a record of the *Concierto de Aranjuez.*

"We don't sell any records here," the owner told them, "but if you want to meet the composer, you only have to cross the street."

And that is how we met the Petrequins, an attractive couple who became our good friends.

* * *

In a nightclub, a singer is singing *Aranjuez, mon amour*. A patron says to his friend, "See what a great song that is. They've written a whole concerto from it!"

* * *

One day, on the beach of Cullera, an unknown bather approached Joaquín, and transfixed him thus: "Are you the one—the man who wrote—that concerto—?"

The Birth of Cecilia

On January 27, 1941, at dawn, Joaquín called a taxi to take me to San Luis de los Franceses Hospital. At eight o'clock that evening the baby came into the world: a world in the midst of war, full of horrors, misery and atrocities.

"It's a lovely little girl!" announced Dr. Harguindey, with satisfaction.

"And what about her eyes?" I asked weakly.

"They're magnificent, blue!"

After hearing those words, I fell into a deep sleep.

When I awoke, they showed me the baby, dressed in blue and white, with a little lace cap that covered her head. She looked like a doll taken from a toy shop's window, with golden hair and rosy cheeks.

Joaquín was out of his mind with happiness, and wanted to hold her in his arms to rock her and caress her.

Ten days later we went home, for our friends had found a capable young woman to care for the little one. I was very thin, and did not weigh more than eighty-five pounds, but the phlebitis had disappeared.

Feeding the baby caused us many headaches, for there was a scarcity of everything in Madrid. But we were finally able to solve the problems. She soon became "a model baby," according to the pediatrician, Dr. Muñoz Seca, who took care of her health until she married.

On February first—a very cold day—the baby was baptized in the Church of San José, with Federico Sopeña and Lola Rodríguez Aragón acting as god-parents. She was given these names: Cecilia, because her father was born on the feast day of Saint Cecilia, the patron saint of music; Amadea, because she was born on Mozart's birthday; Sofía and Juana, for her grandmothers; Lola, for her god-mother; and Gloria, because we liked that name.

After the baptism a group of friends, almost all musicians, gathered at our home. There were the composers, Joaquín Turina and his wife, Obdulia, Regino Sáinz de la Maza with his wife, Josefina, Padre Nemesio Otaño, Director of the Conservatory, the Director of the Orchestra, Pérez Casas, with his wife Angelita, Maestro Izquierdo and a few more.

The refreshments were frugal, for in those days neither bread nor anything else prepared with flour could be found. So the tiny canapés had to be made with almond paste. Sugar had vanished completely, and one of the most prized gifts our baby received was a paper cone of white sugar lumps.

The conversation was very lively. The guests were telling jokes and celebrating the occasion, when Federico appeared, terribly excited, and shouted "We're going to war! It's just a matter of hours!"

There was a deathly silence. We looked at each other, horrified.

"Surely it's a mistake?" someone asked in a tremulous voice.

"They must be false rumors," affirmed Joaquín, trying to reassure us.

That day I had gotten out of bed for the first time in honor of our guests, but by the end of the afternoon I was overcome by such an enormous fatigue that I had to leave the room to collapse beside the little crib, where the baby was sleeping soundly. Suddenly, I heard the sound of footsteps in the dark room, and saw a black silhouette, very tall and slender, coming toward the bed. I was about to scream with terror when I recognized Padre Otaño, who wanted to bless the little one before leaving the house.

It was a day full of emotions and shocks, but fortunately, Federico's dire prediction was not fulfilled.

The year 1940-41 was a year of great significance in the life of Joaquín Rodrigo.

His two children: one of his flesh, and the other of his spirit, were born almost at the same time.

For him and for me these two accomplishments have been an inexhaustible source of joy and satisfaction.

Concierto de Aranjuez

PROGRAMA

REGINO SAINZ DE LA MAZA

GUITARRISTA

PRIMERA PARTE

SINFONIA DEL NUEVO MUNDO . . . A. DVORACK

a) *Adagio - Allegro.*
b) *Adagio.*
c) *Allegro.*
d) *Allegro vivo.*

SEGUNDA PARTE

CONCIERTO DE ARANJUEZ (estreno). . J. RODRIGO

a) *Allegro ma non troppo.*
b) *Largo.*
c) *Allegro.*

Solista: R. SAINZ DE LA MAZA

TERCERA PARTE

LOURD . . . . J. S. BACH
VARIACIONES . . . . SORS
REVERIE . . . . J. TÁRREGA

Solista: R. SAINZ DE LA MAZA

SERENATA (estreno). . . . . A. CASELLA

Marcia.
Notturno.
Cavota - Musette.
Cavatina.
Finale.

Concierto de Aranjuez

MUSICA

9.11.40

Estreno del "Concierto de Aranjuez", de Joaquín Rodrigo

BARCELONA, 10.—Anoche, en el Palacio de la Música, se ha estrenado, por el guitarrista Sáinz de la Maza y la Orquesta Sinfónica de Barcelona, el magnífico "Concierto de Aranjuez", para guitarra y orquesta, original del gran compositor levantino Joaquín Rodrigo. La obra, bellísima e inspirada, obtuvo un estruendoso éxito, siendo aclamados con insistencia los ejecutantes y el autor.

Entre otras personalidades, asistió al estreno de la obra de Rodrigo el subsecretario de Educación Nacional, camarada Rubio.

Concierto de Aranjuez

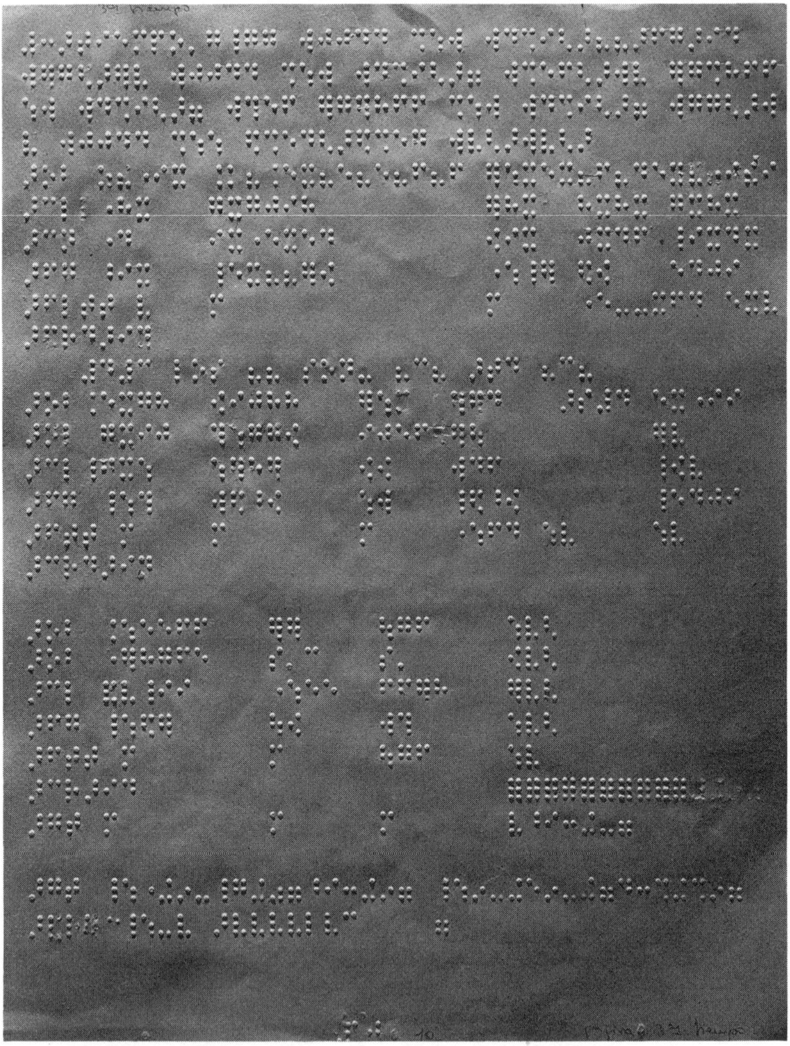

Page of the manuscript in Braille of *Concierto de Aranjuez*

Part III

Chapter VIII

On the Road to Fame

The years following the birth of our daughter Cecilia were among the happiest of our lives. After the success of the *Concierto de Aranjuez*, Joaquín had reached the peak of fame, and it seemed that the specter of poverty and penury had definitely abandoned our door-step.

In her cradle, upholstered in pink fabric, our precious baby would lift her fat little arms toward us, while the small sweet voice would say clearly, "Papá" and "Mamá."

Joaquín was in seventh heaven. He had just completed his *Homenaje a la Tempranica* [*Homage to La Tempranica*] with "the scraps from the *Concierto de Aranjuez*," as he put it.

As he never lacked a sense of humor, he began to compose the *Gran Marcha de los Subsecretarios* [*Grand March of the Undersecretaries*] for four hands, dedicated to two pianists, friends who at that time were occupying that position. One of them, Jesús Rubio, would become Minister of Education, while the other, Antonio Tovar, would achieve great fame as a philologist, and author of many important books, such as the *Life of Socrates*.

The *Gran Marcha* was performed for the first time at the Círculo Medina of Madrid by the composer and Luis Galve. Later Joaquín and I included it on all our tours: in London, Paris, Puerto Rico, Caracas, Turkey, Japan, Portugal, etc.

It was recorded by Odeon, along with several piano pieces, played by Joaquín.

Returning to the topic of our family life, I remember that during the summer of 1941 the heat in Madrid was tropical. As it was usually cooler at night, the wide terrace of our modest apartment would fill with friends who gathered to breathe the fresh air that blew from nearby Retiro Park.

But the baby in her crib suffered from the heat, and her crying filled us with grief and anxiety. Doctor Muñoz Seca, who watched over her health, earnestly advised us to get out of the capital as soon as possible and to find a place with a more temperate climate.

But where could we go with a six-month old baby at that time of draconian restrictions? After considerable thought we decided to move by auto-bus to Piedralaves, a little village near the Gredos mountains, which was well supplied with meat, according to some reports. There were also two or three hotels there.

But unfortunately, our experience in Piedralaves was disastrous. It was very hot, and I also contracted food poisoning. We immediately returned to Madrid.

There a series of real disasters awaited me: the baby, accustomed to nursing, adamantly refused to accept formula from a bottle. She began to lose weight rapidly, and within a few days our "model baby" had become an emaciated, hungry little creature. Joaquín and I were desperate.

To top off our misfortunes, bad news arrived from Paris, now occupied by German troops. Mamá and my sister were in grave danger, and in great need.

All these calamities overwhelmed me, and very soon I suffered a nervous depression that forced me to enter a sanatorium. The baby was entrusted to an experienced nurse, who was able to feed her with cow's milk.

A few weeks later, completely recovered, I was able to return home, where I had the pleasure of finding the calm and beautiful baby I remembered so well.

During all of this, Joaquín's greatest comfort was his music.

To celebrate the first birthday of our "Mimina"—as everyone called her—we gave a little party, to which several children were invited. I made a chocolate cake on which I placed a pink candle. The baby contemplated it, fascinated, and then stretched out her little hands to grasp the flame, adamantly refusing to blow it out, as we encouraged her to do. Of course, she had her way.

And from then on "Mimina" never gave us any problem. She grew up, sound in mind and body, attractive and bright, affectionate with her parents, and obedient.

And further, news arrived from France that relieved our fears: Mamá and Mathilde had found refuge in the little house in Mirmande, and, thanks to our friendship with a French diplomat, we were able to send them a package of food, from time to time, which they welcomed like manna from heaven.

On June 4, 1942, Joaquín gave a concert of his works in the Circulo Medina, where the *Marcha de los Subsecretarios* had already been presented.

There we met journalist Andrés Revesz, a man of the world, very cultured. We talked a while, and finally he asked me why I didn't keep a personal diary, noting everything relating to music and to my husband's career, as well as events in my own life, which seemed very interesting to him and sounded like a novel.

I told him that when I was an adolescent, I had indeed kept a diary, to which, like all the preparatory school girls in Vienna, I confided all my joys and sorrows. His suggestion seemed excellent to me, and I promised Revesz I would resume the practice that very day.

As a matter of fact, since that time I have continued to write down all my impressions almost daily, never expecting that one day they would be published as the story of our adventurous life.

One morning, while walking along the Castellana, we met Ricardo Viñes. He told us that he planned to present several concerts in Madrid, and that he wanted to come to our home to get Joaquín's advice on the preparation of his programs.

That same afternoon he walked up the five floors and knocked, panting, at the door of our flat. As the elevator happened to be working, Joaquín asked him why he hadn't used it.

Ricardo, smilingly replied that he hadn't known which button to press, and had not wanted to bother the porter, who was outside getting some fresh air.

The incident is typical of this great artist; he was truly self-effacing and kind, and had the heart of a child. Viñes would die soon after, in April of 1943.

At that time we began our friendship with Eduardo Vicente, who later painted portraits of Joaquín and Cecilia. His picture, "Villagers Musicians," occupies a place of honor in our house. The famous painter, Amadeo Roca, was also our close friend.

In June, Joaquín finished a work for violin and piano, entitled *Rumaniana*, which was commissioned for the Competitions of the Madrid Conservatory. It is written on themes of Rumanian folk dances, which I had heard in my childhood.

We spent the summer that year in Mallorca, invited by a sister-in-law who owned a luxurious place in the village of Paguera, near a peaceful beach. Cecilia's first contact with the sea made a great impression on her. Very soon she became a devotee of life at the beach. The days spent on that beautiful island agreed with her wonderfully. Joaquín and I, stretched out on the sand, would listen complacently to the little one's laughter, and as a background, the murmur of the sea.

From time to time in the distance one could see a small boat or a sail boat, impelled by the breeze. The island seemed deserted, since in those years very few tourists or bathers visited it.

Elias Canetti's observation that "the sea is always solitary" was never more apt.

In 1942 the National Award for Music competition was announced, requiring a concerto for piano and orchestra.

In September of that same year, Joaquín began to work on his *Concierto Heroico*, for all his friends were advising him to compose a work which could command a broader audience than the *Concierto de Aranjuez*. Despite the notable success it had achieved since its world première, the *Concierto* seemed unlikely to be often performed, for at that time the use of a guitar as a concert instrument was very unusual.

Joaquín wrote this work in a few weeks, and dedicated it to the Ruins of Sagunto, his native city, famous for its heroic resistance to Hannibal's troops in ancient times. It was completed about the middle of November, and won the National Award.

The world première took place in Lisbon, April 6, 1943, performed by the pianist Leopoldo Querol, and the National Orchestra, conducted by Ernesto Halffter.

It was impossible for me to attend this concert, because I could not leave Cecilia, who was still a baby.

Joaquín called me that night to tell me that the success had been enormous, that the work was as popular with the audience as with the critics. The work was soon performed for the first time in Madrid, May 7, 1943. The hall had been sold out since the day before, and the audience rewarded the composer and performers with endless ovations. The soloist was again Querol, but this time the orchestra was conducted by Maestro Bartolomé Pérez Casas.

At the end of the concert Gonzalo Soriano, moved to tears, embraced Joaquín, telling him that it had been one of his greatest emotional experiences in music. Later he whispered in my ear, "Long live the composer of the *Concierto de Aranjuez*!"

Gaspar Cassadó and Maestro Moraleda congratulated me very effusively.

The *Concierto Heroico*, despite performances by illustrious concert pianists, such as Lazare Lévy, Alicia de Larrocha and others, has not yet attained the popularity which was predicted. There are works which catch on strongly from the beginning, and, by the same token, others take longer to become popular, without our ever knowing why. But if they are good, sooner or later they make it.

In the fall of that year the Berlin Chamber Orchestra, conducted by Hans von Benda, presented the *Zarabanda Lejana y Villancico* [*Villancico-Christmas Carol*] very well received by both public and critics. And so began our long, firm friendship with this great German conductor.

We celebrated Cecilia's second birthday with a party for several little friends of her age. She was very "grown-up" and quite precocious.

When her papá asked her, "What did Daddy buy?" She answered promptly, "Rice, on the black market!"

In March we made an escape to Valencia to see the Fallas. All the excitement, the noise of the fire-crackers, the fire and smoke, made a vivid impression on me. Walter Starkie has called it, quite accurately, a "terrible fiesta."

To celebrate the triumph of the *Concierto Heroico*, the Café Lyon Club of Madrid gave a banquet in honor of Joaquín. There were more than forty guests: musicians, literary figures, painters, critics. Also attending were the Spanish Ambassadress to Portugal, Isabel de Franco, and Doña Elisa de Sousa Pedroso. Eugenio D'Ors and Díaz Cañabate were speakers; Manuel Machado and Emilio García Gómez read verses; and finally, Joaquín sat down at the piano to play and sing his works. It was a memorable evening, full of happiness and emotion. For a few hours we forgot that the specter of the bloody world war surrounded us day and night.

In the summer of 1943 we went with our little daughter to Benicasim, where we spent two months in a very primitive little house, right on the beach. The murmur of the waves and the cries of the sea gulls were the inspiration for one of Joaquín's most personal works: the *Concierto de Estío* [*Summer Concerto*] for violin and orchestra.

In it are reflected the happiness and emotions inspired by the games and laughter of our graceful child, as she ran across the sand along the edge of "Mare Nostrum." It is music full of light and love.

The work was written rapidly and presented for the first time, also in Lisbon, on April 11, 1944.

There is a picturesque anecdote concerning the première of this concerto, chronologically his third.

In 1943 there were two outstanding violinists in Madrid, Enrique Iniesta and Luis Antón, both Joaquín's good friends, and both eager to present the work. Which of the two should he choose? It was a thorny problem. Joaquín wracked his brain over it, until he hit upon the solution: they would draw lots for it.

In the capacity of his position in the National Organization for the Blind, he ordered the drums brought to the house that are used for the daily lottery prize drawing, and in the presence of José María Cossío, who served as notary, a spectacular raffle was carried out, as previously agreed to by both parties.

Luck favored Enrique Iniesta, professor of the Conservatory of Music and concert master of the National Orchestra.

The world première in Lisbon was a resounding success, and the première in Madrid, on the third of May, in the Palace of Music, was even more successful, if possible. Both concerts were directed by Pérez Casas.

The work was recorded by Christian Ferras with the Paris Orchestra, conductor by George Enesco, and some years later Agustín León Ara recorded it with conductor Ros Marbá.

In April, 1944, we had to make a brief journey to Barcelona, where we were invited, along with all the critics from Madrid, to attend the concert of presentation of the Municipal Orchestra, conducted by Maestro Toldrá. It was a great success, and all of us who were guests enjoyed the magnificent concert enormously.

But afterward, we spent several very upsetting days, full of emotion and fear. It so happened that on the day before this concert, June 6, 1944, at six in the morning, the Allied invasion of France had begun. We learned of it from the "extra" editions of the newspapers which inundated Madrid, and we remained hopeful, since this was the presage that the end of this atrocious war was near; perhaps at last there would be peace on earth.

However, the war would continue for almost another year, with enormous losses. Fortunately for us, the battle zone had not reached Mirmande, where Mamá and Mathilde were safe.

We spent our summer in Liencres, a village in the province of Santander. We rented two rooms with "kitchen rights" in a very rustic house. The beach was not too close, and we had to take a long walk with the baby and our niece, Belinde, to reach it.

The fresh air, sun and the relatively abundant healthful food agreed with all of us, and we returned to Madrid very pleased with the summer vacation.

While there, Joaquín had composed his *Capricho* for violin solo, commissioned by Radio Madrid, in honor of Sarasate.

The concert season began with the performance by the Portuguese conductor, Pedro de Freitas Branco. He often came to Madrid, accompanied by his wife, the excellent French pianist, Marie-Antoinette Levêcque, and soon a great friendship developed between us, which the years have not diminished.

On December 24th the *Concierto Heroico* was played again, conducted by Enrique Jordá, with the same success as before.

At this time Joaquín was spending a great deal of time with the Radio and with the National Organization for the Blind. In addition, he held the position of music critic for the newspaper "Pueblo," which obliged him to attend all the concerts and operas. All this kept us involved in the city's social life, which was fairly intense at that time.

We lunched several times at the "House of Velázquez," where the director, Maurice Legendre, served us delicious meals. We enjoyed the company of illustrious artists who were passing through Madrid.

We often attended receptions at the embassies, the French Institute and Walter Starkie's discussion groups at the British Institute.

On Candlemas day we gathered with several friends at the home of Eugenio D'Ors, where Nucella prepared the traditional *crêpes* for us according to an old recipe.

On February 15, 1944, we left for Barcelona with Cecilia and Belinde. It was not a pleasant trip, for Joaquín had a terrible cold, and we arrived, after two o'clock in the morning, several hours late. The next day Joaquín was so much worse that we had to postpone the concert at Sabadell and cancel the one at Lérida. Fortunately, by the day of the tribute, at the Catalan Palace of Music, which took place on the twenty-second of February, Joaquín had recovered sufficiently to play his pieces for the piano.

The program included *Zarabanda Lejana y Villancico*, the *Concierto Heroico*, with Leopoldo Querol, the *Concerto de Estío*, with Iniesta, and songs, sung by María Cid, who was accompanied on piano by the author. The Municipal Orchestra was conducted by Maestro Sabater. The hall was filled to overflowing, and the audience rewarded the author and the interpreters with long ovations.

I have observed that the Barcelona audiences have always shown great affection for Joaquín, as much in the premières of his works as in his recitals and lectures. We will never forget the successes achieved there with *Ausencias de Dulcinea* [*Longing for Dulcinea*] and the ballet, *Pavana Real* [*Royal Pavane*], truly extraordinary ovations.

There was also a tribute at the French Institute, with a concert presented by Joaquín and singer María Cid, followed by toasts to the artists. The dinner afterwards, also hosted by the French Institute, was attended by Walter Starkie and the director of the British Institute of Barcelona.

On another occasion we were guests of Frank Marshall, noted pianist and pedagogue, who was Alicia de Larrocha's teacher.

We saw Federico Mompou almost every day, enjoying long walks with him through the suburban areas which he was to immortalize in his pieces for the piano. However, our last days in Barcelona were not very pleasant, for it rained continuously, and all communications were cut off. Finally we were able to leave for Valencia, where Joaquín gave the final concert of his tour.

And how was Cecilia during all this? Although she sometimes drove me wild with her mischief, we knew that she was really a sensitive and good child.

I recall one day, during one of our morning walks, when she declared, "Mamá, I love you so much, so much! It makes me very happy!"

She was very witty, and we often laughed at her remarks.

On one occasion, while watching me make a chocolate custard, she asked, "How do you do it, Mamá?"

"In the baño María." ("*Bain Marie*" or double boiler).

"And why not in the baño José? Didn't San José bathe?"

During January of 1945 Joaquín worked on his *Concierto de Estío*, which was published some years later, in Paris. And I, in spite of all I had to do, amused myself by writing—as a commission for Radio Madrid—short biographies on the love lives of the great musicians, or entitled *Liebeslied* [*Song of love*]. At that time I was working on the story of Edvard Grieg, whose piano pieces I had known since childhood.

The concert season had begun under the best auspices. Alternating as conductors of the National Orchestra were Toldrá, Freitas Branco, Pérez Casas and Argenta. Among the pianists who performed were Magaloff, Galve, Javier Alfonso and Geza Anda. There were ballet performances by Manuela del Río and Elvira Lucena, which surely delighted our daughter.

The most important event was the sensational debut of Victoria de los Angeles at the Cultural Center, on March fifth. She sang two of Joaquín's songs: *Serranilla* and *Coplas del Pastor Enamorado* [*Song of the Shepherd in Love*], with a purity of style and diction, and a sensitivity that left us enthralled. And what a voice she had! That twenty-year-old girl was already a diva!

The concerts by the Russian conductor, Igor Markevitch, attracted large audiences. He lunched several times in our home, with Luis Galve and Gonzalo Soriano, and was delighted with the Turkish coffee that I served him.

And now, an unforgettable concert: it took place on the ninth of May, at the British Institute. It featured an excellent vocal quartet, and, during the intermission we received the glad news, longed for by everyone: the world war had just ended!

Overjoyed, we drank toasts with the glasses of champagne offered by Walter Starkie, director of the Institute, to celebrate this memorable event.

At last peace reigned on earth!

On May 27, 1945, in the Athenaeum of Madrid, there was a concert in honor of cellist, Ruiz-Cassaux, during which Joaquín's *Dos Piezas Caballerescas* [*Two Chivalresque Pieces*] for an orchestra of violoncellos was played for the first time. That same month we made a four-day journey to Barcelona, where Joaquín gave a lecture in the Athenaeum on contemporary musical life in Europe. On the following day we made an excursion to Montserrat. Fantastic! But we arrived half an hour late at the banquet honoring Joaquín.

On May 29th, we attended the concert of the Radio Chamber Orchestra, conducted by Ataulfo Argenta. I will always remember that day, for it was the debut of a man who was to be one of the most famous Spanish conductors.

It was about 1944 when I saw Ataulfo Argenta for the first time, during the intermission of a concert in the María Guerrero Theater. I was watching him while I talked with Joaquín; what had caught my attention was his height and his elegance of bearing. Large, dark eyes stood out in his lean face.

"Who is that?" I asked when he moved away.

"He's the pianist, Ataulfo Argenta, who just returned from Kassel with his family. One night, the Allied planes dropped bombs on his house, and it's a miracle that he and his family were saved. He just told me that he is going to give a concert in Madrid soon."

Soon after this, and through Joaquín's efforts, the National Radio Orchestra was created. Several names were being considered to fill the position of conductor: Jesús Arámbarri, Conrado del Campo and Ataulfo Argenta, among others. The majority inclined toward the latter, because of Joaquín's preference, for he recognized in him the talents of a great conductor. Nevertheless, when Joaquín confided to me that the brand new orchestra would make its debut in December of the same year, I was concerned, for this expression of preference meant a great responsibility for Joaquín.

"Argenta has never conducted," I observed, "and if he is a failure, you will get the blame."

"Don't you believe it," replied Joaquín, "Argenta has studied orchestra conducting in Germany, and he is a fine musician. I have faith in him."

The night of the concert arrived. Seated beside Joaquín in a box at the María Guerrero Theater, I saw Argenta go out to the stage. He was deathly pale, almost skeletal, and his full-dress suit, although elegant, was too large for him. The first measures of the Symphony sounded, and there was a feeling of expectation on the part of the audience which filled the hall.

During the intermission, various comments were heard, and some people criticized the style and excessive gesticulation of the new conductor. Joaquín headed for the dressing room with some friends, but as he was a very long time in returning, I began to be alarmed. At last he came to whisper to me that Argenta had just had an acute attack of appendicitis, and that they didn't know whether he would be able to continue. Almost simultaneously, a musician from the orchestra came out to the stage to tell the audience that the conductor had felt indisposed, but that he expected to be able to conduct the second part of the concert.

And in fact, with a superhuman effort, Argenta, tormented by acute pains, got up from the sofa where he had remained for a long hour, and took the baton to conduct Joaquín's *Tres Viejos Aires de Danza* [*Three Ancient Dances*]. The audience applauded warmly, impressed by such great courage.

Once recovered, Argenta began to periodically direct the Radio concerts, with Joaquín's advice. Soon he acquired enough skill to be named Associate Conductor of the National Orchestra, once the veteran conductor, Maestro Pérez Casas, no longer made many public appearances.

It was in May, 1950, that the National Orchestra made its first journey to Paris with Argenta and Narciso Yepes, who had just performed the *Concierto de Aranjuez* in Madrid. Joaquín took part in the expedition, but I had to forego it because I didn't want to leave our little Cecilia and Mamá.

The success of the concert in the Théâtre des Champs Elysées was exalting. The work as well as the guitarist created a sensation, as did the conductor of the orchestra, of whom one music critic would write that "he seemed a Greco come down from his frame." This was the consecration of the two young Spanish artists, to whom all doors were opened, first in France, and later in the rest of Europe.

It was also the beginning of the *Concierto de Aranjuez's* fame. As one music critic would write: "In this work culminated the entire history of the concert guitar, which begins with Tárrega, and which, passing through Falla's *Homenaje a Debussy* and Turina's *Fandanguillo*, is released in a genuinely Spanish work with universal appeal."

Toward the end of June our little daughter was sick and we were very worried. She was coughing a lot—especially at night—was listless and had no appetite. Soon the illness was diagnosed as whooping cough —at that time no immunizing vaccine was available. Inexplicably, I caught it from her, although I had had it when I was Cecilia's age.

There was a few anxious days, for the doctors took quite a while to diagnose my problem. They thought that it could be a symptom of tuberculosis, but the medication they prescribed had no effect.

In that condition I prepared for the move to the little Asturian village of La Isla. The change of climate, the sea and the sun were a real panacea, and both Cecilia and I recovered in just a few days.

We had been invited to spend the summer in Asturias by the conductor of the Oviedo Symphony, Angel Muñiz Toca, a close friend of Joaquín's.

Muñiz Toca's sister-in-law, Laly, a very attractive woman, gay and dynamic, had found us a furnished chalet within our budget, thus solving all our domestic problems. Her twin sons, Fernando and Papío, were playmates for Cecilia.

Cecilia was now a little lady of four, and was taking swimming lessons with Andrea Senén, while Andrea's husband, Federico, a talented violinist and conductor of, "The Friends of Music" orchestra, chatted with Joaquín, both of them stretched out on the warm sand.

At night we would join a group of friends; there were Federico Senén and his wife, the writer Julio Casares, the family of Muñiz Toca and several more. Senén and I would interpret sonatas by Mozart, Schubert and Beethoven, and then we would amuse ourselves by playing poker until the wee hours of the morning.

It was clear, at last, that the world war was over and that we could breathe freely. Now I received direct news from Mamá and my sister, who were still in Mirmande, and I planned to go get them.

And so it was that Joaquín, at the height of our euphoria, composed the inspired piece for piano dedicated to Ricardo Viñes, *A l'Ombre de Torre Bermeja* [*In the Shadow of the Vermillion Tower*], which some months later had its première with José Cubiles, and the *Capriccio,* written in homage to Sarasate, for violin solo.

About the first of September of this year we went to Oviedo, where Joaquín had been invited to offer a course at the University on the history of music. There were five lectures, attended by the city's elite. I did the musical illustrations at the piano for several of the lectures, playing music by Spanish composers.

On the 18th of November, Iniesta was violinist at the première of the *Capriccio*, on Radio Madrid. Soon after, the work was published by the *Editora Nacional*, and several years later, by the house of Salabert, in Paris.

I want to mention the appearance of the German director, Heinz Unger, who created a sensation, soon becoming the favorite of Madrid audiences. Julián Uceda also brought us the eminent pianist, Lelia Gousseau, who presented several concerts, with much French music.

Ricardo Viñes died that year in Barcelona, alone but not forgotten. Soon thereafter the French Institute, in posthumous homage to this master of the impressionist piano, commissioned a piece from each of three composers: Ernesto Hálffter, Federico Mompou and Joaquín Rodrigo. Some time later these pieces were published by the *Editora Nacional*.

Llanto por la Muerte de Ricardo Viñes [*Lament for the Death of Ricardo Viñes*] is the title of the piece composed by Ernesto Halffter, who opens the score in the manner of a funeral march. This is music at once complicated and simple, with a hint of the medieval.

La Canción que tanto amaba [*The Song He Loved So Much*] is the title of the second work, written by Mompou. It refers to a popular Catalan song, Ricardo's favorite, which Mompou was able to harmonize in that personal and subtle manner that is his special gift.

The third work is titled *A l'Ombre de Torre Bermeja*. Joaquín, recalling the profound emotion with which Ricardo Viñes used to interpret Isaac Albéniz's *Torre Bermeja*, wanted to write a work which would somehow paraphrase that piece, and he titled his *A l'Ombre de Torre Bermeja*, half in French, half in Spanish, to express Viñes' personality. He closed the work with a tolling of the bells of that Andalusian tower, in whose shadow Ricardo would have wanted to rest.

Soon after the newspaper *Pueblo* was launched, Joaquín was named its music critic. In 1946 it ceased publication and he was quickly named music critic for the sports daily, *Marca*, a position he held for several years.

The verses of the great Catalan poet, Jacinto Verdaguer, inspired Joaquín to write one of the most lyrical and tender of his works, *Triptic de Mosén Cinto*. He composed the music in a short time, and the première took place in the Palace of Music in Barcelona, on the fifth of October, 1946.

It consists of three songs: *El Arpa Sagrada* [*The Sacred Harp*], *San Francesch i la cigala* [*St. Francis and the Cigala* (cicada or grasshopper)] and *Lo violi de San Francesch* [*The Violin of St. Francis*]. It was performed by Victoria de los Angeles and the Municipal Orchestra of Barcelona, conducted by Eduardo Toldrá.

The audience was electrified by the work's beauty, and as for the performance, it seemed we could hear an angel coming down from Heaven. I don't remember having seen an audience as emotional or as enthusiastic as that one, tirelessly applauding the singer and the composer.

In the same program was a work written in Paris a number of years before. *Four Catalan Songs* was also warmly applauded.

A short time later, Victoria sang the *Triptic* in Madrid with the National Orchestra, conducted by Argenta. On that occasion, too, the applause was clamorous, although the audience did not react in exactly the same manner. Some years afterwards, Consuelo Rubio sang it with the Municipal Orchestra of Valencia. Lazare Lévy, who had performed the *Concierto Heroico* in the same program, marvelled at the work, even though he was known to be a severe critic, and had expressed little confidence in modern composers.

In the fall of that year, Cecilia was enrolled in the Lycée Français near our house. She was very content in those surroundings, and brought home good grades. Besides, she met many friends of her own age there to share her games. Some became friends for life, among them attractive María Victoria Marfany, in spite of the fact that her marriage later took her to Mexico.

Two years later, Cecilia entered *Estudio*, the preparatory school recently founded by Jimena Menéndez Pidal, where she earned her diploma.

Almost at the same time, Cecilia began to study music with me. On her fifth birthday I gave her her first lesson in solfeggio, trying not to make it not too dry. It was a success! The proof was that she asked, "More solfeggio, Mamá!" So we both enjoyed it. At the same time, she began piano lessons. She had a very good ear, a retentive memory and excellent hands for the instrument.

Two years later she was able to perform in public, premièring at the Circulo Medina the work which her father dedicated to her, entitled *Cecilia's Album*, and which she soon played on Radio Madrid. Undoubtedly, she had enough talent for a great career as a pianist, but from early childhood she was attracted by classic dance. We had to take her to London a few years later, where she studied for two years in the Royal Ballet School, returning with her diploma.

With his daughter Cecilia, at the age of five, 1946.

After her return, Cecilia began to teach ballet in Madrid. She performed several times in public, and did some choreographies. Success always accompanied her. I remember that some people asked Joaquín if he was "Cecilia Rodrigo's father," while others said to him, "Joaquín, she is your masterpiece!"

During the summer of 1946 we spent several weeks at the beach of San Juan, which was almost deserted. We returned to Madrid during the hottest summer weather, which made our small top-floor apartment unbearable. It was then that Joaquín's friend, Manolo Chumillas, offered to build us a small house in Torrelodones.

The plot of land pleased us, and we happily threw ourselves into the process of building, forgetting that we had very little money at our disposal.

It was a miracle that we were able to finish and furnish the house. Thanks to the sale of a small gold antique watch, which had been a gift from my father, we were able to buy a colonial-style dining room set. In the living room we placed an upright piano—bought second-hand—and a modest sofa-bed.

But we were floating on air, since at last we had fulfilled our desire to have our own little country home, with its garden planted with trees and flowers.

The house was completed in June of 1947, and we moved in for the entire summer. We called it *El Lirio Azul* [*The Blue Iris*], the title of Joaquín's symphonic poem, which had premièred in Valencia, obtaining the first prize.

Some weeks earlier we had gone to Paris to bring back Mamá, from whom we had been separated for eight years.

Her presence was a blessing for us. Thanks to her self-denying efforts with Cecilia, her vigilance, and her instructions, I could dedicate myself completely to my task of secretary, pianist and copyist, and become Joaquín's inseparable companion, in Madrid as well as on all our travels throughout the world. We knew that our daughter was perfectly cared for and brought up, and this was a great relief.

Mamá, who was very well-educated, spoke several languages. She was a great music lover, and often accompanied us to concerts. She never missed one of Joaquín's premières; she thought of him as her own son.

Federico Sopeña, Cecilia's god-father, came often to the house. One day he told us that he had just finished a biography of Joaquín on which he had been working during the previous months. This news pleased us very much.

The Editorial EPESA published this beautiful book without delay, and it was soon published abroad. Even in Ankara a Turkish musicologist showed us a copy, acquired in who-knows-what bookstore, commenting that he had enjoyed it enormously.

On the 14th of November, 1946, came the sad news of the death of Manuel de Falla in Alta Gracia, news that moved the entire musical world.

So many memories assailed us: his sincere affection, his help, so effective in difficult moments.

On a cold day in January 1947, we left for Cádiz, where all the musicians, intellectuals and artists of Spain had been assigned space. At ten in the morning we were all at the dock to 'receive' his mortal remains, brought by cruiser from Argentina. Accompanying his remains was his sister, María del Carmen, an exemplary woman, who had been devoted to him all her life.

We saw all the delegations and representatives there, as well as the authorities. Presiding were the Minister of Justice and the Subsecretary, Jesús Rubio, who later became Minister of Education.

Afterward we attended the services in the Cathedral, where a Te Deum was celebrated. The Capilla Clásica sang the Requiem of Tomás Luis de Victoria, music that Don Manuel loved so much.

Later the coffin was lowered into the crypt, where one hears the murmur of the waves of this Atlantis which the Maestro had dreamed of.

There is also a strange echo, which repeats a sound sixteen times! We left that place deeply moved.

During the following days there were several concerts dedicated to Falla's works, interpreted by Lola Rodríguez Aragón, Cubiles and the Capilla Clásica, conducted by Padre Tomás. The Andalusian Orchestra, conducted by Ernesto Halffter, also collaborated.

One night we were invited to a supper in Chato's Tavern, where a typical flamenco fiesta was organized. Cubiles played the "tanguillos" (song and dance typical of Cádiz. It involves a hanging wooden figure, made to dance with a whip) of Cádiz, and Lola sang Joaquín's songs. Pemán recited his verses, and Joaquín played his *Concierto de Aranjuez*. With all the activity, we got to bed at three in the morning!

The first of May of 1947 we made the journey to Paris to get my mother. When I saw her at the metro station where we had arranged to meet, I was appalled. How she must have suffered!

As for "Gay Paree," it had lost all its exuberance, and was a city dressed in mourning.

So many friends had disappeared! Among the missing was my beloved Dudú, deported with her husband and two children. What sadness that news brought me!

The few whom we met: Aurelio Viñas, the Trépards, organist André Marchal and Maestro Lazare Lévy, talked only of the horrors of the war, the deportations, the shootings, imprisonments and the constant hunger. It was a tragic era that everyone wanted to forget.

We took advantage of our trip to pick up a packing crate containing a complete set of Bohemian crystal, and porcelains from Sêvres, Saxony and China, all very valuable objects of art, inherited from my parents. It was a real miracle that neither the occupation troops nor thieves had removed them from the warehouse.

As a precaution, we had requested a certificate of transfer from the Consulate, in order to avoid problems at the border.

On arriving at Hendaye, the customs inspector, insisted that the enormous crate be opened. We explained that it contained very fragile crystal, packed by a specialist, and that if it were opened, it would surely arrive in Madrid in pieces. Although we showed him the certificate from the Consulate, the man insisted, "I'm sorry, those are my orders."

He called to an assistant, who approached with hammer and hatchet. My blood ran cold.

"And now you'll have to sign some papers in that office."

"My husband will come with me," I replied, almost in tears.

When we entered the Chief Officer's office, he looked at us closely and exclaimed, "Bless me if it isn't Maestro Rodrigo! What on earth brings you here?"

We explained our situation, and he was aghast, "They'll do nothing of the sort. What blockheads! Don't worry, they won't open a thing."

And then he added, "You don't remember me, but I'm a flautist, and I played with the Orchestra of Bilbao at the première of your *Concierto de Aranjuez*. I'll never forget that!"

We thanked the kindly customs officer, and taking Mamá by the arm, prepared to cross the border—on foot—for the train from Paris stopped in Hendaya. I will never forget that walk—I thought it would never end. But how brave Mamá was, making the whole trip at a good pace, and never complaining. She carried within her heart all the sadness of her separation from Mathilde and from her little grandson. But once on the train, Mamá cheered up, and by the time we arrived in Madrid, she was all smiles.

The first meeting between Mamá and her granddaughter was moving. For some moments they stood face to face, studying each other silently. Then Mamá opened her arms and the little one suddenly confident, ran to her. What a hug they gave each other!

"But you aren't lame," observed Cecilia. "I thought every grandmother was lame and walked with a cane!"

We spent the whole summer in the house in Torrelodones, and returned to Madrid at the end of September. The stay in the country had agreed with everyone except Joaquín, who suffered an acute infection of his right eye, with fever and severe pain.

With time he recovered his health, but did not regain the limited vision that he had had. However, he overcame this crisis with great fortitude, and his serene and optimistic nature did not change in the least. Proof of this is that his *Cuatro Madrigales Amatorios* [*Four Love Madrigals*] date from this period.

Joaquín's first première of 1948 took place at the Círculo Medina, on February fourth. Four magnificent and very young singers, all pupils of Lola Rodríguez Aragón: María Morales, Celia Langa, Blanca María Seoane and Carmen Pérez Durias, introduced the *Cuatro Madrigales Amatorios*, accompanied at the piano by Joaquín. The applause was beyond words, and the Four Songs had to be repeated. This work soon achieved enormous popularity, as great abroad as in Spain, and there are several recordings of it by outstanding singers.

That day another of Joaquín's songs was introduced, whose lyrics I had written at the age of fifteen, and which had been published in a Viennese magazine.

With what emotion I accompanied my "Schifferliedchen" or Barcarole, at the piano.

The following day Joaquín inaugurated the History of Music course, in the School of Philosophy and Letters of the University of Madrid. It was a solemn occasion, and the presentation was made by the illustrious Arabist, Professor Emilio García Gómez, whose words were full of affection and admiration. The amphitheater was crowded with students, and there were also some friends, such as Professor Entrambasaguas and Regino Sáinz de la Maza.

Later Joaquín gave a lecture on the music of Haydn, winning the esteem and sympathy of his future pupils. He would occupy the Manuel de Falla Chair (as it was later called) until 1978.

Some weeks later we received news which brought us enormous pleasure: on the 12th of April, the Cervantes Grand Prize, established to commemorate the fourth centenary of his birth, had been awarded to Joaquín for his symphonic poem, *Ausencias de Dulcines* [*Longing for*

Dulcinea], composed on a text taken from *Don Quixote*. This is surely one of Joaquín's most inspired works.

A few days later, on April 19, 1948, it was premièred with resounding success in the *Teatro Español*, conducted by Toldrá.

This was a very busy time for us. On the twelfth of June we were once again in Valencia, to attend the première of *Numancia*, the immortal work of Cervantes, in the Roman Theater of Sagunto. For this occasion Joaquín had written his *Danza de los Tristes Augurios* [*Dance of the Sad Auguries*], which would be used some years later for the tragedy of José María Pemán and Francisco Sánchez-Castañer, *La Destrucción de Sagunto* [*The Destruction of Sagunto*], which was presented in the same theater, with enormous success.

Around the first of July of this year, Joaquín had been named Interim Chief of the National Organization for the Blind. In that capacity, it was his pleasant obligation to entertain a Colombian mission which came to Spain as tourists. These were Pardo Ospina, head of the Association for the Blind of Colombia, and his secretary, Hernández. They were both attractive, well-informed individuals, and we enjoyed their visit. The Colombian friends were delighted with their pleasure trip through the "mother country."

In July of 1948 we made an escape to Segovia, invited to the "Summer Course for Foreigners." Presiding was Ramón Menéndez Pidal, who gave a sensational lecture on the Spanish "*romancero*."

Joaquín gave two lectures in the University, as did Sopeña, Antonio Tovar, Aurelio Viñas and Joaquín Villanueva, who was then governor of the province.

Consuelo Rubio came to give a concert and Joaquín accompanied her on the piano in her rendition of his songs.

We took advantage of that week to make excursions near Segovia. We visited La Granja, El Paular and the tomb of St. John of the Cross.

At the close of the course, the National Orchestra gave two concerts, conducted by Argenta. In the second, the *Concierto de Aranjuez* was played by Yepes, and the *Homenaje a la Tempranica* was also performed.

Every night we gathered with friends, and the discussions sometimes lasted until dawn.

After its success in Madrid, *Ausencias de Dulcinea* was demanded by Barcelona, where it opened the last of November at the Palace of Music, with the same artists. The work was also acclaimed there.

On the eve of the concert Joaquín gave a lecture on "The Song," at the Athenaeum, with the collaboration of Conchita Badía.

The year 1948 ended with very sad news for us. In the middle of December we received a telegram from Istanbul, telling us that my dear father was critically ill. Two days later another arrived, announcing his death of a heart attack. This was a dreadful blow for Mamá and me, and we were both grief-stricken. I had not actually seen my father since 1936, but in my thoughts he was always with me.

The première of *Ausencias de Dulcinea* took place in Valencia on January 14, 1949, conducted by Hans von Benda. He was delighted with the work, and repeated it at the audience's request. For this occasion, Joaquín made a trip to Valencia with his pupil, Marcelo Tobajas. In February Toldrá conducted the work in Madrid, and it met with the same public acclaim.

In February, Olivier Messiaen arrived for an audition of his compositions. He was accompanied by the pianist Yvonne Loriod—famous for her phenomenal memory—who, some years later, would become his second wife.

About that time, the young French guitarist, Jean Fuller, came to our house. He had come expressly to meet Joaquín and to request the score of the *Concierto de Aranjuez*, which he planned to play on Radio Paris and during his professional tours. I remember that he was an attractive and very elegant young man. Soon afterward, we heard of his death in an airplane accident during his tour of the Far East.

Another well-known composer came to Madrid in April. This was Francis Poulenc, who gave a concert of his works with Pierre Bernac. A few hours before his train departed for Paris, he visited us and expressed his admiration for the *Concierto de Aranjuez* with these words: "It is a masterpiece from the first note to the last."

We also enjoyed visits from the famous orchestra conductors, Clemens Kraus and Hans Rosbaud, and from the Dutch pianist, Cor de Groot.

On February 3rd a tribute had been prepared in the University for Joaquín Turina, who had died some weeks previously. But it had to be postponed because of the illness of Lola Rodríguez Aragón, a famous singer, and instead Joaquín gave a lecture on Berlioz and his *Symphonie Fantastique* in the auditorium, before 800 students.

On March 7th, I went with Joaquín to the first lecture by Ortega y Gasset, who had recently arrived from abroad. It was a cultural event, and the hall of the Athenaeum of Madrid was filled to overflowing with admirers of the noted philosopher, with whom Joaquín would have further dealings later. Pedro Rocamora presided.

During the spring of 1949 I devoted myself to revising the score of the *Concierto de Aranjuez*, which was to be published, and at the end of April I finished it.

On May 13th Malcolm Sargent conducted the National Orchestra, and Gaspar Cassadó played Dvorak's *Concerto*. That night Cassadó had dinner with us and expressed his great enthusiasm for the concerto Joaquín was composing for him, which was already well under way.

I had heard this great artist many years before, in Paris, in a recital with pianist Ciulietta Mendelssohn, and I was delighted to meet him personally. He was a most attractive man, friendly with everyone, and a real charmer. He loved children—he was a bachelor—and he very quickly made friends with Cecilia; he used to send her gifts of balls and other toys that delighted her.

When he played with the National Orchestra, the audience went wild. He drew a full, sonorous tone from his cello, very powerful, and his technique was amazing. It was no wonder that he had a legion of admirers of all ages and all social classes.

One day he had asked Joaquín, "Why don't you write me a concerto? I would play it everywhere, I would record it, and I would see that it was published in Paris."

The proposal was very attractive, and Joaquín quickly fulfilled his wish, within a few months composing the pure and inspired *Concierto Galante* [*Gallant Concerto*]. Once he heard the themes, Gaspar became very enthusiastic, and offered to write the score from dictation himself. During the summer of 1949 he came to spend several days in our little house in Torrelodones, and there, in the idyllic peace of the country, interrupted only by the cry of a night bird, the two friends remained at work until four in the morning. There were restrictions on electric power that year, and often, laughing and jesting, they had to light their labors with candles.

Cassadó premièred the *Concierto Galante* in Madrid, in the fall of 1949, with the National Orchestra conducted by Argenta. Joaquín and I were in Argentina at the time. The second performance was in Rome, in January of 1951 by Cassadó and the Orchestra of Santa Cecilia, also conducted by Argenta. With this incentive, we spent several days in Rome, and then went to Naples.

Cassadó, Argenta and Federico Sopeña were waiting for us at the station in Rome, and accompanied us during our entire stay. I especially want to mention that we were received in a private audience by Pope Pius XII, who had warm and kindly greetings for us.

In spite of Cassadó's pessimistic forecast, the work was well-received, and no whistles were heard among the very warm applause.

Nevertheless, a very disagreeable surprise awaited Joaquín. His concerto, which at first had aroused such enthusiasm in Cassadó, began to seem too long to him once he began to perform it. Neither reluctant nor lazy, Cassadó took scissors to the score, especially in the parts where the soloist didn't play. Joaquín complained bitterly about seeing his work mutilated, and his annoyance affected me. How would we get along with so many erasures when the time came to publish the work? This "little caprice" of Cassadó's seemed a veritable heresy to us!

Some years later Mica Salabert, director of the well-known publishers, acquired the *Concierto Galante*. Only God knows how hard it was for me to revise and correct it! I spent long hours on this job, but finally had the satisfaction of sending an impeccable score to Paris, so that it could be published. There have already been three recordings of this work, the latest by Robert Cohen, in May of 1982, in London.

The date was approaching for our voyage to Argentina, where Joaquín was to undertake a long tour of concerts and lectures, but nothing was confirmed. It was, therefore, a very risky venture, but we were already committed, and could not back out. At first, the departure was set for the first of August, but the ship could not sail until the 26th.

We spent some peaceful days in Torrelodones, enjoying the company of Mamá and Cecilia, and took an excursion to Segovia with them. All this served to distract us until the hour of separation arrived —surely a sad time for all of us.

Chapter IX

Professional Tours

Journey to Argentina

I had always had an enormous desire to travel to Argentina. Since my teacher, Professor George Lalewicz, had moved to Buenos Aires, where he founded an important piano school, I had often received long letters from him, describing this new country, full of promise and possibilities. However, when I asked him what he thought of our making a tour through the country, he very strongly discouraged the idea. The expenses for such a trip, and for a stay would be very high, he wrote, and unless we received a guaranteed contract, with fees which would cover all expenses and leave us a certain profit, it would be folly to set out.

In 1949, after the resounding success of the *Cuatro Madrigales Amatorios* and the *Ausencias de Dulcinea*, I was feeling completely euphoric, for it seemed certain that Joaquín's works would triumph in all the Hispanic countries. And at that point Joaquín was introduced to an impresario who had connections in Argentina, and who promised to organize an extensive tour through the entire country, with lavish fees.

And so it happened that on August 26, 1949, we set sail on the "Monte Udala," a transatlantic liner of the Aznar Line, which sailed from Bilbao.

We spent seventeen boring days on that luxurious floating prison, both quite unhappy, for we had had to leave Mamá and Cecilia in our little house in Torrelodones, in the care of the faithful Teresa and of Emilia, a family friend.

The crossing was not smooth, for we encountered heavy squalls in the gulf of Santa Catalina. The ship danced over the waves like a nutshell on the surface, and the passengers were so seasick that they couldn't leave their cabins. I was the only person who went down to the dining salon with the captain. As a distraction, they played recordings of light music, the "la vaca lechera" kind, always the same. One day, Joaquín ventured into the cabin where they were broadcasting the music and asked the attendant if they had a record of the *Concierto de Aranjuez* for guitar and orchestra.

"No, Sir," he answered drily, "We have only good music here."

Our sole diversion was the stop in Montevideo, where we spent the afternoon with our friends, Carlos Rodríguez Pintos and Maestro Carlos Estrada. We arrived in Buenos Aires on the sixteenth of

September. Unexpectedly, we found a committee on the wharf awaiting our arrival: Antonio Tovar with his charming wife, Chelo, two secretaries from the Spanish Embassy, and the famous Doctor Ara who, not long before, had embalmed the body of Manuel de Falla for the sad journey to Cádiz, and, a few years later, would attend Eva Perón.

However, the impresario who had promised Joaquín a tour of the country had vanished, and was not heard from again.

We were surrounded by reporters and photographers who followed us to the City Hotel, where we were installed in a luxurious suite, as nice as the one occupied by Federico García Sanchiz, whose "chats" were the sensation of Buenos Aires in those days.

The next morning, to our great amazement, we found our picture in all the newspapers alongside one of four stowaways found on the "Monte Udala." Suddenly we were celebrities in the country. And as if this weren't enough, the telephone rang, and a masculine voice asked, "Hello, is this Señor Puccini?"

"Not yet," replied Joaquín. Nevertheless, we thought the mistake was a good omen.

The following day Ambassador José María de Areilza gave a cocktail reception in our honor. Until the end of our stay he continued to show us every interest and affection, and it is in great part due to him that our journey, which seemed so risky, became a fable from the *Thousand and one Nights.*

What a joy it was to see my dear Maestro George Lalewicz again after so many years of separation! We accepted a lovely bouquet of flowers from him, with an invitation to lunch in his home, which was furnished in impeccable taste, and filled with paintings by his wife, Antka. There we met his ex-pupil, Lía Cimaglia, now a famous pianist, who immediately organized a small party in her home, where we met the most outstanding musicians of the capital: Williams, Ugarte, Pessina, Suffern, the young singer Myrtha Garbarini, as well as a number of journalists. Our friend, Alexander Sakharoff, the famous choreographer, was there, too.

At another cocktail party we met several celebrities of the musical world: Washington Castro, Negrini, Pessina, Vehils, García Morillo, Larroque.

By pure chance, at one of Joaquín's lectures in the Krafft Hall, I met my old friend, Jackito. We spent every day with him until our departure.

Joaquín's performances began around the first of October, and numbered about nineteen altogether: at the Law School, at the Society of Friends of the Book, at the "Empire," with the collaboration of tenor Guichandut and singer Myrtha Garbarini.

The "Rodrigo Festival" took place on November 7th, at the *Teatro Colón*. Enrique Iniesta played the *Concierto de Estío*, followed by *Ausencias de Dulcinea*. At this concert García Sanchiz proved himself a real "claque," as did Antonio Tovar and Jackito, who shouted "Composer! Composer!" tirelessly in stentorian tones after each work. It was a noisy success!

One day we had a visitor who seemed typically creole to us, with long, black hair and dark eyes. She was Petronila de Tedin Uribarri, friend and protector of the sightless. In San Isidro, near Buenos Aires, she had founded the Román Rosell Institute, truly a modern palace, where ninety blind boys lived and received an education which would permit them to become independent and to earn a living. She invited us to visit it, and the welcome that they gave us there moved us profoundly.

One of my happiest memories is of our visit to the *Quinta de Petronila*, located some sixty-five kilometers from the capital, where they prepared a creole barbecue for us in an enormous park, filled with century-old trees and populated by an infinite number of exotic birds.

One day the management of the City Hotel told us that the hotel employees would be off-duty on the following day, because Eva Perón, the President's wife, was going to speak in the *Plaza Rosada* [Pink Plaza, the plaza in front of the Casa Rosada, the president's residence], and her speech would be broadcast over the radio. It lasted more than four hours, and I was dumbfounded at seeing this attractive woman, who seemed so fragile, demonstrate strength and an iron will.

As a finale, we made a short three-day trip to Rosario, where Joaquín gave a concert of his works in the great auditorium of the Radio, and, as always, we ended with the *Marcha de los Subsecretarios*. Nevertheless, I never dared to play alone in public. My teacher, Professor Lalewicz, reproached me amicably about this, for he did not forget that I had been one of his favorite pupils.

"You have given up your career," he added, with a touch of annoyance. And I didn't know what to say to him.

On November 4th we began the return trip—in tropical heat—accompanied to the ship by a multitude of friends, who filled our stateroom with flowers, candies and other gifts.

For me, the memory of these days will always be vivid; it was our first important tour abroad.

In April of 1950 we went to Valencia to attend a concert in honor of Joaquín, for which Maestro Lazare Lévy came from Paris to play *Concierto Heroico*. During the second part of the program Consuelo Rubio sang the *Triptic de Mosén Cinto* beautifully. These two important works, among Joaquín's most inspired music, are still little known by the general public, for reasons I cannot understand.

Several weeks later we attended another tribute in Joaquín's home town, with music and *paellas*. In those peaceful and picturesque surroundings we felt very happy.

We spent the first part of the summer in Torrelodones, moving at the end of July to Santander, where we had been invited to take part in the Menéndez Pelayo summer course, at the Madgalena Palace.

The director of the course was Antonio Lago Carballo, a friendly and greatly refined man, with whom we formed a solid and enduring friendship. Among the professors were Pedro Laín Entralgo, Fernández Miranda, the German professor Leibbrand and many more.

Joaquín gave a course on Bach, in celebration of the second centenary of his death. Cecilia and I did the musical illustrations for his lectures, and she performed some excerpts from the *Libro de Ana Magdalena Bach* [*The Book of Anna Magdalena Bach*] and was warmly applauded by those attending.

Through the recommendation of Professor Walter Starkie—a man whose erudition was as great as his musical ability—, we were invited by the British Council to spend two weeks in London, and it was time that we put to very good use.

We left for London on the 26th of February, 1951, and were received with great affection by both the director of the Spanish Institute, Xavier de Salas and his wife, as well as by Aurelio Valls and his wife, Carmen. We were also very well looked after by representatives of the British Council.

I remember the supper given by Sir Ian Frazer in honor of Helen Keller, that extraordinary woman who overcame her tremendous handicaps; in spite of having been left deaf, dumb and blind by meningitis at the age of two, she completed her university studies and wrote notable books. Her autobiography, which I read at the age of eighteen, had deeply impressed me.

The concert of his works which Joaquín gave at the Spanish Institute was a success. There were a number of well-known personalities present: the Duke of Sanlúcar, several ambassadors, representatives of the British Council, of the B.B.C., of the Chester publishing house, etc. I found several members of my family there, among them my aunt

1951, In London at the Parliament House of Commons,
as a guest of the blind Member of Parliament Sir Ian Fraser.
Next to Joaquín Rodrigo the famous writer Helen Keller.

Elvira with her two daughters, and Elías Canetti, the future Nobel prize winner, who wanted to write the storyline for a ballet, with music by Joaquín.

Among the many invitations we received, I want to mention those from Michael Wood, director of Covent Garden, of the pianist Harriet Cohen, of Arnold Haskell, director of Sadler's Wells and of Harold Livermore, director of Canning House, whose wife Ann, a singer and musicologist, became a great friend of mine.

We met composers Arthur Bliss and Lennox Berkeley, guitarist Julian Bream, Tom Goff and Brossa (Brossa was a teacher on the course at Santiago de Campostela).

We were to return to London several times. The audiences always welcomed Joaquín's works with the greatest pleasure, especially the *Concierto Pastoral* and the *Concierto como un divertimento* for violoncello, on the occasion of its world première.

Once, in Heathrow Airport, the official who checked our passports asked Joaquín,

"Are you the musician?"

"Yes, I am he."

"It is an honor for us," he said.

* * *

During the first months of 1950, the death of violinist Antonio Fernández Bordas, left a vacancy in the Academy of Fine Arts of San Fernando, and Joaquín's friends urged him to offer himself as candidate. There was only one competitor, José Subirá, who had a long career as musicologist, but was not a composer. But he was considerably older than Joaquín and was being presented for the second time, so that he was a very strong candidate.

Joaquín and I began to make the required visits to the different academicians, for we weren't completely pessimistic. But when we called on the Conde de Romanones, Director of the Academy, our rising hopes were quickly dashed, for he told us that he had already committed himself to the other candidate. However, he assured us that Joaquín could count on his vote on the next occasion. Discouraged, we rose to take our leave, and then realized that the count's secretary, who had been present at the interview, was speaking to him in lowered tones.

"Has the Count noticed that Maestro Rodrigo is always accompanied by his wife? It would imply a great deal of fatigue for her to have to make all these visits again..."

"You have a point," replied the count. "In that case, we should give him precedence—."

"Rodrigo," he said aloud, "You may count on my vote."

Joaquín was elected to the Academy unanimously, and the ceremony of investiture took place the 18th of November, 1951. His speech was entitled, "Technique Taught and Inspiration not Learned," and Prince José Eugenio of Bavaria made the reply. As a finale, Joaquín played his *Cinco Sonatas de Castilla* [*Five Castilian Sonatas*] for the first time.

Although it had rained ceaselessly all day, the hall was filled, and the audience was most select. I saw Minister Ruiz Giménez, the Rector of the University, the French Ambassador, Madame Hardion, many academicians and our close friends. Mamá and Cecilia were seated behind us. I remember that the roof leaked, and that many drops fell on my new hat.

Joaquín played his *Cinco Sonatas de Castilla* confidently, and was roundly applauded. The session lasted a little more than an hour, and afterward, we gave a small reception at home for our friends.

* * *

The World War had completely severed my communication with my teacher, Lazare Lévy, although indirectly, from time to time, I had received news of him. He had had the sorrow of losing his son, René, a fighter in the Resistance, and he had begun his classes in Paris again. I was overjoyed when he was contracted to direct a two-week course in the Madrid Conservatory.

I went to all his classes, which were very well attended. In general, the Maestro seemed content with the level of the class, but the two students who stood out above all were Manuel Carra—"His Debussy was of the stature of Gieseking," said the Maestro—and also Achúcarro. He predicted a brilliant career for both of them, and he was not mistaken.

During his stay in Madrid we spent every day together. There were a number of receptions given in his honor, and he had many funny stories to tell about notable musicians like Moszkowski, Blanca Selva and others.

One day we made a pleasant trip to Toledo with Mamá. The Maestro was delighted with the museums, the churches and the "cigarrales" [a typical country home of Toledo located in the hills above the city]. When we returned, he gave no sign of weariness as we took him to the reception given by José Cubiles. On the contrary, he sat down at the piano to play pieces by Chopin and Schumann. When he left Madrid, we all felt bereaved.

On March 5, 1952, with great anticipation, I accompanied Joaquín to Barcelona to attend the grandiose tribute given in his honor by that city's Theater of the Lyceum. This had been initiated through the efforts of Antonio Fernández Cid. We were received by all the musicians with the greatest affection. Our room resembled a flower garden, and the fragrance was intoxicating.

On the night of the concert the theater was filled with a very select audience. The program included three of Joaquín's most important works: *Ausencias de Dulcinea*, the *Concierto de Estío* and the *Concierto de Aranjuez*, with soloists of the stature of Narciso Yepes, Christian Ferras and Corbella. Maestro Toldrá conducted. It was an enormous success, praised by both audience and critics.

In Madrid on May 3rd, the *Two Sephardic Songs* were introduced by the University Chorale, and in the afternoon the *Twelve Spanish Songs* were introduced in the Atheneum. There was a full house, and it was a smash hit. Marimí del Pozo was magnificent, and I accompanied her at the piano better than I had hoped. Joaquín played his works and had one of his best days.

The collection, *Twelve Spanish Songs*, was entrusted to Joaquín by the Barcelona Institute of Musicology, and the twelve songs which comprise the album were chosen right there, with no specification as to which region they belonged. Joaquín enjoyed doing this composition, which he accomplished quickly, and he was always satisfied with the result.

We recorded these songs with Marimí del Pozo in October of that same year. I think I accompanied her in eight of them, and Joaquín on the other four. The first edition of the songs sold out rapidly; later they were re-issued by the Schott House of London.

May 13, 1952, is an important date in Joaquín's career. That was the day of the establishment of the Manuel de Falla Chair in the History of Music in the University of Madrid, a professorship which Joaquín would hold until 1978. The auditorium of the School of Philosophy and Letters was crowded; there were speeches and music. It was a brilliant event.

On November 18, 1952, the Young Peoples' Musical Groups [*Juventudes Musicales*] were inaugurated in Spain; the program already operated in several European countries. Joaquín was asked to speak at the opening session.

Juventudes Musicales has done excellent work for many years, organizing concerts all over the country, and is now enjoying considerable popularity.

At that time Joaquín was busy with the composition of eight Christmas carols, which he wanted to enter in the National Competition. Two of them were written after verses of Lope de Vega, four based on my poems, and the last two based on anonymous texts.

The judging took place on December 21st, and the first prize was shared by Joaquín and García Leoz the composer. Of the eight Christmas Carols, two of them: *Pastorcito Santo* [*Blessed Little Shepherd*] and *Coplillas de Belén* [*Little Songs of Bethlehem*], would make a tour of the world.

* * *

On February 6, 1953, the première of the ballet of *Concierto de Aranjuez* took place, featuring the classic dancer Pilar López. The theater was filled, and Joaquín and Pilar received many ovations. The work was in the headlines until the departure of the company for Cuba, ten days later. The ballet would be performed in several countries, and there were a number of revivals in Spain.

About that time I received a commission to write the Spanish version of the libretto of the opera *Wozzeck* by Alban Berg, for the

National Radio, a commission that kept me busy for several weeks. The book, by the Austrian author, Georg Büchner, is a masterpiece that is as fine as the music.

Conducted by Argenta, Alicia de Larrocha played the *Concierto Heroico* with the National Orchestra, and soon after, Yepes performed the *Concierto de Aranjuez* with the same conductor.

In April we enjoyed a visit from the German ballerina Ilse Meudtner, who had staged the *Concierto de Aranjuez* in the Berlin Opera, under the title *Alborado* (sic). In view of its success, her husband wanted to use the music for a motion picture. I believe that the project was never realized.

In March of that same year the composer, Conrado del Campo, died. He had been very active as a teacher—for many years he was a professor of the Conservatory—and as Orchestra Conductor. His death was a great loss to Spanish music.

Around the end of April, Cemal Resit the orchestra conductor, arrived from Istanbul. He enjoyed considerable prestige, for he was also composer of numerous works: pieces for the piano, songs, chamber music and an opera, *Celebí*. He was a fine and sensitive man, greatly cultured. He knew almost all my family and had been a friend of my father's. He directed two concerts in the Athenaeum with much success.

At the end of May, 1953, we made a professional tour to Morocco.

In Tetuan we were received by the cultural delegate, Miguel Baena, an excellent and very pleasant person. He and his wife accompanied us to Ceuta, where Joaquín gave a lecture, followed by a recital of his works.

One afternoon we attended a tea given in our honor by Garrido, director of the Conservatory. It was made more delightful by the Arab orchestra which we were accustomed to hear on the radio—the best in the area—and which went to Granada on the occasion of the visit of King Abdullah. Its conductor, Sidi al Hami, was a notable man; at the age of 84, he had four wives, the latest no more than nineteen years old!

He was a Shereef, descended from the Prophet, and was a personal friend of General Franco. I thought that the Moorish tea, with mint and spices, was excellent. We were served along with all the professors.

On the following day Joaquín gave a concert of his works in Tetuan.

Another day we went to Tangier, invited by the Society of Friends of Music. There Joaquín played in a large hall crowded with people. The most applauded works were *A l'Ombre de Torre Bermeja* and *Preludio al Gallo Mañanero*.

The summer of 1953 was very hot, and on the first of July we left for Torrelodones with Cecilia and Mamá. Joaquín made a quick trip to Valencia, as he did every year, to help judge a band concert.

Several days later I accompanied Joaquín to Sagunto where, on July 30th, he was honored with a fantastic tribute. First, his admirers gave a banquet lasting three hours, during which the typical dishes of the region were served. That afternoon a plaque was unveiled on the house where Joaquín was born, and in the evening there was a concert of his works in the Roman Theater: *Per la Flor del Lliri Blau*, the *Concierto Heroico* and the *Cuatro Madrigales*. It was estimated that from eight to ten thousand people had gathered there to cheer their illustrious countryman.

To end the vacation, we took Cecilia on a short trip to San Juan de Luz, but the beach was a disappointment. How different from the bright, sunny beaches of the Levant!

About that time, Joaquín got in touch with Rafael Gil, who wanted him to write background music for his films. Joaquín wrote first the music for *Sor Intrépida* [*The Heroic Nun*], which was quite successful. Soon after, he wrote the music for *El Hereje* [*The Heretic*] and *La Guerra de Dios* [*God's War*]. We used the honorarium from this last film to buy our modest apartment on Villalar, which we had always rented.

One day it occurred to me that I, too, could make a contribution and, in order not to hold back I embarked on an unusual musical and literary activity, which soon bore fruit.

I got in touch with the Valencian flautist Ribelles, with whom I recorded the Bach Sonatas, some works by Gaubert and by other composers, for the radio. I accompanied the Chilean violinist Pedro d'Andurain on piano in works by Hindemith, Bartok, etc., the singer Marimí del Pozo in Songs by Schubert and Brahms, and I also did some work with the Finnish singer, Viola Wynne.

All this let me earn some money, and more importantly, served as a diversion.

Late in 1953 we made a trip to Turkey, where our friend Cemal Resit had organized several "Rodrigo Festivals." We made a stop in Athens, and at the airport had the pleasant surprise of being met by the Spanish Ambassador, Señor Romero, accompanied by José Bustinduy, the Basque violinist, and his daughter María.

They took us to the English Hotel, where we rested a while, and later went to the Embassy, where our hostess served a luncheon based on typical dishes of the country. I noticed that she was speaking Greek to our fellow diners, and, I enthusiastically joined in the conversation. Everyone was amazed.

"And how do you, a Spaniard, speak the language of Homer?" asked the Ambassador. "My wife is Greek by birth, but you?"

"I am Byzantine," I answered, "and therefore your neighbor, and I have spoken Greek since childhood."

Yes, we were in Athens, and I thought I was dreaming. Pindar called it "the radiant, crowned with violets and famous in song, cornerstone of Hellas, magnificent Athens, divine city."

I will never forget our walk through the Acropolis, where we contemplated the Parthenon and the Erecteon, glowing in the light of early morning. Everything there, the great and the small, shows the grandeur of man.

That afternoon Joaquín gave a concert of his works in Radio Athens, where the *Preludio al Gallo Mañanero* caused a sensation.

Two days later we were in Istanbul, my native city. We visited Ankara, Bursa and Smyrna during our three week stay.

In Istanbul we stayed at the Pera Palace, the oldest hotel in the city, across from the building where I had lived with my family. There were reunions with my cousins, Tanica and Vitali, with Jackito and other members of the family, as well as with a number of friends who still remembered me. We were showered with attention by everyone, and our room was filled with flowers and delicacies.

The Rodrigo Festival was an event, and from the very first day, all the seats were sold.

The program featured the *Concierto de Aranjuez* with Manuel Díaz Cano, and the *Concierto Heroico* with an excellent Turkish pianist. Cemal Resit conducted the orchestra with great authority.

We took the little steamer at Gálata to cross to Smyrna, where Joaquín presented a concert of his works. Later there was another concert in Bursa.

Nor could we fail to visit Ephesus, where the ruins of the temple of Diana are grandiose. There, too, is the tomb of St. John.

We went up to *Panaya Capulu*, the "House of the Virgin," where, according to an age-old legend, the Virgin Mary lived and died at the side of St. John. Upon the cross, Jesus had said to the disciple, "Behold thy mother," and to his mother, "Woman, behold thy son."

In front of the tiny house runs a little stream, where the Virgin washed her clothes in the shade of leafy olive trees. Every year, on the 15th of August, the faithful from all the surrounding countryside gather for a pilgrimage to *Panaya Capulu.* There, time stands still.

The concert in Ankara, with the same program, was even more successful. The enormous hall was crowded, and all the critics, musicians and intellectuals of the city were present. The government officials were also present, and we initiated our friendship with Ercole Michelini, the cultural attaché of the Spanish Embassy, and his attractive wife, Evelina.

On our return to Istanbul, Joaquín and I spent time on long walks through the city, while I described to him the places where I had spent my childhood.

How nostalgically I revisited the Garden of the Taxim and the streets of old Istanbul with their mosques, among them Santa Sofía, which reminded me of the legends that my father used to tell me! And the Golden Horn, the Bosporus, the "Maiden's Tower...."

In spite of the cold wind blowing from the Black Sea and the snow flakes which were beginning to fall, we also went to Besiktas to see the house where I was born. It was so shabby and neglected that it was soon torn down and replaced by a skyscraper.

Joaquín thoroughly enjoyed his stay in that city, so charged with history, which had opened its arms to him as to a favorite son.

We did not imagine that, some years later, we would have the occasion to return for another Rodrigo Festival.

* * *

In March of 1954 I traveled to Béjar with Marimí del Pozo, the young singer who was at the height of her operatic career.

We prepared an interesting and varied program, ending with the *Cuatro Madrigales Amatorios*. We were warmly received and the audience rewarded us with much applause.

During our entire stay we were royally entertained by José Agero, the attractive president of the Philharmonic Society, and we got along famously.

In April of 1954 we bought another apartment in the same building, 9 Villalar, where we had lived since 1940. The new apartment was considerably larger, and relatively comfortable, but it was in very bad condition. We had to refurbish it completely before moving into it, in December.

During this time we became acquainted with several well-known painters. Julio Moisés, one of Joaquín's colleagues at the Academy of Fine Arts, painted my portrait, a real masterpiece, and Gregorio Prieto did first, a portrait of Joaquín with enormous art and sensitivity, and later, one of me, as successful as the first. Then too, began our long friendship with Amadeo Roca, the Valencian painter, a great lover of music, whom we encountered at almost every concert.

José María Pemán, a great friend of Joaquín's had asked him to write the incidental music for his tragedy, the *La Destrucción de Sagunto*. The extensive score was composed quickly, and on the first of June they began rehearsals in the Roman Theater of Sagunto. The première, on June 7th, was a success of heroic proportions. The music, truly Valencian in inspiration, touched the hearts of the people, who tirelessly applauded the authors and the performers.

Cecilia made her debut in a public performance of the *Danza de los Tristes Augurios* [*Dance of the Sad Omens*], which the temple priests danced with youthful grace. I think that this number and the spectacular fire at the finale were the high points of the production, which attracted thousands of spectators during two consecutive weeks. Some time later the work was repeated, and triumphed again, with different performers.

On December 28th, Spain's Day of the Innocents [equivalent in custom to April Fools' Day], we decided to play a fine "inocentada" [trick] on our close friends. We invited them over for a drink, without telling them that we had moved to the new apartment.

When they rang the bell, a stranger opened the door and told them that the previous owners had moved, leaving no forwarding address. There was general consternation! Julián Uceda was the most upset. Lola Rodríguez Aragón, Cecilia's godmother, thought that they had knocked on the wrong door, and gave a half turn to check it out. Sopeña, the godfather, very grim, muttered something under his breath. Gloria and Odón Alonso felt hurt that we had not told them about something so important. On the other hand, Lula de Lara seemed very pleased, remarking that it was about time that the Maestro Rodrigo had an apartment worthy of him!

Finally, the truth was revealed, and the group gathered around the big table, we had recently brought from Valencia, to toast the occasion with champagne. They admired the furnishings, curtains and lamps acquired in El Rastro. We thought that it was a very original house-warming.

* * *

In July of 1954 we went to Paris for a week to attend the Louis Braille International Congress, as delegates from Spain. It was most interesting, for there were many important decisions made to benefit the blind.

One morning while I was reading the newspaper aloud to Joaquín, I was horrified to learn that the famous painter André Derain had been run over by an automobile, dying a few hours later. We were stunned, recalling the Derain had agreed to design the scenery for the ballet Joaquín had planned to prepare with musicologist, Roland-Manuel. It would have been staged in Paris, at the Opera-Comique.

But the outbreak of the World War had interrupted those plans, and we had lost touch with our good friend, Roland-Manuel, a great Hispanist, who had dreamed of producing a work honoring the vihuelists, whom he greatly admired. And now we had lost Derain too, in such a tragic manner. He had been one of my favorite painters.

"Goodbye, ballet," sighed Joaquín, "Now everything's fallen apart."

"Why?" I replied. "We have fine painters here in Spain who could certainly design adequate scenery."

"Well and good, but without Roland-Manuel, who's going to write the book?"

"I'll do it myself," I answered with aplomb. "There has been a lot written about the Spanish vihuelists, and I could spend some time in the National Library to research it in depth. Surely I'll find something to serve as a plot for your ballet."

No sooner said than done. Once we returned to Madrid, I set about studying all the literature regarding the vihuelists, especially the writing of Luis de Milán, author of the interesting book, *El Maestro* [*The Teacher*], published in 1535 in Valencia.

By pure chance I came across the autobiography of this great vihuelist, entitled *El Cortesano* [*The Courtier*], in which he describes in great detail the manners and customs of the Court of Germaine de Foix, wife of the Viceroy of Valencia. There are only three or four copies in the world.

Drawing from these sources I wrote a simple plot, in which all the characters were historic, and on which Joaquín composed one of his most inspired works, his ballet, *Pavana Real*, which was presented on December 17, 1955, in the Lyceum in Barcelona, with memorable success. Some years later, it was performed in Buenos Aires, and in Chile and Peru.

In October, they informed us that the date for the ballet's première had been set for December eleventh. Joaquín and I were hopeful and began to make preparations for the event. We organized several meetings in our home so that some fragments of the work would become known. Among those who attended were the Director of the British Institute, Arthur Montague and his wife, Oscar Esplá and his wife, Aurelio Valls and Carmen, the Valverdes and some critics.

The music was a hit, and everyone predicted a rousing success for us. We were in contact with several painters, among them Santiesteban, who showed us the models he had made for Antonio Ruiz, Pilar López, José Greco and others. They seemed excellent to us, but the choice was not ours, falling instead to the Management of the Lyceum. We had to wait several weeks longer.

At last the longed-for moment arrived for our departure for Barcelona. The première had to be postponed, because the properties for the work *La Lola se va a los Puertos* [*Lola Goes to the Ports*] which formed the first part of the program had not arrived on time. These circumstances were much in our favor, since on our arrival we found the ballet was still in limbo. The week we lost was in reality our gain, for it gave us time to edit the program carefully, make contact with the corps de ballet and to attend rehearsals.

Adrián Sardó, the conductor of the orchestra, along with Juan Magriñá, the principal dancer and choreographer of the Lyceum, were very enthusiastic about the preparations. I was delighted with the way Magriñá had staged the work, and I liked Aurora Pons, the prima ballerina, Alejandra Dimina and all the corps de ballet, as well as the guitarist, Renata Tarragó, whose part in the orchestra was important.

The one thing I did not find acceptable was the scenery, worn and threadbare, which had been used in Meyerbeer's opera, *The Huguenots*. But on the whole, the effect was not bad.

The night of the opening of *Pavana Real* will be engraved on my memory as long as I live. When I came into the great hall of the Theater of the Lyceum, holding Joaquín's arm and with Cecilia beside me, I felt quite content, even happy; the theater was completely filled, and I was sure that a cultivated audience would appreciate a work of the caliber of our ballet.

My long dress, a simple design of black taffeta, became me, and I felt sure of myself, as co-author.

But we had to sit through the first part of the program, also a première performance. Would it be a success? This was the unknown, but it would serve as a thermometer for ours.

I can't say that *La Lola se va a los Puertos* filled me with enthusiasm. It lacked grace, and the music seemed monotonous and dull to me. Therefore, I did not anticipate enthusiastic ovations at the end of the performance.

But when the curtain fell, there was a sepulchral silence instead of courteous applause. No foot-stomping, nor whistles, nor protests: absolute immobility. The spectators, rigid in their seats, seemed to be carved of stone.

My blood ran cold, and I felt at the point of tears.

During the intermission, friends visited our box with words of encouragement and affectionate embraces. Someone brought me a glass of orange juice, but my hand was shaking so that I spilled it all over my dress. A disaster...!

When Maestro Sardó mounted the platform, there was applause at last. Then the first measures of the ballet sounded, and the curtain rose on the first scene, the fiesta in the palace of the Viceroy of Valencia. The audience seemed interested, above all when the lovely Doña Mencia and the Duke of Calabria executed their *Zarabanda de Amor* to languid and melodic music. At the end of the first act there was long applause. At the end of the second act, after Durandarte's song, the whole hall applauded enthusiastically, and when the work ended, its success was assured!

Joaquín and I had to go up on the stage with Maestro Sardó, Renata Tarragó, Magriñá and the entire corps de ballet to acknowledge the audience's applause. It was the greatest surprise of our lives.

On February 1, 1955, the Seminar of History of Music was inaugurated in the School of Philosophy and Letters, and Joaquín gave a lecture on concrete music before a large audience of students.

To celebrate, we invited José María de Cossío and Federico Sopeña to lunch in our new dining room, and I outdid myself with a civet of hare which they, as great gourmets, knew how to appreciate.

About the middle of March, Joaquín and I made a short concert tour through the Levant: to Alicante, Murcia and Lorca.

We were received everywhere with the utmost friendliness, especially in Murcia, where the director of the Conservatory, Señor Massotti, put us up in the Upper College, Cardenal Belluga.

In Madrid we never missed attending a concert. The pianist, Weissenberg and Kempff, the Vienna Philharmonic conducted by the extraordinary Karl Bohm, are the ones who impressed me most.

In June we presented a concert of Turkish music: the pianist Yüksel Koptagel, the singer Sofía Noël and I, following a lecture by Joaquín. The songs of Cemal Resit, Turkey's most outstanding composer, made a hit.

With the arrival of summer, Joaquín and I set out for Paris, Brussels and Baden-Baden. It was a short trip, lasting only three weeks.

During that summer the Music Festival of the S.I.M.C. took place in Baden-Baden. As Oscar Esplá, President of the Spanish Section, was not strong enough to undertake the journey, Joaquín, who was then Vice-President, had to substitute for him as the delegate from Spain. On our arrival, some of the delegates received us with a certain misgiving. The delegate from Brazil greeted us with these words:

"You are from the Spain of Casals, aren't you?"

To which I replied, "No, simply from Spain."

The most disagreeable individual of the group was the delegate from Norway. We learned later that she was a friend of Casals'.

On the other hand, Martell, the French delegate, Nils Vigge Bentzon, from Denmark, and the Italian delegates could not have been more pleasant.

The German delegate, Heinrich Strobl, was politely discreet, but we noted a good deal of "behind the scenes" activity on his part. His purpose was to create two Spanish sections: one composed of the Spaniards "of Franco," and the other of the "expatriate Spaniards," a proposition which Joaquín strongly opposed. The debates went on for more than five hours, and finally came to a vote.

Meanwhile Joaquín and I had to leave the hall to wait outside in the hallway during the long hours it took the delegates to reach an agreement. At last Strobl came out to tell us that we could return to hear the decision: Spain was readmitted almost unanimously to the International Society of Contemporary Music. There was only one vote against, and two abstentions, but the vote was secret, and we could learn nothing that day.

However, the next day we met the Italian delegates in the dining room of the Hotel Golf, and they congratulated us on our success.

"Won't you tell us who voted against us?" I asked, smiling.

"We can't say a thing. You will have to guess."

"It wouldn't surprise me if it were the delegate from Norway!"

"Bravo!" exclaimed one of the Italians. "You hit the nail on the head! And now I will tell you who abstained: Canada and Yugoslavia."

"Nice people!" I exclaimed, and everyone burst out laughing.

The next day almost all the delegates marched in parade; Joaquín and I were among the last.

And what shall I say of the concerts at the Festival? To me they all seemed the same, monotonous and not very interesting. The only one that stood out was the presentation of *La Marteau sans Maitre* [*The Unguided Hammer*] by Pierre Boulez, perhaps the only work which has been retained in the repertory of European orchestras.

From Baden-Baden we went first to Cologne, travelling by boat along the Rhine. In Cologne Joaquín gave a recital of his works on the Radio, with much success.

We spent several very pleasant days in Cologne, and we visited the Cathedral which, miraculously, was not destroyed by the bombs of the World War.

We went also to Bonn, where we visited Beethoven's birthplace, and the tombs of Robert and Clara Schumann.

And finally, we set out for Brussels, where we were received by the guitarist, Nicolás Alfonso. He introduced us to pianist René van Arenbergh and to the Marissal family, in whose house we spent four or five very interesting days, making excursions to Bruges and Antwerp.

On our return to Spain, Joaquín received a commission to write the music for a production of Edmond Rostand's *Cyrano de Bergerac*, which opened on October 15th, 1955, in the Teatro Español. I was not enthusiastic about it, except for a few scenes which seemed very well done to me, and the costuming, which was in good taste. Joaquín's music was inspired and appropriate to the action. The show was on the boards for quite a long run.

In January of 1956 I became a member of the General Society of Spanish Authors, as a writer and composer. I was required to pass a not-too-difficult examination.

I continued to accompany Joaquín to the classes of History of Music at the University. During those years we often organized good concerts in the Auditorium at the University.

On the 28th of January, Mozart's opera, *Bastien et Bastienne*, was presented, and much appreciated by the students.

In February Loren Maazel conducted the National Orchestra, and since Joaquín's *Cuatro Madrigales Amatorios* was the program, he and his wife paid us a visit. Toñi Rosado sang the *Madrigales*, and Maazel made a great impression on me, for his musicality and his conducting technique. He was very attractive and elegant.

Soon after, Freitas Branco conducted the *Cinco Piezas Infantiles*, and Pilar López was again soloist in the *Concierto de Aranjuez*. There was no doubt that Joaquín stood in the limelight!

I continued my piano practice, and with violinist Angelina Velasco, I ventured to give a recital of Mozart's sonatas at the University. It did not turn out badly, and we were warmly applauded by the students.

"Overture on Making Music" was the title of the series of eight lectures which Joaquín gave in the Athenaeum at that time. The talks were well-attended, and their success was flattering.

* * *

Joaquín used to go to a barbershop near our house, and the barber's messenger boy, a lad of about 13 years, would always accompany him on his return. When Joaquín asked him what he wanted to be when he grew up, Paco invariably answered:

"A torero" [bullfighter].

"If you are," Joaquín told him, "I will dedicate a 'pasodoble' to you."

Some years later young Paco, accompanied by his agent, a newspaper reporter and a photographer, unexpectedly presented himself at the house. He announced that he was now a *matador* [the torero who kills the bull], and for that reason the magazine *Semana* wanted to publish an interview, with photographs of him with Joaquín. Paco won in the bullring and Joaquín soon composed the cheerful pasodoble, *Paco Alcalde*, which soon became popular all over Spain.

Soon after that Paco invited us to his wedding, and, to the best of our knowledge, he is still fighting bulls.

* * *

Joaquín had met the illustrious Basque Harpist Nicanor Zabaleta during one of Zalabeta's professional visits to Madrid, and was his great admirer. So when Zabaleta asked him to write a concerto for him, Joaquín accepted immediately. Zabaleta told him that he would prefer a work inspired by classic harp music rather than by the romantic style.

At first Joaquín directed his efforts toward the impressionist harp, but later he abandoned this project and thought about a concerto which would evoke the music of the beginning of the 19th century, especially in its taste for the popular everyday life in Madrid.

This characteristic is most apparent in the first movement, "Estudiantina" [Student Serenade]. The second movement is written in the form of a canon, followed by a fugue. And the third movement, "Sarao" [Soiree, evening party with music and dancing], is perhaps the most genuinely Spanish, with several themes and refrains, which end in *Seguidillas*, [an Andalusian dance form].

In 1951, Joaquín was able to deliver the completed score to Zabaleta, who came to pick it up in the station at San Sebastian, where the train stopped for a few minutes during our journey to London. Zabaleta was delighted with the work and lost no time in presenting it.

However, the première in Madrid did not take place until November, 1956, with the National Orchestra, under the baton of Paul Klecki. Its success was very gratifying, and soon after, Zabaleta recorded the *Concierto Serenata* conducted by Maerzendorfer, making it known world-wide.

Other recordings of this concerto exist, one by the French harpist, Catherine Michel, and the other by the Russian, Ada Tougay. It was also performed as a ballet by a company in Paris.

In April of 1956 we went to Pamplona and to Barcelona, where Joaquín gave three lectures in the University and another in the Athenaeum, at which the singer Conchita Badía and I presented the *Twelve Spanish Songs*. Several days later Joaquín gave a concert of his works at the home of José Bertomeu, whose hospitality was proverbial. There we visited with all our old friends.

On our return to Madrid we became acquainted with Robert Shaw, director of the American Chorale, who came to our home to learn more about Joaquín's work. He was enthusiastic about the *Concierto de Aranjuez*, and thought it ridiculous that it had never been played in the United States. Coincidentally, at that time the guitarist, Rey de la Torre, who lived in New York, was in Madrid. He was able to speak with Shaw that same night, and between them they set a date for the première in New York.

On the other hand, in spite of all our efforts, our ballet, *Pavana Real*, had not been performed, either in Valencia, or Madrid, or abroad. It had been accepted by the Munich Opera, and Joaquín had signed the contract. But a few days before the opening night, the principal dancer was run over by an automobile!

In May of 1956 the famous Leopold Stokowski came to direct the Symphony Orchestra in an eclectic musical program. In the first part, featuring Spanish music, there was Joaquín's *Homenaje a la Tempranica*, *Psyche and Eros*, by Esplá, and *La Fantasía Castellana*, by Conrado del Campo. In the second part we heard *Betafogo*, by Darius Milhaud, and Tchaikovsky's *Fifth Symphony*. The great conductor really shone in this last work, achieving a thousand marvels, for he had a special grace for that music. The success was overwhelming!

A few days later, Joaquín and I set out for Portugal to give one concert each in Porto and Lisbon. For us this trip had a special significance, for we were fortunate to be received by the Count and Countess of Barcelona, parents of the present King of Spain, at their residence in Estoril. Villa Giralda gave the impression of a very

Spanish house, at once charming and majestic. Both Don Juan and Doña María were very kind and affable, and I have a very pleasant memory of our visit.

During the summer of 1956 we made a tour through Europe, stopping for a few days in Paris, Frankfort, Munich and Vienna. We wanted to forget the sadness that we had felt after we sold our chalet in Torrelodones. I hadn't realized how much it had meant to me, above all the garden, with its trees, which we had planted ourselves, its roses and the blue iris.

Would we be able, some day, to find a place—perhaps on one of the Levantine beaches—to build ourselves a summer house? This idea obsessed me. How could I guess that my dream would soon become a reality!

One fine day, some good friends told us of a little beach along the Costa Blanca, some 35 kilometers from Valencia, where they were thinking about buying a piece of land. The village was called "Faro de Cullera."

One weekend we drove down there with them and were amazed at its beauty: a peaceful beach with the finest sand, which extended to the edge of a leafy pine grove, thick with rosemary, thyme and lavender. There were only a few houses, but on the crest of the hill, a medieval castle was reflected in a sea the color of turquoise. It couldn't have been more romantic!

We were introduced to the Mayor of Cullera, Leandro Más, an intelligent, cordial man, very fond of music, and promptly expressed our desire to buy a building site in the pine grove. He agreed, with the proviso that we promise not to cut a single tree in building the house. I promised, but actually three or four were cut, to my great annoyance.

* * *

On October 5, 1956, Seneca's tragedy, *Tyestes*, adapted by José María Pemán, had its première in the *Teatro Español*. The music by Joaquín was beautiful and moving. The actors, Mejuto and Seoane, did a splendid job, and the audience applauded warmly.

About that time a close friend of Joaquín's, the pianist and composer Joaquín Nin Culmell, whom we called "the younger Tocayo" [namesake] made a visit to Madrid. We had dinner together several times, and he told us about his life at the University of California at Berkeley, and about his sister, Anais Nin. She had become quite a celebrity with her extensive *Diary*, which had been translated into several languages. I read only three volumes—I believe there are ten in all—and I must confess that, without being prudish, I found many of the chapters shocking. Nevertheless, I recognize that this woman, whose beauty had so impressed me when she was introduced to us in Paris years before, had an enormous talent. She died in America, of cancer.

For some time Joaquín had been thinking of composing an opera-oratorio on a text of José María Valverde, titled *La Azucena de Quito* [*The Lily of Quito*]. The book, which recounted the life of Saint Mariana de Jesús, an Ecuadorean saint who died in the eighteenth century, was very moving. We thought that it was an interesting detail that she also played the guitar very well.

But to dedicate himself to this project, Joaquín needed to request a grant from the March Foundation. When we heard that they had awarded him one hundred thousand pesetas to compose the work during a period of one year, we were enormously pleased.

Joaquín wrote several inspired arias, which were presented in a concert organized in the Ministry of Information and Tourism, on the occasion of Joaquín's 60th anniversary. However, the work, which was to have had its première in Quito, was never finished.

* * *

On the tenth of January, 1957, we went to a concert of the National Orchestra, conducted by Argenta, in which Victoria de los Angeles, at the peak of her career, was brilliant.

Our daughter, at the time an avid autograph collector, insisted on getting one from the hands of the illustrious singer, and Joaquín had no choice but to call the hotel where she was staying. He spoke with her husband, Enrique Magriñá, to ask this favor, and told him, as well, that he had composed two songs that she had not yet heard.

"If that is so," replied Enrique, "we will come to your house right now and pick them up."

The pleasant visit lasted more than two hours, as we chatted and listened to Joaquín's records. Victoria told us that she was going to sing in Paris on February 2nd, and that she would put *Pastorcito Santo* and *Coplillas de Belén* on her program.

Beginning on that date, she sang them in all her concerts, and thanks to her unique art, they toured the world.

About that time the writer, Sánchez Silva—author of *Marcelino Pan y Vino* [*Marcelino Bread and Wine*]—came to the house to talk to Joaquín about the music for a motion picture, *The Heretic*, whose script he had just finished. The score, very extensive, and very moving, was quickly written. Nevertheless, the picture was not very popular. I saw it and liked it fairly well.

In mid-February we made a short trip to Paris when Joaquín was invited to give a concert of his works at the Spanish Library and another at the College of Spain.

On our return to Madrid we began to make preparations for our trip to Caracas, where we were guests of the Latin American Music Festival, as delegates of Spain.

Venezuela

Music came to Venezuela through the front door, thanks to the José Angel Lamas Institute, which in 1954 organized the first Latin American Music Festival, celebrated with the participation of the most important figures of the musical world of Spanish America.

The second Festival, which took place from March 19th until April 6th, 1957, was larger, with nine symphony concerts and a number of recitals and lectures. It was attended by numerous guests of honor: foreigners of great prestige, an enormous gathering of well-known professionals, and music lovers from the entire country.

We arrived in Caracas with perfect weather on the sixteenth of March, and were met at La Guaira Airport by, Señor Valdés, the Spanish Ambassador and Señor Vaca de Osma, Secretary of the Embassy. We stayed at the recently opened Hotel Tamanaco, a veritable palace, in the company of the other delegates: Edgar Martin of Cuba, Roque Cordero of Panama, Blas Galindo Chávez and his wife, of Mexico, Alberto Soriano and his wife, of Uruguay, Cuvelier of Belgium, as founder of the Young Musicians Groups, Guillermo Espinosa, head of the Pan-american Union, Valenti Ferro, of Argentina, Domingo Santa Cruz, of Chile, Gilbert Chase and his wife Kathleen, of the United States, Campos Parsi, of Puerto Rico, Héctor Tossar, of Uruguay, Escobar of Cuba and several more. Later arrivals were Virgil Thomson, Copland and Taubman from the United States, Guarnieri, Iturriaga, Rey de la Torre, Alfonso Letelier and Julian Bautista.

The concerts followed each other daily in the Concha Acústica; the first was directed by Jacha Horenstein, and attended by the President of the Republic, Marcos Pérez Jiménez, as well as the entire Diplomatic Corps.

The first recital featured two great Venezuelan artists, Fedora Alemán and Alirio Díaz, who executed works by Villa-Lobos and Letelier.

During the final symphony concert the four award-winning works were presented, by Roque Cordero, Iturriaga, Blas Galindo and Guarneri.

It is a curious fact that the cultivation of Venezuela's famous coffee is linked to that of classic European music. The introduction of the coffee plant dates back to the years 1783 and 1784. It was first grown on several plantations in Chacao, called "Blandín," "San Felipe," and "La Floresta," which belonged to Bartolomé Blandín and to the priests Soho and Mohedano. It was considered an exotic ornamental plant. In 1786 two German naturalists, Bradmeyer and Schult, arrived in Caracas and established a friendship with Padre Soho, presenting him, on their departure, with some musical instruments and several scores by Haydn and Mozart. And the zeal for music took a great leap forward in the shade of the coffee groves and orange trees. The first cup of coffee was served on Blandín's plantation towards the end of the year 1786, during the course of a memorable fiesta, where quartets by Mozart and Haydn were heard for the first time.

It was this fiesta which Eva Melchort de Arizmendi tastefully evoked for us in a recreation in the gardens of her country place, full of orchids. It was an occasion where we met a most select group of the ladies of Caracas.

I also want to recall the affectionate tribute offered to us by the Ministry of Justice. There was a section called "Work with Music," where the employees used to listen to good records: Beethoven, Bach, Schumann, Schubert, Brahms, Mozart. They also played recordings of Spanish music, among them Joaquín's *Concierto de Aranjuez* and *Cantata*. One morning about eleven o'clock, a committee headed by Blanco Valeira, Rosal and three others—almost all Gallegos—called on us themselves in an official car, preceded by a motorcycle escort, to accompany us to the Ministry, where we were received by all its officials. Rafael Dávila, a man of great talent and sentience, read a speech of welcome. Joaquín replied with his usual Levantine eloquence.

On the day of our departure from Caracas we were accompanied to the airport by a number of friends, among whom, to our great surprise, was a committee from the Ministry of Justice, who presented us with a bouquet of orchids and a parchment full of signatures. We were accompanied to the plane by Dávila, Valeira and Rosal, and we parted from all of them with real regret, but also with the hope of meeting them again in Spain. Three hours later we landed in Puerto Rico.

Puerto Rico

On the thirteenth of April we arrived in Puerto Rico, where they were celebrating the *Pablo Casals Festival.*

On the same day Joaquín gave a lecture, followed by a concert of his works in the *Casa de España.*

The next day the pianist Sanromá accompanied us to the home of the renowned cellist Pablo Casals, who received us very cordially. We spent almost all afternoon there, talking of music and listening to his anecdotes. Finally, he invited us to attend the Festival, an invitation which we accepted with pleasure. I remember that he seemed as physically strong and agile as a young man. His face was smooth and unwrinkled!

Three days later Héctor Campos Parsi gave us some bad news. Don Pablo had become ill during a rehearsal, and the diagnosis was a coronary thrombosis. He would not be able to take part in the Festival, and that implied a double catastrophe. It was clear that many reservations for the Festival would be cancelled, beginning that day.

Joaquín and I were able to attend the rehearsals, accompanied by Sanromá, Luis Antonio Ramírez and several other musicians.

Joaquín recorded some of his works for the Radio and also gave a concert at the University.

One morning Héctor came to pick us up in his car to take us to El Yunque, a mountain covered with giant ferns, coffee plantations and hibiscus. There we heard the songs of thousands of birds and of the *hylas*, those curious little frogs of the Island, which sing day and night. It seemed to me an earthly paradise.

In the home of Irma Isern we met the great Puerto Rican singer, María Esther Robles, and her husband, the journalist Márquez. They were an attractive couple, and we were soon the best of friends.

Joaquín was interviewed several times for the press. One of the journalists was Rafael Montañés, uncle of Martita, the young girl who would become Casal's wife.

Shortly before leaving Puerto Rico, they told us that Don Pablo was much better and that he was out of danger, which was an enormous relief to everyone.

We left the lovely, hospitable island with regret, never dreaming that we would return six years later as professors, engaged by the University of Rio Piedras to give a course on the History of Music.

New York

I had an enormous desire to visit New York, that gigantic city, melting pot of so many races, so many civilizations, where so many artists of all countries had been recognized, achieving universal fame after many years of struggle.

We were met at Idlewild Airport by the Consul General of Spain, Sr. Presilla, the kindest of men, who took us under his wing, and by the composer Carlos Suriñach and several newspaper reporters.

Suriñach, who remained with us during our entire stay, introduced us to the most outstanding composers, and the great publishers of the country.

We also ran into our good friend, Joseph Bloch, who was professor of piano at the Juilliard School, where we enjoyed a lunch with all the professors.

We saw Andrés Segovia almost every day. He invited us to dinner at his home, or he took us to lively parties where we were introduced to many celebrities in the world of the arts.

And after many years, I again met a childhood friend, Rachel de Leeuw, in whose Manhasset house we spent the most delightful hours. I went with her to visit the United Nations and the Metropolitan Museum of Art, where Dalí's "Christ" was the focus of attention, with an unending line of viewers passing before it.

One day Suriñach took us to the Ricordi House, where we had a lengthy conversation with the Director. I remember him as a fine and charming man, but extremely cautious.

Joaquín suggested to him that they publish his complete works including the *Concierto de Aranjuez*. The sum offered by Ricordi House seemed acceptable to us.

But at the last minute, the Director changed his mind, and I recall our great disappointment when we received his letter, in Madrid, alleging that a concerto for a guitar and orchestra had no commercial value. He was not, of course, a very good prophet.

We devoted our last days in New York to socializing, under the aegis of Andrés Segovia. We went with him to a cocktail party given by the pianist Ania Dorfman, where we met a number of well-known artists, including Vladimir Nabokoff.

Of particular interest to us was our visit to the Foundation for the Blind, where they showed us the studios for recording "talking books," and also demonstrated the latest models of typewriters, etc. It was a most interesting visit.

The Rodrigos playing four hands, New York, 1958.

Madrid

We returned to Madrid on the tenth of May, delighted with our long trip to America. I had taken a large notebook with me, in which I jotted down all the events and experiences. On re-reading those accounts now, I remember them as among the happiest and most interesting of our life.

We immediately renewed all our activities, which were more demanding than ever.

I recall that we had a domestic crisis, I was unable to find household help, and that Mamá helped me in every way possible. My day's work began at eight in the morning, and never ended until almost time to go to bed. Sometimes almost until dawn!

Joaquín was busy recording some pieces that the writer, José López Rubio, had entrusted to him, and spent long hours in the Chamartin Studios.

He continued his classes at the University, and also his duties with ONCE and the Radio.

We spent our summer vacation in Faro de Cullera with Mamá and Cecilia, who had passed 'with distinction' the examination for her degree.

On the 4th of September Cecilia and I set out for London. She insisted on studying at the Royal Ballet School, for her dream was to become a dance star. For two years she submitted to the iron discipline of this School, the most important in Europe, whose director was Arnold Haskell and after a great deal of work, she received her diploma.

How empty the house seemed when I returned from London! Joaquín and Mamá, both nostalgic, reproached me for having taken Cecilia to a country so far away, and told me that all the happiness had gone from the house.

As before, we attended every concert, and one which made an unforgettable impression on me was by Victoria de los Angeles in the hall of the *Monumental*. She made a true masterpiece of *Pastorcito Santo* and of *Coplillas de Belén*, which she recorded soon after. They were published by the House of Schott.

About the first of July we had a visit from the Sanjuan brothers, documentary film directors, who gave Joaquín a commission to write the music for a film on the Gardens of the Retiro, which was our favorite walk. The score, entitled *Música para un jardín* [*Music for a Garden*], had great success.

I remember the dinner that we had at about that time for the attractive pianist, Margot Pinter and her husband, Maestro Weissbach. The famous Dr. Schermant, an incorrigible fisherman—he and his wife Concha were among our closest friends—had given us a huge pike, and I spent several hours in the kitchen preparing it according to an old French recipe. The guests did honor to this excellent dish, and Maestro Weissbach wrote the following verse in my autograph book:

"Sie wurden dem schönen Hecht aufs herrlichste gerecht."

("You were worthy of this magnificent pike.")

I can assure you that that pike made me proud.

A little before Christmas we organized a concert of Christmas music in the University Auditorium.

Joaquín gave a lecture as preamble.

I played works by Mompou, Guridi and Joaquín's *Borriquitos de Belén* [*Little Burros of Bethelem*]. Afterward, Isabel Penagos sang popular Christmas carols from several countries, two of Joaquín Nin's and two of Joaquín Rodrigo's. It was a rousing success.

* * *

On January 16th Joaquín gave a lecture at the College of Santa Teresa de Jesús. His topic was the work of Strauss and Debussy.

The following day we went to a concert of the National Orchestra, where Argenta conducted the *Messiah*, with singers Norma Procter and María Stader.

On the nineteenth of January we celebrated our silver wedding anniversary with a party at home. There were more than forty friends from the Madrid musical world, and the house was filled with flowers and gifts. It was a very lively evening, and when the last guests departed it was after two o'clock in the morning. Everyone missed the "young lady of the house," especially her parents.

On January 21, 1958, we received truly terrible news, which left us all stunned: that very morning, Ataulfo Argenta, the orchestra conductor, had been found dead in his home in Los Molinos. Federico Sopeña called us several times; he had been urgently summoned to take charge of the situation, for Argenta's wife, Juanita, had left the night before for Switzerland.

An autopsy was performed, and the cause of death determined as monoxide poisoning from his automobile, which had been left with windows closed and the motor running.

General consternation reigned, and many rumors began to circulate. According to some, he died "in the odor of sanctity," because only two days before he had conducted Handel's *Messiah*. With his death, Spain lost one of her most prestigious orchestra conductors.

* * *

After several years' absence, Andrés Segovia had returned to his native land, and between tours, would appear in Madrid's concert halls. He performed almost every year in the festivals in Granada, but Joaquín and I didn't take part in those until 1963.

If I am not mistaken, we saw Segovia for the first time at a ballet performance by Pilar López, in which she had included the *Concierto de Aranjuez*. That night, guitarist Luis Maravillas had suffered a real ordeal, for he played the soloist part completely by ear, as he could not read scores. Directly in front of him, seated in a parquet box, he saw Segovia, serene and majestic, and his fingers began to fly at such a rate that it hurt to watch him. It was clearly a real exploit for Maravillas—who lived up to his name ("Marvels")—from which he emerged successful.

It was in 1951 that Segovia asked Joaquín for a new concerto for guitar and chamber orchestra. In order to exchange ideas, he came one summer afternoon to our chalet in Torrelodones, and stayed to have supper with us. Not long before this, Joaquín had dedicated *Tres Piezas para Guitarra* [*Three Pieces for Guitar*], *Fandango*, *Pasacalle* and *Zapateado* to Segovia, which had pleased him enormously.

After the triumph of *Concierto de Aranjuez* in Paris, Joaquín felt no great desire to compose another concerto, and he postponed the work. One day, however, he told me that he had thought it over and that he would write a "Suite" on themes collected by Gaspar Sanz, the famous guitarist of the court of Felipe IV. The title would be *Fantasía para un Gentilhombre* [*Fantasy for a Gentleman*], and he would also dedicate it to Andrés Segovia, whom he greatly admired, as a tribute.

We carefully reviewed the works of Gaspar Sanz, and together we selected the themes which would serve as basis for this new work.

At Christmas, Andrés Segovia unexpectedly came to our house, asking to look over the score of the *Fantasía para un Gentilhombre.*

Just as I was accompanying him at the piano in the first measures, there was a power failure, and the whole apartment was plunged into darkness.

Thanks to two candles, we surmounted the difficulty. The work played marvelously under the great artist's fingers, and the tenuous light lent an archaic atmosphere, very fitting, above all for the "dance of the torches." It was not difficult to predict the same success for this work as that achieved by its elder brother, the *Concierto de Aranjuez.*

Soon afterward, the date was set for the première in San Francisco, under the direction of Enrique Jordá. We were invited to attend as guest of the San Francisco Symphony Orchestra, and the trip's expenses were underwritten by the Del Amo Foundation.

San Francisco

We left for San Francisco the 27th of February, 1958, and on the 6th, 7th and 8th of March, Segovia presented the *Fantasía para un Gentilhombre* in the great Opera House of that city.

At the San Francisco airport, Andrés Segovia was waiting for us, with Enrique Jordá and his wife, Audrey, and some reporters. They took us to the Francis Drake Hotel, where we had a short time to rest. The rehearsals began at once, for only a few days remained before the première.

Then followed the rounds of the press, interviews, parties, dinners with the artists and the critics. Nothing was omitted that would characterize this première as a great event. And the success was complete, unanimous, enthusiastic. In all three of the successive concerts, the audiences who filled the hall applauded the soloist and the composer with fervor. During the intermissions people surrounded us, with radiant faces, to congratulate us, to request an autograph, a photo. It was thrilling!

Several weeks later Segovia recorded the *Fantasía para un Gentilhombre* in New York, with the Orchestra of the Air, under the direction of Jordá.

From then on, the work began its worldwide career, versions multiplied, and it can now be said to compete with the *Concierto de Aranjuez*, whose fame has not diminished in all these years.

Fantasía para un Gentilhombre
World Première. San Francisco, March 1958.
Program Cover

SAN FRANCISCO SYMPHONY ORCHESTRA

Enrique Jordá, Conductor

46th Season - Tenth Program

Wednesday, March 5, at 8:30; Thursday, March 6, at 8:30
Friday, March 7, at 2:15

ANDRES SEGOVIA, *Guest Artist*

SUITE FROM *CASTOR AND POLLUX*.......... *Rameau*

Overture
Gavotte
Air Gai
Menuet
Tambourin
Chaconne

FIRST PERFORMANCE IN SAN FRANCISCO

FANTASIA PARA UN GENTILHOMBRE,
FOR GUITAR AND ORCHESTRA .... *Rodrigo*

Villano y Ricercare
Españoleta y Fanfare de la Caballería de Napoles
Danza de la hachas
Canario

MR. SEGOVIA
WORLD PREMIERE

INTERMISSION

GUITAR SOLOS:

GAVOTTE AND MUSETTE.................... *Bach*
PRELUDE AND STUDY.................. *Villa Lobos*
TORRE BERMEJA.......................... *Albéniz*

MR. SEGOVIA

SYMPHONY NO. 5, IN D MAJOR....... *Vaughan Williams*

Preludio
Scherzo
Romanza
Passacaglia

Presented by

SAN FRANCISCO SYMPHONY ASSOCIATION

KENNETH MONTEAGLE, President **HOWARD K. SKINNER, Manager**

Patrons who occasionally find they are unable to attend concerts may make a worthwhile contribution to the Symphony by returning their tickets to the Box Office for resale prior to the performance. Proceeds will be used to benefit the San Francisco Symphony Orchestra's Pension Fund.

437

Fantasía para un Gentilhombre
World Première. San Francisco, March 1958.
Program

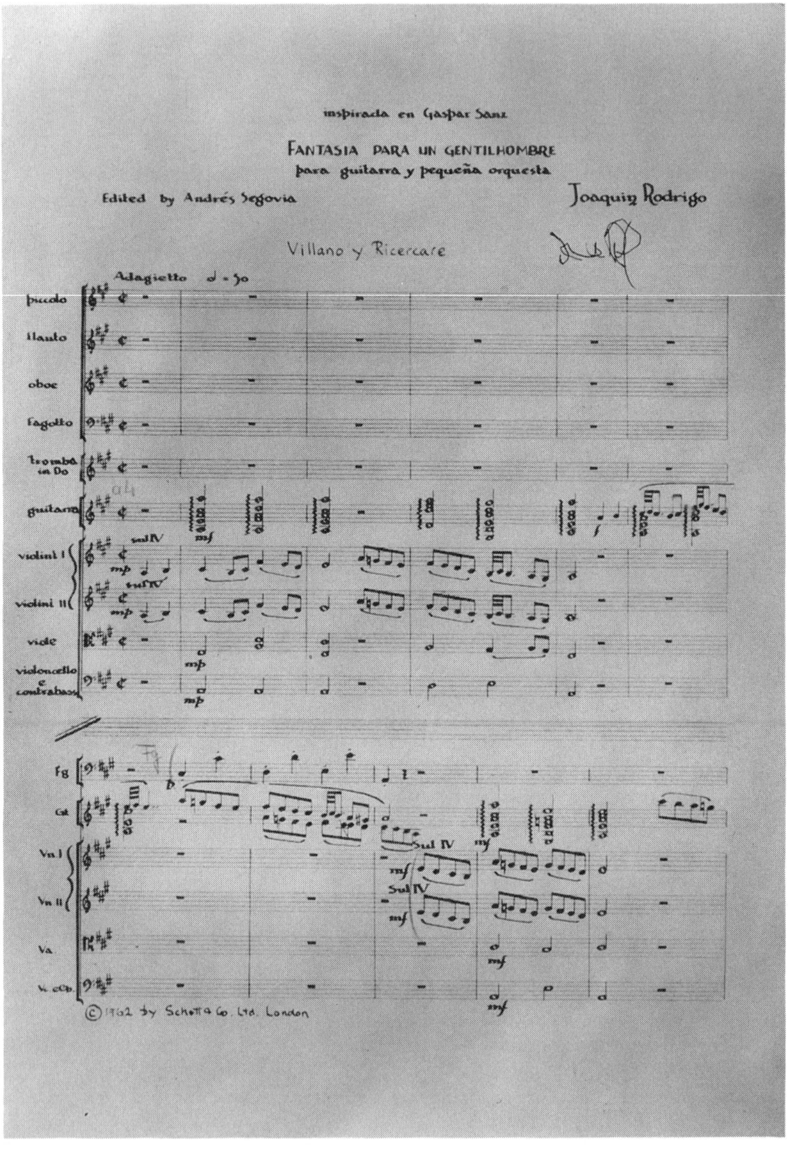

Fantasía para un Gentilhombre
World Première. San Francisco, March 1958.
1st page of Manuscript

Joaquín Rodrigo at the world première of *Fantasía para un Gentilhombre* with Andrés Segovia and music critic Alexander Fried. San Francisco, March 1958

March. 1958

Segovia and Composer Share Symphony Honors

By ALEXANDER FRIED

GREAT RICHES and mysteries of tone color made fascinating music in a beautiful concert of the San Francisco Symphony last night at the Opera House.

First they emerged with a miniature jewel-like charm in the new "Fantasia para un Gentil-hombre" by the Spanish composer, Joaquin Rodrigo, with the unique Andres Segovia as guitar soloist.

Later, in Vaughan Williams' Fifth Symphony, they broadened into full orchestral splendors and rapturous tonal atmospheres in which Conductor Enrique Jorda inspired our symphony to some of the finest, most luminous playing of its career.

Such a performance showed again that within the past two years Jorda—by keen training and shrewd choice of players—has raised the orchestra to an entirely new level of quality. I have no doubt he has further levels in mind beyond that.

Rodrigo's "Fantasy for a Nobleman" uses themes of a late 17th century composer named Gaspar Sanz. Segovia is the present-day "musical nobleman" Rodrigo had in mind in writing his charming work. Its classic motifs recall an age in which a nobleman at the Spanish court could play the guitar as a genuine "dilettante"—that is, for his own and his Lady's exquisite pleasure.

True to the dimensions of its solo instrument, the "Fantasy" makes no big pretensions. But it makes a delightful blend of classic dignity and Spanish musical flavor. The blend is fastidious, piquant in its dance rhythms and veiled with a peculiar melancholy.

One of the wonders of our noise loving age is that a huge audience in a huge hall will listen with such silent joy to the neatly quiet, aristocratic, glowing sound of Segovia's masterly guitar.

Jorda's leadership, in the "Fantasy," balanced the sound flawlessly with the accompanying texture of a cleancut, subtly savory small orchestra. The composer himself—who by the way has been blind since infancy—was present to share in the audience's great applause.

For good measure, Segovia produced a series of beautiful unaccompanied guitar solos—in Bach, Villa Lobos, Albaniz and an unidentified encore.

As to the Vaughan Williams Symphony, it is relevant to mention he dedicated the work to Sibelius. For the symphony (completed in 1943) is a sensitive English reinterpretation of the epic Sibelius spirit.

Its scope is epic even though many, many of its pages are raptly or mysteriously quiet. Its Sibelius type of long, exalted gaze and grand personality takes on a lightened English flavor of lyricism and folk song.

The Fifth is a masterpiece in at least three of its movements. The final "Passacaglia" lets the work down a bit because while its structure is skillful, its ideas are not so valuable.

The program, beginning with a Rameau "Castor and Pollux" Suite, will be repeated tonight and tomorrow afternoon.

Fantasía para un Gentilhombre
World Première. San Francisco, March 1958.
Press Reviews, San Francisco

March. 1958

Segovia and a Premiere at Symphony

By Alfred Frankenstein

Composers all too infrequently have occasion to bow from a box at the Opera House in acknowledgement of the applause for a world premiere, but Joaquin Rodrigo did just that at Wednesday night's San Francisco Symphony concert, and the applause that came forth after Andres Segovia, Enrique Jorda and the orchestra had performed his "Fantasia para un Gentilhombre" was justly enthusiastic, warm and prolonged.

For Joaquin Rodrigo is himself a "gentilhombre," in the broadest meaning of that word. His fantasy is based on dances by the 16th century Spanish guitarist, Gaspar Sanz, and in his version for guitar and orchestra they provide a fabric of subtle, piquant and delectable sounds requiring hairbreadth balances for their proper expression. This is the kind of music in which the contrast between a plink on the guitar and a plunk on a violin, pizzicato, is a major event, and if either the plink or the plunk is ever so slightly miscalculated, the whole thing falls apart.

Tunefulness and delicate humor are also of Rodrigo's essence. The five short movements of his work remind one a little of what Domenico Scarlatti was to accomplish in the famous harpsichord sonatas he wrote in Spain three-quarters of a century after Sanz's time. Scarlatti, too, knew all about the sophisticated use of popular dance music for the guitar, and he would have envied the Sanz-Rodrigo idea of basing a piece of musical gossamer on the bugle calls of the Naples cavalry.

The fantasy is a virtuoso piece for all concerned, and it was given an enchanting performance. Since the guitar is inevitably a trifle under wraps when playing with an orchestra, Segovia also presented some solos. As always, he played them gorgeously, but only one of them, a gavotte and musette by Bach, was of the substance and quality one expects at a symphony concert, solo or no solo.

The Rodrigo fantasy is light, and so Jorda balanced it at the end of the program with the loftiness, radiance and grandeur of Vaughan Williams' fifth symphony. His performance of this work some years ago has lingered in memory as one of his finest achievements, but Wednesday's performance was even finer. Few things in modern music are more moving, beautiful and properly described with that overworked adjective "great" than this symphony by the English composer, and Jorda is one of its most penetrating interpreters. This department will not be satisfied until he does a whole Vaughan Williams cycle, including all nine of the symphonies, and the tuba concerto with Ralph Murray as soloist.

The concert opened with the noble severity of Rameau's overture and dances for "Castor and Pollux," the texture of which was not quite so flawlessly achieved as it might have been. The concert will be repeated this afternoon.

Fantasía para un Gentilhombre
World Première. San Francisco, March 1958.
Press Reviews, San Francisco

THE WASHINGTON POST *and* TIMES HERALD
Sunday, April 13, 1958 A 7

Blind Pianist Rodrigo Plays His Own Music

By Richard Salem
Staff Reporter

Joaquin Rodrigo went virtually blind when he was 3 years old.

But he could still see enough the following year to stand in front of a bookcase and, making believe the books were musicians, conduct his orchestra while his older sister pumped the player piano.

That's when his family became convinced he would be a musician. Rodrigo is now one of Spain's most highly acclaimed composers. Yesterday he gave a piano recital at the Cosmos Club, one stop on his concert tour of the United States.

"I don't think I would have been a musician if I had not been blind," Rodrigo said during an interview. "I love history, and had I been able to read I think I would have become a professor of history or English."

He still enjoys history and is professor of the history of music at Madrid University.

Rodrigo weaves the history of Spain into his music.

"I try to capture the spirit of 16th, 17th and 18th centuries in Spain and put it to music—not traditional Spanish music, but I modernize and intellectualize it."

Spanish critics believe he has achieved his goal. One review of his major work, "The Aranjuez Concerto," which was premiered in 1939, said:

"Rodrigo intentionally avoids folk song as subject matter and . . . sallies in search of themes that are the cries of folk people."

Rodrigo came to the United States primarily to hear his "Fantasia Para un Gentilhombre," for guitar and orchestra, premiered last month by Andres Segovia and the San Francisco Symphony Orchestra. The work was highly praised by West Coast critics.

One of Rodrigo's compositions, "Preludio al Gallo Mananero, led to a meeting with a young Turkish pianist whom he later married.

"I was thrilled when I heard the Prelude," Victoria Kamhi Rodrigo recalled. "We were both in Paris studying music at the time and I was determined to meet the composer. It took me about three months to meet him and three years later we were married."

Rodrigo prefaces his concerts with a 10-minute talk on Spanish music and his music. He speaks in Spanish and his wife translates.

The Washington Post
JOAQUIN RODRIGO
. . . to capture the spirit

Fantasía para un Gentilhombre
World Première. San Francisco, March 1958.
Press Reviews, San Francisco

A Modern Spanish Composer

FROM A CORRESPONDENT (DEREK PATMORE)

British concert-goers and listeners to the B.B.C. are now familiar with the *Concierto de Aranjuez* for guitar and orchestra by Joaquin Rodrigo, and recently the Spanish composer passed through London on his way from a two months' tour in the United States and *en route* for his native Spain. Now recognized as one of the most important of living Spanish composers, Rodrigo is himself a gifted pianist, and during his tour in America he gave a number of recitals in New York, Washington, and San Francisco, but, as he told the writer of this article, "I only like to play my own compositions."

A shy, typically reserved Spaniard, Joaquin Rodrigo has been blind since the age of three, but this disability has not prevented him from having an astonishing musical career. Born in 1902, in Sagunto near Valencia, he soon displayed an unusual talent for music. Then, following the example of other Spanish composers such as Albeniz, Falla, and Turina, he went to study composition in Paris in 1927. He studied under the composer Paul Dukas and soon became one of his favourite pupils. When asked whether he had been influenced by the French composer, Rodrigo replied: "I learnt a great deal from Dukas, but studying under him I became even more Spanish than I was before. Indeed, I feel that composers to-day must keep to their national idioms. So much of modern music is monotonous because all the very young composers will write in the same atonal style."

Rodrigo told the present writer that he had learnt much from his great compatriot, Manuel de Falla, and undoubtedly he follows in the musical footsteps of this master. Valencia, like Granada and Cadiz, has long been a centre for popular Spanish folk music and dancing, and Rodrigo has used many of these regional melodies in his music. At the same time, he has been greatly attracted to the musical traditions of Old Castile. As he said: "Valencia had very close relations with Castile, and I have always felt a close affinity with the spirit of this noble part of Spain. Indeed, one of my favourites among my own compositions is *Ausencias de Dulcinea*, which won the Cervantes Prize and is scored for full orchestra, a bass voice and four sopranos."

Undoubtedly, there is a strong mystical streak in Rodrigo's character, for some of his finest music has been inspired by the great Spanish mystical poets, and at present he is working on a full-length opera based on the life of St. Maria de Quito, the saintly nun who devoted her life to helping the Indians of Peru. This work is called *La Azucena de Quito*. "The opera is in three acts," he said, "and I hope to complete it this summer. Its world *première* will be in Quito, as it has been commissioned by the Peruvian Government." The composer added that he had started a symphony which he hoped to finish soon.

The Times, Monday, 19 May 1958

Fantasía para un Gentilhombre
World Première. San Francisco, March 1958
Press Reviews, London Review

Letter from Andrés Segovia
November 7, 1954

Mi querido Rodrigo : Aunque parezca mentira,esta es la tercera carta que le mando desde que recibí su anuncio referente a La Fantasia para un Gentilhombre. Estoy persuadido de que ni el Correo de Suiza ni el de los Estados Unidos merecen reproches de mi parte.En cambio temo que haya entre los funcionarios de dentro de la Administración española amantes de autógrafos o,más vulgarmente,inocentes que imaginen que mis cartas,sin certificar,pueden contener billetes de banco. Eso ó simplemente descuido y falta de pundonor en el desempeño del cargo.No se explica de otra manera pérdidas tan irritantes.

Esta irà certificada.Las otras no he podido porque estoy en pleno torbellino desde mis conciertos de Paris,sin disponer de una hora para irme al edificio de Correos.Hoy estoy en Chicago,pero salgo mañana para otro lugar y continuaré asi hasta el 17 de Diciembre,fecha de mi regreso a Nueva York para un descanso de 12 dias.El primero de Enero tocaré ya en otra ciudad y seguiré viajando hasta el 23 de Marzo.En total 48 conciertos...sin contar los recitales de Town Hall ni la Television.

Estoy encantado con la noticia que me da V.y ardo en deseos de echarle la vista encima a esa obra.El Titulo es delicioso.Me pondré a trabajarla enseguida que me sea posible,aun en los vagones de ferro-carril que,por desgracia,son el medio menos frecuente de transporte que utilizaré este año.Quiera Dios librarme de accidente y conservar mi salud para trabajar bien la"Fantasia"de modo que tengamos ambos satisfaccion,V.en oirla como le guste y yo en tocarla segun su deseo.

No quise decirle nada pero,conociendo la obra de Gasper Sanz,me parecia demasiado endeble el fundamento del trabajo que iba V.a emprender.Menos mal que,como la araña,saca V.de si mismo el hilo con que tejer la obra.

Si hay en ella frecuentes cambios de ritmo o entradas dificiles con la orquesta le agradeceré que haga una reduccion para piano y guitarra,con el fin de trabajarla a conciencia.Con la guitarra se tiene que ir a la Orquesta requeteaprendida la obra, de lo contrario se sufre Horrores porque es humanamente imposible improvisar posiciones.Aunque intelectualmente conozca uno la obra a la perfeccion si los dedos no estàn aconstumbrados a ir,como automatas,a los pasajes, se rompe uno la crisma.

(Continued)

Letter from Andrés Segovia
November 7, 1954

Lanzo esta carta otra vez al azar porque es domingo y ha pasado la hora de certificarla. Le agradeceré que me ponga unas lineas si la recibe. Dirijalas a mi apartamento. Y tambien, naturalmente, la copia de la Fantasia; pero certifíquela y asegurela.

Por cierto que se me ocurre - ya le hablé de esto en una de las cartas extraviadas - que deberia V. mandar hacer el Cpyright de la Zarabanda Lejana y de la Suite. La primera porque ya està impresionada en disco y la segunda porque enseguida que esté trabajada la daré en conciertos, radios, television y tambien en discos. He hablado con Williams Strecker, propietario de la casa Schott, que es amigo intimo de larguisimos años, y està dispuesto a publicar la Suite, en cuanto la haya yo tocado en mis conciertos en Europa y América durante la próxima temporada. Si V. no tiene otro proyecto, tambien le hablaré de la Fantasia. La espera a que someten la publicacion de las obras no es imposición mía, conste, sino precaución de ellos para lanzar las obras cuando sus numerosas audiciones y criticas han despertado el interés del publico suceptible de adquirirlas.

Nada más que repetirle mi impaciencia por conocer la Fantasia y... por tocarla.

Saludas afectuosos a su esposa, a su mamà politica, y a la simpatica y dinàmica chiquilla.

Y le abraza cordialmente su amigo y admirador,

[signature]

Chicago 7 de Noviembre de 1954.

My dear Rodrigo: Believe it or not, this is the third letter I've written to you since receiving your announcement about the *Fantasía para un Gentilhombre*." I am certain that neither the Swiss Post Office nor the U.S. Post Office deserves my reproaches. Instead I am afraid that among the Spanish postal workers there may be some autograph collectors, or perhaps some fools who think that my letters, even if they are not certified, may contain currency. Either that is the correct explanation, or else it is carelessness or dishonesty in doing their jobs. There can be no other reason for such an irritating loss of mail.

This letter is being sent 'certified' the earlier letters could not, as I am living in a whirlwind since my concerts in Paris, without a free hour's time to go to the Postal building. Today I am in Chicago, but tomorrow I leave for another city, and will continue to travel in like fashion until December 17, the date of my return to New York for a 12-day rest. On January 1, I'll be in another city and will continue to tour until March 23. Forty-eight concerts in all—without counting the Town Hall recital or television appearances.

I am thrilled about the news you sent and am burning with desire to get a look at the work. The title is delicious. I'll start to work on it as soon as possible, even if I have to do it in railroad cars which, unfortunately, will be the form of transportation I'll be using least often this year. May God keep me safe from accidents and preserve my health, so that I will be able to work on the "*Fantasía*" to both our satisfactions—you in hearing it as you prefer, and I in performing it according to your taste.

I hadn't wanted to say anything, but being familiar with Gaspar Sanz's work, I'd felt that the funding for the basis for the work you were starting was very weak. Fortunately, like a spider, you produce the thread you need to weave your own work.

If there are frequent changes of rhythm or different entrances with the orchestra, I'd appreciate your preparing a reduction for piano and guitar, so that I can really work on it. With the guitar, one must approach the orchestra "super-prepared," to perform the work, for otherwise it's a horrible mess, because it is humanly impossible to improvise positions. Even if, intellectually, one knows the work to perfection, if one's fingers are not used to moving, like robots, to the passages, the performer will break one's neck in performance.

I will have to also mail this letter while trusting in fate, because today is Sunday and it's too late to have a letter certified. I'd appreciate hearing from you if you receive it. Write to my apartment. And of course, also a copy of *Fantasía*, but be sure to *certify* and *register* it.

I also feel—I mentioned this in one of the letters that got lost in the mail—that you should definitely order the copyright for "Zarabanda Lejana" and the "Suite." The first because it's already available as a recording because it'll be heard during my current tour in concerts, radio, television and also on records. I have spoken to William Strecker, owner of the Schott house, a close friend for many years, and he's willing to publish the *Suite*, once I have performed it in my concerts in Europe and America during the upcoming season. If you do not have any other plan, I'll also mention the *Fantasía* to him. My hope that you'll present these works for publication is not an imposition on my part, rest assured, but is instead a precaution of theirs, taken once numerous hearings and critical reaction to it has awakened the public's interest in acquiring the music.

I'll close by repeating my impatient desire to see the *Fantasía* and...to play it. Affectionate greetings to your wife, your mother-in-law and to that attractive and dynamic little girl.

A warm embrace from your
friend and admirer

Andrés Segovia

Chicago, November 7, 1954

Letter from Andrés Segovia
July 10, 1957

Buenos Aires, 10 de Julio de 1957

Maestro Joaquín Rodrigo

Mi querido Rodrigo:

He aquí la justificación de mi silencio. Cuando ustedes salieron de Nueva York no tuve sino unos días tranquilos, después de los cuales pasó por mi riñón izquierdo una arenilla que me tuvo en un grito durante diez u once días, sin ánimo de pensar en nada ni poder hacer otra cosa que esperar ansiosamente al médico para que me aliviara el dolor con inyecciones de Pantopon o de morfina. Ya en condiciones de ir al consultorio del médico para que tomase radiografías, tuve la buena noticia de ~~que~~ saber que mis riñones estaban vacíos de cálculos y que volvería a mi normalidad después de cumplido todo el viaje del granito perverso de arena.

A los pocos días me trasladé a esta ciudad y comenzó enseguida mi actividad de conciertos, viajes, gentes, estudio, etc. etc.

Estrené el Fandango en el Colón y lo recibió el público con gran entusiasmo. Le guardo unos programas de ese concierto.

Saldré probablemente para Ginebra hacia el 12 o el 15 de Agosto y después de recoger allí ropa y música seguiré para Madrid donde permaneceré hasta los primeros días de Octubre. Este reposo me permitirá el estudio a fondo de la Fantasía. Haga usted sus planes de manera que nos podamos encontrar ahí con frecuencia. Si usted se ausentara durante ese período de tiempo sin salir de España, dígame a dónde se dirigirá. Caso de que fuese en algún sitio con comodidades hoteleras en que no hubiese suciedad, mosquitos , etc. lo mismo me da pasar los días que requiera nuestra mutua consulta acerca de la obra en Madrid o en el lugar en que usted se encuentre y si le puedo evitar la molestia de un viaje la tomaré sobre mí con gusto.

Tengo que anunciarle que además de prometer la audición de la Fantasía a Barbiroli en Manchester, la tocaré también en Londres y después en América del Norte, Brooklyn Academic of Music y seguramente en algún otro lugar antes y después de San Francisco. Lo único malo que tiene ésto es que privamos a nuestro amigo Jordá de la primera audición de la obra, pasándosela en cambio a Barbiroli.

Yo secundaré sus planes tanto como me sea posible en Nueva York. Le sugeriría sin embargo que tratase usted de obtener en México algunas actuaciones. Háblele usted a Quesada. Desde allí podría usted venir a Nueva York y, aunque conoce usted por Suriñac lo difícil que le será, mejor dicho, que nos será conseguir alguna audición para usted, ya sabe que puede contar con una parte de mi caché americano. Si esto puede ayudarle, me placerá mucho.

Antes de salir de Nueva York, no pude hablar con Castroviejo, pero no habrá dificultad en retirar del Instituto fundado por su señora algunos centenares de dólares en favor de usted, me-diante su actuación.

Escribí al individuo de Cincinnati sin obtener respuesta. La copia fotoestática que usted me facilitó del documento de Ricordi la conservo siempre.

Con saludos muy afectuosos a ~~su~~ señora y un abrazo para usted créame su devoto admirador y amigo

Buenos Aires, July 10, 1957

Maestro Joaquín Rodrigo

My dear Rodrigo:

Here is the explanation for my silence. After you two left New York I had only a few quiet days, and suddenly began to suffer from a kidney stone that had me in agony for 10 or 11 days, unable to think about anything beyond the arrival of the doctor, who would relieve my pain with injections of Pantopan or morphine. Once I was able to get to the doctor's office for x-rays, I was happy to learn that my kidneys were free of stones and that I would return to normal once the little stones completed their journey.

A few days later I traveled to this city, and immediately resumed my activities—concerts, travel, people, studies, etc.

I premièred the *Fandango* at the Colón Theater, and the audience was very enthusiastic about it. I have saved some concert programs for you.

I will probably leave for Geneva around the 12th or 15th of August, and after picking up some clothing and music I will travel on to Madrid, where I will be until the beginning of October. This extended stay will allow me to study the *Fantasía* in depth. Arrange your schedule so that we can see each other often while I am there. If you plan to leave Madrid to travel to another part of Spain during that time, let me know where you are planning to go. As long as theres a place nearby with adequate hotel facilities—clean, without mosquitoes, etc., it is fine with me if we spend the few days necessary for our consultation together on this work in Madrid or wherever you plan to stay. If I can save you the bother of a trip back to the capital, I'd be happy to do so.

I need to let you know that along with promising to play *Fantasía* for Barbirolli in Manchester, I will also perform it in London and later in North America, Brooklyn Academy of Music and certainly some other performances before and after San Francisco. The only disappointment in this arrangement is that we're depriving our friend Jordá of the honor of being first to hear the work, instead bestowing that honor on Barbirolli.

I will back your plans as much as possible in New York. I suggest, however, that you try to arrange for some performances in Mexico. Talk to Quesada. From there, you could travel to New York; and although Suriñach has told you how difficult it will be for you, or rather, for us, to obtain an audition for you, you know you can use part of my American cachet. If it can help you, it will be my pleasure.

Before leaving New York I was not able to speak to Castroviejo, but it should not be difficult to receive a few hundred dollars from the Institute his wife founded, to support your work.

I wrote to the individual in Cincinnati, but did not receive a reply. I still have the photostatic copy of the document of Ricordi's that you furnished to me.

With very affectionate greetings to your wife and an embrace for you, your devoted admirer and friend.

Andrés Segovia

During one of our visits to Barcelona, the publisher José Janés, a good friend of Joaquín's, told us that the famous American author, William Saroyan, had been very enthusiastic about the *Concierto de Aranjuez*, and had bought the record.

I thought about that on the eve of our departure for America, and I wrote Saroyan to tell him that within a few days Andrés Segovia would be the soloist in the première of another work for guitar and orchestra by Joaquín, adding that we would be honored if he would attend the concert.

Saroyan, who lived in Malibu Beach, enthusiastically made the eight-hour drive by automobile, arriving a few minutes before the beginning of the concert.

He was seated in our box, and I could see that he was delighted with the new work. At the end, during the applause, I asked him which of the two concertos he preferred. His reply was, "Frankly, I don't know. I like them both."

On the 10th of March we left with Segovia for Los Angeles, where we visited the pianist Amparo Iturbi and the composer Castelnuovo-Tedesco, and attended the magnificent concert offered by Segovia.

We arrived alone in New York during a snowstorm, and were met by the composer Carlos Suriñach, who accompanied us to the home of Tina and Coco, whose hospitality we enjoyed for two months. The two sisters were excellent ballerinas; Tina had been Cecilia's teacher in Madrid.

The days we spent in New York were very busy.

We went often to Segovia's home, where he delighted us with his interpretations of various works.

We were also invited to dinner by our friends, Nancy and Bob Barton. The great singer, Lucrecia Bori, gave a dinner in our honor, as did Carlos Suriñach, composer Virgil Thompson and others. We went to a number of parties, where we met many well-known people: musicians, painters, writers and choreographers.

The famous violinist Alexander Schneider, colleague of Pablo Casals, took us to dinner with Tina and Coco one night at one of the best Chinese restaurants in the city. What a banquet they served us!

On March 25th Joaquín gave his concert at the Spanish Institute, which was an enormous success. The hall was crowded, and all our friends had come to applaud him. It was a memorable night.

On Easter there was bad weather, with heavy snow and bitter cold. We didn't leave our room, and Joaquín dictated the Cadenza of the *Fantasía para un Gentilhombre* to me, so that we could send it to the London publishers, Schott and Co., Ltd., who published it soon afterward.

On April 11th we made a short trip to Washington with my friend Rachel. The cherry trees were in bloom, and the entire city seemed blanketed in a cloud of blossoms shading from cerise to palest pink. That was a dream!

I had the joy of seeing my niece Marita again after many years. She was married to Stanley Sokolowsky, director of the Voice of America.

Joaquín gave a lecture, followed by a concert of his works, at the Cosmos Club, which was attended by the members, a number of critics and all our friends.

They asked me to read the English translation, which I did willingly, for it was a very friendly gathering, and the audience rewarded me with warm applause.

I took advantage of those days to visit the famous National Art Gallery, where one can admire the finest Rembrandts, Van Dyke, the French Impressionists and Dalí's "Last Supper."

At the invitation of Guillermo Espinosa, we returned to Washington several days later to attend the Festival of American Music, and we found there all the composers and musical critics whom we had met in Caracas the year before.

On the 29th of March, 1958, we met Maurice Pate, the founder of the United Nations Fund for children (UNICEF) at a cocktail party in New York we'd attended with Andrés Segovia.

I remember him clearly, quite tall, and somewhat corpulent. I thought him very attractive. His abundant hair was almost white and his face, round and ruddy, had a kind and convivial expression. But what held my attention was the direct and penetrating gaze of his clear, blue eyes.

After the usual exchange of courtesies, he sat down to talk to us about the recent première of *Fantasía para un Gentilhombre*, by Segovia, for he was apparently a devotee of music. We talked also about UNICEF, this marvelous work created by him in 1946, which has as its goal the alleviation and eventual elimination of hunger, disease, malnutrition and ignorance in the world's children.

Three weeks later Joaquín and I said farewell to the New World and took the plane to London, to see our daughter, Cecilia, at that time a student of the Royal Ballet School.

We were surprised to find Maurice Pate, smiling and cordial on our flight. He sat down with us, and we renewed the conversation interrupted several days before, which dealt principally with UNICEF. I was amazed to learn of the gigantic ongoing struggle to save millions of children, combatting such diseases as yaws, tuberculosis, leprosy, trachoma, malaria, rickets, etc.

Efforts are being made also to do away with ignorance and superstition: training teachers and nurses, midwives and specialists in the care of infants; creating sanitary centers, maternity wards and schools.

When we landed in London, Maurice Pate ordered, "Here, give me your hand baggage and take care of your husband."

I obeyed, a little embarrassed, handing him two heavy bags, and together we headed for the customs. I watched as the agent saluted him respectfully, without touching his luggage.

I took out the keys to our suitcases and gave them to the customs official with our passports. He glanced at them and exclaimed, smiling: "Don't open a thing, Mrs. Rodrigo, we are all admirers of the Maestro. Just two days ago, we saw the ballet of *Concierto de Aranjuez* on television with Rosella Hightower and Pirmin Trecu. What a gem!"

When Mr. Pate asked us if anyone was coming to pick us up at the airport, we told him that our daughter had arranged to meet us at a café near the School of Ballet.

"Come with me," he said, and grasping Joaquín's arm, escorted us to an official limousine in which the three of us made the trip to the designated café. When he watched us greet our daughter, kissing her repeatedly, a tender smile lit his face.

"What could I do to help UNICEF?" I stammered, as we said goodbye.

"Well," he replied, "Now there is a Spanish section. Get in touch with its president and give her my regards. Goodbye!"

One last handshake and the official car drove away. We would never see him again.

In Madrid I established a friendship with Carmen Cavestany, the president of the Spanish Committee, who appointed me to membership on the newly constituted Board of Directors. Since then the UNICEF has grown in prestige in the entire world. The seed was good, and it has borne magnificent fruits.

But Maurice Pate was to die prematurely in January, 1965. The New York Times had this to say in its commentary on his death: "Few people have heard of Maurice Pate, but tens of millions of children in more than one hundred countries have been fed and clothed because of him."

His successor, Henry R. Labouisse, received the Nobel Peace Prize awarded to UNICEF in Oslo, December 10, 1965.

On the 11th of December, 1971, UNICEF marked its twenty-fifth anniversary. All during that year glittering "Silver weddings" were celebrated all over the world, with lectures, concerts, cinemas, etc., as fund raisers for this fine work.

It was then that I presumed to ask our friend, the celebrated violinist, Henryk Szeryng, whom Joaquín and I had applauded since his first concerts in Europe in 1940, to give a concert for the benefit of Spanish UNICEF. He promised it gladly for, as he said, "UNICEF is a project very close to my heart." His collaborator, the eminent pianist, Pepe Tordesillas, followed suit, so that after overcoming a few difficulties, we were able to organize the concert on the 31st of January, 1972, in the Royal Theater, with complete success.

With Henry Szerying, January 1972.

* * *

On our return from New York, we spent two very pleasant weeks in London. We stayed in the home of the singer and musicologist, Ann Livermore. The house, Sandy Combe Lodge, had been the property of the famous painter Turner, and at that season the garden was full of flowers, and the linnets and blackbirds were beginning to sing.

We went to the Royal Ballet School, where the director, Arnold Haskell, gave us glowing reports of Cecilia.

The next day we were invited to dinner at Covent Garden, with the famous Dame Ninette de Valois and principal dancer Pirmin Trecu.

Later we attended the performance of *The Sleeping Beauty*, in which Trecu shone in the role of the Prince.

At a cocktail party in the home of Arnold Haskell we met the director of Covent Garden, Michael Wood and his wife; Tom Goff, who made clavichords, our friends the Valls and a number of well-known artists.

The great pianist Harriet Cohen gave a reception in our honor, and among the many guests were composer Lenox Berkeley, guitarist Julian Bream, and other musicians.

Cecilia went with us everywhere, and I also had the pleasure of again seeing almost all of the members of my family who were living in England. How we hated to leave London!

That same year Segovia performed *Fantasía para un Gentilhombre* during the Musical Festival of Granada, but we were unable to attend the concert because at the last moment Joaquín caught a dreadful cold. The performance was an enormous success with both audience and critics.

Early in July we received an invitation from our friend, José Bertoméu, to attend a party at his estate, "El Jardí dels Torongers," to celebrate the tenth anniversary of the weekly concerts held in his house in Barcelona.

That night the splendid "Jardí" was filled with a multitude of guests for the gala concert. There were six hundred people!

The Municipal Orchestra was conducted by Toldrá, and the program included Beethoven's Pastoral Symphony and Wagner's Siegfried Idyll.

After the cold supper, everyone joined in singing a hymn with words by our host and music by Narcís Bonet, and as finale, an orchestra of Sardanas [Catalonian dance and music] played works of Toldrá and Larra, and the famous "nuns' sardana," danced by all the guests.

* * *

During the summer of 1958 we spent a short vacation in Altea, with Cecilia, after much difficulty in obtaining reservations at the Hotel Gasthof near the beach.

On the first of September, Cecilia left for London to resume her ballet classes.

On the 24th and 26th of October Segovia presented *Fantasía para un Gentilhombre* in the Sala Monumental of Madrid. All the seats were sold by the day before the concert, which had a rousing success.

In November I made a short trip to the Portichol, Jávea, where with the aid of our friends, the Lamberts, I bought two lots, the smaller on the edge of the sea, facing the Mongó, and the other, a lovely, dense pine grove, fragrant with thyme and rosemary.

I planned for us to build a small summer hours on one of them, but it was a desire not to be realized, for soon after this, these good friends died. Almost at the same time, I bought "the little house in the orchard," in Villajoyosa.

On my return from these short trips, I saw that Joaquín did not look well. He was tired and nervous, with no desire to work or to compose.

The worry about his health kept me sleepless, leaving me with no energy—almost exhausted. The arrival of Cecilia, who took advantage of her Christmas vacation to come see us, and the presence of Mamá, with her unshakeable serenity, were my only comforts during those unpleasant days.

Some of our friends became alarmed and called Dr. Marañón, who promised to come see Joaquín as soon as possible.

One morning he appeared unexpectedly at our house, saying to Cecilia, who opened the door for him, "I am Dr. Marañón." And she replied, without a change of expression, "And I am Cecilia."

The visit of the illustrious physician lifted Joaquín's morale, but as for his health, there was no change.

The Christmas holidays were sad and monotonous. Except for visits from the Argentine orchestra conductor, Rodríguez Fauré, who came often to distract us with charming conversations about his professional tours, I don't remember any visit.

After the Feast of the Magi, Cecilia had to return to London, to rejoin the Ballet School. Her departure left an aching void. It was then that Mamá and I noticed an improvement in Joaquín's health, thanks to the eminent psychiatrist, Dr. López de Lerma, who treated him with genuine affection and self-abnegation.

During January, 1959, I devoted myself to the correction of two of Joaquín's important works: *Fantasía para un Gentilhombre* and the suite *Soleriana,* in the first and second proofs. Near the end of February Joaquín finished the *Sonata Giocosa* for solo guitar, and the *Aria Antigua* for piano and flute.

Around the first of February we went to Salamanca, where Joaquín gave a lecture, the theme of which was "Castile in the music of Joaquín Rodrigo." The great hall was crowded, and the Civil Governor, the University Rector and other notables were present. After the lecture, Conchita Rodríguez played Joaquín's *Cinco Sonatas de Castilla,* and there was lengthy applause for the author and the musicians.

During these days in Salamanca, we were constant companions of Antonio Tovar, who was then Rector of the University, and his wife, Chelo.

* * *

It was about that time when we met a young couple, Walter and Pilar Rubin. He was Director of the Spanish program for the American base at Torrejón de Ardoz, an authentic prototype of the intellectual American, simple and unassuming. He had principally devoted himself to the study of the works of Pérez Galdós, of which he had profound understanding.

Pilar, daughter of an Andalusian mother and an Italian father, was a painter of great talent. Very attractive, she had the grace of the women of Seville, and was gay and vivacious. They were both delightful, and their company was a joy, as much for Mamá as for Joaquín and me.

We met them again in 1970 in their home in Houston, where he had been named professor of Spanish literature in the University of Houston, and later in 1978, on the occasion of the première of the symphonic poem, *A la busca del más allá* [*In Search of the Beyond*] composed in celebration of the Bicentennial of the United States and commissioned by the Houston Symphony Orchestra.

During the spring of 1959 we had a visit from the illustrious French writer, Jean Giono, a great admirer of the *Concierto de Aranjuez*, who wanted to meet its composer.

The 18th of October, 1959, was a memorable day for us. A tribute was offered to Joaquín by the city of Aranjuez, with a brilliant celebration, during which a plaque was unveiled for a street newly renamed "Joaquín Rodrigo." Early that day we set out in the automobile of our friends from Torrejón, followed by another car with more American professors from the base. We all gathered in the City Hall, where the Mayor, Manuel García, had prepared a "vino de honor" reception in a salon where the painter Alberto was exhibiting his paintings. There we found our friend María Luisa Martínez, ex-commentator of the Radio and organizer of the tribute, with her husband, Manolo Sánchez Beato.

At 12:30 we all gathered in the broad avenue which was to be named "Joaquín Rodrigo," along with more than a thousand other people. In an impressive silence, we mounted the podium, Joaquín, Mamá and I, with the mayor and dignitaries.

The mayor spoke briefly, with warmth and affection, and then Joaquín spoke for more than twenty minutes. When they unveiled the tablet of white marble with its gold inscription, I was profoundly moved, remembering all the long road traveled since the day when we walked in Aranjuez for the first time, on our honeymoon.

* * *

We had spent the month of July with Mamá and Çecilia in Villajoyosa, where we inaugurated the new house, "Villa Victoria." There we were surrounded by friends who extended themselves to make our stay in the village pleasant. There were Cristóbal Zaragoza, a most talented writer, later awarded the Planet Prize, and his attractive wife, Amparo; the Aragonés brothers, and Ambrosio, who took care of the small garden.

In August a "Rodrigo Festival" took place there, with *Concierto de Aranjuez* performed by Narciso Yepes. The Municipal Orchestra of Valencia was conducted by Maestro Correll. It was quite an event.

On leaving Villajoyosa, Joaquín, Cecilia and I made a short trip to Cádiz, where Joaquín gave a course in the summer program of the University. Later we spent several days on the beach at Punta Umbría, invited by Juan Lafita, the very popular journalist.

On our return to Madrid we received some good news from Buenos Aires: Our ballet, *Pavana Real*, had been presented on October 18th in the Teatro Colón, with great success. It was staged by Antonio Truyol.

I remember that, soon afterwards, the Barenboims, father and son, whom we had met in Salzburg in 1954, presented themselves at our house. Daniel, at seventeen years of age, had a contract to present a concert in Madrid. He played the *Waldstein Sonata* and an *Impromptu* of Schubert with great mastery. It did not take a prophet to predict a brilliant career for him.

On the 19th of November we left for Paris, where on the 22nd, Saint Cecilia's day, *Fantasía para un Gentilhombre* was presented in the Théâtre des Champs Elysées. Segovia had one of his best days and received an ovation, as did Joaquín.

We were in Paris a whole week, during which Joaquín gave a lecture in the Spanish Embassy on a recently introduced work, and another in the Spanish College on *Ausencias de Dulcinea.*

* * *

It was early in 1960 when Cecilia gave us some news which overwhelmed us. We had gathered for lunch when she rose from her chair to announce very solemnly:

"I have something very important to tell you. Agustín has asked me if I will marry him. And I want to!"

Ever since she had travelled with Joaquín to Sanitago de Campostela she had been very interested in Agustín León Ara, a young violinist from the Canary Islands, whom she had met in the Music Course. Apparently it had been love at first sight, and we gave them our blessing.

On January 22nd, our future son-in-law played Lalo's *Symphonie Espagnole* with the National Orchestra, conducted by Schmidt-Isserstedt. It was a revelation, and we were deeply moved by the long ovations given him by the demanding audience at the Palace of Music.

After the concert we gave a late supper in honor of the engaged couple and the German conductor, who was very friendly and paternal. Maruja, Cecilia's future mother-in-law, and my Cousin Bucia, who was living in Brazil, were among the guests. The house was full of flowers and we all happily toasted the future bride and groom with champagne. Watching Cecilia's radiant face, I felt that I was dreaming. Now I could no longer treat her like a child.

At the end of February Joaquín and I escaped to Villajoyosa to enjoy a few days of rest in the new little house. Flowers were springing up in the garden, and the orange and lemon trees were covered with blossoms. An enormous rose extended its branches, laden with buds, up to the roof, wrapping everything with a mantle of red silk. The ground was studded with violets, and the finches and blackbirds sang tirelessly. From the flat roof the view encompassed meadows and orchards, and in the distance, the blue mirror of the Mediterranean.

We visited the American military base of Aitana to see the Commanding Officer, Major Milton Weiss and his wife Helen, and spent a night in their chalet on the Albufuera. They were an enchanting couple, with whom we very soon formed a close friendship.

On June 6th there was an informal ceremony in the House of Velásquez, during which the French government's decoration "Arts and Letters" was awarded to Spanish artists.

Joaquín, Oscar Esplá and Jesús Guridi were named *Officiers*, and Antonio Iglesias and the painter Amadeo Roca, *Chevaliers*. Christiane Deneumostier received the "Academic Palms."

A few days later a "Rodrigo Festival" was presented with the title, "The Musical Adventure." Spanish Radio-Television organized it in the

Sabatini Gardens. Cecilia made her debut there as a classical dancer, and her numbers from *Pavana Real* and *The Sleeping Beauty* were a resounding success, which filled Joaquín and me with parental pride. Sáinz de la Maza was the soloist in the *Concierto de Aranjuez*, Isabel Penagos shone with *Cuatro Madrigales Amatorios*, and as a conclusion, Joaquín played several of his pieces. This was the last concert of the season.

I cherish wonderful memories of that summer, in our little house of the "Villa," finally renovated and furnished, where later on, we would put an upright piano.

Our friends organized another "Rodrigo Festival" in the village square, which turned out to be excellent. Several notables attended: the governor of the province, the widow of General Moscardó, Major Weiss and his wife and many others. Josefina Salvador presented the *Concierto de Estío* and Gonzalo Soriano played several works for the piano.

On our return to Madrid, we received a communication from Paris, announcing that the ORTF had sponsored a competition titled "the guitar cup" to award a prize for the best piece composed for the guitar.

The organizer, Robert J. Vidal, a good friend of ours, was pressing Joaquín to present a work, but he told me that he felt no desire to write something new for that instrument.

At that point I remembered that Joaquín had some years before written an inspired work for Regino Sáinz de la Maza. We had no copy of the manuscript, but one was found in Regino's house. It was a rough draft in pencil—full of errors—which we had to pick up to revise and correct. We were off and running!

We produced a clean copy in very little time and sent it to the ORTF, where it arrived just a few hours before the end of the allotted time!

The work, *Invocation et Danse* [*Invocation and Dance*], a tribute to Manuel de Falla, was to the jury's liking, and won the prize. In addition to the cash, the prize included a lovely edition of Mistral's book *Mireille*, which we were able to pick up personally soon afterward, on a trip to Paris.

The prize-winning piece was published by the French house *Editions de France*, and at present is included in the repertory of all the great guitarists.

We enjoyed a very pleasant visit from the Presti-Lagoya duet. We had met Ida Presti in Paris, at the home of the composer Brocua. She was then twelve years old and was considered the "child prodigy" of the guitar, for she was master of almost the entire repertory of Andrés Segovia. After launching a very successful career, she married the guitarist Alexander Lagoya, with whom she formed a duet, and together they had toured the whole world. Now they wanted very much to commission a concerto for two guitars and orchestra to present on their next tours.

Joaquín took several years to write his *Concierto Madrigal* for them, and they planned to present it for the first time in the Pleyel Hall in Paris.

Unfortunately, this project was never realized, for Ida died suddenly at the age of 42, in a clinic in Rochester, and was mourned by the entire musical world. She was not only an inspired artist, but also an enchanting woman. Small and slender, she had large dark eyes, and an abundance of curly black hair. How vividly I remember her!

As for Alexander, the loss of Ida left him shattered. Little by little he managed to recover. At present he is a professor at the Paris Conservatory and has renewed his professional tours as a soloist. When we heard him at the Music Festival of "La Rougerie," he was accompanied by his second wife.

On the 22nd of April at the School of Philosophy and Letters, we organized a tribute to composer Hugo Wolf. Isabel Penagos sang the Spanish Song-Book, which I accompanied at the piano. Joaquín gave a very well-received lecture as introduction.

I very much enjoyed the interpretation of these songs, real jewels of German lyric poetry. We had a flattering success, with a full house.

Near the end of May, Joaquín and I made our first trip to Tenerife, where he gave two lectures and a recital of his works. We spent a very pleasant week there, with the León Ara family and many friends.

On the first of June we were in Paris, invited by Robert J. Vidal to receive the *Coupe de la guitare* prizes. We were guests at the luxurious Hotel Bedford—the favorite of Andrés Segovia and Villa-Lobos—, and for a few days we felt like millionaires.

What a wonderful time we had with all our friends in Paris!

One day publisher Mica Salabert took us to the "Chez Maxim" restaurant, a temple of French gastronomy. The setting was most elegant, the service perfect, the dishes delicious, and I recall that the table wine had been replaced by a fine champagne. Naturally, we left there feeling very happy and optimistic.

Madame Salabert wanted this banquet to celebrate the signing of a contract for the publication of the *Concierto Galante* for violoncello and orchestra.

We spent the whole summer at our house in Villajoyosa. On our return to Madrid, I began to work on the correction of orchestra material, and the editing for piano of the *Concierto Serenata*, which the Spanish Musical Union was planning to publish. We resumed our social life, and we didn't miss a single concert.

Among a number of visitors, the one I remember best is Antonio Truyol, who had staged our ballet, *Pavana Real*, in the Teatro Colón of Buenos Aires. Along with Prokofiev's "The Love of Three Oranges," it had been the season's greatest success.

On November 24th, 1961, the world première of *La Atlántida* in concert form took place in the Lyceum of Barcelona. For that occasion, Joaquín and I made a quick visit to the noble city.

The theater was crowded with an elite audience. All the ministers, diplomats and the aristocracy were there. There were relatively few artists, but the critics were out in force.

Victoria de los Angeles sang the two beautiful arias of de Falla's score in her matchless voice. The *Salve*, too, seemed very good music to me. The choruses and the orchestra were undistinguished. As for Maestro Toldrá, he seemed exhausted, and people were saying that he had spent many sleepless nights.

On Sunday the concert was repeated, and the audience warmly applauded all the performers, as well as the composer, Ernesto Halffter, who had rescued this work from oblivion with his valuable collaboration.

On our return from Barcelona we had a visit from the violinist, Philip Newman, whom Queen Elizabeth of Belgium, a great music lover, had favored with her friendship. He frequently went to the Laeken Palace to delight her with his music. At our house he played the *Capriccio* for violin solo, and Joaquín gave him some advice, for he was planning to include it in his repertory. He had three or four Stradivarius violins with him, which he carried everywhere, for fear that they would be stolen from his hotel! We were always laughing with him, for he was very witty and charming.

A few days before Christmas, Isabel Penagos and I gave a concert of Christmas carols at the University of Madrid, introduced by Joaquín, who also gave commentaries on the selections. The hall was crowded with a youthful audience, enthusiastic about the music.

In March we took delivery of our first little car, something we had hoped for for some time. It was a Dauphine, and we gave it its maiden run on a trip to Aranjuez, driven by Cecilia, who was our only chauffeur until the day of her wedding. She was an excellent driver, and took us to Toledo, to El Escorial, to the pine groves of Valsáin and to many other places. We never had a mishap with her at the wheel.

On the fifth of April, a famous dinner took place, honoring the "One Hundred Most Illustrious Persons of Spain." It was organized by Emilio Romero, director of the newspaper *Pueblo*, at the Hilton Hotel. There more than 150 of us gathered, with all groups represented. Joaquín was named Musician of the Year.

The Festival of Bordeaux

The spring of 1962 was a particularly busy time for us. I will never forget the days of the Bordeaux May Musical, organized in the Chateau de la Brède, a scene immortalized by Montesquieu, the celebrated eighteenth century French writer.

We left Madrid on the ninth of May with Fedora Alemán, the famous Venezuelan singer, a very charming and endearing woman who was to première the work commissioned from Joaquín for this Festival: *La Grotte* [*The Cave*], a tribute to Debussy, composed on a text by the poet Louis Emié, who wrote it to commemorate the 100th anniversary of the birth of the great French musician.

Joaquín had promised to accompany this song at the piano, but during the days preceding our journey, he felt very tired and without the spirit to perform in public. At that point I had no choice but to master this work—a very difficult one—with all speed. I rehearsed it carefully with Fedora, an artist of great talent and sensitivity, and on the day of the opening it came out so beautifully that we had to repeat it at the audience's insistence.

Joaquín had another world première on the same program: *Invocation et Danse*, tribute to Manuel de Falla, played by the guitarist Alirio Díaz.

Among the notables in the audience were Chaban-Delmas, who was then mayor of Bordeaux, writer André Maurois, composer Gustave Samazeuilh and Valéry-Larbaud.

The day before the concert, we had to record the entire concert for the radio.

We spent several very pleasant days in that lovely city, where we did honor to its famous gastronomy. The Commissar General of the Festival, George Delort, received us very warmly and presented us with tickets for all the events, among them the performance of Alessandro Scarlatti's opera, *Mithridate Eupatore*, which was being staged for the first time in France.

After our concert we were invited to a reception in the Château de la Brède, and on the following day there was another at the home of Louis Emié. Of course, we visited the very complete Debussy exhibit. Claude Rivière, a poet of great talent, was the companion who showed us the most interesting parts of the city.

During our stay, guitarist Alexandre Lagoya came on a flying visit to remind Joaquín that he wanted a concerto for two guitars and orchestra. This would be the *Concierto Madrigal*, first performed in Hollywood in 1970.

The Gulbenkian Festival

At the end of that spring we went with Cecilia and Agustín to Lisbon to attend the Gulbenkian Festival. The program included *Fantasía para un Gentilhombre*, with Narciso Yepes, *Concierto de Estío*, with Agustín León Ara, and *The Three Cornered Hat*, as well as two works by Portuguese composers: *Piano Concerto* by López Graça, with the pianist Helena de Sá e Costa, and a *Suite* by Freixas. The hall was filled and there was much applause for artists and composers.

While we were in Lisbon, Joaquín gave two recitals of his works for the piano: one at the Gulbenkian Foundation and the other at the Spanish Embassy, organized by the cultural Attaché, Pedro Rocamora. Ambassador Ibáñez Martín and his wife, the Countess of Marín, welcomed us very cordially.

We accompanied them on a magnificent excursion to Estoril, Cascais and Santarem. On our return we had the pleasant surprise of finding our English friends, Professor Harold Livermore and his wife Ann, with whom we spent the last hours of our stay in Lisbon.

During the summer vacation of 1962 we went to Villajoyosa with Mamá and Cecilia, returning to Madrid the last day of September. We missed the sunny beach and the small orchard with its orange and lemon trees, and most of all, the long chats with our congenial neighbors.

A few days after our arrival in Madrid the courses of History of Music began at the University, where every Thursday the auditorium would fill with students.

I devoted myself to correcting the proofs of the orchestral score of *Fantasía para un Gentilhombre*, which Schott & Co. of London was publishing. I accomplished that task in a few weeks.

The first of November we made a quick trip to Alicante with Teresa Tourné, the singer, to give a concert at the Savings Bank of the Southeast. I accompanied Debussy's melodies and the songs of Joaquín and other Spanish composers.

On November 22nd we celebrated Joaquín's sixtieth birthday and Cecilia's Saint's day with a rollicking party. Father and daughter were inundated with flowers and gifts, and the house was filled with friends.

All the musical world was present, and there were many newspaper men, who did interviews for radio and press. It was a very lively gathering, which went on until ten o'clock that night.

Immediately afterward we went to an evening party at the home of the decorator, Duarte Pinto Coelho, who had invited a number of musicians, painters, writers and diplomats to listen to Joaquín's works. Isabel Penagos, Teresa Tourné, Blanca María Seoane and Francisco Navarro performed, and I accompanied them on piano.

Joaquín and Gonzalo Soriano played several pieces, and as a finale, Odón Alonso and Marita Halffter collaborated in the humorous piece *Gran Marcha de los Subsecretarios*.

After the concert Duarte served us an American supper, featuring a monumental cake with sixty lighted candles. Everyone had a wonderful time, especially Cecilia, who was very lovely in her green mousseline gown, dancing tirelessly with her young admirers!

On the 24th of November the Ministry of Information and Tourism organized a concert-tribute under the sponsorship of Manuel Fraga Iribarne. Its success was outstanding. The hall was crowded with an enthusiastic audience; there were even people standing in all the aisles. Many people heard this concert on the radio, which broadcast it to all of Spain.

The principal piece of the program was, naturally, the *Concierto de Aranjuez*, with Regino Sáinz de la Maza. Isabel Penagos sang several songs, and introduced two arias from the opera-oratorio *La Azucena de Quito*. The National Orchestra was conducted by Cristóbal Halffter.

In our box, besides several of our friends, was the Papal Nuncio, Monsignor Rivero, who was seated beside me. At the end of the second movement, the famous *Adagio*, he asked Joaquín what he was thinking of as he was writing those pages, so full of emotion and nostalgia.

"My wife," was the reply.

On December 6th, the Tribute to Debussy took place at the French Institute.

As an introduction Joaquín gave a forty-five minute lecture, followed by renditions of Debussy's songs by Monique de la Torre, and several piano pieces by Manuel Carra.

During the intermission the Advisory Minister of the French Embassy awarded Joaquín the Medal of Knight of the Legion of Honor.

To conclude, Monique and I interpreted *La Grotte, Homage to Debussy*, which had had its première in Bordeaux. I don't know how I managed to accompany this very difficult piece, for I was very nervous.

About that time the moving pictures theaters of Madrid were showing a short feature titled "Joaquín Rodrigo at Home," which featured all the members of our household.

A little before Christmas we went to Valencia to attend the Concert-Tribute organized by the City Council. The program couldn't fail to include *Concierto de Aranjuez*, with Yepes, nor the symphonic poem, *Per la Flor del Lliri Blau.*

From there we went to Sagunto, where further tributes awaited us.

That year the Christmas season was extremely cold. The thermometer sank to ten degrees below zero, the pipes froze, and we were left without water. Later the pipes burst, and the stairs were flooded up to the entrance hall.

We spent the holidays quietly, with the family, Mamá, Cecilia and Agustín.

Journey to Barcelona

The year 1963 began with less cold, but with heavy rains.

We renewed the same busy routine as always: visits and visitors, interviews and concerts. At the same time, I devoted myself to correcting the proofs of *Fantasía para un Gentilhombre* and *Soleriana.*

In the middle of January we made a quick trip to Oviedo where Joaquín gave a lecture at the University with the title: "The Music of Joaquín Rodrigo in relation to the University." We took advantage of those days to visit the orchestra conductor Muñiz Toca, a close friend of Joaquín's, and the friends of the Organization for the Blind.

On our return Joaquín began to compose the work he would promise Marisa Robles as a wedding gift, *Sones en la Giralda* [*Sounds in the Giralda*] (La Giralda, a famous tower in Sevilla), which was first heard soon after on the B.B.C.. It is one of my favorite works, and several recordings have been made of it, including one in France and one in the Soviet Union.

On January 30th of 1963 Joaquín had the pleasant surprise of receiving the nomination for the Manuel de Falla Chair, granted by the Ministry of Education. We were very happy!

Within a few days we made a trip with Cecilia to Barcelona, invited by the Spanish Television to take part in the broadcast, "This is Your Life," directed by Federico Gallo.

Before the cameras, Joaquín recalled the most important events of our life, while in the background was heard *Concierto de Aranjuez*, as well as *Preludio al Gallo Mañanero*, the work I fell in love with without knowing anything about the author!

Afterward came the great surprise: our close friends began to file past, brought from Madrid: José María Cossio, Isabel Penagos, the violinist Manolo Bel—this time without his "boys," who accompanied him at the Café de Paris. Finally came Agustín, Cecilia's fiancé, just arrived from Brussels to take part in the party.

Afterwards we saw, on the screen, our dear friend, Amalia Carrasco, now very old, and her ancient piano, on which the *Concierto de Aranjuez* had been composed in Paris.

All of this was very emotional for us. And as a finishing touch, Cecilia, who was preparing for her approaching wedding, was named "Bride of the Year."

A few days later we were all in Madrid again, where further surprises awaited us: first, a visit from the German orchestra conductor, Hans von Benda, always an assiduous interpreter of Joaquín's works, and then one from the great painter, Luis Mosquera, who was beginning to do a portrait of Cecilia as a wedding gift.

Cecilia's Wedding

Gifts for the bride and groom poured in, ranging from a modest ashtray, purchased at a fair by a guitarist of scarce means, to the crocodile bag from the house of Loewe, the tortoiseshell toilet case and the antique ring with a ruby and diamonds, Mamá's gift. Soon they were able to make a display of gifts in their apartment.

Two days before the wedding my sister Mathilde and her son, Rafael, arrived from Paris, and my cousin Irene, from London.

On the fifth of April the formal request for her hand in marriage took place, attended by the whole family, except for the father of the groom, who had a bad case of flu. There was the traditional exchange of gifts. Cecilia received a pretty ring, and we presented a watch to the bridegroom.

The weather was very cold and rainy. Cecilia caught a bad cold, and had to spend several days in bed.

The wedding was celebrated on the sixth of April in the Church of University City.

Cecilia, now recovered, looked lovely under the white veil. Her blue eyes shone with happiness.

The speech by Federico Sopeña, her godfather, was to everyone's liking, and Joaquín's *Cánticos Nupciales*, written for the ceremony, were lovely.

The church was filled, and almost all our friends were there.

Soon after the young couple left for Villajoyosa, where they wanted to spend their honeymoon.

I was completely exhausted and had to go to bed, as did Mamá, for so much activity and excitement had been too much for our resources. Joaquín was the one who stood it best, but how sad he was at the separation from our Cecilia.

After a few days of rest, Joaquín and I left for the Canary Islands, to attend the "International Competition for the Interpretation of Spanish Music." Besides Joaquín, members of the Jury included José Cubiles, José María Franco, and Magda Tagliaferro, Carmen Pérez, Henriette van Lennep, Antonio Lecuona and Agustín León Villaverde. The first prize was unanimously awarded to Jacinto Matute.

At the end of May we made a brief trip to Cullera, where architect Giménez Cusí was building us the chalet we wanted, facing the beach, in the midst of a leafy grove of pine trees. It fulfilled, at last, our greatest desire.

The plan he drew was a good one, for although the house consisted of only four rooms, with a bath and kitchen, it would be our solution to summer vacations for many years to come. We would gather together there: Mamá, the children and our little granddaughters, sometimes even a few guests. On one occasion, the Japanese publisher, Shimpei Matsuoka, spent two days there with us. He had come from Tokyo expressly to pick up a score, and we showed him the village, the beach, the lighthouse, and the "Island of Pansies," all of which he found delightful

On our return from Tenerife, Joaquín had finished his *Cuatro Canciones Sefardíes* [*Four Sephardic Songs*], published by the Max Eschig House. Shortly afterwards, his *Cuatro Estampas Andaluzas* [*Four Andalusian Images*] were published by Unión Musical Española. These works were recorded by several pianists, both in Spain and abroad.

Professor Criado de Val, who had asked Joaquín to write a ballet for the Festival of Hita, invited us to a picturesque supper on the Feast of Corpus Christi in that Castilian village, which still preserves all its medieval flavor. They served us an abundant dinner of roast lamb, "figados" and "migas," all excellent dishes.

The spectacle which followed included scenes from *Don Carnal* and *The Dance of Death*, composed by Cristobal Halffter.

In mid-June we made a trip to Vitoria, when Joaquín was invited to give a lecture on a little-known work of Beethoven's: *Wellington's Victory*.

We took advantage of these days to visit the city's principal monuments: the Provincial Museum and the Portalón, a Gothic building which houses the Museum dedicated to Wellington and the allied troops' victory over Napoleon.

Joaquín gave a very well-documented lecture, and we listened to a recording of the work by the London Symphony, during which the cannon shots and other sounds of the fighting are heard, reproduced with such genius by Beethoven.

On June 24th we left for Granada with Cecilia and Agustín where he was to play the Mendelssohn concerto under the direction of Frühbeck de Burgos.

At that time the concerts in Granada were held outdoors and the evenings were usually cold. The audiences were not generous with their applause and "bravos" were very rarely heard.

For that reason we didn't expect a resounding success for Agustín whose interpretation of Mendelssohn's work was brilliant. However, we were told that the audience was "very happy" and praised enthusiastically the young artist from the Canary Islands.

The next day Nicanor Zabaleta performed Joaquín's *Concierto Serenata*. Unexpectedly, the audience was warmly touched and both composer and artist received a long ovation.

Afterwards, one of the music lovers attending the concert came over to Joaquín to pay him a strange compliment: "I congratulate you not only for your work but also for the audience's applause." We were quite perplexed...

After the concerts we usually went to the "tertulia" at the restaurant to eat the *churros* [fried pastries] and hot chocolate which warmed us up, and to talk things over. We never got to bed before three in the morning.

During the day we would stroll through the gardens of the Generalife, a spot unique in the world, which has inspired so many immortal works. I never tired of admiring the flowers, the ancient cypress trees, the fountains and little streams. That was paradise!

We also visited Manuel de Falla's "Carmen" [A summer house in Granada], where we were received by its proprietress, the Duchess of Lécera.

We regretfully bade goodbye to Granada, and left for Madrid in our little Dauphine car, driven by Cecilia.

Two days later we attended a concert by Montserrat Caballé, organized by the "Friends of Music in Compostela," at the Prado Museum. After some *Lieder* of Schubert and Strauss, she sang Joaquín's *Cuatro Madrigales Amatorios* to overwhelming applause.

At the University of Puerto Rico

Early in 1963, Joaquín had been contracted by the University of Rio Piedras in Puerto Rico to teach a course on the History of Music. The financial terms were very good, but the prospect of leaving Madrid for nine months disturbed me. Above all, so long a separation from Mamá didn't seem wise. Finally, our problem was solved by the arrival of Mathilde, who would be Mamá's companion for several months.

We left for Puerto Rico on August 10, 1963.

We were met at Isla Verde airport by the pianists Irma Isern and Elías López, and Roger Martínez, Head of the Department of Music, who drove us to our apartment, located in the faculty residence.

Soon Joaquín's course began at the School of Humanities, with all of the students and several professors present, so that we met a new group of friends right away. The following Monday Joaquín gave his first lecture. His assistant, William Menéndez, attended that class, but some weeks later, I began to substitute for him, because he was too busy with coursework. However, he always drove us to the School in his car, sometimes accompanied by his wife, Lili, who taught Spanish literature.

A few days later we had a surprising telephone call: Major Milton Weiss, with his wife Helen, and their three children were in Puerto Rico. They had arrived the same day we did.

The Major, who had been commanding officer at the American air base at Aitana, was now stationed at the Ramey Naval Base, as a professor.

When they came to visit us at the Residence, with their son, Howard, and an American couple named Samuels, we were overjoyed, for now we had old friends on the island.

Milton told us that they were living with their children on the Naval Base, some sixty miles from Rio Piedras, but that they would manage to come see us often. They treated us as the closest of friends.

At a cocktail party at the University we were introduced to the prominent musicians of the area, many of them Spaniards, such as the singer Angeles Otteín, María Rodrigo, Alfredo Romero, Verdaguer and professor Matilla. There were also composer, Héctor Parsi, the pianist Sanromá, singer María Esther Robles, López Cruz, Figueroa and many more. Everyone was very friendly. In fact, I don't believe that there are many places where we have met such warm hospitality as in Puerto Rico.

Soon after our arrival, I suggested to Joaquín that he come with me to the grocery store to buy some supplies, for we were tired of eating at the Faculty Club.

Setting out, we found ourselves in a thick forest of coconut palms and other tropical trees, but as there were no definite paths, we began to have difficulty with weeds and undergrowth. Suddenly a middle-aged man appeared in our path, who greeted us in a friendly manner and asked us where we were going.

When we explained our purpose, he exclaimed, "Don't go that way! The path is dreadful and the grocery is quite far. But even worse, there are apt to be hoodlums who will steal everything you have with you. Tomorrow I am going to shop with my wife, and we will be delighted to take you with us."

He introduced himself as Professor Luís Hernández Aquino, adding that he remembered having met us in the home of Juan Ramón Jiménez, in Moguer.

He is also a poet of considerable talent. Some time later, Joaquín set his poem *Bajo el Cupey* [*Under the Tree of Heaven*] (The Cupey is a tropical tree native to Cuba and Venezuela), to music.

One day Sanromá asked us to go with him to the airport to meet Pablo Casals, who was returning from London with his young wife, Martita. Also gathered there was a committee of professors from the Conservatory and a group of friends of the illustrious musician, so beloved on the Island.

Joaquín and I went several times to visit him at his home, near the beach. We felt very much at ease there, and always found interesting people with him. The topic of conversation was always Music. It was there that we first heard his oratorio, *El Pesebre* [*The Manger*] on magnetic tape.

On November 6th the Rodrigo Festival took place in the Grand Theater, with Narciso Yepes participating as soloist in *Fantasía para un Gentilhombre*, and María Esther Robles singing *Dos Poemas* [*Two Poems*], by Juan Ramón Jiménez, two Christmas carols, and *Cuatro Madrigales Amatorios*. The orchestra was conducted by Donald Thompson, a professor at the University.

We had already made many friends, and almost every day we received some invitation, whether for dinner or a party, an excursion to El Yunque or to the beach.

All of our neighbors in the Faculty Residence were our friends. One day Professor Gautier presented himself at our door with a platter of rice cooked in milk, according to the traditional recipe, and this kindness was followed by many others. The Litvinoffs, from Argentina, came to see us every day, asking if they could assist us in any way.

However, not everything was rose-colored; the hurricane season was approaching, which terrified me.

We did get one, rather violent, which obliged us to stock up with provisions for several days, for it was very dangerous to go outside. Besides that, I caught a heavy cold, and we were afraid it might be dengue fever [an infectious disease, transmitted by the Aedes mosquito, with high fever and racking joint pain. Also called Break-bone fever], which was frequent in those tropical latitudes. Happily, it was not, and I recovered in a few days.

Saint Cecilia's day was approaching, and we were thinking of giving a little party at home.

After lunch on November 22nd, I was in the garden of the Residence, when I heard our neighbor Helly give an ear-splitting scream,

"The President! The President!"

"What has happened?"

"An attack. They have killed him in Dallas," she answered, sobbing.

All of the neighbors came running into the house to watch the television. There were blood-curdling scenes which I don't like to remember.

The next day they announced that President Kennedy had died, and that the presumed assassin, Oswald, as he was being escorted from the jail to an armored car which was to take him to another prison, had been shot down by Jack Ruby. Half an hour later, Oswald would die also, in the same hospital as the President.

There was an outpouring of sympathy and emotion, followed by days of anxiety and sorrow in the entire country.

* * *

The Christmas holidays were approaching, and with them, I had the familiar feeling of homesickness.

Many friends thought of us, and we received more than one invitation to join a family celebration on Christmas day. Finally, we decided to go to the home of Hernández Aquino, whose apartment, lined with books, was very welcoming. It was a family with whom we were very happy.

* * *

I think that it was a little before New Year's Day when we were awakened one night by music, very sweet and tuneful, beneath our window. We got up, intrigued, and were surprised to see a full chorus of young people, girls and boys, who were singing popular Puerto Rican music. They sang and played for a long time, to our delight. Dawn was breaking when they slipped silently away, like a chorus of ghosts.

The next day our friends explained that it was an old Island tradition to compliment guests of honor with a midnight serenade, prepared with great secrecy.

A few days after that, we had a lively gathering at our house. José Greco and his company, who had just performed at the Caribe Hilton, gave us a "fiesta flamenca," to which we invited all our friends, among them Sanromá and María Esther, who played and sang Puerto Rican music, Hernández Aquino, who read his poems, Fernando Díaz Plaja and many more.

It may seem illogical, but in spite of so many satisfactions, we were thinking of cutting short our stay on the Island. In truth, we were feeling exhausted from the strenuous life, far from our family and far from our Madrid apartment, so calm and comfortable. Besides, Joaquín was not well; his hernia was making him very uncomfortable, and he wanted to have an operation as soon as possible.

When our Puerto Rican friends learned of our decision, they protested vociferously, trying to make us change our minds, as did the professors at the University—and even the students!

Their show of affection was very touching, but our departure was inevitable.

A little before we left, our pupil, Oscar Hernández Vargas, honored us with a banquet in the oriental fashion, featuring delicious dishes which had been familiar to me since my childhood. Oscar and his wife,

Nadellda, came to Madrid on several occasions, and we formed an enduring friendship.

As for Major Milton Weiss, he and Helen invited us to spend a few days in their home at Ramey Base, and we made an excursion with them to Mayaguez to attend a guitar concert, at the end of which Joaquín and I presented several pieces at the piano.

On the day of our departure, February 2, 1964, a large group of friends accompanied us to Isla Verde airport. Many photographs were taken, to be published with laudatory articles.

We left the Island with real nostalgia, and when we boarded the plane, there were tears in my eyes.

We arrived in Madrid on February 3rd after having spent six months in Puerto Rico—the entire first semester.

Joaquín was operated on the twenty-sixth by Dr. Mariano Zúmel in the clinic of Our Lady of Loreto, where he spent ten days.

His recovery was relatively rapid, but he delayed the renewal of any activities because he suffered from a mild depression. A few days of rest did him a world of good.

On April 9th, radio, television and press had news which brought us a happy surprise: Joaquín was named *Doctor Honoris Causa* by the University of Salamanca. Also named were the ophthalmologist, Dr. Castroviejo, and diplomat José Antonio Mora. The investiture took place on May 22nd; it was a solemn and moving ceremony, unforgettable for us.

Early in June we received bad news: our great friend, "Uncle" Federico García Sanchiz, had died suddenly of a cerebral thrombosis. The famous "charlista" [speaker—"Charla" is a chat. Sanchiz was famous for his informal talks on the radio, on many subjects, always introduced by "Pues, Señor." He was universally popular], had created a medium of which he was the only representative. Since we first met in Argentina, we had maintained strong bonds of friendship with him and with his wife, María Isabel. When I went to give her our condolences, she told me, in tears, that Federico had kept three papers always with him: one, some reflections of Jovellanos, another referring to Michelangelo, and the third, a poem dedicated to me. It was probably a reply to my poem which I had dedicated to him, entitled "Pues, Señor," the words with which he introduced all his chats. He was a man of great talent, completely original, typically Valencian.

We spent the summer vacation with Mamá, half in Villajoyosa, and half in Faro de Cullera, where we took possession of the new chalet, "The Pines," now almost finished. Cecilia and Agustín arrived from Brussels to keep us company for a month, and with them our Belgian friend, Claire van Walleghem, an enchanting girl, and a very talented harpist.

We were very happy on this beach, in spite of the tropical heat that prevailed there. The only unpleasantness was that the coast was beginning to fill with tourists, and transistor radios were heard everywhere. How much everything had changed in such a short time!

In September we returned to Villajoyosa to enjoy the silence and savor the delicious fruit from our small orchard.

A few weeks later, we were in Madrid, in preparation for the première of the lyric comedy *El hijo fingido*, [*The Impostor Son*] which involved a great deal of work, but which culminated satisfactorily in the Zarzuela Theater, on December 5, 1964.

El Hijo Fingido

It was during the summer of 1955 when we had a visit at our chalet in Torrelodones, from the well-known playwright and librettist, Jesús Arozamena. It was our first personal contact with him.

He was a middle-aged man, plain and affable, with an ever-present smile. He visited us unexpectedly to make Joaquín a proposition which he considered extremely interesting. It was to set to music a comedy by Lope de Vega, adapted by Arozamena, with the title *Where does it come from*, in order to present the work in the competition announced by the National Ministry of Education. The prize of one hundred thousand pesetas was very generous for the period, and the alloted time period of one year seemed reasonable. And so Joaquín let himself be tempted, and promised to get to work on it very soon.

A few days later, Arozamena returned to give us a reading of the completed book, which he titled *El hijo fingido*, and which seemed pleasant to us, but no more.

However, there were several sonnets and trios by Lope himself intermingled in the manuscript, which impressed Joaquín vividly. They would inspire him to write several arias of great beauty.

Joaquín composed all the music for this lyric comedy in a short time, and the two authors were actually able to present it to the National Competition.

Nevertheless, they had no luck, and the work did not win any of the three prizes. The excuse the jury made was that it lacked the traditional choirs. The first prize was awarded to Manuel Parada, whose work, insofar as we knew, was never performed.

Years passed, and Joaquín and I lost all hope of seeing the work produced. It was Lola, Cecilia's godmother, who suggested to Joaquín that he compose some additional numbers, including the inevitable choirs, which he did without delay. When he had completed the score, we initiated the steps for the opening performance.

And when we received the news that *El hijo fingido* would be presented during that same season, in the Zarzuela Theater, we were happily surprised.

And then came the most hair-raising task: to present an impeccable transcript to the theater's management. Although the score for the orchestra was completely finished by the composer, it lacked all the bowings and dynamics. And naturally, all this work was incumbent on me. Besides that, I had to take upon myself a most annoying job: that of correcting the book, which apparently had never been revised by the author.

It was a mismash, with some verses by Lope himself, lyric and musical, and on the other hand, some attempts at dubious and trivial comedy, inadmissible in a classic text.

Joaquín had often asked the librettist to cut out the superfluous passages which had no relation to the original text, in order to create a unity of plot, but it was in vain. Apparently, the work no longer interested Arozamena, and the proof is that he didn't even attend the opening performance, using the pretext of a trip to Bordeaux.

So I had no choice but to revise the book, availing myself of Lope's original comedy, and adding some verses from another very funny comedy, *Ramilletes de Madrid* [*Bouquets from Madrid*].

For many days I pored over various works by the illustrious playwright, most of which had fallen into oblivion. With a few judicious cuts, as is done with the works of Shakespeare and other classic authors, they could be staged perfectly, which would enrich the repertory of the classic Spanish theater.

By a stoke of luck, we found two magnificent sopranos, Isabel Penagos and Ana Higueras, to alternate in the role of "Angela," the play's heroine. The part of "Barbara" was sung by Ines Rivadeneyra, an excellent mezzo-soprano, and that of "Leonardo," by Villarejo, a good baritone.

The staging, by Luis Escobar, was very skillful, as was the scenery by Burgos and the costuming.

The ballet, directed by Alberto Lorca, seemed rather weak. It was apparently because the amount of money alloted by the management did not permit the hiring of enough professional dancers. But one couldn't be too demanding!

On opening night the Zarzuela Theater was completely filled. There were many well-known people: writers, painters, and so forth.

By chance, a number of our friends had come, as well as one hundred students of SEU, devotees of Joaquín.

In a word: the opening night of *El hijo fingido* was more than an artistic success; it had already achieved success at the box office.

* * *

Early in 1965 Joaquín finished *Concierto Madrigal*, commissioned by the Presti-Lagoya duet, and we hastened to revise it as quickly as possible in order to send it to two great artists.

Joaquín once again began his classes at the University, more crowded than ever.

About that time there was a performance of *Concierto de Aranjuez* by Alirio Díaz and the National Orchestra, conducted by Rafael Frühbeck, which received enthusiastic acclaim. The Sala Monumental hall was crowded with an audience which enthusiastically applauded the magnificent guitarist, one of the best interpreters of this work.

We frequently saw Lucero Tena, a great ballerina and magnificent virtuosa of the castanets, who came to see us often, with her attractive mother, Doña Luz.

More than once we went with friends to the *Corral de la Morería* to enjoy her performances. Joaquín wrote *Dos Danzas Españolas* for her.

Early in March we attended the rehearsals of a work on commission for the "Week of Religious Music" in Cuenca: *Himnos de los Neófitos de Qumran* [*Hymns of the Novices of Qumran*], written about the Dead Sea Scrolls, the recent discovery of which had caused a sensation in the entire civilized world. The inspired work is written for three sopranos, a male chorus and a small orchestra. The world première took place on the 15th of April, 1965, at St. Michael's Church, in Cuenca.

The next day we left for Brussels, where we enjoyed the company of our children for two weeks.

Queen Elizabeth of Belgium's love of music was well-known, as is the interest she showed in the talented young musicians whom she took under her patronage. Our son-in-law, who was awarded a prize in one of the "Queen Elizabeth Competitions," spent three years in *La Chapelle* , where he was able to pursue his studies in an ideal environment.

One day we were invited with our children to visit Laeken Palace, the residence of the Belgian sovereign. The Queen received us very cordially, and at tea time, she served Joaquín's tea with her own hands, which implied a great honor, for, as we were told later, this was something which she never did with her guests.

From Brussels we began a journey to Israel.

Journey to Israel

Himnos de los Neófitos de Qumrán

I

I will pray day and night at all the times that the Lord has decreed,
When the sun blazes at the height of the heavens,
When its rays light the darkening west
Where God reveals to us his secret treasures.
When the shadows conquer the light of day,
When the night rises with all its stars,
And when the white dawn gleams anew.
When the moon shines over the peaks,
And when they are gathered together in the divine bosom,
And when the natural seasons begin,
When the months are born, when winter comes
And illuminates the sacred feasts of summer,
I will comply with that decree engraved on the tablets
Of stone by the imperious divine finger,
The duty to lift up the prayers of my lips
To the eternal Love. Amen, Amen, Amen.

In April of 1965 the Victoria Agency informed us that *Concierto de Aranjuez* was going to be premièred in Israel by Alirio Díaz and the Haifa Symphony Orchestra, under the baton of Sergiu Comissiona.

A few days later we set out for Brussels, where Joaquín had been engaged by the Viscount de Berryer, the ex-Ambassador from Belgium to Spain, to give a lecture-concert in the "Cercle Gavlois."

It was there that we received some upsetting news from Comissiona: there were only a few days remaining before the opening performance, and the parts for the orchestra had not yet arrived! There was only one solution: to take the material to them ourselves. This was providing that we could acquire the scores in Brussels, which was problematical.

Someone—I don't remember who—told us that the young Basque guitarist, Iturri, had gone to live in Brussels, and that he had recently performed the work. We contacted him, and were very happy to learn that he had the material available. We then hurried to the Israeli Consulate, where Mr. Harman had the kindness to give us a V.I.P. visa.

When we landed at Lod airport, my nerves were in such a state that I scarcely recognized the friends and relatives who had come to welcome us! It all seemed like a dream!

Two days later we set out for Haifa, where we were met by Alirio Díaz, Comissiona and the entire orchestra.

The *Concierto de Aranjuez* was exquisitely performed two days later, and the audience greeted it with endless ovations. At the reception which followed the concert, we met many prominent people, among them Nora Baruh, an attractive woman and excellent guitarist, who would become our close friend.

The next day we began our pilgrimage to the Holy Places, accompanied by my cousin Bubi, an active and determined politician, who was our guide during our entire stay.

The bus to Jerusalem was crowded with people, tourists from everywhere, Sabras [a person born in Israel] and Arabs. As we approached the city, the famous "golden walls" appeared in the distance, welcoming us.

After a short visit to the Spanish Consulate, we set out for the Mount of Olives. "It doesn't seem very big," I observed, "And that little wire gate at the back, what's behind it? Wouldn't they let us go through?"

"I wouldn't recommend it," replied Bubi, drily. "The other side is Jordan, and they would shoot you before you knew what happened."

From there we went to the Conservatory of Music, where we were honorees at a luncheon. Among the other guests were the Minister of Culture, the Spanish Consul, the entire faculty and my family. We visited all the rooms, as well as the interesting Museum, where one can see musical instruments of every kind from many countries, ranging from the most ancient and primitive to the contemporary.

The following day we were again in Jerusalem for some intensive sight-seeing. We went to Rachel's tomb, to King David's tomb, to the Damascus Gate and the Golden Gate.

To finish, we visited the Archaeological Museum, where the famous Dead Sea Scrolls, discovered at Kirbet Qumrán, about twelve miles from Jerusalem, are preserved under a modern dome. The scrolls were found in a number of caves, stored in large earthen jars by members of an Essene community called "The Alliance." Some of the manuscripts, such as the *Scroll of Habakuk*, were written more than two hundred years before the time of Christ.

The most notable were the inspired hymns which the novices used to sing, in a solemn ceremony, on the day of their admission into the community. Some of these hymns, with music by Joaquín, had been heard in Cuenca a month earlier, as a commission for that year's "Week of Religious Music."

On the day of that première we had never expected to soon be admiring them in their own setting. What surprises fate has for us!

We also went to Nazareth, where we visited the Basilica of the Annunciation and the cave which had served as a dwelling for the Virgin Mary.

Nor did we miss an excursion to the Sea of Galilee, where we visited Caperneum and Tiberius. We contemplated the blue mirror of the Dead Sea and the ruins of Sodom and Gomorrah. There were pillars of salt everywhere under a blazing sun.

I was vividly impressed by the *kibbutzim*, especially by Givat Brenner, devoted to agriculture, research and the arts. Its hospitable director showed us all the installations and served us an excellent coffee with homemade pastries.

I want to mention the symphony concert we attended at the Mann Auditorium. What acoustics! Zubin Mehta conducted and Vladimir Ashkenazy was soloist in Tchaikovsky's *First Concerto*, if I recall correctly.

The day of departure arrived, and we had to forego an excursion to the port of Eilat, the ruins of Masada, and other historic places, because of lack of time. But we hoped to be able to visit them on another visit to the Holy Land.

* * *

On our return to Spain, we immediately went to Galicia with Cecilia and Agustín, who was to give a concert in La Coruña, on July 26th.

On the 29th, at the same place, Joaquín's new work was performed for the first time. This was *Rosaliana*, a cycle of four songs on poems of Rosalía de Castro, commissioned by the City Council. The songs were performed by Ana Higueras and the Municipal Orchestra, achieving an enormous success.

At the end of October I attended the first Board meeting of "The Friends of UNICEF," whose president was Carmen Cavestany, a women of great warmth and culture.

From that time on I was a zealous supporter of that magnificent project, attending all the weekly meetings and participating in all the campaigns to support its services. When UNICEF was awarded the Nobel Peace Prize on October 26, 1965, it was a source of immense joy and satisfaction to all members of the Board.

On that occasion each of us received a telegram of congratulation from Mr. Labouisse, the President of UNICEF, which encouraged us to continue our work.

In November of that year we had a visit from the director of the Pittsburgh Orchestra, Mr. Boudreau, who came to commission a work by Joaquín for the Festival of Spanish Music which he was organizing in that city.

Joaquín soon sent him the *Adagio* for wind instruments, which would be published by the house of Peters, in the United States. It is a work which is frequently performed, and always with great success.

On November 18th the world première of the *Cuatro Canciones Sefardíes* for voice and piano took place in the Atheneum. They were interpreted by Fedora Alemán, with great style and sensibility.

Shortly thereafter they were published by the Max Eschig House, of Paris.

This year, Spanish Television came to the house to film some scenes for "Maestro Rodrigo's Christmas Eve."

We celebrated Christmas and New Year's Day with Mamá, who had returned from Paris after spending time with Mathilde and her grandson. They were peaceful, pleasant holidays.

During the first weeks of 1966 we scarcely left the house, for Joaquín was composing his *Sonata Pimpante*, for violin and piano, written through the initiative of the Viscount de Berryer. Agustín was the soloist at the première on February 26th in Brussels.

February was very busy: Joaquín was dictating the *Concierto Madrigal* for the Presti-Lagoya duet and I devoted myself to correcting the cantata *Música para un Códice Salmantino* [*Music for a Codex of Salamanca*]. At the same time, we were editing *Album de Canciones* [*Album of Songs*].

Every Thursday we went to the School of Philosophy and Letters, where the classes in the History of Music continued to be crowded. I remember that one day we took a taxi to the University. The driver, a grey-haired, middle-aged man, looked like a good fellow, and I asked him if he would wait until we came out after class. He agreed, provided that the guard would let him park.

"Just tell him that you're waiting for Professor Joaquín Rodrigo, composer of the *Concierto de Aranjuez*."

"I already know that. I recognize him," he replied.

When we reached our house, he got out to help us out of the cab and he refused a tip.

"This afternoon, at 4 o'clock, listen to "The Voice of Madrid," he told us, "You'll hear the taxi driver's salute."

Sure enough, we were able to listen, and we clearly heard the salutation of the music-loving taxi driver, with the *Adagio* as background music.

Disturbances at the University were increasing. There had been student sit-ins and demonstrations in Political Science, and above all, at the Law School, where they broke the glass in the doors and windows, shouting, "Unite, Unite! We want freedom of the press!," and similar slogans.

In March, Maestro Sergiu Comissiona came to conduct the National Orchestra. He had conducted the *Concierto de Aranjuez* in Haifa a year earlier, and in his honor we gave a small reception, attended by a number of close friends who were also his admirers.

We organized an interesting concert at the School of Philosophy and Letters on March 12th. Although the Dean would not allow us to announce it, for fear of student demonstrations, the auditorium was packed from wall to wall. *Cantores de Polifonía* [*Singers of Polyphony*] were conducted by Jesús López Cobos. There was thunderous applause.

We will always remember Good Friday, 1966. We saw no one that day, for Joaquín was very preoccupied with the composition of the *Concierto Madrigal* for two guitars.

I went to bed at the usual hour, but I had slept very little, when I was awakened before six in the morning by a noise like the explosion of a bombshell.

"I was dreaming," I thought, and went back to sleep.

At eight o'clock I went out on the terrace to see whether the sun was shining, or if there had been a storm during the night. I was horrified to find the terrace covered with debris: bricks, chunks of cement, glass! The wrought iron chairs and table were completely bent and twisted. At first I thought of an earthquake, later, that perhaps workmen above had thrown the debris down on our terrace.

The doorman came up, looked around, and discovered the cause: the double partition of our wall had collapsed.

Just the day before, as the weather had been fine, Cecilia had spent the entire afternoon on the terrace, sun-bathing. Suppose this had happened a few hours earlier—it was better not to think about it!

On the first of April, as he did every day, Joaquín turned on the radio at breakfast time. What interested him most was the weather report. But the announcer immediately began to read a list of those who were to be decorated with the Grand Cross of Civil Merit. We listened to several names we didn't know; then we heard those of Ciriaco Pérez Bustamente, Dr. López Ibor and others, and finally that of Joaquín Rodrigo.

"They've given it to *me*?" he exclaimed, astonished. "That can't be me, there are many others with the same name!"

At that moment a friend called to congratulate him; later there were more phone calls, and congratulatory telegrams began to arrive from people in important positions, from Ministers, among them one from Manuel Fraga, from writers, etc. And as this went on, Joaquín was finally convinced that the Grand Cross was for him.

The ceremony of investiture took place on April 21, 1966, with the attendance of renowned musicians, high officials of the Ministry of Information and Tourism, music critics and many friends. A committee from the City Council of Sagunto, which had defrayed the cost of the Cross, arrived for the occasion. Manuel Fraga's speech, which outlined Joaquín's career, moved me deeply, as did Joaquín's words of response, which he ended by saying that he offered this Cross, which was so great an honor, to Vicky, his wife, who had helped him to accomplish his work.

On the following day, Igor Markewitch conducted the *Concierto de Aranjuez* in the auditorium of the Ministry of Information and Tourism, crowded with people. Both he and Yepes met an enthusiastic response, and for Joaquín there were interminable ovations.

It was May, and the History of Music course in the University would soon be over. However, that day we noticed something unusual; there were few people in the classroom or in the hallways. So, when the doorman advised us to get out of there as quickly as possible, Joaquín didn't finish the lesson, and the few students who were there remained to listen to the tape recording of the *Sonata en la*, which had been premièred in Brussels in February.

We rapidly went down the stairs, and made the foolish mistake of getting into our small car to return home. But we couldn't go very far because just a few yards from the campus a gang of enraged students blocked the way, shouting, "Freedom! Freedom!" At the same time they threatened us with stones, one of which struck the car, making a dent in a door. I have seldom been so frightened!

On the thirteenth of May we were invited to a concert in the Palace of Liria, residence of the Duke of Alba. The "Boccherini Quintet" played five quintets of that famous Italian composer, in fine style. This was the closing performance of "Boccherini Week."

In June we had bad news from Tenerife: Maruja Ara, our son-in-law's mother, died of cancer at the age of 52. She was an enchanting woman, with many virtues, and very artistic. She had been professor of piano at the Conservatory for many years, where she was much loved by all her pupils and colleagues. Joaquín and I were very fond of her.

We spent the summer vacation in Cullera with Mamá and Cecilia.

On our return to Madrid a great surprise awaited us: the radio announced that Joaquín had been awarded the Gold Medal for Merit in his Work.

As a result, there were a number of interviews for press and radio. Congratulations poured in from everywhere. Of course, Joaquín richly deserved that award.

Igor Markewitch congratulating Joaquín Rodrigo at the awarding of the Gold Medal of Meritorious Work.

On October 13th Joaquín resumed his classes in the University. There was a new faculty member, Professor Valbuena, a very agreeable man and an ardent devotee of music.

That same day marked the opening of the new Royal Theater, with the attendance of the Chief of State and all the Government Officials. The great hall had been completely redone, on the site of the old, historic Royal Theater, and a select audience filled every seat. The program included the *Homenajes* [*Tributes*] of Manuel de Falla and Beethoven's 9th Symphony.

The young conductor, Frühbeck de Burgos, wielded the baton. I recall that it rained in torrents during the entire concert and all night long. The comments were generally favorable, although some were of the opinion that they should have built a concert hall *ad hoc*, reserving this lovely theater for opera performances.

About that time we had an unexpected visit from the singer Richard Anthony, accompanied by the French publisher, Labbey, and the English publisher, Hal Shaper. We had some drinks, and there was talk of the vocal adaptation of the *Adagio* from the *Concierto de Aranjuez*, which he referred to as *Aranjuez, mon amour* [*Aranjuez, My Love*], and which was already being performed in the Paris nightclubs. That day we attached no importance to this "fantasy" of his, and we parted as good friends.

We don't know whether he was acquainted at the time with the record by the American trumpeter, Miles Davis. If that was so, it is possible that it may have suggested to him the idea of committing this act of piracy. Actually, this was the signal for the assault that the musicians of jazz and pop music made on this work. The song, *Aranjuez, mon amour*, began to circulate through the entire world, performed—with more or less success—by an infinite number of singers of every category. For a long time it was number one on the French "hit parade."

There was no way of stopping this avalanche, and it is a real miracle that it has not—from sheer repetition—diminished, or even destroyed, the popularity of the original.

Rather, it has served as promotion, and while the pop records lasted only two or three seasons, the recordings of the concerto for guitar continued to multiply. I could tell many anecdotes: in New York, for instance, the taxi driver, a Sevillian, who drove us to the Spanish Institute, recognized Joaquín and, full of admiration, asked for his autograph.

In a typical restaurant in Tokyo, the waiter, a fan of guitar music, requested an autograph. And in Istanbul, the Italian pianist at the Park Hotel, who was adding charm to the dinner hour with various musical selections, played the *Adagio*, without suspecting that the author was in the room, applauding him. At the end, when we went to congratulate him, he almost wept with emotion, throwing out his arms and exclaiming, "O! que musica bellissima! Lei è un genio!" ["Oh! What beautiful music! You are a genius!"]

There is no doubt that during those years the *Concierto de Aranjuez* was the most popular work of contemporary symphonic music.

The year 1966 was running out. Unexpectedly, Joaquín received a commission from the guitarist Celedonio Romero, a Malagueño [native of Malaga, a seaport in the south of Spain] living in Hollywood, to write a concerto for four guitars and orchestra.

In spite of the difficulties offered by a work of such scope, Joaquín composed his *Concierto Andaluz* in very little time. The première took place in November of 1967 in San Antonio, Texas.

Immediately after the performance, they placed a long distance call to us to congratulate Joaquín on the tremendous success and to announce that they were planning to record the concerto on the following day.

Since then this work has figured in their repertory and is famous in America and in Europe.

On Christmas Eve we left for Brussels to be present at the birth of our first granddaughter, Cecilita, which took place on January 2nd of the new year. She was a pretty baby, with a lot of dark hair and big blue eyes. At last we were happy grandparents.

That winter of 1966-67 was very raw. The streets were covered with snow and frost, and it was my duty to leave the house very early in order to bring back a cartload of groceries. I was in charge of the house until Cecilia returned from the hospital.

When the time came for leave-taking—much too soon—I felt such sadness that I couldn't hold back my tears as we boarded the train for Paris.

We spent three days there, seeing our friends and visiting the Picasso exhibit in the "Grand Palais."

On February 24th, I accompanied Joaquín to the Palace of Justice to be present at the hearing of the suit against the SGAE, which had authorized the transcription of the *Concierto de Aranjuez* for trumpet and jazz, recorded by Miles Davis. Joaquín's lawyer, Manuel Escobedo, was brilliant in his presentation. He spoke for almost an hour, with admirable warmth, feeling and nobility.

On the other hand, the lawyer for the defense spoke for only a few minutes, and his remarks were vague.

Nevertheless, we lost the case, for the judge's opinion was that, since Miles Davis' record had granted author's rights to Joaquín, he had no redress against the SGAE.

We spent a very happy summer in our chalet in Cullera, with Mamá, Cecilia and Cecilita, our enchanting granddaughter, who was already six months old, and the joy of the household. Her favorite lullaby was the *Españoleta* from *Fantasía para un Gentilhombre*, which her grandfather never tired of singing softly to her, to put her to sleep.

In September we went to Belgium, invited by the violinist Louis Poulet, to form part of the jury in the Lièges Guitar Competition. There we had the opportunity to hear several very gifted young guitarists, such as Barberá, Betove and others.

In mid-November we were in Granada, where Joaquín gave a lecture on *El Retablo de Maese Pedro* [*Master Peter's Puppet Show*], attended by María del Carmen, Manuel de Falla's sister, who, at the age of eighty-four was as alert as ever. It was a pleasure to talk to her.

Joaquín resumed his classes in History of Music, and the students came in large numbers. That year the lessons dealt with the contemporary composers.

It was during that autumn that we had the pleasant visit of an Australian couple, the Kohrys, of Melbourne. John Kohry was a lover of the guitar—he played it very well—and he had done a great deal on behalf of this instrument in Australia. As he was a great admirer of the *Concierto de Aranjuez*, we introduced him to the *Concierto Andaluz* and to other works for the guitar.

He and his attractive wife came often to Spain, and we took them to Aranjuez and to other typical places. On every trip they would bring us lovely mementos from their country, and I still have a set of precious opals from them. Punctually, on every St. Cecilia's day, a great bouquet of flowers would arrive with their good wishes. However, we missed them in 1983, and in their place we received a letter from Mrs. Kohry, telling us of her husband's death. With his death we lost one of our most cherished friendships.

In mid-December we had a call from the newspaper *Pueblo* to tell us that Joaquín had been chosen the "Most Popular Musician of the Year" for his *Concierto Andaluz* and his song *Aranjuez, mon amour*.

In January of 1968 the grand dinner for the "Populars" took place in the Hotel Ritz, with more than three hundred attending. Fraga Iribarne, the Minister of Information, presented Joaquín's trophy—a very artistic work by the sculptor, Avalos. As a finale, Guardiola sang

En Aranjuez con tu amor [*In Aranjuez with your beloved*] with words by Alfredo Segura for a change.

During the entire spring semester of this year it was impossible for Joaquín to present his classes in the School. Strikes and sit-ins were the order of the day. Not until mid-May did tranquility return, and one Thursday we went to the School. Only five students attended, but it seemed to me that that was a good beginning.

Through a commission of National Radio, Joaquín began the composition of *Cantos de Amor y de Guerra* [*Songs of Love and War*], which he completed very quickly. The première took place on March 16th, in the auditorium of the Ministry of Information, with Ana Higueras, conducted by Odón Alonso. The next day, the same program was repeated in the Palace of Music, with even greater success.

In late June we met the guitarist, Celedonio Romero, who had premièred the *Concierto Andaluz* in Texas in 1967, with his three sons, Celín, Pepe and Angel. He had come to Madrid with his wife, Angelita, to spend a few days before going to Málaga, his native province. They were delightful people—Angelita was a typical Andalusian beauty. From the first we were close friends, and every one of our meetings became a celebration. Two years later we would be guests in their house in Beverly Hills, on the occasion of the première of the *Concierto Madrigal* in the Hollywood Bowl in Los Angeles.

In July and August we spent a happy vacation in our little house at the beach with Mamá, the children and our little granddaughter, Cecilita. We had to leave them in September, but planned to meet them in Brussels a month later. First we went to Paris, invited by Robert J. Vidal to attend the International Competition, *La Coupe de la Guitare* [*The Guitar Cup*], organized by the O.R.T.F.

The weather was dreadful, cold and rainy, and I caught a bad cold, arriving in Brussels with a sore throat and high fever. I had to spend several days in bed, well cared-for by Cecilia, and accompanied by Cecilita, who would not leave my side.

On our return to Madrid we were told that the National Orchestra had programmed a concert of Spanish music in whose first part appeared the *Homenaje a la Tempranica* and the *Concierto de Aranjuez.* The soloist, Oscar Ghilia, was a pupil of Andrés Segovia.

The audience at the Royal Theater seemed very cool toward the guitarist, but not toward the composer. Especially at the Sunday performance there was a veritable apotheosis. Joaquín received ovations, not only in the auditorium, but also in the lobby and in the aisles during the intermission. An entire group of young people, boys and girls, crowded around us, applauding enthusiastically and asking for autographs. What popularity he had attained! And how moving this youthful fervor!

On November 14th, the press and radio announced bad news, which saddened all of Spain: the illustrious writer and polygrapher, Don Ramón Menéndez Pidal, had just died. In only a few months he would have reached one hundred years of age. His death took away one of Spain's most unique figures.

Don Ramón had many links with the Sephardic world and had compiled an enormous number of folk songs in the Balkan countries as well as in North Africa, which he had visited with his wife.

It was he who had finished the themes which Joaquín used for his work *Dos canciones Sefardíes del Siglo XV* [*Two Sephardic Songs of the Fifteenth Century*]: "Ill was the King's Son" and "The King who Rises Early" for a chorus of mixed voices, as well as the theme of his *Cuatro Canciones Sefardíes* for voice and piano.

I will never forget the afternoon we spent in his house *El Romeral* [*The Rosemary Garden*], leafing through the huge collection of Sephardic songs, to choose the themes which Joaquín would use for his compositions. It was an inexhaustible source!

When we said goodbye to him, I asked permission to make a few cuttings of the fragrant rosemary from his garden to take to our little house in Torrelodones, where I planted them on Palm Sunday.

How amazed we were to discover, a few days later, that they had all rooted! And a year later we would have the satisfaction of seeing in our own small garden an abundance of shrubs from the rosemary given to us by Don Ramón Menéndez Pidal.

In early December we received two very pleasant news items: the first was from Paris, informed us that the *Concierto de Aranjuez* was still number one on the hit parade. The other was a letter from Leopold Stokowski, telling us that he had conducted the *Concierto de Aranjuez* with Alirio Díaz, warmly congratulating the composer.

We often had telephone calls from newsmen who wanted interviews for news agencies or for the radio. Joaquín always received them cordially, although such interviews cost him a great deal of time.

We spent the Easter vacation at our chalet in Cullera with Cecilia and Cecilita, who came to enjoy the sun which they missed so much in the humid cold of Brussels.

But we were surprised by unusual cold weather, and I had to buy woolen blankets for all of us. We spent the days in front of the fireplace, for it rained ceaselessly.

It was a fiasco! At the very end of the vacation the weather improved, so that we were able to enjoy a sunny beach. There the little one suddenly let go and began to walk alone across the soft sand, unafraid of falling. It was a touching sight, especially for us, the grandparents.

The first day of 1969 was disastrous, for soon after midnight Mamá had an attack of dizziness and fainted, fracturing one arm, near the humerus.

We spent a miserable night, without closing an eye. I didn't leave Mamá's side, applying hot pads and giving her what comfort I could. The next morning our physician, Dr. Trápaga, came, and later the surgeon, who said that the injuries were not serious and that the arm would heal without complications. A few weeks later she could leave her bed, and little by little she continued to recover. What a relief for everyone!

* * *

In late January, Fina de Calderón gave a lecture in the French Institute with the title: "Colette and Spain, an imaginative and intuitive process." The audience which filled the hall represented all of diplomatic, cultural and political Madrid. Fina used the "Adagio" of the *Concierto de Aranjuez* as background music, creating a romantic and evocative atmosphere.

About the first of June we had a visit from Dr. Isao Takahashi, eminent oculist and promoter of the classic guitar in Japan. He had worked for eight years in Lambarene with Dr. Albert Schweitzer, and was broadly cultured. From our first meeting we formed a firm friendship. On this occasion he was accompanied by his wife, Take, a delightful person, and we chatted a while about one thing and another. As the door leading to the terrace was open, we could see flocks of swifts, swooping and darting in incessant flight, uttering their cheerful calls.

"How beautiful!" exclaimed Take, marvelling. "Why doesn't Maestro Rodrigo write a work which would reflect the flight of these lovely birds, a symbol of spring?"

"Nothing easier," replied Joaquín, smiling. "It will be a piece for the guitar, and I will dedicate it to you."

"Magnificent! Then, the première will be in Tokyo, and on that occasion, we invite you to visit our country."

Joaquín kept his promise, and three years later he sent his new work, *Pájaros de Primavera* [*The Birds of Spring*] to Tokyo, dedicating it to Mrs. Takahashi. But she was then critically ill, suffering from incurable cancer. She heard the work from her hospital bed, interpreted by a guitarist friend, on the eve of her death.

Dr. Takahashi also kept his word, and through his initiative, we were both engaged by the impresario Tetsuyi Matsuoka to make a concert tour of Japan. When, in every concert, we listened to this inspired piece played by the guitarist, Parkening, our hearts were filled with sadness.

Now it was June. The heat was intense and we were thinking of moving to the house in Cullera, as we did every year.

On June 22nd, Mamá had her ninetieth birthday, and we gave a grand tea in her honor, not forgetting a monumental cake, adorned with ninety candles.

All of the friends gathered to wish Mamá happiness, and she held up perfectly through all the excitement her health much improved. It was a very happy day.

That same afternoon we had a visit from our American friend, Ramsey Rams, a most attractive and congenial woman, who had been hostess of the program "The Bridge of Triumphs" on Radio Madrid.

Many famous people had appeared on that program, among them Joaquín and Cecilia, who had just graduated from the Royal Ballet School of London. Ramsey had married Dale Wasserman, author of the libretto of the musical comedy, *Man of la Mancha*. They lived most of the year in Benalmádena, where they had built a splendid home.

We stayed on the terrace talking until one in the morning, and Ramsey promised to come again soon, with Dale.

We went to Cullera early in July, where we enjoyed almost two months of rest. On September first we left for Portugal, where Joaquín had been engaged by the Summer Course of Music to give classes of musical analysis. The theme chosen was "Classic dance and its development."

The classes were held every afternoon in the Guimarães Museum of Cascais. There were about twenty-five students registered, young men and women, of various nationalities.

Helena de Sá e Costa and Professor Karl Engel, of Basle, were in charge of the piano classes; Sandor Vegh in charge of those of violin. The professor of violoncello was Maurice Eisenberg, and the professors of voice, Lisie Egger and Professor Schilhawski of Salzburg.

In this ideal spot, surrounded by illustrious artists and enthusiastic students, we passed a very pleasant fortnight. Our only disappointment was the beach, for the sea was so cold that we could not swim even once. We made the journey by automobile, which permitted us to admire the scenery.

In October we made a quick trip to Seville, where Joaquín took part in the Seminar devoted to "Music in the University." In addition, he gave a lecture on "Musical Creation."

Some days later, at the end of October, we left for Valencia for Joaquín's admission into the Academy of Fine Arts of San Carlos, as an honorary member.

The President of the Academy, Javier Goerlich, read a highly laudatory speech, and also praised my work at the side of the new Academician.

The following day he invited us to his house in Navajas, where the extensive garden, full of trees and flowers, was the most carefully tended in the area.

About that time León Davico, the son of my cousin Luisa, arrived from Paris. Familiarly known as Loni, he was the Chief of Information for UNICEF in Europe, to which the Spanish Delegation also belonged. He had come to Madrid for the purpose of asking Spanish Television to broadcast the gala he was organizing in Paris for December 4th. His wife, Gabi, is from Berlin, a delightful person, with whom I maintain an assiduous correspondence.

Montserrat Caballé had been chosen as delegate from Spain, but Loni also wanted Joaquín to take part in the gala, playing the "Adagio" of the *Concierto de Aranjuez* on the piano, with orchestral accompaniment.

We invited him and his aide, Mr. Danois, to dinner at the *Corral de la Morería*, where Lucero Tena was performing every night. They were both enthusiastic about Lucero's grace and elegance and her artistry with the castanets, and Loni engaged her on the spot for the gala the following year.

As to that year's gala, in spite of our being officially invited, Joaquín made only a brief appearance, for at the last moment a number of complications arose.

The gala concert, in which famous artists took part, was brilliant, but it was Peter Ustinov, as announcer, who stole the show; his comic timing was flawless. The audience was very select: in a box in front of us sat Princess Grace of Monaco, Prince Rainier, and the Begum. Within the auditorium were a number of Ministers, Ambassadors, artists and the cream of Parisian society. Loni was a great success as an organizer.

We wound up our trip in Brussels, where we had two weeks of rest with our children enjoying our granddaughter Cecilita, who was almost three years old.

She was very funny little girl, clever and affectionate, who followed me like a shadow all day long, asking me to draw her a little house, a dog, a tree. And every few minutes she would say to me, "Grandmamá, I love you so much."

We returned to Madrid on Christmas Eve, to celebrate the holiday with Mamá, who was waiting for us impatiently.

In 1970 Joaquín had resumed his classes at The University of Madrid, which were very popular. The number of students increased each year.

On March 26th we went to Cuenca to attend the second performance of the *Himos de los Neófitos de Qumrán*, poetically conducted by López Cobos.

On April 22nd we had a telegram from Brussels telling us that Cecilita had a little sister. It was very happy news, and we hoped to fly there to attend the baptism of little Patricia Sofía. However, it wasn't possible, for various reasons, primarily because we didn't want to leave Mamá alone.

In July Cecilia and our two little granddaughters arrived in Madrid, and we all went to Cullera, where we spent several happy weeks.

We had to cut short our vacation, because Celedonio Romero had invited us to attend the première of the *Concierto Madrigal* by his two sons, Pepe and Angel, at the Hollywood Bowl in Los Angeles.

We spent a very pleasant week in this typically Andalusian household of artists. Angelita, Celedonio's wife, had grace and charm, and with her very personal style, she never passed unnoticed.

They had another guest, Father Madina, the eminent Basque composer, whose funny stories kept us all amused.

We spent a whole day with Pepe in Disneyland, a wonderland for young and old. And we paid a visit to the pianist, José Iturbi, who despite advanced age, had attended all the rehearsals.

On the night of the première, the Hollywood Bowl, with a capacity of twenty thousand, was crowded. The success was flattering, although the lack of rehearsals could be detected. To top it off, the sound system failed during the performance of the *Concierto Madrigal*. The engineers set to work on it immediately, and after exhausting all their technical resources with no result, someone gave the apparatus a kick. Faced with such a drastic argument, it began to function normally.

There was generous applause for the composer, the two soloists and the conductor, Frühbeck de Burgos.

We could not stay more than a week in Hollywood, for our Houston friends, Walter and Pilar Rubin, were insisting that we pay them a visit. Their house, surrounded by a shady garden planted with tropical flowers, resembled a museum of modern art. Pilar's landscapes and still-lifes reflected her far-off fatherland: Andalusia, Madrid, Toledo. They had organized a full schedule for us: parties, receptions, excursions.

The most notable was our visit to NASA as guests of honor. The astronauts received us with the utmost cordiality and invited us to a luncheon in their own dining room. Joaquín had permission to touch all the objects on exhibit there: the modules, various instruments, the moon rocks.

Another day we were guests of the Institute of Hispanic Culture, where there was a very moving ceremony, followed by a concert of Joaquín's compositions, performed by young Houston artists.

We would return to this city eight years later, on the occasion of the première of the symphonic poem *A la Busca del Más Allá* [*In Search of the Beyond*], composed in honor of the Bicentennial of the United States, and dedicated to NASA.

We returned to Madrid on August 12, 1970, enchanted with our tour, so full of delightful impressions.

October was dry and sunny, and we took advantage of it to make an excursion to the Pantano de San Juan, which everyone was praising to the skies. By chance, we saw a lot there, which I fell in love with immediately. Located on the water, it was surrounded by leafy pine groves, and a profusion of thyme, rosemary and wild flowers filled the air with their fragrance. I thought that our little granddaughter, Cecilita, would love it. She was then three years old, and had begged to go "a paya, a paya" ever since she began to talk.

They told us that the land was for sale, and without further thought, we bought it, expecting to build there, some day, a little house for vacations.

On December twenty-second we were in León for the performance of Joaquín's eight Christmas Carols, which had been premièred in the Atheneum in Madrid in 1953. The soloist was Isabel Penagos, and the orchestra was conducted by Odón Alonso. One of the Carols, titled *Cantan por Belén Pastores* [*Shepherds Sing in Bethlehem*], was being given its world première, which gave me a double satisfaction, since I appeared on the program as lyricist. Both the orchestra and the chorus demonstrated a great deal of interest in these inspired songs of Christmas, which they had prepared very quickly.

The winter of 1971 was very severe. There were heavy snowfalls in Castile and the thermometer fell to 8^0 beneath zero in Madrid. We went out as little as possible. Mamá was sick, with severe headaches and dizziness. Happily, she had a strong constitution, and soon recovered, so that we could resume our normal activities.

As our apartment on Villalar seemed increasingly small, we bought a much larger flat, which was under construction on General Yagüe street. Now I had to look for carpenters, plumbers, electricians, cabinet makers, and decorators. It was an overwhelming task, but it was unavoidable.

In March, the committee for the *Falla de la Plaza del Caudillo* presented themselves at our house to invite us to several days in Valencia on the occasion of the celebration of St. Joseph's feast day. Joaquín had been named "Colossus" of the year 1970, with five other Valencians, and he would go personally to receive the trophy, a reproduction of the Colossus of Rhodes.

There was a gala dinner honoring those who were named "Colossus" this year at the Hotel Monte Picayo, with more than five hundred guests.

On St. Joseph's Day we were invited to the "Mirador," a large apartment where all the members of the *fallera* committee gathered to witness the *nit del foc* [night of fire] and *la cremá* [the burning of the *fallas*].

It was after one o'clock when they began to launch the rockets, which burst into fabulous castles of fire; the Valencians are masters of the art of fireworks.

It was while they were setting fire to the gigantic Colossus erected in the Plaza, crowded with people, that the tragedy occurred: a rocket, dampened by a sudden shower a few minutes earlier, exploded on the ground, killing two young men and injuring a number of others.

The panic was indescribable, people were running in every direction, knocking down whoever got in their way.

More and more ambulances began to arrive, to pick up the victims. It was a Dantesque spectacle which we watched from the Mirador in horror. What a horrible end to the celebration for the city on the Turia.

After many years of separation, I had the great pleasure of seeing Eugenio Bures again. He was Hungarian, and had been my fellow student with Professor Lalewicz. He was the professor's favorite pupil, and had always attended my classes. Now he was making a tour of Spain with his wife Heidi, the daughter of the Austrian composer Franz Schreker. He was doing well in Buenos Aires, where he enjoyed great prestige as a concert pianist and teacher. We spent a very pleasant evening with them and our friends, the Esnaolas, recalling the good times of years gone by.

The concert season was in full swing, and great artists visited us: the orchestra conductors Leinsdorf and Watanabe, Szeryng, the violinist, organist André Marchal and pianist Carmen Vilá.

On the fifth of April we mourned the death of José Cubiles, the great pianist and our close friend, who gave the first performance of *Noches en los Jardines de España* by Manuel de Falla.

Two days later the press announced the death in New York of Igor Stravinsky.

Joaquín was invited to give a lecture on *Ausencias de Dulcinea* and his *Concierto Andaluz* in Burgos, and soon afterward, we went to Toledo, where he spoke at the University Center—in the Hall of Culture—on Stravinsky.

About that time we met the American newspaper woman, Kitty Close, an enthusiastic devotee of music, with whom I would form a close friendship.

We spent the last two weeks of the month in Paris, where Joaquín had been named a member of the jury for the Marguerite Long Competition.

Rosette Jacques-Ibert, the widow of the celebrated French composer, had invited us to stay at the Foundation named for her husband, and we felt very much at home there.

We spent several very busy days completely devoted to the tasks of the Competition. The president of the Tribunal was Tony Aubin, and the other members were almost all well-known pianists: Claudio Arrau, Monique Haas, Professor Agosti of Rome, Professor Fliers of Moscow and the music critic Bernard Gavoty.

Fifty-five contestants were presented, all of them very well-prepared, but those who were outstanding were the three Soviets who were awarded the prizes: Felzmann, a prodigy of nineteen, Egorov, seventeen years old, and Viardo.

We spent the first part of our summer vacation in Cullera, with our children and the granddaughters, and from there we went to Bad Gastein, in Austria.

This spa, which had enjoyed world wide fame for many years, thanks to its healthful, radioactive waters, was very different from the place I remembered from the many happy vacations spent there with my family.

Now, one could not reach the shady pine groves without risking life and limb, for the narrow roads were traversed by thousands of cars of every description which passed, day and night, in an endless column.

Our greatest diversion was the tea-room, La Causerie, where costumed blonde girls served exquisite ice creams and pastries. In the mornings we took long walks through the magnificent Par, where the "Kurkapelle" gave very good concerts.

There can be no doubt that the baths agreed with us, and we undertook the journey home feeling completely rejuvenated.

Early in 1972, Joaquín and Federico Mompou had received a commission from the Ministry of Education for a song cycle for voice and piano.

Joaquín chose several texts from the work of Antonio Machado, whom he had always admired enormously, and in a short time composed ten songs under the title, *Con Antonio Machado.*

These were introduced by the young singer, María Orán. The concert had been scheduled for the fourth of October in Seville, but at the last minute we had to cancel our trip. I had been the victim of a traffic accident, from which Joaquín, fortunately, emerged unhurt.

Towards the end of November our son-in-law recorded the *Concierto de Estío* with the Catalán orchestra conductor Ros Marbá. Recorded on the other side of the record were *Música para un jardín*, *Zarabanda lejana* and *Villancico*, all important works.

On December 16th we went to the *Colegio Mayor* [Student Residence at the University] Pius XII, where the orchestra called *Soloists of Madrid* was presented in concert. They played five of Joaquín's Christmas carols as well as the *Zarabanda lejana.* The hall was crowded with students who knew how to appraise this Christmas music with great sensitivity.

* * *

After we had bought the apartment on General Yagüe, we realized how much we needed a summer house in the proximity of Madrid. The piece of land at the Pantano de San Juan, which until then had been used only as a destination for excursions, seemed very suitable.

Luckily, we found the ideal architect in the person of José María García de Paredes, Maribel de Falla's husband, who came early in January of 1972 with plans for the chalet which he was going to build us in San Ramón.

I don't want to overlook an important event in the musical world: the inauguration of the Advanced School of Song, whose founder and inspiration was Lola Rodríguez Aragón. It took place on January 17, 1972, in the Bauer Palace, which had been completely remodeled.

That night Teresa Berganza delighted us with a concert, attended by the most famous musicians of Madrid, members of the aristocracy, high officials, artists and intellectuals. It was a very brilliant evening.

* * *

Our second tour of Turkey, from April 20th to May 5th, 1972, turned out to be almost more successful than the 1953 tour.

This time the guitarist, Alirio Díaz, accompanied us. He was an enormous success, as much in Istanbul as in Ankara.

In Istanbul the concert was held at Taxim Hall, because the new Opera Theater—one of the most opulent of Europe—had been burned by a group of terrorists during a theatrical performance. It happened to be one of Arthur Miller's plays. By some miracle, there were no victims, but many works of art, among them a collection of antique enamels of incalculable value, had been food for the flames, as had dozens of mink coats, left in the coat room by the elegant spectators.

Going back to the Rodrigo Festival: they told us that all the seats, put on sale a week earlier, had been sold on the first day of sale, disappointing many people.

In Ankara, the concert was even more successful, if possible. Joaquín, Alirio Díaz—who was soloist of the *Concierto de Aranjuez*—and singer Suna Korah, who shone with the *Cuatro Madrigales Amatorios* received standing ovations.

The auditorium was crowded, and in the front row I saw Ismet Inonu, then President of the Republic, surrounded by government officials. There was also the entire diplomatic corps, the intellectuals of the capital, artists and music critics. We were happy to see our close friends from the Spanish Embassy, Ercole and Evelina Michelini, and also my long-time friend, pianist Yuksel Koptagel.

On this trip we managed to see the Hittite Museum, full of true archaeological jewels—their art was unique—, and we also toured the most interesting folklore museum.

* * *

On October 18, 1972, we moved from the flat on Villalar to the new one on General Yagüe street in the modern sector of Madrid. It was a day of frantic activity, of nerves and weariness. Fortunately, a few devoted friends helped us through the crisis. Moving the books and the music and records was the most arduous. There were so many cartons!

It was a real problem to transport the two pianos, especially the Bechstein concert grand. It was completely dismantled, and even so, it was very difficult to get it up the narrow stairways. But what a relief it was, when everything was finally in place, some two weeks later!

The new flat really was larger and more comfortable. But I missed the old place on Villalar, where we had spent thirty very happy years. Actually, I missed the district of Salamanca, so typical of Madrid, with its Retiro Park, the Cibeles fountain, Recoletos boulevard with its tall trees and its cafés, the shops, all so familiar to me.

Here we missed the "sereno" [the watchman who guards the block and lets you in or out after 11 o'clock at night], Pepe, of pure Asturian stock: he who, at night, would see us coming from afar, and would hasten with his heavy handful of keys to open the door to the vestibule. How different all this was! I had the feeling of having moved to another city.

In mid-March, we became acquainted with two Japanese, with whom we would form an enduring friendship. Tetsuyi Matsuoka was director of a concert agency, and his companion was the guitarist Nakabahashi. They came to the house to meet Joaquín, and we went with them to Aranjuez, where they took many photographs.

As the radio forecast fair weather, we decided to spend Holy Week in Cullera. But toward the end of April Joaquín had a mild nervous depression with a great loss of weight, which weakened him considerably.

When we returned to Madrid, we resumed our customary social activities, and we attended the most important concerts: as, for instance, that of the National Orchestra conducted by Lorin Maazel, and the concerts of those extraordinary violinists, Itzhak Perlman and Leonid Kogan.

We had a surprise visit from the eminent guitarist and vihuelist Emilio Pujol, our old friend from the days in Paris.

We spent the summer vacation in Cullera where the rest on the beach did Joaquín a world of good.

On October 22nd we were saddened by news of the death of Pablo Casals, who had been in a coma for several days. It was an enormous loss for music and for all of us who had the privilege of being his friends. There is no doubt that he was the greatest cellist of all time, and moreover, supremely humane.

The première of the *Concierto Madrigal* in Madrid took place in the Royal Theater on November 16th. Pepe and Angel Romero were the soloists, and the National Orchestra was conducted by Maestro Atzmon. Both guitarists were magnificent in technique and musicality, and Atzmon knew how to inspire great poetry, nostalgia and passion from the orchestra. Soon after, this work was recorded by the Romeros and the Orchestra of St. Martin in the Fields, and soon became a "best seller."

* * *

Journey to Japan

On November 18th Joaquín and I boarded the plane for Japan, where Tetsuyi Matsuoka had organized a concert tour for us.

The trip didn't seem too long, and we arrived in Tokyo feeling quite refreshed. We were met at the airport by Dr. Takahashi, the guitarist Nakabahashi and an attaché from the Spanish Embassy.

When I saw the immense metropolis, extending before us in a sea of lights, I exclaimed,

"I can't believe that we're in Japan! It's a dream!"

And witty Dr. Takahashi replied, "Your great poet Calderón has already said it, 'Life is a dream' ."

We were installed at the Hotel Prince, one of the finest in the capital, an old palace. There were several flower arrangements in our room, and a bottle of whiskey with two glasses of cut crystal, compliments of the kind impresario Matsuoka.

From the first day, press interviews and meetings with various societies of guitarist followed, one after the other, for two days.

On November 21st, with only one day's notice, our impresario, Shimpei Matsuoka, and Dr. Takahashi gave a large party to celebrate Joaquín's birthday. A number of guitarists were there, and also Gaspar Cassadó's widow, the Spanish Ambassador, Gutiérrez Cano, the cultural attaché and other dignitaries. Joaquín's works and Japanese folk music were played on an instrument called the "koto."

On the following day we were taken to the Imperial Palace to hear a concert of "Gagaku," traditional Japanese music.

The first Rodrigo Festival took place on November twenty-third. The program included the *Concierto de Aranjuez*, with guitarist Christopher Parkening, and *Concierto de Estío*, with the Japanese violinist Isako. Joaquín played selections from his works, and we concluded with the *Marcha* for four hands. The room was full, and the success resounding. The second concert also took place in Tokyo, the third in Nagoya, and the fourth in Osaka.

The Japanese trains never ceased to amaze me. Such speed! (More than 120 miles per hour). And such comfort! Such service! There was nothing in Europe to compare with them.

In Nagoya we visited the famous Yamaha house, where Joaquín performed some of his works.

One of my happiest memories is of our excursion to Kyoto, which we made as true tourists. What charm it has! And what enchantment we found in its enormous temples, its colorful streets and houses, and its curious gardens with their diminutive trees and plants. And there were jewelry stores everywhere, overflowing with pearls!

We were interviewed for the radio on several occasions, and we visited the Institute for the Blind, where the children enthusiastically applauded the concert which we dedicated to them. When it was over, they overwhelmed us with gifts which they had made themselves.

Our friend, Doctor Takahashi, had obtained an audience for us with their Imperial Highnesses, Prince Akihito and Princess Michiko. When Joaquín and I entered the music room, accompanied by Doctor Takahashi, the imperial couple, with their three sons and several members of their household, were waiting to receive us, surrounded by their maids of honor. I counted eighteen people, all standing, waiting to welcome us.

Joaquín gave an inspired performance of his works, and at the end, the *Marcha* for four hands sounded better than ever.

After the concert, the prince and princess offered us tea: first, Japanese green tea, and then English tea with pastries. Dr. Takahashi and the Spanish Ambassador were with us. Princess Michiko chatted with us in English. Her voice, soft and melodious, was a real delight, and she resembled a porcelain doll, much prettier than in her pictures and on television.

"We have filled the vases with chrysanthemums in your honor, so that you may take with you the memory of their fragrance," she said to Joaquín with a sweet smile. When they bade us good-bye, the prince and princess presented us with a lovely silver goblet, engraved with the royal emblem, the chrysanthemum.

The day before our departure, friends took us to the home of the composer Goka, who received us with the utmost courtesy. To acquaint us with his music, he played some recordings and, finally, he presented us with a doll of marvelous craftsmanship, a real work of art, and with orchids and persimmons from his garden.

From there we went to the home of the Yamaha family, relatives of Tetsuyi, where we were served a sumptuous luncheon, with typical dishes of the country.

Tetsuyi wanted us to take some memento from him back to Spain.

"What would you prefer," he asked, "pearls or something else?"

When he insisted, we confessed that we would need a suitcase to carry all the mementos of Japan which we had already received.

The next day we found two magnificent suitcases in our room, instead of one!

When the time came for our departure, all our friends accompanied us to the airport, and when we embraced them all in parting, my heart was heavy. How much I regretted leaving this extraordinary country—a mixture of progress and tradition—which could serve as a model for so many, so-called "civilized" countries.

In mid-January of 1974, Joaquín renewed his classes at the University, and I devoted myself to revising the manuscript of his *Concierto Heroico.*

In early March we attended two concerts by the Paris Orchestra, conducted by Georg Solti. During the first, Bernard Ringeissen performed Ravel's *Concerto*. The second was an even greater success with the *Symphonie Fantastique* of Berlioz.

About that time we met the American organist, Peter Gray, a fervent admirer of Joaquín, who had come from Kansas City expressly to meet him personally.

Every year, at Christmas, we receive a large package from him, containing a traditional fruitcake or some homemade sausages. His letters and post cards come from all parts of the globe, for Peter is an inveterate traveller. I regret that we have never been able to accept his invitation to visit him at his home in Kansas, where he cultivates all manner of plants and trees.

On April 14th—it was Easter Sunday—Mamá fell in her room, breaking her hip. The surgeon told us to move her to the hospital immediately, for it was necessary to operate as soon as possible. What a sorrow for all of us! However, thanks to a strong constitution, Mamá emerged well enough from the operation, and we were able to move her out of the clinic before summer.

About that time we had a visit from the composer, Albert Hemsi, author of several collections of very interesting Sephardic songs. He gave us his latest portfolio, which we keep as a memento of a fine musician and a very sensitive man.

In mid-May we made a short trip to the Costa Blanca to attend the wedding of a friend from Cullera.

While on a visit to the coast, we went to Villajoyosa, where a disagreeable surprise awaited us. The wide wooden door of our little house, which opened to the garden, had been split with an axe, and vandals, using that entrance, had looted the entire house. All the bedding, clothing and tableware were gone. The pretty antique oil lamp we had acquired in the Rastro had been smashed with a stone, and broken pieces covered the floor, as did parts of the old sideboard, all the pictures, the lamps. It was a disaster!

On our return from the Costa Blanca, Joaquín was named Musical Advisor of the Atheneum of Madrid, whose president, Carmen Llorca, had gathered around her those individuals most outstanding in their own specialties: Carmen Conde, Campoy, Vallejo Nájera, Marta Portal.

There was a large reception on the eighteenth of May, attended by writers and newspapermen from all over Spain. It was a good beginning, and it is a great shame that all these activities have not been continued.

On May 24th the first concert was given there, and turned out brilliantly. The chorus of the RTVE [Spanish Radio and Television] performed under the direction of Odón Alonso, and the program included a Cantata of Bach, Joaquín's *Música para un códice salmantino*, *La libertad sonríe* of Luis de Pablo and Messiaen's *Couleurs de l'Empire céleste*.

On the twenty-second of June we celebrated Mamá's birthday in the German Hospital. All her friends came to wish her happiness, and she received many flowers and sweets. It was her final birthday, and I will always remember it with deep emotion.

Our friend, Robert J. Vidal, had invited us to attend the *Recontres de la guitare* at Arles, in whose framework he had included a tribute to Joaquín.

We left Madrid on July 19th to drive by way of Barcelona. The gala concert took place on the twenty-fifth in the *Théatre Antique* with the following program:

Part I

Guitar recital by Alirio Díaz
Piano recital by Joaquín Rodrigo

Part II

Fantasía para un Gentilhombre	Rodrigo
Concierto de Aranjuez	Rodrigo

by Alirio Díaz

conducted by Maestro Mule

Gran Marcha de los Subsecretarios	Rodrigo

There was quite a large audience, in spite of the "mistral" which was blowing violently, scattering orchestra parts, scarves, etc., in all directions. It was a great success, and the very pretty "Queen of Arles" presented me with a bouquet of flowers after the performance of the *Marcha de los Subsecretarios*.

The next day Joaquín gave a lecture on compositions for the guitar.

We spent a week in this lovely city in the south of France, so full of ancient monuments, which was immortalized by the composer Georges Bizet with his *Suite l'Arlésienne*.

We found several old friends there: Dr. Takahashi and the guitarists Menahem Baguiche and Nora Baruh, among others, and enjoyed the reunions.

On August 1st we were in Joaquín's native city to attend the revival of *La Destrucción de Sagunto* in the Roman Theater. There we met José María Pemán and Francisco Sánchez-Castañer, authors of the play. As before, the Theater was filled to capacity, and as always, the "Assault on Sagunto" with the spectacular fire was the most applauded.

On August 24th we were in San Sebastián, where Nicanor Zabaleta performed the version for harp of the *Concierto de Aranjuez*. Rafael Frühbeck conducted the National Orchestra. The hall was full, and one sensed a feeling of curious anticipation. In spite of the fact that Zabaleta gave an impeccable interpretation of the work, with much emotion in the *Adagio*, this version was not convincing either to Joaquín or to me, for the harp is a rather cold instrument, whose tone conveys neither the warmth nor the color of the guitar. Nevertheless, Zabaleta made it known around the world; the record sells well, and now there are many harpists who request the score in order to perform it in their concerts.

In Madrid, the concert season began on September 30th, with concerts by the Royal Philharmonic Orchestra, conducted by Leinsdorf and López Cobos. The soloists were Rafael Orozco and Erich Gruenberg.

On October 4th we attended the opening of the Atheneum by the famous French dramatist, Eugene Ionesco, who gave a lecture entitled: "Culture, what purpose does it serve?" There was an impressive crowd, with many people standing.

Journey to Mexico

The date was approaching for our departure for Mexico with our friend Enrique Figueroa. I was very reluctant to leave Mamá, but since this trip had already been postponed once, we couldn't cancel it again without offending the Mexican composers who had so kindly invited us.

We left on the fifteenth of October.

We spent a busy fortnight, in that extraordinary country, and we were able to see the most important things. We talked to the people, the common people, who told us their joys and sorrows. And I loved the little dark-eyed boys, barefoot and ragged, who swarmed through the streets and alleyways, hoping to pick up a few coins.

Cecilia's childhood friend, María Victoria Marfany, was the guide who showed us the most interesting and picturesque places. We saw the Palace of Fine Arts, the Cathedral, and much more.

We went with Enrique Figueroa to the Anthropological Museum, which houses innumerable prehistoric treasures of the ancient civilizations—Maya—Aztec—etc.

From there we went to make a tour of the University City, and visited the sculptor Peraza in his studio, where we could admire his very personal works.

I recall meeting "Cantinflas," whom we liked very much.

One night we attended a concert at the Palace of Fine Arts, where the Symphony Orchestra, conducted by Remoortel, played the *Concierto de Aranjuez*, with the excellent Mexican guitarist Alfonso Moreno.

The next day we went with Figueroa to Acapulco, the elegant beach which attracts well-to-do tourists from all the world.

In spite of the tropical heat, Joaquín caught a frightful head cold and had to go to bed in the bungalow of the Villa Vera, where we were lodged in luxury, because all of the hotels were full. That week, we learned, the Congress of Communications was meeting in Acapulco.

The first night there was a thunder storm, followed by a veritable deluge. We were frightened, for we were quite alone in that secluded bungalow, and there were no neighbors to be seen anywhere.

But the next day, Figueroa installed us in the Hotel Acapulco Royal, where they put us in a suite, facing the sea.

On Wednesday, October 23rd, the Symphony Concert took place in the Cultural Communications Center. Enrique Bátiz conducted. It was almost a Rodrigo Festival, for the program consisted of the *Zarabanda Lejana*, the *Concierto de Aranjuez*, with Alfonso Moreno, and the *Fantasía para un Gentilhombre*, with López Ramos. Then, Joaquín played his *Preludio al Gallo Mañanero*, and was rewarded with a great ovation.

We left Acapulco to visit Cuernavaca and Taxco, the famous silver center. What marvels of workmanship can be seen in those innumerable silversmiths' shops, which attract thousands of visitors!

We had lunch at the home of Antonio Pineda, the silversmith. His house was surrounded by a splendid garden filled with tropical plants of a thousand colors.

On the last day we were received by Pedro Domecq and Antonio Ariza in their famous "bodegas." Here was truly a world in itself, a faithful replica of Jerez, with its lovely gardens, its bull-ring, its gaiety!

On October 31st we were back in Madrid.

During these weeks, Mamá's health had improved, so that we could bring her home. But shortly afterward, she had a relapse. From then on she grew weaker every day. Dr. Sánchez Trápaga, who had cared for her for so long, with such affection, could do nothing for her this time.

We went, with friends, to attend the tribute in honor of Vicente Escudero, now far advanced in years, who had been one of Spain's best male dancers, and whom I had applauded, many years before, in Paris.

The concerts at the Atheneum, which Joaquín and I organized, had acquired a reputation and were now attracting large audiences.

First, we heard the young harpist, Ana María Martini, in an extensive program.

Later, María Orán, accompanied by Miguel Zanetti, performed Joaquín's song cycle, *Con Antonio Machado*.

The French pianist Bernard Pommier offered a concert of very hackneyed pieces. Beethoven's *Sonata in F. major, Op. 10*, and Debussy's *Children's Corner*, which was a bit monotonous. On Christmas Eve García Navarro conducted the *Messiah* in the Royal Theater.

During these sad days preceding my mother's death, music was my only consolation.

We had the good luck of finding a young Portuguese nurse, very competent and caring, who was a great help to us at this painful time.

Without Deolinda, I don't know what would have happened, for I was completely exhausted, and at the point of desperation.

It was in the early morning hours of December 24th when Mamá closed her eyes forever, those beautiful blue eyes, full of kindness and tenderness.

On that same day Cecilia arrived unexpectedly from Brussels, with little Patty, who was then four years old, a child of amazing sensitivity. During the two days they were with us, she never left my side; she even emptied her toy bank to be able to buy me "a gold necklace and bracelet." Children's love is the very best balm in our hours of sorrow.

And so we passed the holidays of Christmas and the New Year—the saddest of my life—and in January resumed our usual routine of work.

* * *

In late March, 1975, we went to Cuenca for the première of the second part of the *Himnos de los Neófitos de Qumrán*. This première, in the framework of the "Religious Week," was more moving and dramatic than the first, if possible. The work pleased the audience, and the critics were extravagant in their praise.

Two days later, Joaquín and I left for Brussels to spend the Easter feast days with our children and the little granddaughters, Cecilita and Patty. As always, we spent many pleasant hours with the Van Walleghem family and our other Belgian friends.

In April we had a visit from my childhood friend, Rachel de Leeuw, whom I had met first in Paris, then in Amsterdam, where she lived as a newlywed, and finally, in New York, where she had since located.

Now we spent long hours, chatting of things past and present. They were very pleasant conversations, for Rachel was one of the most intelligent and erudite of my friends. She had worked for a long time at the United Nations.

Among other curious facts, we recalled that our respective grandfathers had been close friends, just as we were.

In mid-May we were invited to a show at the Queen Victoria Theater staged by Mexican performers. At the end Joaquín was awarded the "Silver Spur," as were several other notables with Mexican connections, Pedro Domecq, among them.

The next day the unveiling of the monument to the Mexican composer, Agustín Lara, took place in the Corrala. The plaza was crowded; there were people on the balconies and leaning out windows, and some small boys had perched on walls or climbed to the tallest branches of the trees. There were many speeches, and at the end they played the famous schottische, *Madrid, Madrid, Madrid*, with everyone present joining in the chorus.

The monument, created by Peraza, who was present at the ceremony, was placed in the center of the plaza, and that night there was a great celebration in the Plaza Mayor. Taking part in that were two hundred "charros" [Mexican horseman, elegantly attired], the singers Nati Mistral, Lola Flores and many others. The festivities went on until daybreak.

* * *

Summer came, and after a few weeks of rest at the beach in Cullera, Joaquín and I were once more in Madrid.

The summer interruption of the concerts at the Atheneum had not lasted long, and on October 30th they presented the young Japanese violinist, Takayoshi Wanami, who was beginning a brilliant international career. Blind from birth, he had brilliant technique and great musicality. The audience approved of all his interpretations, applauding him warmly.

The Infante Luis de Baviera almost always sat in the honorary box with us. He was a great music-lover, who rarely missed a good concert.

On St. Cecilia's day a number of friends came to wish Joaquín happiness. It was a very lively gathering.

We celebrated Twelfth Night in 1976 with several close friends, and the next day we left for Palma de Mallorca, where our son-in-law played the *Concierto de Estío* with the Symphony Orchestra conducted by Julio Ribelles. The concert took place in the Auditorium, an enormous hall of modern design, difficult to fill. But this performance attracted a large audience, and there was warm applause for the composer and his interpreters.

The program also included Joaquín's symphonic poem, *Per la Flor del Lliri Blau*, *Karelia* by Sibelius, and *Acuarelas* by López Chavarri.

We were most cordially received by members of the City Council and their respective wives.

Joaquín enjoyed this excursion as much as Agustín and I did.

In February, 1976, my friend and compatriot, Yüksel Koptagel, came to Madrid to give a concert in the Círculo Medina. During the two weeks that she spent in Madrid we were together every day, and I was sad as I accompanied her to the airport to take the plane to Paris.

During March Joaquín and I were invited to a cocktail party at the home of the director of the United States Cultural Center, Mr. Murville. On that occasion my attention was called to a young woman guest, very elegant, of singular beauty. She was tall and slender, with fair skin and lovely violet eyes in an oval face. She introduced herself to Joaquín and me as Mrs. Farrell, saying that she was a great devotee of music and that she admired Joaquín's works enormously.

A few days later I paid her a visit in the "Rastrillo," where, she had a shop in the Rembrandt Pavilion, featuring products from her country, Holland. I went home loaded with cheeses, chocolate and cookies, all truly delicious!

That was the beginning of my friendship with Ilonka Farrell, and every time I find myself with her, whether to visit an exhibit of paintings, to go to a concert or to make some excursion, I am happy. We share the same taste, the same affinities and almost the same training. She combines all the moral and spiritual qualities and has a broad education. Her husband, Edward, an American international lawyer, is very fond of salmon fishing and is a great hunter of hare in Ireland, which we have sampled several times in Madrid and in their house in Marbella.

On March 9th we attended the funeral of our good friend, Paul Guinard, ex-director of the French Institute, who had been the victim of a traffic accident. A great hispanophile, he had published several studies on the history of art. His death grieved us deeply; only a few days before we had seen him walking briskly through the University City, where he occupied a Chair in the Complutense.

José Tamayo staged a revival of *La vida es Sueño*, with incidental music by Joaquín.

Shortly thereafter we were at the Atheneum, where the duet, Javier Alfonso-Teresa de los Angeles, gave a fine concert, performing Joaquín's *Cinco Piezas Infantiles*, with great success.

The final concert of the Atheneum was given by the Trio Juvenal, made up of three extraordinary young Israelis.

A few days later they played again in the Graduate School of Scientific Research. Queen Sofía was present and was seen applauding warmly. Her love of music is proverbial, and it is well-known that she never misses a good concert.

At the end of May my sister arrived from Paris in a pathetic state. She was suffering from rheumatoid arthritis and walked with great difficulty, leaning on a cane. I was heartsick to see her so changed. The doctor who came to see her recommended vigorous treatment at the thermal baths at Benicasim, where I took her in July. The stay at the spa was beneficial, and in September she returned to Paris, much improved.

Joaquín and I joined Cecilia and the granddaughters in our house in Cullera.

To entertain ourselves we bought a television, which let us watch the Olympic games in Montreal, which began on July 17th. This was our major diversion during the summer.

On October 12th, the day of Spanish Unity, Joaquín and I left for Paris, officially invited to the gala concert which took place in the Théâtre des Champs Elysées to commemorate the thirtieth anniversary of the creation of UNESCO.

My nephew, León Davico, Chief of Public Relations for UNESCO, had provided tickets for all the family, so that Agustín, Cecilia and the children came flying in from Brussels for a twenty-four hour visit to celebrate the occasion.

The program included the *Concierto de Aranjuez*, with John Williams. Yehudi Menuhin played Chausson's *Poem* and Kiri Te Kanawa, a most attractive young soprano, enchanted the audience with her art. Nevertheless, it was *la garde republicaine*, stationed on the monumental staircase of the Theatre, which most impressed Cecilita and Patty.

This time Omar Sharif introduced the artists, and Natalie Delon drew the tickets for the charity raffle. The theater was crowded with a very distinguished audience, and I recognized the Prince and Princess of Monaco, the Begum, and other notables. It was an important cosmopolitan event in Paris.

In Madrid Joaquín and I renewed our usual activities. On October 28th we were objects of a very moving tribute organized by the painter, Dina Cosson, President of Club 24, where we were named honorary members. First, we gave a concert in which Joaquín and I played his pieces for the piano. During the second part, Ana Higueras, accompanied by Miguel Zanetti, delighted us with several songs. The hall was crowded, and the audience overflowed into the street. The ovations were interminable!

Since that day we have had a close friendship with Dina and her husband, Pedro Cosson.

The next day we went to Málaga, where the street named "Joaquín Rodrigo" would be officially opened in a new district where all the streets bore the names of famous musicians.

That afternoon we attended the concert in the recently completed Conservatory, where the Oporto Symphony Orchestra played the *Concierto de Aranjuez*, conducted by Maestro Izquierdo. The soloist was José Tomás. The room was filled, and the audience warmly affectionate.

We dedicated Sunday to sight-seeing with our friends, Pedro and Mercedes Sánchez. We had lunch in a small restaurant on the waterfront, where they served us "pescaito" [small fish, fried whole and very crisp] and shell fish in abundance. We had a stupendous day!

That year we celebrated St. Cecilia's Day in fine style with a cocktail party. About fifty friends gathered to wish Joaquín happiness on his seventy-fifth birthday. There were many gifts and, as always, the fragrant bouquet of flowers from the Australian guitarists. And a reporter from the radio showed up to record some interviews.

We celebrated the feast of Christmas and New Year's Day completely alone. In spite of the intense cold and the unceasing rain, all our neighbors in the Amazonas building had gone on vacation. The streets were deserted and absolute silence reigned in our neighborhood. We spent our time resting!

We celebrated the Fiesta de Reyes [Feast of the Magi] with good friends, who, in spite of the formidable downpours of rain which had fallen on Madrid, came to share the traditional *roscón* [a sort of sweet cake, customary for Twelfth Night] with us.

It was at this time that I began to work seriously on my "Memories," which I had neglected due to lack of time.

Since 1942 I had jotted down something almost every day about the vicissitudes of our busy life and the most important events of the Madrid musical scene.

With Joaquín—a music critic for many years—I had attended all the symphony concerts, recitals, lectures with musical illustrations, concerts in the University Residences, in the Circulo Medina, the Atheneum, and the different Institutes, and also the recitals at the Institute of Hispanic Culture.

We saw almost all the performances of the Opera, and naturally, all of the artistic presentations at the University.

At home we often received notable musicians and artists: Argenta, Freitas Branco and his wife, the pianist Marie Antoinette Levêcque, Markewitch, Klecki, Toldrá, Unger. The pianists Cor de Groot, Lazare

Lévy, Gonzalo Soriano, Helena de Sá é Costa, Katchen and many others.

Others who came were Segovia, Yepes, Alirio Díaz, the Romeros, Ernesto Bitetti, Gaspar Cassadó, Nicanor Zabaleta, Rafael Frühbeck de Burgos. Great singers like Victoria de los Angeles, Montserrat Caballé, Pilar Lorengar, Lola Rodríguez Aragón, Isabel Penagos, Marimí del Pozo.

During that winter Joaquín composed two works. The first, *Sonata a la breve*, was a commission of the Ministry of Education, which wanted to publish a collection of works for the cello, as a tribute to Pablo Casals.

Soon after, he wrote the *Sonatina para dos muñecas* [*Sonatina for Two Dolls*], for four hands, dedicated to our granddaughters, Cecilita and Patty, who were not long in learning it. It is a work which delights them, and they play it beautifully.

Early in March we went with all the family to Sagunto, where Cecilita had been named "Junior Queen of the Fallas."

When they had completed the preparations for the fiesta, Joaquín and I took the first plane for Madrid, where we went directly to the "El Escuadrón" restaurant, invited, with several friends, by the writer Carmen Llorca. The lunch was delicious, and we enjoyed ourselves, but as we were leaving, Joaquín gave us a dreadful fright when he collapsed in a faint, probably from sheer exhaustion.

When he recovered consciousness, I took him home and immediately called the family doctor, who ordered him to bed for two days. Fortunately, it was nothing serious, and within the week he could resume his normal schedule.

Two days later we undertook a second journey to Sagunto, arriving in time to attend the parade of the *falleras*. Cecilita was radiant on her throne on an enormous float, tossing toys and candies to the onlookers, who applauded her enthusiastically.

The *cremá* took place on the night of the Feast of St. Joseph. In a short time, all the *fallas* were food for the flames, while the children amused themselves shooting firecrackers.

On May 10th Joaquín and I went to Rome, where we were met by the director of the Spanish Academy, Juan Antonio Morales, and his wife Elena. We stayed at the Academy, a true palace, where the young students led an enviable life.

Two days later Joaquín gave a lecture on "The theatrical music of Manuel de Falla," in the Spanish Institute of Language and Literature, which is directed by Manuel Sito Alba. Among those whom I remember at the lecture were Maribel de Falla and her husband, the ambassador to the Holy See, Sanz Briz, Ambassador Robles Piquer and the Mayor of Seville, who was in Rome at that time.

I was deeply moved to find my first cousin Mathilde there. She had lived in Rome since the World War, and she seemed so old, so worn. The happiness that she felt at our meeting was reflected in her face.

The following day auditions began for the "Fernando Sors" competition, with Joaquín a member of the jury. It went on for three days, and prizes were awarded to three contestants: Ligos, Matrona and Corona.

During the final days we enjoyed the company of Alirio Díaz and his wife Lina. We took long walks together, visiting St. Peter's and other churches. On the last evening we undertook the return journey under a torrential rain.

On the eleventh of June we gave a reception in our home for our American friend, Professor Walter Rubin, and his class from the University of Houston which had come to Spain on a study tour. I counted twenty students, young men and women. We also invited a few of our close friends, and to add to the party we asked the young harpist Ana Maria Martini to give us a concert. As ever, Joaquín's works were prominent in her program. The party went on until midnight.

On June 25th of this year I was awarded the Ribbon of Alfonso X, the Wise, an honor which filled me with pride and satisfaction, for it was proof that my work at Joaquín's side was recognized and appreciated.

To celebrate this event, the Board of UNICEF in Spain organized a banquet in the Madrid Casino. Presiding were H.R.H. the Infanta Margarita de Borbon, Duchess of Soria, and her husband Doctor Zurita, Duke of Soria. President Ernesto Garrido's speech was very moving, and afterwards, Joaquín told of our meeting in Paris, thanks to our mutual friend, Alexander Demetriad, and to Joaquín's composition, *Preludio al Gallo Mañanero*, which he called "the match-making cockerel." Finally, I read some lines recalling my meeting, many years before, with Maurice Pate, founder of UNICEF and great friend of children, who inspired me to join UNICEF.

* * *

At the end of September we made our second trip of the year to Italy, to attend the annual competition for the guitar in Alessandria, a small city of great charm, completely surrounded with woods and vineyards. That year the competition was a tribute to Joaquín.

The organizer, Michele Pittaluga, director of the Antonio Vivaldi Conservatory, is a dynamic and cheerful man, of broad education. He welcomed Joaquín and me most cordially, as well as the other members of the Jury: Robert J. Vidal, Alirio Díaz and José Tomás.

Ten young guitarists took part in the contest, but one, a Japanese named Yamashita, stood out immediately. He was 17 years old, but appeared to be no more than twelve. He was small and slender, but his supple fingers drew an amazing tone from the instrument. The works required were the *Fandango* and *Invocación y danza*, by Joaquín, and in the second test the contestants played fragments from the *Concierto de Aranjuez*. Naturally, it was Yamashita who took the honors, performing the entire *Concierto de Aranjuez* with orchestra in the closing concert, which took place in the Church of Santa María.

Back in Madrid, we were invited to dinner by Juan Garrigues Walker with the members of the new Spain-USSR Cultural Association. Joaquín was named an honorary member, as were other notables, almost all politicians. We were introduced to Dr. Jesús Caldas, Dr. Osorio and to three famous Russians: the cosmonaut Popovitch, the cardiologist Bukharin, Lenin prize winner, and the sociologist Grenkow. The cosmonaut kissed me on the cheeks several times. When someone told him that I was the wife of the composer Joaquín Rodrigo, he smiled and answered: "One has only to look at her to realize that he is a very fine person."

Chapter X

Premières and Tributes

On November 16th, 1977, Joaquín and I went to London as guests of the British Council, through the recommendation of the Director of the British Institute, George Sanderson. He and his wife were great fans of music and had become very fond of us.

The Birmingham Orchestra had programmed *Fantasía para un Gentilhombre*, with John Williams, and he had invited us to stay overnight in a hotel in London to be present at the concert, but thanks to Sanderson, the British Council gave us three days.

The concert took place in the Royal Festival Hall, with a full house. John Williams was sensational, and Louis Frémaux conducted the orchestra with much musicality.

In London I had the pleasure of meeting with my cousins Irene, Lottie and Gladys, whom I had not seen in many years.

The next day Michael Emmerson, manager of James Galway, "The Golden Flute," presented himself at our hotel to arrange the details concerning the concerto for flute and orchestra which he had commissioned from Joaquín. We came quickly to an agreement, and the première was scheduled for the following year.

We boarded the plane at 4:30, and by 5:00 we were in Brussels, where our children and the granddaughters awaited us at the airport. Nevertheless, I enjoyed very little of their company, for I was exhausted, and had to go to bed as soon as we arrived at the house. My rest was brief, for the next day Cecilia gave a large reception in our honor.

During that week two of Joaquín's important works had been performed in Brussels: the *Concierto Andaluz* for four guitars, by the Romeros, and the *Sonata Pimpante* for violin and piano, by Agustín and José Tordesillas. This last was played in the concert organized by the King and Queen of Spain in honor of the King and Queen of Belgium.

Everyone missed us, and Cecilia had to explain the reason for our absence.

We spent several days in Brussels, where I soon recovered. And then, regretfully, we undertook the return trip to Madrid.

* * *

The year 1978 began with sunny weather and pleasant visits.

In January we had a visit from Herbert Chappell, of the British Broadcasting Company, who wanted to make contact with us, for the following month James Galway was arriving to play the Mozart concerto with the orchestra of the RTVE, and Chappell wanted to take advantage of his stay to make a documentary on Joaquín's life and work, to be continued in Switzerland and in England with Galway. He returned a month later, accompanied by his assistant, Marjorie Russell, and the technicians from the BBC, who began to shoot the telefilm.

They worked at the house for three days, examining recordings, scores, pictures and photographs. Then Marjorie came to take us to Aranjuez. The weather was splendid, and they were able to film us in the park near the *Casita del Labrador* [*The Farmer's Cottage*], strolling, and then resting on a bench.

The next day Galway arrived. I was really shocked to see him come into the room in a wheelchair; he had been the victim of a serious traffic accident in Switzerland, and had fractured both legs. But he had overcome the crisis, and it didn't prevent his continuing his activities as concert artist and lecturer. He seemed very young, the typical Irishman, happy and jovial.

With his "golden flute," he played the part for the flute in Joaquín's concerto at first sight. What tone! What technique! What musicality! He left us amazed.

When he finished playing Galway remarked that he liked the work very much and that he was thinking of introducing it in the fall of that same year, that is, in 1978. Before leaving for London he sent Joaquín a bottle of a special whiskey, made in Ireland ten years earlier. A real nectar! That same week Joaquín completed the third movement of the *Concierto Pastoral*, still influenced by the strong impression of that meeting.

On the 19th of March we were in Houston, guests of our good friends Pilar and Walter Rubin.

Through a suggestion of Pilar's, Joaquín had composed his symphonic poem, "A la busca del más allá" ["In Search of the Beyond"], dedicated to the astronauts of NASA whom we had visited as guest of honor during the summer of 1970. We had struck up a friendship with Walt Cunningham, hero of Apollo 7, a most congenial man who played the guitar and knew the *Concierto de Aranjuez*. For that reason, one might say that it was the first work to reach the moon! He was very tall, and so slender that he seemed almost transparent. A real featherweight!

The work had been commissioned by the Houston Symphony Orchestra, conducted by Lawrence Foster, in commemoration of the Bicentennial of the United States. To illustrate it, Pilar had painted a lovely picture, full of symbolism.

During the two weeks that we spent in Houston we were the honorees on several occasions: first at the Institute for the Blind, the Lighthouse, and later at the University of Houston, where Joaquín gave a lecture on his works. The Mayor of Houston honored us with the key to the City.

The première took place in Jones Hall on March 27th, conducted by Ros Marbá. The program also included the *Alpine Symphony*, by Strauss, and Liszt's *Second Concerto*, with Rafael Orozco.

The next day the concert was repeated with the same success.

Pilar's painting, exhibited in the lobby of Jones Hall, was greatly admired. It was later acquired by NASA, and several reproductions were made. The first was taken to the White House, where President Carter personally received the Spanish painter. Finally, we received one of the reproductions, which occupies a place of honor in our house.

An urgent task awaited me in Madrid. After having finished the definitive correction of the *Concierto de Aranjuez*, I began to write, from Joaquín's dictation, the work for the clavichord which he had composed for Genevieve Galvez, with the title, *Preludio y Ritornello.* It did not take me long to finish it, and I sent it to the Max Eschig House in Paris, which published it soon after.

I don't want to omit the "Gala Dinner" organized by the Department of Tourism and the International Inn Keepers Association in the Hotel Meliá Palace. Those honored were, with Joaquín (as Outstanding Musician of the Year), Pilar López, Fernando Rey, Carlos Saura, the spectacular, "300 millions," which was seen every week on television, and a few others from the Innkeepers Association. The trophy was a golden bull on a block of white marble!

In June we spent a week in Brussels, which was enduring a heat wave, with very high temperatures, something unheard of in those latitudes.

On the first of June Joaquín was enrolled in the Royal Academy of Sciences, Letters and Fine Arts of Belgium, as a corresponding member, in the vacancy left by Benjamin Britten.

On the same day, the Academy invited us to a luncheon attended by the Spanish Ambassador, Aguirre de Cárcer, a great devotee of music. Joaquín's speech was entitled "Notes on Manuel de Falla," and the welcoming address was read by composer René Bernier.

The next day we were invited to a dinner in the Spanish Embassy, attended by a number of musicians, diplomats and newspapermen.

A day later the Festival of Dance took place in the House of Culture organized by Cecilia with her Academy. The pupils did very well, but Joaquín and I were most admiring of Cecilita in *Clave de sol* and of Patty, who performed as a "little bird." They were both very graceful.

Back in Madrid we were invited to a reception at the Palace of Aranjuez given by President Giscard d'Estaing for the King and Queen of Spain. It was a brilliant affair, attended by ministers of state, military officers of high rank, famous artists and writers. We were able to greet the King and Queen, who were pleasant, as always.

Joaquín and I left the Palace at midnight and walked toward the park, where a large crowd of the people of Aranjuez had gathered. Suddenly, they began to applaud. Joaquín, surprised, asked me,

"What's happening? Are their Majesties here?"

I couldn't help laughing as I answered him, "The only guests in this place are the two of us. The applause is for *you*!"

During the summer of 1978 we spent two very enjoyable weeks in the chalet of Vicente Vayá and his wife, in El Perechil, a small planned community about seven miles from Sagunto. There were pine groves everywhere, silence and clear fresh air. Vicente had just published his biography of Joaquín, which he had worked on tirelessly to finish.

We ended the vacation in our own house at San Ramón, and by the last week of September we were once again in Madrid.

The première of the *Concierto Pastorale* was set for October 16th, in London. And off we went for the second time that year.

Joaquín and I were present at both of the rehearsals with James Galway and the orchestra. The Mexican conductor, Eduardo Mata, managed the work to the composer's complete approval. As for the flautist, it was hard to know what to admire most: his velvet tones, his musicality or his technique!

On the day before the première, we were invited to a concert at Wimbledon, where Galway performed *Fantasía para un Gentilhombre* in the version for flute and orchestra, with resounding success.

On the night of the première, the Royal Festival Hall was crowded. Galway was fantastic, and the orchestra sounded first-rate. The audience applauded with enthusiasm, and at the end Joaquín had to go up on the stage on Galway's arm.

With James Galway, rehearsing before the World Première of the *Concierto Pastoral*, London, 1977.

From London we went directly to Paris, for Joaquín had been named a member of the jury in the Twentieth Competition for guitar, organized by the ORTF, which continued for a week.

Also on the jury were our friends, Isao Takahashi, Michele Pittaluga, Robert J. Vidal and Alexandre Tansman. It was a good competition and, as always, we spent several very pleasant days with them.

We had a very rainy autumn in Madrid and, therefore, I left the house as little as possible. However, I wanted to go with Joaquín to Prado del Rey, where he taped an interview for television, playing his *Berceuse de Primavera* [*Lullaby of Spring*] at the end for a group of youngsters gathered there, who waited for him at the exit to applaud him with enthusiasm. This is the greatest stimulus an artist can have, for it comes from the heart, and it touches the heart!

Winter came, and encouraged by our friends, the Farrells, we decided to spend Christmas in Marbella, where we made a reservation at the Marbella Club.

During the two weeks that we were there, we spent much time with Ilonka, who showed us all the sights of interest at this deluxe beach, frequented by millionaires from Europe, Asia and America During that year the petro-dollars had not yet erupted in that oasis.

On New Year's Eve the Farrells invited us to their house, where we were served a succulent civet of Irish hare, bagged by our host.

The year 1979 began auspiciously. Newsman Millán Clemente de Diego telephoned Joaquín to tell him that on January 15th he would receive the F of the "Famous" at a cocktail party given by the "Tertulia" in the Hotel Atlanta.

This was an award made by a group of outstanding newsmen, artists and writers.

It was a very nice event. Joaquín was introduced by Clemente de Diego, and later, Matías Prats and David Cubedo spoke very affectionately of both of us. Luciana Wolf sang *De los álamos vengo* [*I come from the poplars*], and finally, a "vino de honor" was served.

We spent the last week of March in London, invited by Herbert Chappell to attend the press preview of the film about Joaquín and James Galway which he had made the previous year.

This took place in the Picadilly Club, and the room was crowded with reporters. The film lasted precisely fifty-nine and one-half minutes, and was a big hit.

On Easter Sunday it was broadcast on television throughout the United Kingdom, and was later shown in Australia and America.

We took advantage of those days to do a little sightseeing with my cousins. On the morning when we visited the famous Tower of London, the rain fell in torrents and a freezing wind was blowing hard enough to take one's breath away. Nonetheless, all went smoothly, and on the following day we returned to Madrid, very pleased with our trip to London, the third within a year.

In late April our friend and "matchmaker," Alexander Demetriad, arrived from Bucharest. We had not seen him since the Paris days, when we were fellow students of Lazare Lévy and Paul Dukas. At the airport, it was he who first recognized us. He had probably changed more than we, perhaps because of the tragic circumstances of which he had been victim. What he needed most was warmth and affection, and he was deeply moved that his old friends had not forgotten him.

The three weeks that he spent with us were very busy, with excursions to Toledo, El Escorial, the Valley of the Fallen and Segovia. We took him to the Prado Museum and to the Rose Garden in Retiro Park.

Finally, we gave a reception in his honor, to which we invited a number of artists and writers, among them Carmen Llorca and Gregorio Prieto, Lucero Tena, Pilar Primo de Rivera, the Princess Ghika, the

Marqués and Marquesa Prat de Nantouillet, George Sanderson and his wife, Ilonka Farrell and several others.

Alexander was inspired in his rendering of works of Chopin and Brahms.

For me it was a great satisfaction to be able to listen to him after so many years. For a few minutes I imagined that I was back in my parents' house on the rue de Passy, when I was a young pianist full of dreams, and that he was playing for me.

It was a miracle that we had been able to meet again after so many vicissitudes.

A few days later Alexander left for Paris, leaving a great void. He promised us another visit, as soon as possible and, two years later, he kept his promise.

It was about that time when we struck up a friendship with the cultural attaché of the Mexican Embassy, José Fuentes Mares, and his wife Emma. A writer of great talent, he gave us his book, *La nueva guía de los descarriados* [*The New Guide for the Misguided*], a parody on Maimónides. It was a well-documented and very amusing work, which we read with real delight. Later he sent us his *Biography of Hernán Cortés*, which was very successful.

In mid-June we had a visit from Stanley Sokolowsky, accompanied by his son Michael, who had been director of "The Voice of America" in Washington. There he had met Marita, the daughter of one of my cousins, whom he married soon after.

The two days that they spent with us were devoted to sightseeing. I showed them old Madrid, the Rose Garden in the Retiro Park and Toledo. We went with Joaquín to Aranjuez, where we visited the Palace, the Farmer's Cottage and the Costume Museum, which I had not seen before. The collection of fans amazed us.

We made a long walk through the park where the magnolias were in full bloom.

A group of Japanese tourists was walking toward us, and one of them, catching sight of Joaquín, exclaimed, "Look, there's the one who was such a hit in Japan!"

Every one of them seized his camera, and they asked Joaquín for autographs. Stanley was dumbfounded.

"I knew you were famous in your own country, but I had no idea that you were that well-known halfway around the world!"

On the same day that Stanley and Michael left, Alfredo and Ignacio Amestoy came to see me, to tell me that they were planning a television program about Joaquín.

According to their description, it would somewhat resemble the one which Federico Gallo had produced a number of years before, titled "This is his life."

This program was inspired by Vicente Vayá's biography of Joaquín, and they called it "The real Joaquín Rodrigo." And they wanted more details. They wanted to gather a number of people with whom we had contacts, and of course, our family, including the children and granddaughters from Brussels. And all this had to be kept in absolute secrecy. The recording of the program was set for July 22nd, and very little time remained.

Two days before the date we went to the Club 24, where Dina Cosson had organized a dinner as a tribute to "Five Great Figures of Spanish Music": Andrés Segovia, Moreno Torroba, Ernesto Halffter, Regino Sáinz de la Maza and Joaquín Rodrigo. Dina said a few very touching words, and there were some speeches. An atmosphere of cordiality and affection reigned in the room. At the close, we saw the opening of the exhibition by the photographer, Juan Gyenes. They were truly artistic creations; one, for instance, was a composition of a fragment of a Beethoven score, arranged with his sources of inspiration.

I think that the initiative shown by Dina merits praise, and that this beautiful example, coming from one who is herself an artist, should be imitated by those who only go to concerts and attend openings of art exhibitions, but who show no interest in direct contact with the creators.

Finally, the great day arrived for the recording of Amestoy's program. Joaquín was in fine spirits. The new dress designed by my Basque modiste made its debut and won me many compliments.

Amestoy was the Master of Ceremonies, and participants were: Vicente Vayá as biographer, the critic Andrés Ruiz Tarrazona and the composer García Abril, as well as Maestro Odón Alonso and García Asensio. Then came the surprises as, one after another, friends and relatives paraded across the stage: Joaquín's older sister Isabel, torero Paco Alcalde, our friends Alfredo Ríos and Domitilio, the faithful factotum of the ONCE (National Organization for the Blind in Spain, so-called from its initials in Spanish); Lucero Tena, Regino Sáinz de la Maza, Dr. Castroviejo and Dr. Takahashi, brought from Japan expressly for the occasion.

But the great sensation was made by our children and the granddaughters, Cecilita and Patty, who performed a piece for four hands before throwing themselves into the arms of their happy grandparents.

This program was broadcast all over Spain and was as big a hit as the earlier program dedicated to Montserrat Caballé had been.

We were the "couple of the hour!" And Joaquín and I were the ones most surprised by this popularity. Wherever we went we heard, "There goes Maestro Rodrigo!"

I was much amused by a group of workers unloading sacks at the door of the restaurant where we had just had dinner with some friends. They stood watching us for a few minutes, and then one of them nudged his companion, saying,

"Yes, it *is* Maestro Rodrigo!" At which point they all stood up straight to give us a proper salute.

The same sort of thing happened in San Ramón, where drivers would stop their cars to offer us a ride, and a few weeks later, in Sagunto, where men, women and children would come up to us in the street to shake hands and tell us the the *Concierto de Aranjuez* was their favorite work.

A few days after the completion of our chalet in San Ramón, we had an unexpected visit from Karl Musil, the principal dancer and choreographer of the Vienna Opera, accompanied by his wife, Irina Boronova, famous ballerina of Buenos Aires' *Teatro Colon*.

They had driven from Vienna, after having spent some time in Toledo, and the object of their visit was to ask Joaquín to compose the music for a ballet based on Musil's plot, *The Jewess of Toledo*, with himself as protagonist.

Joaquín was intrigued by the project, and promised to get to work on it as soon as he received more details.

A lengthy correspondence was established between us, which was interrupted by a tragic event during the summer of 1981. The Musil family, just after opening their summer home in the suburbs of Vienna, suffered a horrifying accident, when an airplane flying overhead burst into flames and plunged into their house, setting it on fire.

Karl, Irina and their two children barely had time to get out of the house. They escaped through the flames, but suffered severe burns. They were all rushed to the hospital, where the two children were treated and released within a few days, but Karl and Irina took quite a while to recover. As Karl said to a reporter who interviewed him, "It's a miracle that we are alive!"

Nevertheless, he gave up his career as a dancer to devote himself exclusively to teaching.

During the New Year's Day concert, the ballet of the Vienna Opera was bereft, for Karl could not appear as he had in previous years. But we will always remember this enchanting couple and the visit they paid us on that lovely summer day.

The French Festival

Some months earlier, Joaquín had received a letter from Pierre Petit, a French composer and director of the Paris Ecole Normale de Musique, proposing that Joaquín compose a piece for solo guitar. It would be introduced within the framework of the "French Festival of Music" celebrated at the castle of La Rougerie, the property of Joelle Bellon. This was apparently a genuine sponsorship, for she was underwriting all the expenses, including inviting us to the première. The artist who would introduce Joaquín's work was none other than Alexander Lagoya, widower of Ida Presti.

When Joelle Bellon asked Lagoya which composer he would prefer for the new work, he designated Joaquín without hesitation. Joaquín composed the *Triptic: Prelude, Nocturne* and *Scherzino*, a moving and very personal work.

We left on July 30th for Bordeaux, where we were met by a private car which took us to the "castle." A young secretary was our escort from there to the Hotel du Centenaire in "Les Eyzies," in the Dordogne. This is a region famous for its prehistoric caves, which attract many tourists, especially during the summer months.

Our hotel was located in the country, and the view from the balcony encompassed green fields and shady woodlands of ancient walnut trees.

On the following day we were received in the "castle" by our hostess, a lovely woman of forty, tall, slender and very elegant.

She welcomed us very cordially and introduced us to Pierre Petit and to the orchestra conductor, Pol Mule, as well as to the new Madame Lagoya.

The concert, attended by more than a thousand people, took place on the night of July 21st. The audience was very elegant, the ladies displaying models of Parisian "haute couture," with jewels by Cartier and other jewelers of the Rue de la Paix, and the men in dinner jackets.

As for Joelle, she looked like a fairy princess, with her turquoise gown, fabulous jewels and an artistic coiffure which emphasized her beauty.

The program was not long. Lagoya played the two concertos of Vivaldi, under the conduction of Pol Mule, and afterward introduced Joaquín's *Triptic*, which had a warm reception. To conclude, the orchestra played the *Divertimento* by Bela Bartok.

After the concert, a midnight supper was served in the park. The menu was worthy of Perigord, a region famous for its gastronomy: canteloupe melon with ham, poussins with a salad of truffles—a specialty of the region—, pastries, Bordeaux wines and a special champagne. A fantastic display of fireworks put the final touch to this brilliant Festival of Music.

* * *

One autumn afternoon, Joaquín and I were invited to the home of the new Ambassador of the Soviet Union, Yuri Dubinin, where we met Dr. Jesús Caldas, Juan Garrigues Walker, Professor Vinogradov from the University of Moscow and two or three other guests. Madame Dubinin, a very attractive woman, welcomed us cordially.

At this gathering we learned of the proposal for the creation of a Spanish-Russian Association, to promote a cultural interchange between the two countries through concerts, lectures, exhibits, films, ballets....These would be the vehicles which would bring us closer to this great country of which we knew so little.

However, Joaquín's music had already made its appearance in the U.S.S.R. The *Concierto de Aranjuez* was as popular there as in other countries, and his other works were also performed. Ada Tougay, the eminent harpist with whom we maintained an assiduous correspondence, played all of his pieces for the harp. And M. Waisbord, a renowned musicologist, had published an album which included several of his works, and was planning to organize a Rodrigo Festival in Moscow, with our assistance.

I want to mention my participation in the annual Flag Day, a benefit for the Red Cross. It was my good friend Elena Carnicero, who was devoted heart and soul to this charitable organization, who named me chairman of a "table," in Serrano Street.

Even though the nomination was a great honor for me, I didn't accept at first. But at her insistence, I got to work and managed to gather together a few friends of good will to help me in the task.

The great day fell on November 7th, and we enjoyed sunny weather, almost like spring. All our friends responded to our invitation and came personally to make their contributions. The youngsters came, too—boys and girls—emptying their savings banks full of coins and bills.

The result was excellent, and when I went home, after having spent many hours at the table, I was not at all tired. Neither, they assured me, were my co-workers. It was a happy day.

Journey to Mallorca

In late November, 1979, we left for Mallorca to attend the "Second International Andrés Segovia Competition for the Guitar," for which Joaquín had been named President of the jury.

We were met at the airport by Padre Bernardo Juliá, director of the Conservatory of Music and of the Capella Clásica, which was founded by that other excellent musician, Padre Thomas, and by Gabriel Barceló, of the Savings Bank.

The concert of the finalists, in the large auditorium, was crowded; the first prize was awarded to the Belgian, Storms, the second to Grandona, an Italian, and the third to the Argentinean, Pellegrini.

This year we didn't celebrate St. Cecilia's day as usual. Instead, we flew to Valencia, invited by the Primitive Band of Liria, which had won a great many prizes in musical competitions. On November 22nd, we attended a banquet honoring St. Cecilia with the Valencian musicians.

On the following day we went to the Conservatory of Music, where the one hundredth anniversary of its creation was celebrated with great pomp. Joaquín's task was to unveil the commemorative plaque.

We also attended the concert at the Principal Theater, where the Liria Band played, and diplomas were distributed to the students of the Conservatory.

Later, our friends Vayá and Adam, with their respective wives, accompanied us to Liria, a picturesque town with a great musical tradition. The Band gave another concert there, for which Joaquín delivered a commentary and played some of his own works for piano.

A few days later, I was called to a meeting at the headquarters of UNICEF, on Mauricio Legendre Street, because of the symphonic-choral competition being organized through the efforts of the president, Ernesto Garrido Jiménez.

The works presented were to have a connection with childhood, and were dedicated to the children of the world.

I was named a member of the Jury—as a director of UNICEF—along with well-known musicians: Ernesto Halffter, president, and Xavier Montsalvatge, Antonio García Abril, Antonio Ros Marbá, Tomás Marco y Román.

The prize was substantial: 500,000 pesetas. However, only seven works had been presented, three of which were retained, all of first rank. With one exception, works of tonal line were eliminated from further consideration.

There were two sessions, and after lengthy discussions the first prize was awarded to *New Moon*, based on a text from Rabindranath Tagore. The work titled *Universal Child* took second prize, which was offered by UNICEF.

After the decision there was a banquet, presided over by the Infanta Margarita, Duchess of Soria, accompanied by her husband, Dr. Zurita, in La Taberna restaurant. the press was well-represented, and several academics attended: Andrés Segovia, Ernesto Halffter and Joaquín, as well as the conductor of the orchestra, the Duke of Alba and the Duchess Cayetana.

The envelopes were opened and it was announced that the winner of the first prize was the young composer Lladó, fellow of the Spanish Academy of Rome. The second prize went to the Valencian composer Amando Blanquer.

Joaquín and I spent the holidays of Christmas and New Year's Day together and alone.

One day we invited three academic friends for lunch: Ernesto Halffter, Federico Sopeña and Regino Sáinz de la Maza. How many years had passed since Regino had played for the first time—and with such apprehension—the *Concierto de Aranjuez*, which is now conspicuous in the repertoire of every guitarist in the world!

* * *

At the end of February, 1980, we made another trip to Valencia, invited by the Committee of the Falla del Pilar, and this time our friend Ilonka Farrell went with us.

They had organized a concert in the Principal Theater as a tribute to Joaquín. The program included the *Concierto de Aranjuez*, with Narciso Yepes, the *Concierto de Estío*, with León Ara, and the symphonic poem, *Per la Flor del Lliri Blau*. The orchestra, conducted by Bernardo Adam, played very well, and the soloists were of the same stature.

During the intermission, Joaquín and I had to go up on the stage, where forty *falleras* had been placed, with the chief *fallera* at the head. What an attractive, colorful spectacle it was, and typically Valencian!

The presiding officer, Vicente Giner, introduced us to the audience with words filled with affection and admiration. Everyone sang the Valencian anthem, and at the end we were presented with an artistic Lladró porcelain and a silver tray, sent by the City Council of Sagunto. All the ladies had been given bouquets of violets and camellias, so that the room had the gay appearance of a spring garden.

Several days after our return to Madrid we received a number of telephone calls from friends who wanted to congratulate Joaquín on receiving the Gold Medal of Fine Arts. The news had been broadcast on radio and had appeared in the press, but we had not been informed. However, the telegram from the Ministry of Culture soon arrived. Guitarist Narciso Yepes and composer Federico Mompou had also been honored. The recently appointed Minister of Culture, Ricardo de la Cierva, had remembered music.

On February 15th we were invited to the commemoration of the 22nd anniversary of the Red Cross campaign for blood donors. This was attended by the Duchess of Alba, as president, the Princess of Bavaria, Elena Carnicero, Dr. Vallejo Nájera and a number of physicians. There were several speeches, and Joaquín was honored with a commemorative plaque, in recognition of his work for the Red Cross.

That same day the radio brought us news which moved all of Spain: Félix Rodríguez de la Fuente had just died in an airplane accident, in Alaska. He was the great friend of wild animals, and he had succeeded in spreading his love for them even to people who had spent their lives removed from nature.

He was cast in the same mold as St. Francis of Assisi, the "poor little one" whose *Little Flowers* is one of the most inspired and moving works of world literature.

Rodríguez de la Fuente had presented to us on the television screen a multitude of wide creatures: birds, foxes, squirrels, bears and horses in their natural environments. Even the "fierce wolf" had found favor with us, thanks to him.

This great-hearted man was also a friend of children, and more than once had collaborated in special events for the benefit of UNICEF.

* * *

On April 8th, in intensely cold weather, Joaquín and I went to Chamartín Station to pick up my sister Mathilde, who was arriving from Paris, accompanied by her son Raphael. I had a presentiment of what was to come when I saw her being helped down from the Pullman coach in a wheelchair. Her lovely face was ashen, and her great dark eyes were expressionless, vacant.

We took her to a nursing home recommended by a friend—the only place that would admit her, for she could do nothing for herself. She stayed in that inhospitable place for a few days, where the atmosphere was most depressing.

When I went to see her—as I did three or four times a week—she greeted me with tears in her eyes, and we would weep together, for I saw no solution to this urgent problem. She was too sick to be cared for in our house, and it was not easy to get her into a hospital in Madrid in her extreme condition.

By pure luck we came in contact with Dr. Félix Berdugo, chief of the section of traumatology in a Madrid hospital. Besides being an excellent physician, he was a very humane person, and he treated her with affectionate care. At the same time, I had been able to rent a room in the home of a trustworthy person, and I hired a nurse to care for her. Everything possible was done to cure her, but unfortunately she had arrived too late.

On April 14th the cellist Julian Lloyd Webber arrived from London. He wanted to meet Joaquín, with the objective of commissioning a concerto for his instrument.

When he came to the house I was amazed to see a tall, athletic young man, with chestnut hair and blue eyes. He had brought his cello to play some pieces for us.

We played a few of Joaquín's records for him, and his preference was the *Concierto Andaluz*.

We spent a very pleasant evening with him and a few friends, invited in his honor, and Joaquín promised to write him a concerto within a year. Julian returned to London the next day, entertaining high hopes for the promised work.

May was a very busy month. On the 8th we attended a reception in honor of Poul Hartling, High Commissioner for Refugees in the United Nations, and there I had the pleasure of greeting my nephew Loni Davico, Chief of Public Relations for that organization.

May 16th was the date for the "Tribute to the Rodrigos," which was organized by Elena Calero and took place in the Círculo Medina.

The spacious hall was full of people, and the Minister of Culture was represented by his sister, Blanca de la Cierva, and their mother. The program of our concert was not long. Joaquín played three of his works, and afterward I played pieces by Chopin, Schumann and Rodrigo. We finished with the *Gran Marcha de los Subsecretarios*.

After the concert cocktails were served—a tradition in the Círculo Medina—and Elena presented us with a beautiful album with the signatures of all those who were present.

On May 29th the presentation of the Gold Medals of Fine Arts took place in the Ceremonial Hall of the Prado Museum. The King and

Queen attended, along with the Minister of Culture, Ricardo de la Cierva, and other notables.

Joaquín was chosen as spokesman to express the thanks of the musicians who were medalists: Federico Mompou, who came for the occasion from Barcelona with his wife, Carmen, and Narciso Yepes, who had delegated his wife, Marisa, because he was in Tokyo.

After the ceremony we greeted the King and Queen, who were pleasant and affable, as always.

On the same day there was a grand reception in the Palace of the Zarzuela, attended by the most prominent artists of Spain: musicians, painters, sculptors, actors, architects, newsmen, etc., etc.

During those days my great concern was for my sister. Under Dr. Berdugo's treatment her health had improved visibly. What cheered her most were her conversations with him and with the friends who came to visit her. But her legs remained paralyzed; she could not take a step. Nevertheless, one could see hope in her eyes.

July came and, after the activity of the year, Joaquín and I needed a few weeks of rest. Encouraged by Dr. Berdugo, who had promised to look after Mathilde, we left for Cullera on July 1st. From that time, we enjoyed a warm friendship with him, and with his charming wife, Delia.

On July 5th we were in Vall d'Uxo, a village of the province of Castellón, to attend a concert-tribute in honor of Joaquín. Our friends, the Vayás, accompanied us.

Vall d'Uxo is famous for its subterranean river, which flows through pre-historic caves, where the stalactites take fantastic shapes which are truly impressive.

First, there was a cocktail party for guests at the City Hall. From there the Mayor, Sr. Zaragoza and his wife, accompanied us to the street in a new neighborhood which would bear the name "Joaquín Rodrigo." We were preceded by a band of musicians, who were playing to the accompaniment of noisy rocket fireworks, launched in our honor.

The concert began at nine-thirty. There were three bands and an audience of six thousand. In the program was, among other works, the *Concierto de Aranjuez*, and a folkloric ballet was the opening number of the celebration, which closed with an informal speech by the eloquent master of ceremonies, Sr. Pérez, and moving responses by the Mayor and Joaquín.

We returned to Cullera, but we were not able to enjoy many days on the beach, for on July 12th we received an urgent telegram calling us to return at once to my sister. We left immediately, but by the time we arrived in Madrid, just before midnight, she had died.

Dr. Berdugo had transferred her to the hospital at the first symptoms of crisis, but despite his efforts, could not save her. Her last words were, "And Victoria, where is she?"

Mercifully, Félix had told her, "She's here, beside you."

This was her final comfort.

Sadly, we returned to San Ramón to finish our vacation, with a further brief interruption at the end of August.

* * *

In the spring of 1980, the Mayor of Benicasim, Domingo Tárrega, a jovial, dynamic man and a great devotee of music, had come to our home to offer Joaquín the presidency of the Tribune of the "Tárrega Competition for Guitar," which was held annually in Benicasim. Furthermore, he invited us to spend a week at that Mediterranean beach.

On August 23rd we took the plane for Valencia, where the Mayor came to pick us up himself.

It was what is called "a good competition," in which as almost always, the Japanese guitarists stood out. The winner that year was Otani.

Members of the Jury, besides Joaquín, were; Robert J. Vidal, of France, Michele Pittaluga, of Italy, Gordon Cressky, of Great Britain, Leopoldo Querol and Manuel Cubedo, of Spain.

The weather was fine, and we spent long hours on the beach, acquiring a tan, or in the Hotel park, always in stimulating company.

We finished our vacation in San Ramón, and by mid-September were again in Madrid, where Joaquín dedicated himself exclusively to the composition of the cello concerto for which Julian Lloyd Webber kept calling impatiently. He had interested the conductor López Cobos, and its première had been set for April, 1982, with the London Philharmonic.

The television "Weekend Show" had sent Alan Benson to exchange comments and impressions with us regarding the film which they wanted to screen with author and cellist to promote the new concerto.

I was very busy with our house in San Ramón. I was making innumerable trips to complete the task of putting it in order and making it more comfortable.

It was about that time that Lola Rodríguez Aragón, Director of the Advanced School of Song, was honored at an event attended by Queen Sofía, Subsecretary Antonio Lago Carballo, representing the Ministry of Education, and other notables. The entire faculty was there, as well as students and friends of the honoree. She was retiring, after having played a primary role in the postwar musical world of Spain, as performer and teacher.

Her School produced many renowned singers; the most famous was probably Teresa Berganza. Lola was godmother of our daughter Cecilia, for whom she felt a deep affection, which was fully reciprocated.

Toward the end of November we had the pleasant surprise of seeing Enrique Figueroa appear on our doorstep in one of his quick visits. He had brought Joaquín a commemorative medal from Mexico, and he took many photographs for publication in the newspapers.

But Joaquín was depressed and gloomy, and nothing could distract him. His creative work had stagnated during the last months. This depression was perhaps due to the hair-raising news coming from abroad as well as from Spain. Italy had been devastated by an earthquake which created thousands of victims, leaving many people without shelter. Many of the survivors were forced to live in makeshift camps, during rain and snow.

Meanwhile, Julian continued to send insistent letters from London.

He assured us that if he could receive at least the first movement of the cello concerto, he would be satisfied, for he could begin to study it. However, Inspiration failed to respond to Joaquín's call.

We heard very few concerts during December. The most interesting was the one in the Soviet Embassy, which featured an excellent singer from Radio Moscow, and the pianist, Vladimir Plotniov, who displayed a dazzling technique in the Sonatas of Scarlatti. The violinist featured on the same program did not appear, because shortly before the concert his violin and his suitcase were stolen from the hotel where he was staying. We never learned whether he recovered them or not.

I visited several exhibits of painting and sculpture with Ilonka, and together we attended the opening of the exhibit of "Heads" in the studio of Pablo Serrano by the American sculptor, James Knowles, whose work I had admired at the March Foundation.

I thought that the head which Knowles made of Joaquín was very well done, for he had managed to capture the expression typical of his moments of inspiration. He promised to make us a gift of a replica in bronze, which we would receive as soon as it was finished. Two years later his promise was fulfilled.

On December 17th we attended the concert-tribute in honor of Victoria de los Angeles, which took place in the *Teatro Real* with the collaboration of the Chamber Orchestra, Andrés Segovia and Luis Galve.

It was a moving occasion for us, after so many years to hear this great artist, with whom we had a long and deep-felt friendship. Joaquín and I had attended her debut in the Cultural Society of Madrid when she was twenty. Now her name appeared among the most prestigious of Spanish music.

We celebrated Christmas Eve that year in the home of Julia and Ramón Esnaola, with their family. Julia had been an able pupil of Professor Lalewicz, and he had put us in contact when she moved to Madrid, where she married soon after. Since then we had had a close friendship with this charming couple, made closer by our mutual love of music.

That night Julia and I revived the *Sonatina para dos Muñecas* [*Sonatina for Two Dolls*] for four hands, which Joaquín had dedicated long ago to Cecilita and Patty, managing to give it a youthful and "Christmasy" air.

Later we went over the new digital recordings of *Concierto de Aranjuez* and *Fantasía para un Gentilhombre*, recorded by the Mexican conductor, Enrique Bátiz.

On the other hand, there was no gaiety on New Year's Eve. Joaquín and I spent it alone, just the two of us, in our apartment in Madrid, longing for the company of our children and grandchildren, who were still living in Belgium.

* * *

Early in 1981 Father Merino, an erudite and pleasant Franciscan priest, paid us a visit, accompanied by the famous aviator Juan Ignacio Pombo, who was then retired. The purpose of their visit, they told us, concerned the celebration, during the autumn of 1982, of the 800th anniversary of the birth of St. Francis of Assisi, founder of the Franciscan order. For this occasion they hoped to commission from Joaquín an Oratorio composed on a poem written by the Saint. They quickly received his consent, for Joaquín, as well as I, had a predilection for the "poor little one," friend of the beasts of the forest and the birds of the fields.

Joaquín was enthusiastic about the poem selected by Father Merino from the *Little Flowers*, and a few months later the Oratorio entrusted to him was completed, under the title *Cántico de San Francisco de Asís*.

On February tenth the Soviet Embassy organized a grand party in the Centro Cultural de la Villa. There was a concert, and singers, guitarists and dancers took part in the entertainment.

Joaquín played only one selection, *A l'Ombre de Torre Bermeja*, and he was warmly applauded.

There were many speeches. The first speaker was our friend, Dr. Caldas, followed by the Ambassador Yuri Dubinin and others. It was interesting, and I wasn't bored.

On March third, Joaquín and I were in Valladolid with Elena Calero, for "The Biennial of Sound," organized by Father Verdú. The concert, dedicated to Joaquín's works, took place in the Borja Hall, full of music lovers, who enthusiastically applauded Ana Higueras and Félix Lavilla, interpreters of his songs, and the composer, who played several pieces. Need I say that we closed the program with the *Gran Marcha de los Subsecretarios*?

When we asked the concierge at the hotel what he could recommend as the most typical thing to take home, he replied, "Bread."

We thought he was joking, but he was quite serious. It just so happens that the white bread from that city is the best bread that we have tasted in all of Spain, so we took home a generous sample, accompanied by an excellent wine, the gift of kindly Father Verdú.

On March 8th we went to a concert at the *Teatro Real* [*The Royal Theater*] to hear—one more time—the *Concierto de Aranjuez*, with Diego Blanco, winner of the Queen Sofía prize, who was generously applauded by the audience.

A good while after the guitarist had left the stage, there was an outburst of applause. Joaquín had been noticed in an orchestra box and was the object of a warm demonstration of affection and admiration.

Chapter XI

The Mexican Adventure

Some time earlier Joaquín had entrusted to our good friend, cellist Carlos Prieto, a composition to be presented for the first time at the Mexican Rodrigo Festival, on March 17, 1981. As a tribute to the Prieto family, who were originally from Asturias, it had been inspired by an Asturian song and was entitled *Como una Fantasía* [*Like a Fantasy*].

We had been invited to spend a few days in this interesting country, which we had visited in 1974 with our loyal friend, Enrique Figueroa, who would again be our companion on this second trip.

We left Madrid on March 10th. It was wonderful to see the faces of many friends at the airport in Mexico City. Among those awaiting our arrival were Isabel and Carlos Prieto, María Victoria Marfany and a number of reporters. We were driven directly to the Hotel María Isabel, where we lost no time in going to sleep after the long flight. The next morning we awoke feeling like new, which was fortunate, as Enrique had planned a crowded itinerary for the entire week.

On the first day we visited the Braille Library of the International Committee for the Blind and were shown all their displays. After the tour, they offered us a "vino de honor," and the pleasant director presented Joaquín with a diploma as a memento.

On Wednesday the president of the Mexican Chapter of UNICEF, María Teresa de Torre de Mar, came to see me. She was an extremely attractive and intelligent woman, accompanied by three of her volunteers, young cultured women, deeply involved and interested in this charitable work. After that we had a visit from the delegate of the Mexican Organization for the Blind, Señora de la Torre, and some reporters.

Friday the thirteenth was a very busy day. The Pedro Domecq Institute of Culture gave a dinner in our honor in the restaurant "San Angel Inn." Beside me at table I had Pedro Domecq himself. A man of the world, courteous and a great conversationalist, he enjoyed enormous popularity in Mexico, where his wineries are as famous as in Spain. We met his wife, an attractive and elegant American, and we found among the guests Antonio Ariza, President of Casa Domecq, Antonio Armendáriz, witty writer and ex-Ambassador, Gustavo de la Serna and his wife, and composer Blas Galindo. Of course, our close friends, the Prieto family, were also there, and our daughter Cecilia had just arrived from Brussels, so that our happiness was complete.

After the banquet Figueroa drove us to Los Pinos, the residence of the President, López Portillo, who received us with great cordiality.

The conversation dwelled on music, and especially on the *Concierto de Aranjuez*, as popular in Mexico as in Spain.

The weather was fine, and everywhere we saw magnificent flowering trees. Nonetheless, I missed the singing birds which flutter around the parks of Europe in that season. Perhaps they have no great desire to live in a capital of fifteen million inhabitants.

On Saturday we made an excursion to Taxco, the city famous for its silver mines, which we visited at length.

From there we went to the lovely country place of Antonio Castillo, the music-loving silversmith, where we were served a typical luncheon. After lunch, Joaquín was presented with an artistic silver plaque, and at the same time was named favorite son of Taxco, where a street would bear his name. And I asked myself: how many streets are already named for my husband? I had counted seven in Spain, plus the "Plaza de Joaquín Rodrigo" in Buenos Aires!

That night the writer Edelmira Zúñiga and her husband Florencio Gregori came to pick us up at the hotel to drive us to the "El Parador" restaurant. There, in the "Salón Aranjuez," a gala dinner was served on the occasion of the presentation of diplomas to the award-winning artists, writers and actors of 1980.

We found a great many old friends there, among them Angeles Calcaño, of the Manuel Ponce Institute, who always visits us when she comes to Spain.

On Sunday we went with Enrique to see the "lanchas," in my opinion the prettiest sight in the city, where the picturesque appears everywhere. These boats, which have a characteristic coloring, remind me of the Venetian gondolas. But while those that remain in Venice seem rather sad these I speak of are full of euphoria and happiness.

During the afternoon, Manuel López Ramos, the guitarist we had met during our trip to Buenos Aires in 1949, came to visit us, accompanied by his pleasant wife, Corita, and three of their six children, among them Joaquín's godson, a bright, handsome lad.

On Monday morning we were on State Television, where James Fordson had engaged us for an interview of at least two hours. I suppose that is the longest interview we will ever make! Nevertheless, affable Fordson would have prolonged it, but we were exhausted. Anyway, the program, which included the *Concierto de Aranjuez*, was a success.

Later, Corazón Otero, the young musicologist, came to see us. She was a fine and sensitive person, who had just published the biography of the great Mexican composer Manuel Ponce. Joaquín's friend and fellow-student at the Ecôle Normale of Paris. She had included in her book a photograph and a few lines from Joaquín.

On that same day there was a dinner-tribute hosted by the SACM, the Mexican Society of Authors and Composers. When we arrived at the recording center, a spirit of gaiety reigned in the hall. Two small orchestras added to the charm of the occasion.

Those at our table included the president of the SACM, Consuelo Velásquez, the President of the Vigilance Committee, Rodolfo Halffter and his wife Emilia, and the Director General, Carlos Gómez Barrera. The orchestra played the *Concierto de Aranjuez* in a version for marimba, which was quite exotic.

On Tuesday Joaquín and I were invited by the EFE Agency to a luncheon at the "El Parador" restaurant, in the Aranjuez Salon. Among the numerous fellow-guests were Luis María Anson, Antonio Ariza, Enrique Figueroa, the Spanish Ambassador and several reporters.

We returned to the hotel in late afternoon, and Joaquín went to bed immediately, for he was suffering an attack of gout, with a swollen foot and much pain.

Soon after, I also laid down on the bed and picked up a book about Mexico, which I began to read aloud to take Joaquín's mind off his troubles. We decided not to go down to the restaurant, for that morning Joaquín's admirers from the "Música Buena" record shop had presented us with a huge basket filled with exquisite fruit: mangos, avocados, papayas and bananas, all surrounding an immense, honey-colored pineapple.

"This will be our supper," I said, and Joaquín agreed.

It was about eight-thirty when I heard a strange crackling sound quite near our room. "I wonder what that noise is?" I asked, interrupting the reading.

"It's nothing, some noise from next door," Joaquín assured me.

I went on reading, but a few minutes later I stopped suddenly, alarmed, for the crackling noises were growing louder and I heard something that sounded like a muffled explosion. I jumped out of bed and ran to the window overlooking the street, and what I saw there was hair-raising! Huge chunks of brick, glass and stone and wooden beams were falling from above, a real avalanche! The noise was infernal. And when I looked up, I was horrified: from the window of the room above us, on the eighteenth floor, a huge burst of flame leaped out, with a cloud of black smoke.

"Joaquín, get up!" I cried, "Put some clothes on, quick. We have to get out of here to the fire escape. The place is on fire!"

He got up as quickly as possible, and put on his slippers and a light dressing gown.

Meanwhile, terrified, I grabbed the two suitcases (empty) which were on the luggage rack, and went out in the hall to ask for help.

But no one answered; everyone was downstairs, in the dining room. I pushed the buttons for the three or four elevators, but they were not working. Now I felt real panic, but I didn't lose control.

Suddenly, I saw the freight elevator coming up, and two young maids emerged.

"We remembered you. Come, quickly."

They seized Joaquín's arm, and together we went down to the garage, full of frightened people.

I had left the door of our room wide open, but in order to save time, I didn't go back to close it. Everything was there, clothes, luggage, records, and the most important, an antique ring, Mamá's last gift, and a gold chain which Joaquín had given me.

A patron of the hotel, who was ready to leave in his car, offered us a lift and drove us to the Paseo de la Reforma, where he called a taxi, which we entered.

Joaquín, clad in only a silk robe, was chattering with cold, but I had fortunately thrown a wool bed-jacket over my shoulders before settling on the bed. In March, the nights are cold in Mexico City.

From the cab window we could see what was happening at the María Isabel: the fire had spread to the 19th floor, while on the 17th only our two rooms burned! We watched the fire trucks arriving, counting about thirty of them, and listening to the lugubrious wailing of the sirens.

A helicopter tried to land on the flat roof, and the firemen's hoses launched huge streams of water from its side windows.

The nightmare lasted for a long hour and when, at last, we could return to our hotel, the disaster was under control.

I had to ask for a wheelchair for Joaquín, and they gave us rooms in another wing of the hotel, which was almost empty. As the restaurant was closed, they didn't serve us dinner, and all I could find in the refrigerator in our room was a bottle of orange juice and a bag of potato chips.

That night we got no sleep. The telephone rang constantly. All our friends were worried about us, for the television had broadcast the news shortly after it happened.

Cecilia had called about 9 to ask about her father's health, but the operator, between sobs, told her, "At this very moment the Hotel María Isabel is burning!"

Cecilia almost fainted. A short time later she and her husband came to the hotel, but the police would not let them in.

The next morning—a little after 6—the phone rang. They were calling us from the hotel office to tell us that we had lost everything in the fire! Tears sprang to my eyes, thinking first of all of Mamá's ring and Joaquín's gold chain, which I wore constantly. Besides these, of course, we had packed our nicest things for the trip. Dresses, records, two new suitcases, Joaquín's clothes, with a "Celine" tie for the day of the concert, photographs, diplomas, flowers and the splendid basket of fruit. Everything had been food for the flames! But Joaquín and I were safe and sound, miraculously, and for that we should be thankful.

Our friend Enrique appeared about 9 o'clock in a fine state of emotion. He had almost lost us forever! We told him everything in detail, and he congratulated me on my presence of mind.

Because the hotel would not let us go into our suite—by police order—he offered, in his capacity as a newsman, to take a look around it.

He came back after a while, all commiseration. In the sitting room, he said, everything was gone without a trace. As for the bedroom, a thick layer of ashes covered the floor, and almost all our clothes, hanging in the closet, were ruined.

"Enrique, do me a favor," I pleaded, "look in the drawer of the little night table and see if you find anything there."

He went upstairs again and returned triumphant; in his hand were my chain and the ring, intact! He went back to the bedroom again, and returned with a moccasin and my small overnight bag, partly burned, from which we rescued our passports, also undamaged.

And under a bed he had found all of the things we had brought from the silver shops in Taxco. They were in leather bags, dripping wet, but in perfect condition.

We checked out of the Hotel María Isabel that same day, with only the clothes on our backs. The Prietos had offered us the hospitality of their house—a real palace—and we spent the last days of our stay in Mexico there, in complete euphoria.

The Rodrigo Festival which had brought us to Mexico took place on March nineteenth. The Netzahuacoyotl Hall was crowded with people, among whom we saw many good friends. Joaquín, who was still limping because of his attack of gout, had to appear in slippers.

The program included the *Concierto de Estío* with Agustín, the *Concierto de Aranjuez*, with Alfonso Moreno, the *Concierto Galante*, with Carlos Prieto, who afterwards premièred the work *Como una Fantasía*, and finally, as a great surprise to us, *A la busca del más allá*. The orchestra was conducted by the prestigious Mexican conductor Enrique Bátiz, with great precision and musicality.

There was clamorous applause. The composer as well as the performers were awarded with long ovations. I was given lovely flowers, and Joaquín received a veritable mountain of neckties!

In addition, I was praised for my "courage and calmness worthy of an Amazon, in the face of danger," and was awarded the Gold Medal of the City of Mexico.

Two days later we returned to Madrid, where the news of the fire in the hotel was already well known. The press, as well as the radio and television, had immediately broadcast the following item: "Maestro Joaquín Rodrigo escaped unhurt from the disaster, having been rescued by the hotel manager."

This misstatement annoyed me, since there was no mention of me whatsoever. Hadn't everyone seen that I was always at Joaquín's side? And at the same time, I felt profound sadness, for it just so happened that the manager of the hotel had been one of the three or four victims of the fire. I remember him as a very nice young man, very attentive to the guests. In an effort to rescue his family, who were on the top floor, he had been trapped. The firemen, who had arrived in time to save them, were unable to rescue him from the smoke and flames.

Journey to London

In April Joaquín finished his *Concierto como un Divertimento* for cello and orchestra. Julian received it with great enthusiasm, and began to study it earnestly.

His manager, Alan Benson, director of the "London Weekend Television," told us that the film to promote the work would be shot on September 21st, 22nd and 23rd at our chalet in San Ramón.

At the time I had the joy of meeting again, after many years of separation, my best friend Luise Ungar. She had been my classmate at the Luithlen Lyceum in Vienna, but during the year that we studied together we were not very close, because she was the best friend of Franzi Hegenbarth, daughter of the renowned sculptor and granddaughter of the famous composer Karl Goldmark. Our friendship began after graduation, when I left Vienna with my family. Then an assiduous correspondence began which would last until now.

Luise was the prettiest girl in our class. Of medium height, a little plump, she had olive skin, very black hair and magnificent dark green eyes.

Reunited after so many years, we had a lot to talk about. Our separation had been interrupted by only a few brief encounters in Vienna, Paris and Salzburg, the latest in 1974.

Her marriage had been happy, but she was soon widowed early. She had no children of her own, but was a second mother to her stepchildren, who lived in the United States.

Always a lover of nature and of music, Luise had retired to the picturesque village of Altaussee, near Salzburg, in the heart of the Alps, which had always been her world.

I told her in great detail of my life with Joaquín, of our successes and our failures: of our recent adventure in Mexico and our miraculous escape. She felt a deep admiration and a fraternal affection for Joaquín, and she had always, ever since our schooldays, had faith in me. "You are cut from the same timber as your grandfather," she used to say to me. "You will be a fighter like him. I'm sure that you will reach your goal, too."

All these and other youthful memories we relived with nostalgia. And those three weeks of our final encounter went by like a happy dream.

That year we were again invited by the Mayor of Benicasim, Domingo Tárrega, to the International Competition for the guitar. The revelation of that year's contest was the young Valencian, Picadiza.

On the jury, presided this year by Narciso Yepes, was the German guitarist Yiri Knobloch, of Munich, who had come with his attractive wife, Renate, and their two children. We were friends from the first day, and we spent long hours with them on the sunny beach, where we formed a *tertulia* [a discussion group] with Mathilde and Josefina Salvador, Jaime Asulin, of the University of Jerusalem, and a few other friends.

After those days of cheerful activity, we retired to our chalet on the Pantano de San Juan, where the profound silence was broken only by the chirping of birds.

Near the end of September, Julian Lloyd Webber and Alan Benson came to San Ramón on three consecutive days with all the television equipment, to shoot the promotional film for the *Concierto como un Divertimento*, which was premièred in London on April 15, 1982. The first performance in Madrid took place on February 22nd, 23rd and 24th, 1985.

Those were busy, happy days, in which the filming alternated with animated conversations, jokes and laughter.

Julian played for quite a while, accompanied by me and by Ramona Sanuy, and Joaquín played one of his works.

Altogether, there were eleven of us, and the barbecues organized in our garden were a major attraction.

The film, which I saw in London, seemed very successful to me.

St. Cecilia's day was approaching, and Joaquín would celebrate his eightieth birthday. The Ministry of Culture organized a concert-tribute in the *Teatro Real*, which took place on November 19th.

Joaquín chose the works to be included in the program, and among them were two premières: the *Concierto Pastoral* and *A la busca del más allá*. Also, of course, the *Concierto de Aranjuez* and one of his first pieces, *Per la Flor del Lliri Blau*.

The soloists were Lopátegui the guitarist and Barbara Held, the young American flautist. The orchestra conductor was Max Bragado Darman, who studied the works with great interest. The auditorium of the *Real* was completely filled, and Joaquín heard long ovations from an emotional audience.

An additional tribute had been scheduled soon after in Sagunto. On the following day, we set out to drive there, arriving about nightfall. All of our friends were worried by our delay, and Vicente Vayá told us that a committee had gone to the Sagunto railroad station to welcome us. We had no alternative but to drive to the little village of Puzol to catch a train which would permit us to arrive in Sagunto as scheduled. More than a hundred people were waiting for us there with a band playing a lively march, as well as a number of gracious "Muses," dressed in white, who presented me with bouquets of flowers.

The concert-tribute took place in the *Salon-Cine-Musical*, crowded with people. An atmosphere of expectation, conviviality and affection reigned in the room. The lengthy program was charming. After the opening speeches, the San José Chorale presented two songs, followed by soprano María Antonia Mendoza. The Saguntine pianist Mario Monreal played the *Preludio al Gallo Mañanero*. The final presentation was the *Concierto de Aranjuez*, with guitarist José Pechman, accompanied by the musical group, *Lira Saguntina*, and conducted by Jesús Juan Oriola.

During the intermission, the Mayor of Sagunto named me an adopted daughter of the city, an honor to which I responded with a few words of thanks in the Valencian dialect. I recalled that, in a composition written as a school-girl in Vienna at the age of twelve, I had mentioned not only fearsome Hannibal, but also the heroic resistance of the people of Sagunto, a piece of work which won me an "outstanding" and which I still keep. The performance ended after two o'clock in the morning.

On the following day a "Brotherhood Meal" for five hundred people was served at the Ebro restaurant, situated on the beach of the Port. We listened to a great many speeches and spent all afternoon in that warm and friendly atmosphere.

On the final day we visited the "Colegio Ausias March," where some thousand students received us with "vivas" and applause. All of the little ones wanted to shake hands with us. At the end, the children's chorus entertained us with several pretty songs.

Later we walked a while in the orchard, where we could pick juicy oranges and mandarins from the trees.

* * *

Soon after our return Joaquín finished the work he had been requested to prepare in commemoration of the eight hundredth anniversary of the birth of St. Francis of Assisi. It was composed on the Saint's inspired hymn:

> Good Lord, most high, most powerful,
> Praise, glory and benediction are thine.
> Thine alone are they, O Lord most high,
> And no man is worthy to speak thy name.
> Praise be to Thee, my God, with all thy creatures,
> And above all our brother Sun.
> He who is day, through whom you give us light.

On December 19th there was a concert-tribute at the March Foundation. On the program were pieces for guitar solo, played by José Luis Rodrigo, and songs for voice and guitar, with Ana Higueras and Rodrigo. Federico Sopeña made the presentation, as he had done on the occasion of Joaquín's sixtieth birthday. The hall was crowded, and author and performers were rewarded with long ovations.

On January 19, 1982, the forty-ninth anniversary of our wedding, I attended a meeting of the Board of the Red Cross, of which I had just been named a director. The president at that time was the Duchess Cayetana de Alba.

When I returned home, Joaquín himself opened the door and greeted me with, "I congratulate you and I congratulate myself!"

"Whatever has happened?" I asked, amazed. (Could this be one of the jokes he was so fond of playing on me?)

"They've given me the National Award for Music! It's going to be announced on television right this minute!"

Sure enough, a few minutes later Joaquín appeared on the screen, while the commentator announced that he had received this important award, as had Nicanor Zabaleta.

"Bravo!" I replied, "and now I'm going to give you another piece of good news. A letter has just arrived from the University of Southern California telling you that you have been named *Doctor Honoris Causa* by the University, and that the investiture will take place in May."

All this was no joke, but the simple truth. What better anniversary gift could we have dreamed of?

The première of the *Concierto como un Divertimento* for cello and orchestra had been set for April 15, 1982.

We left for London on the tenth and were met at the airport by the director of RCA, Madeleine Kasket, a young, attractive brunette. At almost the same time, our daughter and the two granddaughters arrived from Brussels.

The days preceding the concert were full of activity: press rounds, interviews, receptions. We were filmed for both Spanish and English Television. The second project took the whole family to Trafalgar Square, where we were told to feed the pigeons while the cameras rolled. How the children enjoyed that!

Julian's pretty young wife, Celia, went with us everywhere, but we didn't meet his brother, Andrew Lloyd Webber, the famous composer of "Jesus Christ Superstar," "Evita" and "Cats."

At last the night of the première arrived. The great auditorium of the Royal Festival Hall was crowded, and there were many members of the Spanish colony among the audience. I recognized the Spanish Ambassador and his wife, the Marqués and Marquesa de Gubea, and several of my own relatives.

There was an air of expectancy, since the work had been highly promoted for a number of days. And the audience would not be disappointed. Julian Lloyd Webber and Jesús López Cobos had succeeded in expressing with fine sensitivity all the Rodrigan Hispanicism, an Hispanicism which never falls into the obvious or the crude. The London Philharmonic was at its very best, and the success was resounding. In the following work, Schubert's Symphony in D, López Cobos excelled. What a great conductor he is, and how justified is his international reputation!

On the following morning the directors of the publishing house, Schott & Co., came to the hotel to congratulate Joaquín, expressing their desire to publish this work, as they had some years before published his *Concierto Pastoral* for flute and orchestra with James Galway. This was a wonderful sign.

With cellist Julian Lloyd Weber, conductor José Luis Lopez Cobos and London Philharmonic Orchestra, at the World Première of *Concierto como un Divertimento*, London, 1982.

Chapter XII

The Last Journeys

After returning to London, we enjoyed several days of rest at home. Then, on the ninth of May we undertook the journey to Los Angeles, invited by the Dean of the University of Southern California, for the occasion of Joaquín's investiture as *Doctor Honoris Causa.*

Pepe Romero met us at the airport. Pepe is a long-time friend, and one of the best interpreters of Joaquín's works. We spent the first day peacefully at the Hotel University Hilton, the usual accommodation for visiting professors.

On the following day we attended a "master class," during which several of Pepe's pupils played Joaquín's works. Pepe's parents, Celedonio and Angelita, came expressly from Del Mar, more than a hundred miles south of Los Angeles, and were with us constantly during our stay.

At dinner that night we met Mrs. McKay, a wealthy rancher, who had come from Fort Worth, Texas, to meet Joaquín. She seemed very young, elegant and attractive, and was very friendly and straightforward. She had two daughters, Alden and Laurie, who were about to make their social debuts. I believe that at that time they were seventeen and nineteen years old. When their parents asked them what they would like as a gift to commemorate the occasion, they were unanimous in choosing as their fondest hope a concerto for guitar and orchestra by Joaquín Rodrigo.

Encouraged by Pepe, Joaquín set to work right away on the composition of the commissioned piece, the *Concierto para una Fiesta*, which had its première on March 6, 1983, in Fort Worth, during the brilliant occasion which brought together some of Texas' most distinguished families.

We were not able to accept Mrs. McKay's invitation to attend the debutante ball because of Joaquín's prolonged illness, which made it impossible for us to travel at that time. However, we were represented by Cecilia and Agustín, who returned filled with enthusiasm, as much for the ball as for the Concerto, for which Pepe was soloist. Guitarists from all the world are already displaying interest in this work, which is of a very distinct inspiration and composition. It was published by Schott & Co., of Mainz.

The investiture took place on Thursday, May thirteenth. We had to rise at dawn that morning, for Pepe came to the hotel very early to drive us to the University, where Joaquín was attired in cap and gown. More than 18,000 people were gathered on the campus: students and their families, professors, authorities and visitors. It resembled a giant anthill.

The ceremony lasted an hour. The excellent University Chorus sang two or three songs, and then there were several speeches. Pepe's introduction of Joaquín was affectionate and moving. Afterward there was a cocktail party and dinner, hosted by the University.

We went from there to Del Mar with the Romeros, where we were guests of Celedonio and Angelita. Celedonio and his three sons—all guitarists as distinguished as their father—had built lovely houses near the beach. We spent the time there in long walks and excursions.

On the day before our departure, Celín, the oldest son, invited us to a barbecue. The entire Romero clan was there, with a few friends. We said goodbye to them sadly, but with the hope of meeting again, whether in Spain or America, but always brought together by music.

We returned to Madrid on the nineteenth of May. Early in July we moved to our chalet in Cullera, where we enjoyed sun and sea, accomplishing feats of swimming under the watchful eyes of good friends, who were always with us.

However, we had to cut short our stay at the beach, because we were expected in Castres, a picturesque city in the south of France, where Robert J. Vidal organizes the "International Meetings for the Guitar" every year. That year he had organized a concert-tribute dedicated to Joaquín.

We found all the programs very interesting. On the first day we attended a concert by the Argentinean guitarist, Eduardo Falu, and on the second day the show of the Flemish artist "Merengue" with his company.

The concert dedicated to Joaquín took place on July 24th, with the following program: *Tonadilla para dos guitarras*, [*Light Music for Two Guitars*], with the Brazilian brothers Assad, who also played the *Concierto Madrigal*. As a finale, the young Cuban-American guitarist, Manuel Barrueco, offered the *Concierto de Aranjuez*. All three artists were magnificent and were generously applauded, as was the composer.

After the concert we attended a reception in the City Hall, with the Mayor of the city, who had invited us to the Festival, his wife, the city officials and the performers.

At the end of August we went with Cecilia and the granddaughters to Benicasim, where Joaquín had been named a member of the Jury for the International Competition for the Guitar.

This year there were more contestants than ever—about fifty—and the award went to guitarist Domínguez Buitrago, from Madrid.

We spent several very pleasant days in the company of our friends, the Knoblochs, Marie-Antoinette Levêcque, Matilde and Josefina Salvador and many more.

We ended our vacation peacefully at our house in San Ramón.

Now we were on the eve of a very important journey. We had been invited by the University of Jerusalem to attend a Rodrigo Festival of a week's duration, which the University had organized with several concerts, recitals, lectures and a "master class" by Joaquín. They had also scheduled excursions, press interviews, reception, and a four-day stay in a kibbutz.

But man proposes....

Joaquín, who at that time was feeling very tired and nervous, seemed to me in no condition to undertake a professional tour. And I did not have the heart to urge him, despite the hopes I cherished of returning to Jerusalem.

When at last we made our decision to postpone the invitation, I was deeply disappointed.

A few days before the date of our projected departure, we had had a visit from the director of the publishing house, B. Schott's Söhne Mainz, who came to sign a contract with Joaquín regarding his work *Concierto como un Divertimento*, for cello.

We would be in very good company with this important publisher: with Hindemith, Karl Orff, Penderecki and many others.

And then one morning Joaquín became dizzy and collapsed, pulling me down with him. Those were dreadful days which I would like to forget.

Honorary Degree of Music awarded by the University of Southern California, 1982.

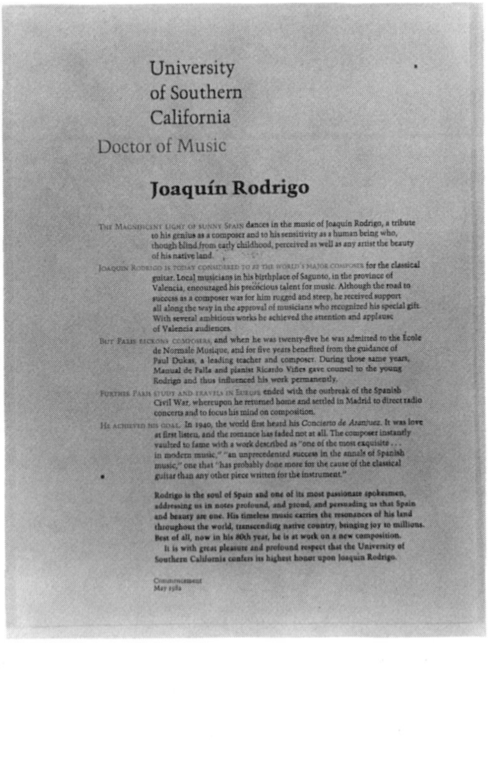

University
of Southern
California

Doctor of Music

Joaquín Rodrigo

THE MAGNIFICENT LIGHT OF SUNNY SPAIN dances in the music of Joaquín Rodrigo, a tribute to his genius as a composer and to his sensitivity as a human being who, though blind from early childhood, perceived as well as any artist the beauty of his native land.

JOAQUÍN RODRIGO IS TODAY CONSIDERED TO BE THE WORLD'S MAJOR COMPOSER for the classical guitar. Local musicians in his birthplace of Sagunto, in the province of Valencia, encouraged his precócious talent for music. Although the road to success as a composer was for him rugged and steep, he received support all along the way in the approval of musicians who recognized his special gift. With several ambitious works he achieved the attention and applause of Valencia audiences.

BUT PARIS BECKONS COMPOSERS, and when he was twenty-five he was admitted to the École de Normale Musique, and for five years benefited from the guidance of Paul Dukas, a leading teacher and composer. During those same years, Manual de Falla and pianist Ricardo Viñes gave counsel to the young Rodrigo and thus influenced his work permanently.

FURTHER PARIS STUDY AND TRAVELS IN EUROPE ended with the outbreak of the Spanish Civil War, whereupon he returned home and settled in Madrid to direct radio concerts and to focus his mind on composition.

HE ACHIEVED HIS GOAL. In 1940, the world first heard his *Concierto de Aranjuez*. It was love at first listen, and the romance has faded not at all. The composer instantly vaulted to fame with a work described as "one of the most exquisite . . . in modern music," "an unprecedented success in the annals of Spanish music," one that "has probably done more for the cause of the classical guitar than any other piece written for the instrument."

Rodrigo is the soul of Spain and one of its most passionate spokesmen, addressing us in notes profound, and proud, and persuading us that Spain and beauty are one. His timeless music carries the resonances of his land throughout the world, transcending native country, bringing joy to millions. Best of all, now in his 80th year, he is at work on a new composition.

It is with great pleasure and profound respect that the University of Southern California confers its highest honor upon Joaquin Rodrigo.

Commencement
May 1982

Epilogue

Memory sleeps,

and hope sleeps.

Miguel de Unamuno

-I-

The Christmas holidays were sad that year. Since November, Joaquín and I had lived almost in seclusion, with doctors and nurses our only companions.

During nights of insomnia I relived the past, recalling the good times of my life, and trying to forget the others.

The joys of childhood are engraved forever in our memory, and their recollection helps us to patiently bear the trials and disappointments of our adult years and old age.

Elias Canetti has said that: "Memory is good because it increases the measure of the Knowable." And Agatha Christie writes in her autobiography: "Memories are the compensation of old age."

And now, I wanted to remember. To remember the people dearest to me: my parents, my sister, my grandparents, my closest friends. And all the years I spent at Joaquín's side....

I recalled the different Christmases and New Year's Eves I had lived in the course of so many years. How many images paraded before my eyes! It was like an immense kaleidoscope.

-II-

I saw, as if on a screen, a joyous event when I was seven. My sister and I were walking with my Uncle Vitali along the main street of Perá. We stopped in front of the shop window of the "Bon Marché," where there was a display of toys. I fell madly in love with a blonde doll dressed in pink, seated in a swing. During the rest of the walk I could think of nothing but that doll. What happy little girl would own her?

When we returned home, there was the coveted doll in my room, seated in her white swing! It was a gift from my Uncle Vitali! I will never forget that joy I felt then....

-III-

Another happy New Year's Eve memory:

Now I am in Vienna, an eleven-year old boarding-school student in the Institute Szanto.

To celebrate the holiday, they have served us fried fish with potato salad, and for desert a *Sachertorte* [a chocolate cake made famous by the Hotel Sacher in Vienna], a real event at that school.

After supper, there would be a drawing for a raffle, and the prizes were placed on a little table in the dining room.

I was looking toward the prizes on the table, fascinated by a large white cardboard box, decorated with a beautiful Angel. This was first prize in the raffle, and all the girls were eyeing it covetously. Who would be the lucky winner? This obsessed me all during supper.

When the Head-Mistress announced the winning number, I almost fainted, for I had won the box with the angel, which contained a complete outfit for the doll my aunt and uncle had just given me for Christmas. It had all been done, in secret, by the teachers. Was that not a miracle?

-IV-

Several years have passed, and another New Year's Eve rises from the past: I am in Paris, with my family and loyal Dudú. Our beautiful apartment on the Rue de Messine is full of guests. My parents are giving a lively party in honor of my cousin Luisa, on the eve of her marriage to Sami. There are flowers everywhere, music, and the sound of champagne corks popping.

Mamá is very elegant in her black lace dress, and Papá is full of funny stories, which elicit loud laughter. The evening goes on until almost dawn.

And more memories assail me with amazing clarity: have I really lived all this?

-V-

Now we are in an elegant flat on the Rue de Passy. In the spacious drawing room, the furnishings are Aubusson; there are costly lamps, paintings, antique Chinese jars, vitrines filled with precious bibelots. Of course, there is a Pleyel concert grand piano. However, there is no happiness in this house. Only a few months before, a business failure had wiped out our entire fortune in a few hours. My parents no longer could give even a simple party....

To celebrate New Year's Eve that year we went with Dudú to a neighborhood movie, and at midnight we drank a hot grog, trying to dissemble our sorrow with pallid smiles.

-VI-

Two years later I am with Mamá in Menton, the pretty city on the Côte d'Azur. Our doctor had recommended that they get me out of the Paris smog to cure me of a persistent head cold. I will never forget this gesture on my mother's part, for it was a sacrifice for her to be away from the rest of the family during the holidays.

We spent two very happy weeks in a modest hotel, with excursions to Nice, Monaco and Monte Carlo. We also went to the Casino, and I remember that I refused to play roulette, because I didn't want to risk becoming a gambler.

When we returned to Paris, Mamá was in good spirits and my catarrh had disappeared.

-VII-

Years have passed, and now I am many miles from the Côte d'Azur, in the little Valencian village of Estivella, with Joaquín. We are still honeymooners, but beset with problems, for our financial situation is disastrous. Joaquín has not found employment, and his annual income from author's rights is only fifty pesetas!

The only solution was for us to separate for a time, since my parents were anxious for me to return to them. Mamá had come to get me, and only a few days remained before our departure, which was set for the 19th of January, our wedding anniversary.

Despite our problems, we celebrated Christmas happily, with our friendly neighbors for company, and attended Midnight Mass with all the people of the village.

The following year, miraculously, Joaquín and I celebrated our New Year's Eve in a Madrid café, surrounded by Spanish musicians.

-VIII-

Suddenly I have a vision of a very different landscape. Joaquín and I are in the Black Forest, now clothed in white—for Spain is devastated by the Civil War.

Thanks to the kindly director of the Freiburg Institute for the Blind, we have found refuge in an asylum for the aged.

There was a festive supper on New Year's Eve, and everyone received gifts, donated by the Friends of the Blind: *Stollen, Lebkuchen,* dates and candies.

My heart filled with nostalgia as I watched the snow falling in thick flakes. How far away from this cold German city were my family, my friends, everything! When would I see them again?

-IX-

More years have passed, and we are no longer in the Black Forest, but in a top floor apartment on Villalar street in Madrid. Only a few days remain before the birth of our daughter, Cecilia.

But I am seriously ill, with double phlebitis, and I have been in bed for more than two months, on a liquid diet of grape juice and broth.

On Christmas Eve Dr. Harguinday, urgently summoned, was very pessimistic: "This patient will not do well," he said as he left.

During Christmas Eve, a few close friends remained at our house, sitting, waiting for the fatal outcome that they all believed imminent.

However, the next morning Dr. Harguinday gave us all a happy surprise when he reported a notable improvement, saying that I was out of danger.

And fortunately, a beautiful baby was soon born, on January 27, 1941, the day of St. John Chrysostom and also Mozart's birthday. That New Year's Eve was the happiest of our lives!

-X-

Many years have gone by since that day. So many events that it is impossible to remember all of them.

Twelve strokes of the clock in the Puerta del Sol announce the arrival of 1983. Unexpectedly our children have arrived from Brussels, with Cecilita and Patty, who want to give encouragement to their "dear grandparents." In their young eyes there is such an expression of love and tenderness that my heart is suddenly filled with hope and joy. I am sure that Joaquín will recover from his illness, and that we will celebrate more New Year's Eves together—as of old.

The girls know that in a few days, on January 19th, we will celebrate our golden wedding anniversary, and they promise us "a nice surprise" on that occasion.

We are no longer alone, but comforted by the certainty that they would always be with us, they and our children.

A musical occasion at the Spanish Society of Authors,
with Plácido Domingo, 1987.

Shaking hands with Their Majesties King Juan Carlos
and Queen Sofía of Spain, 1987.

With Jessye Norman and Pepe Romero after a performance in 1989.

With José Carreras, 1989.

Ceremony held at the Academy of Fine Arts the day violinist Agustín León Ara took possession of his newly awarded seat, 1989.

A family portrait: The Rodrigos with daughter Cecilia, son-in-law Agustín and granddaughters Cecilia and Patricia, Summer, 1989.

CONCLUSION

Several years have passed since we celebrated our Golden Wedding. During this time, Joaquín's illness forced him to give up composing initially, though later he began to write again. His name continued to appear in the programs of international music Festivals, to which we were always being invited as guests of honor.

In the brilliant Lisbon Festival of Music and Dance—from May 14 to June 8, 1983—Julian Lloyd Webber played his *Concierto como un Divertimento*, and Dagoberto Linares the *Concierto de Aranjuez.*

During the summer of the same year, the eminent British musicologist and conductor, Raymond Calcraft, devoted an entire concert to him, with works such as the *Música para un códice salmantino, Cánticos nupciales*, and *Concierto de Aranjuez.*

On May 19, 1984, the *Concierto de Estío* was played at the Moscow International Festival.

From the 25th to the 30th of November a "Joaquín Rodrigo Week" took place in Valencia, organized by the City Council, which we also attended. The program included a song recital by Carmen Bustamente, two symphony concerts in the Teatro Principal—sold out!—with the *Concierto de Aranjuez* and the *Fantasía para un gentilhombre*, played by Narciso Yepes, and *A la busca del más allá* and *Per la flor del lliri blau*, all favorite works of the Valencian public. Maestro Manuel Galduf conducted with great authority. It was a tremendous success. Finally, Federico Sopeña gave a magnificent lecture with the title: "The Music of Joaquín Rodrigo in Spanish Culture."

In 1986 we travelled to London once more, this time for the two-week Joaquín Rodrigo Festival, organized and conducted by Raymond Calcraft. With artists such as Angel and Pepe Romero, Julian Lloyd Webber, Agustín, and Joaquín Achúcarro—playing the *Concierto Heroico* for the first time—Joaquín said that this was definitely the most important Festival of his music which had ever taken place. The four concerts and two recitals were a tremendous success, and in the final concert we heard the première of the beautiful *Cántico de San Francisco*, which Joaquín later dedicated to Raymond Calcraft. Our friend Ilonka Farrell and many other friends came to this event, which included a reception at the Spanish Institute in London. How sad we were to have to leave at the end!

On November 26, 1989, all the family attended an important ceremony at the Royal Academy of Fine Arts in Madrid, when Agustín took possession of his seat as a member He was presented by Joaquín and Narciso Yepes. After an excellent speech on the history of violin schools, he gave a brilliant recital of music by Bach, Luis de Pablo, and his father-in-law—Joaquín's *Capriccio*, in homage to Sarasate.

The mail continues to bring testimonials, honors, announcements of concerts or other affairs in honor of Joaquín and requests for interviews by the press and radio. All of this Joaquín accepts with good grace.

In the spring of 1988 he was named Doctor Honoris Causa by the Polytechnic University of Valencia. The investiture took place on May 31st, and our daughter accompanied us for the occasion, as we were to spend several days there. We had the pleasure of meeting all of Joaquín's family and many of his friends who came to welcome him.

On the day of our arrival the students of one of the college residences invited us to a supper, followed by conversation which lasted until midnight. The next day we went with the Vice Rector, Pilar Roig, to meet Professor Joaquín Arnau, a man of great culture and knowledge who was to serve as sponsor.

The ceremony of investiture was impressive. At noon the officials made their entrance: the Rector of the University, the Mayor, the President of the Assembly, and so on. After the speeches, the University choir sang some of Joaquín's works and, as a finale, the Municipal Orchestra played the *Concierto de Aranjuez* with Narciso Yepes as soloist. It was a memorable day.

A few months later, the same honor was conferred by the University of Alicante. The ceremony there was simpler, but I thought it very moving.

Then, on July 6, 1989, the honorary doctorate was conferred by the University Complutense of Madrid. On this occasion, Joaquín elected to play some of his own compositions for piano rather that to make the customary speech, and that was a great success. The Rector, Gustavo Villapalos, made an address which pleased everyone, and he didn't fail to praise my efforts at my husband's side.

Finally, on July 13, 1990, the University of Exeter named Joaquín Doctor Honoris Causa. For this occasion we had to make a quick trip to England. We left Madrid on July 12th, arriving in London about 2 o'clock. Thanks to our friend, Professor Raymond Calcraft, who met us at the airport, we were in Exeter three hours later, in time to be ready for a full dress dinner at eight o'clock. The room was full of guests, among them the author John le Carré and the Hispanist Jean François Botrel and his wife.

I was seated between Joaquín and Sheila Harrison, the Vice Chancellor's wife, a lovely lady whom we found completely delightful, and we had a very pleasant evening.

Honorary Degree, University of Exeter, July 1990.
Maestro Joaquín Rodrigo sits between famous writer John le Carré and Professor Jean François Botrel.

The program for the following day began with a formal luncheon, attended by the Spanish Ambassador and his wife, as guests of honor, and was followed by the ceremony of investiture, when Joaquín, le Carré and Botrel received honorary degrees. This went on from three o'clock until five. Much charm was added by the performance of the small orchestra of the University.

Afterwards, we were served tea and made our farewells.

The next day was Saturday, and after lunch with Raymond and his wife Mairi we left for London, the airport and Madrid. It had been a very brief visit, but very pleasant and interesting.

Joaquín received a great many honors besides the nominations as Doctor Honoris Causa. It is impossible to name them all here, for, because of the fiftieth anniversary of the *Concierto de Aranjuez*, which has brought him so much fame, there were many celebrations. Here are a few which I attended in 1990:

On the sixth of June, in Aranjuez, there was a concert in his honor with Pepe Romero as soloist. He played Joaquín's *Concierto para una Fiesta* as well as selections from the *Concierto de Aranjuez*.

On June sixteenth, Narciso Yepes took part in another. He, naturally, played the *Concierto de Aranjuez*.

Also in June, in Sagunto, Joaquín was honored at a lovely concert. At eleven o'clock at night the great plaza was filled with his fellow citizens who overwhelmed him with demonstrations of affection. It was very moving.

On July fifteenth, if I'm not mistaken, the "Bandas" of the province of Valencia presented a most original program in honor of Joaquín.

Finally, there was the concert-homage at El Escorial which took place at eleven o'clock at night in the Carlos III Theater. This was attended by Queen Sofía and Princess Irene, with a number of ministers, musicians, intellectuals and a large audience. Many friends and admirers also. At this concert *Líricas castellanas*, the work dedicated to the Queen, was presented for the first time. It is written for soprano solo and antique instruments; I adapted the text. The work met with resounding success, and the soprano, Ana Higueras, and the instrumentalists were enthusiastically applauded. The composer received high praise, and both the Queen and Princess Irene greeted me with affection. It was a deeply moving and very personal concert, the last of the season, and one which I will never forget.

And what have the next winter and the coming years in store for us? What I want most are health and peace for everyone. And for our home, harmony, much music and love.

Victoria Kamhi

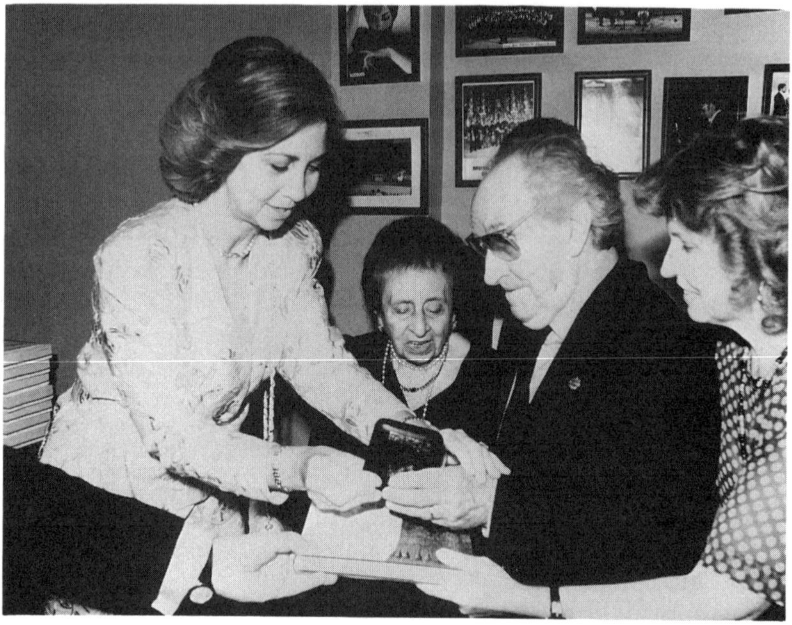

Joaquín and Victoria Rodrigo presenting Queen Sofía of Spain with the manuscript of the work *Líricas castellanas* dedicated to the Queen on the occasion of the World première, July, 1990.

APPENDIX

Letters to Victoria.
Letters to Joaquín Rodrigo.
Note on the work of Joaquín Rodrigo.
Rodrigo and his music by Spanish Writer Gerardo Diego.
Catalog and Index of the works of Joaquín Rodrigo.
Honors awarded to Joaquín Rodrigo.
Honors awarded to Victoria Kamhi.

LETTERS TO VICTORIA

These letters sent from Joaquín Rodrigo to Victoria are herein published for the first time, in English, as a document that will help us to know the Maestro's personality better.

Valencia, October 22

My beloved Victoria: This morning I have received your letter, as anticipated.

I am surprised that you have not received a letter from me in such a long time; the letter I sent on the 12th or 13th was probably lost in the mail. In it I told you that I was sending the serenade, along with something about another, more serious matter.

I told you that we should be thinking about resolving our problem.

Yes, yes, the present situation cannot continue and it is time to end our temporary situation, and our somewhat ambiguous and confusing relationship.

This cannot continue indefinitely, at least it should not be allowed to continue, as I feel more and more certain that such a situation would be worse for both of us.

So then, it is time to end our intrigues, conjectures and doubts by making a decision, don't you agree?

So then, I am ready to travel to Paris to marry my dear friend Vicky, who is my most perfectly ideal companion. Careful, careful! Don't become too conceited, for it is dangerous for a man to marry a woman he thinks is perfect, whom he believes to be an ideal!

Once I have your answer I will talk to my parents. As you know I am unfortunately not independent, so that I will need to ask their approval.

But I want to repeat again, in this decisive moment of our lives, that I must remind you that we cannot live in Paris in a stable and permanent fashion, and that we must live in Spain. You already know the reasons why we cannot stay in Paris. First of all, I don't have enough money. It's so expensive to live there...Secondly, France is an awful place. It is horrible to live at all times as a foreigner, I would not like that at all, and I do not think it is necessary. I think it would be unnecessary and superfluous.

I will tell you about my plans, and let's see what you think of them.

Of course we will marry, once that's settled, when? Whenever. After Christmas, at the end of winter, in the spring. In springtime everything flowers and flourishes, in any case, whenever you please. Then we'll return to Spain, to Valencia. Here we will spend the summer in the ocean and beside the ocean, or in the woods if you prefer. We will spend the summer at my parents' house and when the winter begins we will decide, without speaking a word, to travel to Paris to spend three or four months, perhaps five, depending on how much money we have. I think that this plan is the best, the most practical and the easiest to carry out. If we were to decide to stay in Valencia it would be in our little house...Then...Then...The future cannot be predicted. The future belongs to God. What is the point of calculating all the details with geometric precision, why try in vain to penetrate the dark distance of future years and their hidden designs? It is a useless and sterile exercise. Let's trust in our future and in ourselves.

I feel confident and happy because I know I am holding the right cards from the deck. You are about to lose, dear Vicky, because I am about to win. You deserve much more than I can give you or offer to give you, excepting my boundless affection for you.

So then, let your heart guide you, and don't worry about anyone else's opinion, that's my advice. Anyway, the advice of others is often worthless, and we take it only when it's convenient to do so.

Goodbye, my dear Vicky, write to me soon and often. Until then.

Always yours,
Joaquín

Valencia, November 9

Beloved girl,

At last I'll be leaving tomorrow, as I told you in my last letter (Did you receive it?) dated the sixth.

Yesterday my little poem *Juglares* was performed, as I mentioned. It was not a première, for it has been performed several times in Valencia, so it was the fourth performance. I say that it was performed, rather than heard, because no one heard it (a slight exaggeration, of course.)

The Madrid orchestra played it well, very well. Even though it was not a new work they carefully rehearsed all morning and the result could not have been better. Maestro Pérez Casas is a good conductor, very careful, very meticulous; he does not care for sudden improvisations; he is watchful and also has a good artistic temperament. I—why not tell you?—I can tell you anything—isn't that right? I feel very satisfied with myself. The work sounds really good, Vicky. It has some very well-written passages, and my friends are pleased with it, much more than with earlier try-outs, due to the improved interpretation. The interpretation by performers means everything for composers, and that's why you must apply yourself to the study of piano, so that you will interpret my works better than anyone else can. Even if you don't care much for my music—that's not important.

I might say something to you about maestro Pérez Casas' interpretation of my work. I'm never completely satisfied, I'm one of those composers who really only likes his own interpretation. But that's another matter. I really liked certain musical touches. The practice session took place while I was present, and when the conductor introduced me to the orchestra the musicians began to applaud me and I had to stand to acknowledge their accolades.

As to the audience, that is what least matters to me, I care little for the audience's opinion. Always, regarding my compositions, my own opinion is what influences me, and after that the opinion of a few others, among them my Victoria. The people listened to my little musical piece without praising or damning it, this type of music goes in one ear and out the other for our people, or perhaps they did not hear it at all. In any case, I am quite satisfied.

So then Thursday or Friday I will be with you, but for how long?

I'm very busy packing my suitcase. I repeat the news that I've grown, today I put on a suit from last year and it's a little small for me (it's extraordinary).

Regarding your studies, we are almost in agreement and will soon agree fully—the important thing is to study well.

Dear Vicky, until we see each other; for once it will be very soon.

Many greetings to Mathilde, give her my congratulations, tell her to invite us over for dinner, and not to spend everything at the ice palace.

You know I love you always,

Joaquín Rodrigo

LETTERS TO JOAQUIN RODRIGO

The following letters were written to Joaquín Rodrigo by eminent figures from the world of 20th century music.

HOTEL D'ATHÈNES

TOURNARIE, PROPRIÉTAIRE

21, RUE D'ATHÈNES, 21

(GARE SAINT-LAZARE)

TÉLÉPHONE : GUTENBERG 00-28

R. C. SEINE 204.721

PARIS (IXe) LE 15/12/28

Cher Monsieur,

je ne fais que passer à Paris, venant de Genève et me rendant à Bordeaux et à St Jean-de-Luz.

Je serai de retour le 25 et serais heureux de vous revoir, soit ici, soit à Montfort l'Amaury, si vous êtes encore à Paris à cette époque. Voudrez-vous avoir l'amabilité de me téléphoner, d'abord à l'adresse ci-dessus, puis à Montfort l'Amaury : 89 ?

Croyez, cher Monsieur, à mes sentiments les plus sympathiques. Maurice Ravel

Paris, December 15, 1928

Dear Sir:

I am briefly in Paris, having arrived from Geneva, en route to Bordeaux and San Juan de Luz.

I will return on Dec. 25 and I would be very pleased to see you again, whether here or at Monfort l'Amaury, if you will still be staying in Paris on that date. Will you be kind enough to telephone me, first at the address mentioned above and later at Monfort l'Amaury: 89?

I send you my most affectionate greetings,

Maurice Ravel

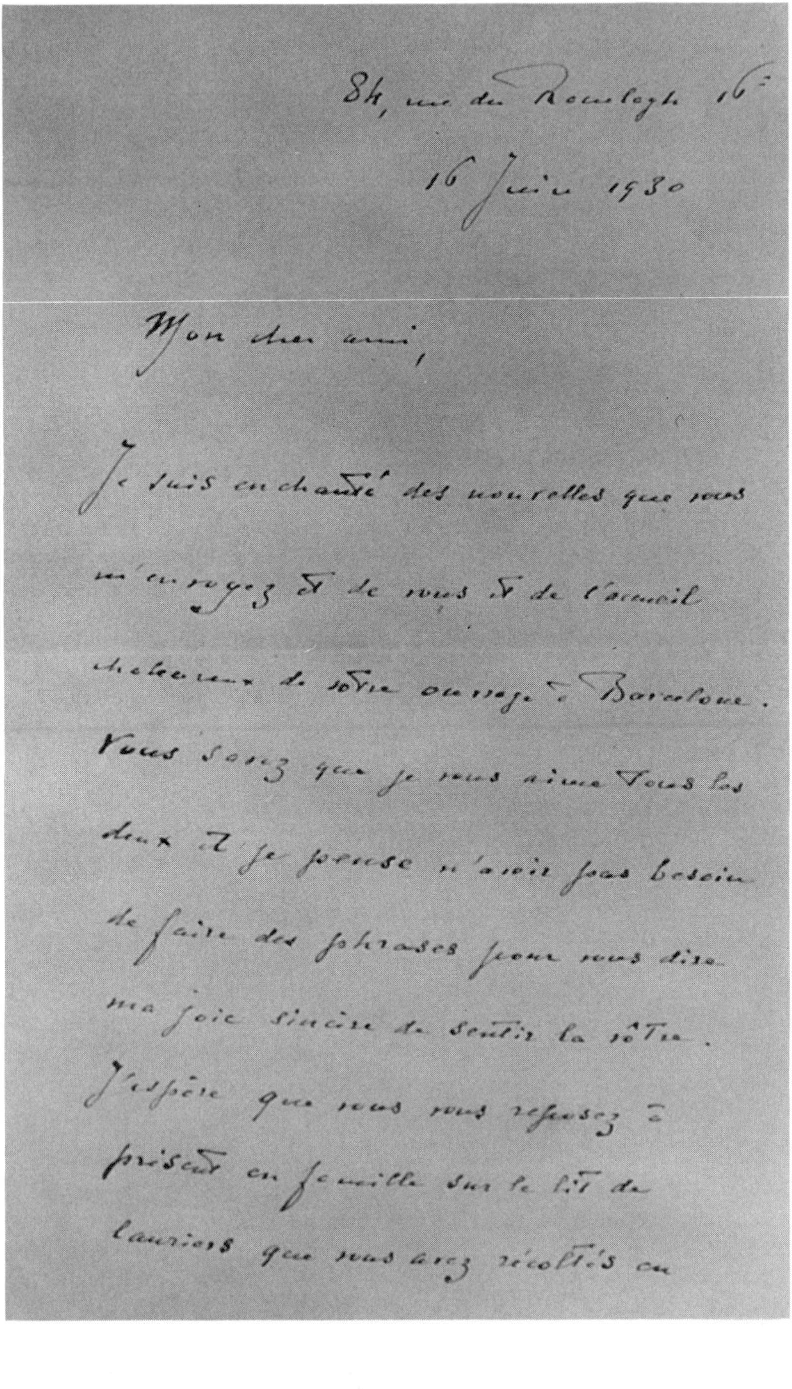

84, rue de Ranelagh 16e

16 Juin 1930

Mon cher ami,

Je suis enchanté des nouvelles que vous m'envoyez et de vous et de l'accueil chaleureux de votre ouvrage à Barcelone. Vous savez que je vous aime tous les deux et je pense n'avoir pas besoin de faire des phrases pour vous dire ma joie sincère de sentir la vôtre. J'espère que vous vous reposez à présent en famille sur le lit de lauriers que vous avez récoltés en

Catalogue. Et comme je sais que vous ne vous y endormirez pas je suis tranquille pour l'avenir en me réjouissant avec vous du présent, des invitations agréables qui vous ont accueilli, du dîner intime des jeunes compositeurs catalans etc. etc.. Premiers feux d'une gloire qui grandira sans vous griser — tel que je vous connais — et à laquelle j'applaudis "en connaisseur", si vous permettez!

J'ai lu votre lettre à vos camarades, aujourd'hui, à l'Ecole Normale. Cela a mis tout le monde en bonne humeur, malgré la chaleur orageuse qui alterne depuis trois jours ici, avec des orages épouvantables qui font les gens assez nerveux. Vos amis étaient tous comme moi et, du coup, j'ai trouvé une compensation à votre absence que nous regrettons tous, mais que votre succès nous faisait oublier puisqu'il vous rendait présent parmi nous.

Bonnes vacances musicales et familiales, mon cher ami, et agréez mes sentiments tout spécialement affectueux. J'y joins mes souvenirs les meilleurs pour votre indispensable et si dévouée compagnon!

[signature]

Merci pour le programme, bien arrivé ce matin.

84, rue Remlegh, 16é
June 16, 1930

My dear friend:

I am delighted with your personal news and with the news of the warm reception of your work in Barcelona.

You know that I love you both and I don't think I need special sentences to tell you about my joy to know of yours (your happiness).

I hope you are resting now *en famille*, on the bed of laurels you won for yourself in Cataluña! And as I know that you will not rest on them for long. I am happy about the future and rejoice with you in the present—the pleasant invitations that have welcomed you, the private dinner with the young Catalan companions, etc, etc. The first glimpses of a glory which will grow without flattering you. Just as I know you, I can applaud that fame "as a connoisseur," if you will permit me!

I have read your letter to your friends today, at the Ecole Normale. That has made everybody happy, in spite of the stormy heat that has alternated here for the last three days, with horrible storms that make people very nervous. Your friends were enraptured; like I am, and besides I have found a compensation for your absence, that we all regret, and that is that your success has made up for it by bringing your presence among us.

May your musical and family successes continue, my dear friend, and accept my most affectionate wishes. My best wishes also to your inseparable and dedicated companion.

Paul Dukas

Thank you for the program, which arrived timely this morning.

Granada, 13 Enero 1932

Querido amigo:

Le agradezco muy de veras su carta y correspondo de corazón a sus votos de felicidad para el Año que empieza.

Gracias a Dios puedo trabajar bien en nuestro oficio, pero es lo único que me permiten. Por eso son tan breves estas líneas.

Mucho celebro sus noticias de Ernesto Halffter y de Madame Buquet.

Mi hermana agradece mucho su saludo, enviándole el suyo.

Su afectísimo,

Manuel de Falla

Granada, January 13, 1932

Dear friend,

I deeply appreciate your recent letter and reply wholeheartedly to your kind wishes for a happy New Year.

Thank God, I am able to continue to work in our common field, but that is the only effort they allow me. That is why this letter must be extremely brief.

I am glad to hear the news about Ernesto Halffter and Madame Buquet.

My sister is happy to hear from you, and returns your greetings.

Your most affectionate friend

Manuel de Falla

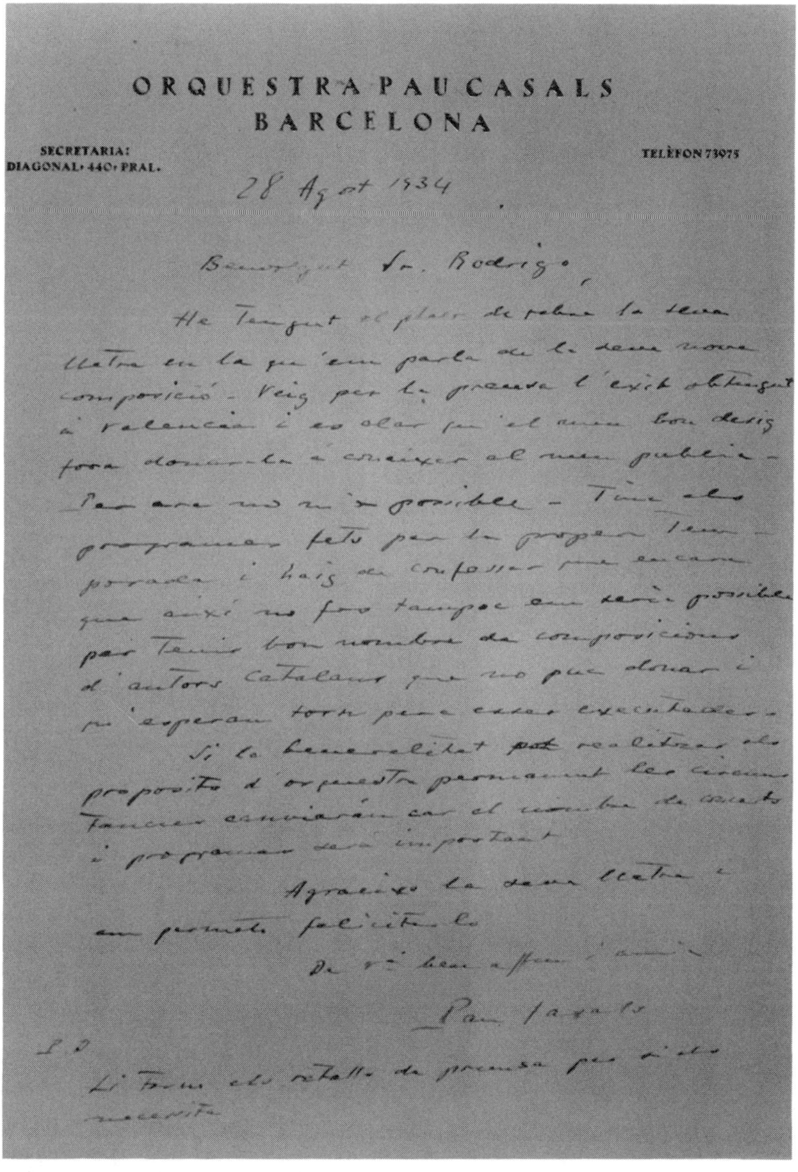

ORQUESTRA PAU CASALS
BARCELONA

SECRETARIA:
DIAGONAL, 440, PRAL.

TELÈFON 73975

28 Agost 1934

Benvolgut Sr. Rodrigo,

He tingut el plaer de rebre la seva lletra en la que em parla de la seva nova composició. Veig per la premsa l'èxit obtingut a València i es clar que el meu bon desig fora donar-la a coneixer al meu públic. Per ara no m'és possible. Tinc els programes fets per la propera temporada i haig de confessar que encara que així no fos tampoc em seria possible per tenir bon nombre de composicions d'autors catalans que no puc donar i n'esperen torn per ésser executades.

Si la generalitat ~~pot~~ realitzar els propòsits d'orquestra permanent les circumstàncies canviaran car el nombre de concerts i programes serà important.

Agraeixo la seva lletra i em permeto felicitar-lo

De V. ben affm. i amic

Pau Casals

P.S.

Li torno els retalls de premsa per si els necessita

August 28, 1934

Dear Sr. Rodrigo:

It was a pleasure to receive your letter, in which you describe your new composition. I recognize the proof of the great success it has had in Valencia, and I assure you of my hope to present it to my audience as well.

Unfortunately, it will not be possible for me to do so at the present time, as all of my programs have been set for the coming season; and I should also admit that even if such were not the case, I would still be unable to present it, due to a large number of compositions by Catalonian composers, whose works I cannot yet present, and who also await their turn to be performed.

If the Generalitat is able to carry out its proposals for a permanent orchestra, these circumstances will change, as the number of concerts and programs will be important.

Thank you for your letter. I congratulate you.

Your most affectionate friend,

Pablo Casals

P.S. I enclose the press clippings in case you may find them useful.

20 Mars 1949

Cher Ami,

J'ai fait parvenir votre lettre à Henry Barraud (adresse: 3 square Moncey – Paris – 9e) en l'accompagnant d'un mot de chaude recommandation pour votre oeuvre.

Merci pour l'exemplaire de votre "Cantique" (St Jean de la Croix) que vous avez eu la gentillesse de m'envoyer. C'est souple de rythme, et la ligne est sobre et belle!

Avec toutes mes bonnes amitiés et mes bons voeux!

Olivier Messiaen

13 Villa du Danube

– Paris – (19e)

March 20, 1949

Dear friend,

I have sent your letter on to Henry Barraud (address: 3 Square Moncey—Paris—9th) with a note strongly recommending your work.

Thank you for the copy of your "Canticle" (St. John of the Cross) which you kindly sent to me. The rhythm is smooth and its line is sober and lovely!

I send my affection and best wishes with this letter.

Olivier Messiaen
13 Villa du Danube
Paris (19th)

NOTES ON THE WORKS OF JOAQUIN RODRIGO

We include the composer's critical comments on some of his compositions.

CONCIERTO DE ARANJUEZ

In the written commentary published to accompany the 1974 recording of the harp version of the *Concierto de Aranjuez* I remarked:

The Spanish composer, as he composes, imagines a phantasmagoric instrument that would combine the soul of a guitar, the tail of a piano and the wings of a harp. Those wings soar as a protagonist in this recording, as requested of me by my admirable friend Nicanor Zabaleta, when he proposed that I write a harp adaptation for the guitar solo in my concerto.

This attempt seemed very attractive and feasible to me, avoiding the natural pitfalls that two such disparate techniques would present. Both are percussive string instruments and can be placed within the same origins, as far as timbre is concerned, although their sonorities are quite distinct.

It is true that the chords of the guitar are deeply imbedded in the soul of Spanish music, and that the guitar merges the classical tradition and the flamenco touch; but the weightless harp can soar, filling the air with crystalline sparks that seem like distant suggestions.

The *Concierto de Aranjuez* is named for the famous royal site on the shore of the River Tagus, not far from Madrid, along the road to Andalucía, and some perceive Goya's shadow in the notes of its music, full of melancholy emotion. Its music seems to bring to life the essence of an 18th century court, where aristocratic distinction blends with popular culture. In its melody the perfume of magnolias lingers, the song of birds and the whisper of fountains, although specific descriptions are not found there.

As we said, the *Concierto de Aranjuez*, a synthesis of classical and popular in both form and emotion, lies dreaming beneath the foliage of the park that surrounds the Baroque Palace, and only wishes to be as agile as a butterfly and as precise as a matador's cape pass.

JOAQUIN RODRIGO

ZARABANDA LEJANA Y VILLANCICO

These two compositions, written a few years apart, still correspond to the same style and were conceived as a single work. They evoke the Spanish music of the 16th and 17th centuries. *Zarabanda lejana* was composed for guitar and soon after orchestrated by the composer as a dialog between the orchestra and its soloists. "The old *Zarabanda* is heard, hidden behind the lattice-work of the arches, enveloped in a mist of muted strings."

The *Villancico* contrasts a more artless and rustic style to the sober refinement of the "zarabanda," one may say that the string orchestra reaches the limits of its possibilities, as far as timbre is concerned. The piece's form is a simple rondo-sonata; in contrast, the writing is extremely complicated. It was given a private première in the Palace of the Princess of Polignac and in public at the Feminine Orchestra concerts in Paris, France.

JOAQUIN RODRIGO

MUSICA PARA UN CODICE SALMANTINO

Among the many new and unexpected experiences of humanity in present times, I want to sing out the experience of a man hearing and listening to himself. A portentous invention has been able to turn on, once and forever, in inscrutable hieroglyphics, of furrows and dashes, the voice and words and song of mankind...And man has been able to hear himself, to have before him a previously unheard image of himself.

So then: I do not know what Eve thought when she was first able to look at and see herself on that first day that the quiet waters reflected the first face of a woman. But I imagine the impression she must have had: Eve did not recognize herself. She did not recognize her own image in the clearest mirror of the clearest waters, just as we who have heard our works for the first time are unable to get past the very novel experience. This experience is in itself disheartening, but is also the immediate consequence of and probably echoes the visual perplexity: we have not recognized ourselves, and we do not like ourselves. We do not like ourselves, because we had maintained an innate and perhaps necessary over-estimation of ourselves; that is to say, that our vanity is wounded. And this would tend to confirm the view of so many psychologists, who apparently paradoxically claim that it is easier to really understand others than to truly understand one's self.

The external aspect and the internal demonstration, the face and the voice, what is commonly called the mirror of the soul and the other, what I call the echo of its own interior, i. e. the voice, have passed through the same trials...and man does not recognize himself and when he finally does he feels mortified, because he does not care for himself, because he had had a much better opinion of himself.

We could multiply, repeat in degrees in a lesser category the event of that scrutiny itself; whenever we become estranged from ourselves, or from our own works, or even from our own actions—the painter who is distanced from his canvas, the composer upon listening to his work, as interpreted by others, feels an unspeakable disappointment,.and it seems changed; and if such is the case, how can we serve as our own critics? Yet, the function of creator demands vigilance, discrimination in application of technique, his innate and acquired tastes, and his instinct, which in art is replaced by sensitivity. And then this need and that inability, I believe, give birth to the tremendous doubt that assaults the creative artist's sense of his value, of the importance or the meaning of his art.

In my case, as always, when I've been asked to say something about my modest works, I'm restrained by perplexity. I must consider my latest work, its ink still wet, which time has not yet affected, or granted a sense of distance from the creator.

However, these expressions of modesty are nearly worthless; rebellion, also just and likewise necessary, forces us to admit that we do in fact know something about ourselves; that we understand a great deal about our own intentions and desires and even about our works. Although such facts may be altogether precise, the sagacious examiner, if we do not mislead him by misleading ourselves, can use them to avoid inquires and deductions that might misdirect or confuse him within the labyrinth of the artist's intentions and desires.

Truly, if not for the suggestion to do so from my dear friend Don Antonio Tovar, the Rector of the University of Salamanca, to compose a sort of cantata for the closing ceremonies of the 700th anniversary of the founding of that university, I would never have turned my attention to Miguel de Unamuno's poetry, although I consider him one of the outstanding contemporary poets of the Spanish language. But was it possible for someone to try to fulfill this difficult duty—doubly honorable—of fusing Salamanca and its University with Unamuno? With the greatest respect and humble devotion I decided to approach Unamuno's words, or as he might have expressed it, to people his poetic world with sonorous ghosts.

JOAQUIN RODRIGO

CONCIERTO-SERENATA

This is the fifth concerto by Joaquín Rodrigo: guitar, piano, violin, cello, and now harp. It was first performed on November 11,

1956 by Nicanor Zabaleta and the National Orchestra, under the direction of Paul Klecki. Here is what Joaquín Rodrigo said of this work:

The gay tinkling of the harp and its suitability for a diatonic music, clear, simple, suggested to me a concerto that would be a sort of message to young people, and would awaken echoes of parties and customs of other eras; that accounts for its title: *Concierto-Serenata.* That is the reason why the piece is set in 19th century Spain, as we have invented it, musically, and are building with raw materials from Padre Soler and Barbieri.

The first movement of *Concierto-Serenata,* "Estudiantina" (Allegro) faithfully follows the construction of the first tempo of a classical concerto, but in contrast to the concertos of the great epoch, the second theme which the orchestra attacks is almost nonexistent; rather than a theme it is a brief refrain. The movement glides along in the form of a march, and it is no surprise that in its development, as in any students' march, one hears the occasional phrase of familiar music.

The second movement, "Intermezzi con aria," is a little aria in the form of a canon, sung by the harp, and interrupted by an "allegretto," a fugue which nevertheless permits the theme of the aria to end pianissimo, after the entire orchestra has joined in its emotion.

The third movement, "Sarao" (Allegro vivace) is composed as a rondo, that is to say, a principal theme that alternates with other secondary themes; but those themes also act as protagonists.

I have tried to do something very difficult: to make everything light, clear, happy, like the harp's own childlike soul, and like a *Concierto-Serenata.*

JOAQUIN RODRIGO

CONCIERTO COMO UN DIVERTIMENTO

This concerto is orchestrated in a simple manner, but with the additional colors of the xylophone and celesta. The first movement begins with the soloist, strumming a *bolero* rhythm. The violins enter with a typically Spanish theme, which is quickly picked up by the violoncello.

Another rhythmic idea leads us to a passage that is diabolically difficult for the soloist. It returns to the first theme, and with a prelude of four octaves we return to the pizzicato of the opening, with which the movement closes.

The slow movement (*Adagio nostalgico*) begins with a delicate acoustic—latticework the solo instrument playing low harmonies. Then, accompanied by the flute, the clarinet and the celesta, a violoncello sings a captivatingly beautiful melody. Half-way through the movement the virtuoso and emotional "cadenza" appears, with its dazzling pyrotechnic adornments with tiny jumps in the seventh, and the left hand's pizzicato. A lively and happy finale leads the Concierto to a brilliant conclusion.

JOAQUIN RODRIGO
April 13, 1982

CONCIERTO ANDALUZ

The *Concierto Andaluz*, for four guitars and orchestra, has been composed as a result of a commission by Celedonio Romero, and is dedicated to him and to his sons, who are all guitar virtuosos. It was written in 1967 and first performed on November 18 of that same year in San Antonio, Texas.

This concerto is composed of themes inspired by Andalusia, but they are the author's own and not taken from popular music. It is written in three movements, and its harmonies are straight-forward for the audience, as is the orchestration. At times the four guitars carry on a dialog together and at other times they dialog with the orchestra. It is a concerto written to feature the performers, although the orchestra is given its opportunities to shine.

The three movements, "Bolero," "Adagio" and "Allegretto," vary in tempo, and are quite different, and they each contain distinct themes of clear importance. The music of this *Concierto* is within the music that Joaquín Rodrigo has dubbed "Neocasticismo" and the entire work, due to the four solo guitars and the orchestration, acquires a great deal of colour, and great evocative power.

JOAQUIN RODRIGO

ELOGIO DE LA GUITARRA

This work is one of the most recent and most important of my pieces written for solo guitar. It demands of the performer a great virtuosity and a sharp insight, for him to be able to penetrate and master the thematic complexities.

The work is composed of three movements and its form is more or less that of the sonata. The first movement presents two themes: the first is more imaginative and the second, more melodic theme releases clear Sevillian inflections.

The second movement, severe in character, evokes an old Castilian cathedral. The tenuous resonance of the harmonic chords that dot the exposition of the two themes, the first from an ancient Gregorian chant and the second a tranquil series of arpeggio chords, work together to achieve this intention, and the movement then fades away into a harmonic vagueness in the high pitched range.

The third movement opens with great gallantry and after scattering various patterns of extreme difficulty, reaches a "presto" of brilliance and virtuosity, the entire explosion concluding with some soft hand knocks against the wood of the guitar box.

JOAQUIN RODRIGO

ELOGIO DE LA GUITARRA (2)

Joaquín Rodrigo has managed to enclose in his composition the brilliant possibilities of classical guitar music, as well as the diabolical requirements made of its player, due to the characteristics of this instrument.

Joaquín Rodrigo has written the following: My intention was to demand a precise and infallible technique of the guitarist, as well as a profound sensitivity to the framework and thematics of the music. I have composed my "challenge" to the guitarist, starting myself rather comfortably with the 'sonata' form.

The first movement "Allegro," is made up of two parts: the first is a chordal progression embellished by scale triplets and passages. It leads to a melodic theme which combines at the end of the movement with the chordal writing.

The second movement "Andantino" has a more serene character and evokes an ancient Castilian cathedral. The firm resonances of the harmonic chords underline the two themes of a distant Gregorian chant. The first theme of the chant ends in a calm series of chords that lead to the second theme in arpeggios. These chords help reach the essence of the theme. The second movement is based on the harmonic register of the guitar.

The third movement, "Allegro," begins with lively triplet figures, and is developed in extended passages of scales, such as those previously heard in the first movement. The second part (indicated "più allegro") is characterized by rapid patterns, which require great virtuosity and lead to a conclusion of sharp contrasts, with notes executed by the left hand alone, which are repeated by the performer as he strikes the guitar's wood with his right hand.

JOAQUIN RODRIGO

CONCIERTO MADRIGAL

The *Concierto Madrigal* for two guitars and orchestra was first performed in 1970 in Los Angeles' immense Hollywood Bowl, performed by that city's famous orchestra under the direction of Rafael Frühbeck de Burgos, with soloists Angel and Pepe Romero. The work, heard by an especially attentive audience, was enthusiastically applauded, a reaction that was later repeated when the work was performed in various U.S. cities.

The *Concierto Madrigal* is built on cadences and phrases taken from an anonymous Renaissance madrigal, which begins: "Happy my eyes which saw in your eyes, Lady, so much goodness." From that phrase and other episodes taken from the madrigal, the piece acquires an archaic and modal flavor. In other sections the melody, which is the thread that unites the entire piece, seems to introduce a more popular tone.

I have used the episodic structure, with a clear designation, throughout this piece, distancing it formally from the more usual architecture. Despite the established dialog and the adaptation of the writing, it leans toward the "Suite" form, even if the element that sustains it is the variation. Each of these variations or episodes is indicated by a title that is related to its atmosphere or its setting,—a light poetic note that smoothly colors the entire musical score. The titles, in order, are "Fanfarre," "Madrigal," "Entrada," "Pastorcito tú que vienes, pastorcito tú que vas," "Girardilla," "Pastoral," "Fandango," "Arietta," "Zapateado," "Caccia a la española."

The orchestra is composed of the following: Piccolo, flute, oboe, clarinet, bassoon, trumpet and strings.

JOAQUIN RODRIGO

CONCIERTO PARA UNA FIESTA

The *Concierto para una fiesta* is the first concerto for solo guitar and orchestra composed by Rodrigo since his irresistibly popular *Concierto de Aranjuez*, written in 1939. It is a piece commissioned by William and Carol McKay of Ft. Worth, Texas, to celebrate the social debut party for their daughters, Alden and Lauri; it was first played on that occasion, in private, on March 5, 1983, performed by Pepe Romero and the Fort Worth Chamber Orchestra, directed by John Giordano.

The new work is an indisputably Spanish piece, exacting in terms of demanding guitar techniques. Guitar virtuoso Pepe Romero has also described it as the most difficult piece he has ever played.

Two themes dominate the first movement, original melodies that are very Valencian in tone. The soloist and the orchestra share the exposition of the first theme in the minor. The second ("Poco piú lento") in D minor, develops from a basic A on the horn, which seems to evoke the spirit of the Cid and Valencia's Moorish past. The atmosphere is elevated by scale motifs scattering through the woodwinds, reminiscent of "Schéhérezade" and which during the second movement acquire a thematic significance. By means of a very demanding work of transition the guitar once again leads the orchestra to the first theme before throwing itself into the written cadenza.

Although the English horn contributes to the principal theme of the introverted second movement for some time, it would be an error to look for—or even, after forty years' time lapse, to hope for—another theme "in the style of Aranjuez."

In fact, despite its construction, this movement is the antithesis of its world-famous counterpoint. Its principal source is the rhythm rather than the melody. Here there is no sign of the rhythmic serenity of the preceding work; instead, there is a constant alternation of two rhythms, from 6/8 to 5/8, and this is further complicated by different groups within the interior of the rhythms (2x3 and 3x2 within 6/8, 3+2 and 2+3 in the 5/8). The result is a continuous and agitated wave, almost restless, through the movement. Then, at the heart of the cadenza (also written) a sort of peaceful rhythm is resolved in 3/4 ("Andante") before being re-expressed by the clarinet below the iridescent chords, once again taking up the initial theme until its magical resolution.

In contrast, the final rondo, where the percussion first appears, is extroverted and suitable for the setting of a party, with a *Sevillianas* as the main recurring theme. Two secondary themes appear, one in the brass, one in the woodwinds, gamboling through the episodes with a nonchalance and freedom, that brings to mind Stravinsky's "Fiesta del Carnaval."

JOAQUIN RODRIGO

EN LOS TRIGALES

(For solo guitar)

This piece forms part of a kind of imaginary Suite that I call "Through the Spanish Countryside." It is one of my most popular works for the guitar. *En los trigales* is set in Old Castile; the Castile region extends to the ends of the earth, as its inhabitants like to remark, and loves strong music. In contrast to the virile dance of the first part, a kind of recitation follows, with the faraway sound of bells, similar to a rest or respite during the difficult work of the harvest.

JOAQUIN RODRIGO

SONATA A LA ESPAÑOLA

(For solo guitar)

I have used the sonata form on various occasions, for different instruments. As an example I can mention *Sonata pimpante* for violin and piano, the *Sonata a la breve* for violoncello, the *Cinco sonatas de Castilla* for piano, and two sonatas for guitar, the *Sonata giocosa* and *Sonata a la española.* The phrase "*a la española*" should be understood as slightly ironic—an irony that becomes more apparent in the bolero, for example. This sonata follows the style of the classic forms and its technique is in the medium range. I composed it around 1970.

JOAQUIN RODRIGO

TIENTO ANTIGUO

(For solo guitar)

This piece evokes the music of the vihuela, an instrument similar to the guitar, and the Spanish version of the lute. This instrument was very popular during the 13th to 16th centuries, and was considered the instrument of elegant and educated society.

JOAQUIN RODRIGO

JUNTO AL GENERALIFE

(For solo guitar)

As in the case of *Bajando de la Meseta* and *En los trigales*, *Junto al Generalife* forms part of the imaginary Suite that describes the Spanish landscape. All the world has heard of the marvellous gardens of the Generalife, near the Alhambra; one can find the murmur of the perfumed breezes, a faraway sound of bells and flowers adorn the ground under the myrtle trees. And there too the guitar lies down and dreams.

JOAQUIN RODRIGO

FANDANGO

(For solo guitar)

This favorite piece of many guitarists forms part of a Suite of three pieces for the guitar (called "Passacaglia," "Fandango," and "Zapateado") composed in 1954, the same year as *Fantasía para un Gentilhombre* for guitar and orchestra. The "Fandango" is a dance that was once enjoyed by all Spanish social classes and should not be confused with the "fandanguillo," which is totally different. My fandango for guitar is a little solemn, but maintains a popular touch, for example in the central section, which contains various echoes of the "seguidilla" which recounts the heroic feats of brave smugglers.

JOAQUIN RODRIGO

ROMANCE DE DURANDARTE

(For solo guitar)

This composition was not originally intended as a piece for the guitar. The music is taken from the ballet *Pavana Real*, on which I collaborated with my wife, Victoria Kamhi. It is taken from a scene in which the female viceroy, Germaine de Foix, who is feeling irritable, dances to the sound of the ballad of Durandarte, the legendary "Knight of the Round Table."

JOAQUIN RODRIGO

EXCERPT FROM A LECTURE ON RODRIGO AND HIS MUSIC BY SPANISH WRITER GERARDO DIEGO

There is much to recall with admiration in Rodrigo's music, as one arrives at an adequate appreciation of his ability to create a musical reflection of the acoustic and optical landscape. I only want to point out the constant happiness with which he adds, separates or contrasts, in his songs, the warmth of the human voice to the silvery cool sound of the delicate, percussive piano. The landscape in this intimate framework acquires a luminous intensity, a sharp differentiation, a power to evoke poetic reality—all quite remarkable. Do you recall Gil Vicente's *Cantiga*? The sea, the mountains, the war have been trapped acoustically within a few notes, within certain rhythms that quickly penetrate directly into the depths of the human heart. How much pain and pleasure and intensive listening must it take to achieve this poetic distillation, this fierce, free essence of nature, integrated yet diverse, in such a winged synthesis? And what can be said about those cuckoo birds, about that audacious and inexhaustible creation of cuckoos that Joaquín Rodrigo gives flight to, allowing them to sing from the branches of vocal and instrumental music? Always faithful to their descending interval, they prefer, however, to appear when least expected, hiding within a counter-rhythm, camouflaging themselves among the irregular arabesques of balancing arpeggios, suggesting a new level of polytonality, sometimes melancholy, at other moments malicious and mocking.

GERARDO DIEGO
Rodrigo's Acoustic Landscape
Colon Theater, Bogotá, Colombia
November 8, 1957

CATALOG OF WORKS BY JOAQUIN RODRIGO

The following is the complete catalog of the musical production of Joaquín Rodrigo, divided into genres. The catalog has been updated, and along with each title presents the date of the composition of each work.

NOTES ON THE USE OF THIS CATALOGUE

This Catalogue contains all the music written by Joaquín Rodrigo from 1923 to the present (1989), which he wishes to preserve. The works are divided into nine large sections, each of which is given a specific letter: A = CONCERTOS, B = WORKS FOR ORCHESTRA, etc. Each work appears within its section in alphabetical order, and with a particular number: D1 = AVE MARIA. All the works, and also each individual piece which forms part of a larger work—each of the songs making up the songcycle CON ANTONIO MACHADO, for example—also appear in alphabetical order at the end, where the reader will find them with their corresponding letters and numbers, together with the page of the Catalogue where they appear.

Each work carries an approximate duration in minutes, its date of composition and the publishing house responsible for its publication or distribution.

The orchestration for each work appearing in sections A, B, C and J is shown in the normally accepted forms.

ORCHESTRATION

O	flauta	flute
(O)	(flautín)	(piccolo)
O	oboe	oboe
(O)	(corno inglés)	(cor anglais)
O	clarinete	clarinet
O	fagot	bassoon
O	trompa	horn
O	trompeta	trumpet
O	trombón	trombone
O	tuba	tuba
T	timbales	timpani
P	percusión	percussion
Str	cuerdas	strings

CATALOGO GENERAL DE OBRAS

A CONCIERTOS

1 CONCIERTO ANDALUZ (4 guitarras y orquesta) 25' 1967
2(1) 2 2 2 4 2 0 0 Str Ed. Joaquín Rodrigo
Schott

2 CONCIERTO COMO UN DIVERTIMENTO 21' 1981
(violonchelo y orquesta)
2 2 2 0 1 2 0 0 Cel Xyl Str Schott

3 CONCIERTO DE ARANJUEZ 20' 1939
(guitarra y orquesta)
2 2 2 2 2 2 0 0 Str Ed. Joaquín Rodrigo
Schott

3*A* *CONCIERTO DE ARANJUEZ* 20' 1974
(versión de Nicanor Zabaleta para arpa y orquesta)
2 2 2 2 2 2 0 0 Str Schott

4 CONCIERTO DE ESTIO (violín y orquesta) 20' 1943
2(1) 2 2 2 2 2 0 0 Str Ed. Joaquín Rodrigo

5 CONCIERTO HEROICO (piano y orquesta) 30' 1942
3(2) 2 2 2 4 2 3 0 P Str Ed. Joaquín Rodrigo
AMP

6 CONCIERTO IN MODO GALANTE 20' 1949
(violonchelo y orquesta)
2 2 2 2 2 2 0 0 Str Ed. Joaquín Rodrigo
Schott

7 CONCIERTO MADRIGAL 30' 1966
(2 guitarras y orquesta)
1 1 1 1 1 1 0 0 Str Schott

8 CONCIERTO PARA UNA FIESTA 27' 1982
(guitarra y orquesta)
1 2(1) 1 1 1 1 0 0 P Str Schott

9 CONCIERTO PASTORAL (flauta y orquesta) 25' 1977
0 CA 1 0 1 1 0 0 Str Schott

10 CONCIERTO SERENATA (arpa y orquesta) 23' 1952
2(1) 2 2 2 2 2 0 0 Str

11 FANTASIA PARA UN GENTILHOMBRE 22' 1954
(guitarra y orquesta)
2(1) 1 0 1 0 1 0 0 Str Schott

11*A* *FANTASIA PARA UN GENTILHOMBRE* 22' 1978
(versión de James Galway para flauta y orquesta)
0 1 1 1 1 1 0 0 Str

B OBRAS PARA ORQUESTA

1 ADAGIO (instrumentos de viento) 9' 1966
3(1) 3 3 2 4 3 3 1 Tx2 Ed. Joaquín Rodrigo

2 A LA BUSCA DEL MAS ALLA 17' 1976
2 2 CA 2 2 4 3 3 1 P Cel Hp Str Schott

2 bis A SAGUNTO 1955
(marcha para instrumentos de viento) Ed. Joaquín Rodrigo

3 CANÇONETA 4' 1923
Vln solo Str Schott

4 CINCO PIEZAS INFANTILES 12' 1924
3 3 3 2 4 3 3 1 P Cel Hp Str Schott

4 bis DEUX BERCEUSES 6' 1933
1 1 CA 1 0 1 1 0 0 P Cel Hp Str
Ed. Joaquín Rodrigo
Schott

i) Berceuse de otoño
ii) Berceuse de primavera

5 DOS DANZAS ESPAÑOLAS 9' 1966
2 2 2 2 2 2 0 0 Str Castañuelas Schott

6 DOS PIEZAS CABALLERESCAS 6' 1945
Orquesta de violonchelos Schott

6*A* *DOS PIEZAS CABALLERESCAS*
(versión para cuatro guitarras)

6 bis ESTUDIANTINA 3' 1962
(Rondalla) UME

7 HOMENAJE A LA TEMPRANICA 4' 1939
2 1 1 1 2 2 0 0 P Hp Str Schott

8 JUGLARES 5' 1923
3(2) 2 2 4 3 3 1 P Hp Str Ed. Joaquín Rodrigo

8 bis MIEDO 10' 1936
1(1) 1 1 1 2 1 0 0 P Hp Str Ed. Joaquín Rodrigo

9 MUSICA PARA UN JARDIN 12' 1957
1 1 CA 1 0 1 1 0 0 P Cel Hp Str Schott

10 PALILLOS Y PANDERETAS 12' 1982
2 2 2 2 2 2 0 0 P Str Schott

11 PASODOBLE PARA PACO ALCALDE 4' 1943
(instrumentos de viento)
2 2 6 5Sax 1 4 2F1 3 2 1 P Ed. Joaquín Rodrigo

12 PER LA FLOR DEL LLIRI BLAU 17' 1934
2(1) 2(1) 3 2 4 3 3 1 P2 Hp Str Ed. Joaquín Rodrigo

12*A* *PER LA FLOR DEL LLIFI BLAU*
(versión para instrumentos de viento)
3 3(1) 6 7Sax 2 4 4 3 2 2 3 2 P T

13 PRELUDIO PARA UN POEMA A LA ALHAMBRA 8' 1928
2 2 CA 2 2 4 3 3 1 P Hp Str Schott

13 bis RINCONES DE ESPAÑA 22' 1990
(versión de Angel Romero para Guitarra y Orquesta)
2(1) 222 2200 Str Ed. Joaquín Rodrigo

14 SOLERIANA 20' 1953
1 2 (1) 1 1 1 1 0 0 Str UME

15 SONES EN LA GIRALDA 10' 1963
2 1 1 1 1 1 0 0 Str Arpa solo Ed. Joaquín Rodrigo

15*A* *SONES EN LA GIRALDA*
(versión de Pepe Romero para guitarra y orquesta)

16 TRES VIEJOS AIRES DE DANZA 8' 1929
1 1 1 1 2 0 0 0 Str Schott

17 ZARABANDA LEJANA Y VILLANCICO 8' 1927/30
Str Ed. Joaquín Rodrigo

C OBRAS PARA VOZ Y ORQUESTA
(*texto)

1 AUSENCIAS DE DULCINEA (bajo y 4 sopranos) 15' 1948
* Miguel de Cervantes
3 2 2 3 4 3 3 1 P T Cel 2Hp Str Ed. Joaquín Rodrigo

1 bis CANTICO DE LA ESPOSA (soprano) 4' 1934
* San Juan de la Cruz
1 1(1) 0 1 1 0 0 0 P Str Schott

2 CANTICO DE SAN FRANCISCO DE ASIS (coro) 18' 1982
* San Francisco de Asís
2 2 2 0 4 2 3 1 P Cel Str Schott

3 CANTOS DE AMOR Y DE GUERRA (soprano) 12' 1965
* Anónimo
i) Paseábase el rey moro UME
ii) A las armas, moriscotes
iii) Ay, luna que reluces
iv) Sobre Daza estaba el rey
v) Pastorcito, tú que has vuelto
3(1) 2 2 0 4 2 0 1 P Hp Str

4 CUATRE CANÇONS EN LLENGUA CATALANA (soprano) 12' 1935
(véanse también H8, H9) Schott
i) Canço del teuladí * (Teodoro Llorente)
ii) Canticel * (Josep Carner)
iii) L'inquietut primaveral de la doncella * (Josep Masso i Ventos)
iv) Brollador gentil * (Joan Guash)
2(1) 1 1 1 2 2 0 0 P Hp x 2 Str

5 CUATRO MADRIGALES AMATORIOS (soprano) 12' 1948
* Anónimo
(véase también H15) Chester
i) ¿Con qué la lavaré?
ii) Vós me matasteis
iii) ¿De dónde venís, amore?
iv) De los álamos vengo, madre
2(1) 1(0) 1 0 1 1 0 0 Str

6 HIMNOS DE LOS NEOFITOS DE QUMRAN (3 sopranos y coro) 15' 1965
* Anónimo
2 0 0 1 0 0 0 0 P Cel Hp Str Schott

7 LIRICAS CASTELLANAS (soprano) 10' 1980
* Anónimo
i) San Juan y Pascua
ii) Despedida y soledad
iii) Espera del amado
Flauta de pico corneta de madera vihuela

8 MUSICA PARA UN CODICE SALMANTINO 14' 1953
* Miguel de Unamuno
(bajo y coro)
2(1) 2(1) 0 0 1 1 0 0 Hp Str UME

9 ROMANCE DEL COMENDADOR DE OCAÑA 5' 1947
* Lope de Vega
(véase también H33)
2 2 2 2 2 2 0 0 Hp Str UME

10 ROSALIANA (soprano) 12' 1965
* Rosalía de Castro
i) Cantar, ei, Galicia
ii) ¿Por qué?
iii) Adiós ríos, adiós fontes
iv) ¡Vamos bebendo!
1 1 1 0 1 0 0 0 P Str

10 bis SERRANILLA (soprano) 3' 1928
*Marqués de Santillana
1(0) 1(0) 1 1 2 2 0 0 Str Ed. Joaquín Rodrigo Schott

11 TRES VILLANCICOS (soprano) 7' 1952
(véase H41)
i) Pastorcito santo * (Lope de Vega)
ii) Coplillas de Belén * (Victoria Kamhi)
iii) Aire y donaire * (Anónimo)
2 2(1) 1 1 2 1 0 0 P Hp Str

12 TRIPTIC DE MOSEN CINTO (soprano) 12' 1936
*Jacinto Verdaguer
i) El arpa sagrada Ed. Joaquín Rodrigo
ii) Lo violi de San Francesch Schott
iii) San Francesch i la cigala
2(1) 1 CA 1 1 2 2 0 0 P Cel Hp Str

13 VILLANCICOS Y CANCIONES DE NAVIDAD 15' 1952
(soprano bajo y coro)
(véanse H20, H22)
i) Cantan por Belén pastores * (Victoria Kamhi)
ii) Duérmete, niño * (Victoria Kamhi)
iii) A la clavelina * (Lope de Vega)
iv) A la chiribirivuela * (Anónimo)
v) La espera * (Victoria Kamhi)
2(1) 1 CA 0 0 2 0 0 0 P Hp Str

D MUSICA CORAL
(véanse también secciones C y J)
(* texto)

1 AVE MARIA (SATB) 3' 1954
UME

2 CANTICOS NUPCIALES (SSS y órgano) 10' 1963
i) Entrada (órgano solo)
ii) Deus Israel * (Libro de Tobías)
iii) Ofertorio * (Salmo 31)
iv) Fughetta (órgano solo)
v) Comunión * (Salmo 128)
vi) Evangelio * (Juan, II)

3 DOS CANCIONES SEFARDIES DEL SIGLO XV (SATB) 4' 1951
* Anónimo
i) Malato está el hijo del rey UME
ii) El rey que muncho madruga

4 TRISTE ESTABA EL REY DAVID (SATB) 4' 1950
* Anónimo Schott

5 YO TINC UN BURRO (SATB) 2' 1933
* Anónimo UME

E OBRAS PARA PIANO
(véanse también secciones A, G y H)

1 AIR DE BALLET SUR LE NOM D'INE JEUNE FILLE 3' 1929
Ed. Joaquín Rodrigo

2 ALBUM DE CECILIA, EL (para manos pequeñas) 10' 1948
i) María de los Reyes (Sevillanas) UME
ii) A la jota (Jota de las palomas)
iii) Canción del hada rubia
iv) Canción del hada morena
v) El negrito Pepo
vi) Borriquillos a Belén

3 A L'OMBRE DE TORRE BERMEJA 4' 1945
Schott

4 ARANJUEZ, MA PENSEE 4' 1968
(versión del 2º tiempo del *Concierto de Aranjuez*)
Ed. Joaquín Rodrigo

5 ATARDECER (4 manos) 8' 1975
Schott

6 BAGATELA 3' 1926
Ed. Joaquín Rodrigo
Schott

7	CINCO PIEZAS DEL SIGLO XVI	10'	1938
	i) Diferencias sobre el Canto del Caballero (Cabezón)		Schott
	ii) Pavana (Milán)		
	iii) Pavana (Milán)		
	iv) Pavana (Valderrábano)		
	v) Fantasía (Mudarra)		
8	CINCO PIEZAS INFANTILES (para dos pianos)	12'	1928
	(véase también B4)		Schott
	i) Son chicos que pasan		
	ii) Después de un cuento		
	iii) Mazurka		
	iv) Plegaria		
	v) Gritería final		
9	CINCO SONATAS DE CASTILLA	22'	1951
	con Toccata a modo de pregón		Schott
	i) Sonata		
	ii) Sonata en Fa sostenido menor		
	iii) Sonata en Re		
	iv) Sonata como un tiento		
	v) Sonata en La		
10	CUATRO ESTAMPAS ANDALUZAS	11'	1946/52
	i) El vendedor de chanquetes		UME
	ii) Crepúsculo sobre el Guadalquivir		
	iii) Seguidillas del diablo		
	iv) Barquitos de Cádiz		
11	CUATRO PIEZAS PARA PIANO	11'	1936
	i) Caleseras (Homenaje a Chueca)		Ed. Joaquín Rodrigo
	ii) Fandango del ventorrillo		
	iii) Plegaria de la Infanta de Castilla		
	iv) Danza valenciana		
12	DANZA DE LA AMAPOLA	2'	1972
			UME
12 bis	DEUX BERCEUSES	6'	1923/28
	(véase 34 bis)		Ed. Joaquín Rodrigo
13	GRAN MARCHA DE LOS SUBSECRETARIOS	5'	1941
	(Para 4 manos)		UME
14	PASTORAL	2'	1926
			Ed. Joaquín Rodrigo

15	PRELUDIO AL GALLO MANANERO	4'	1926 Ed. Joaquín Rodrigo Schott
16	PRELUDIO DE AÑORANZA	2'	1987 Ed. Joaquín Rodrigo
17	SERENATA ESPANOLA	4'	1931 Ed. Joaquín Rodrigo Schott
18	SONADA DE ADIOS	3'	1935 Ed. Joaquín Rodrigo
19	SONATINA PARA DOS MUÑECAS (4 manos) i) Empieza el día ii) Alegres peripecias iii) Recogimiento iv) Vuelta del cole	7'	1977 Real Musical
20	SUITE PARA PIANO i) Preludio ii) Siciliana iii) Bourrée iv) Minué v) Rigodón	10'	1923 Ed. Joaquín Rodrigo Schott
21	TRES DANZAS DE ESPAÑA i) Rústica ii) Danza de las tres doncellas iii) Serrana	5'	1941 Schott
22	TRES EVOCACIONES i) Tarde en el parque ii) Noche junto al Guadalquivir iii) Mañana en Triana	10'	1981 Schott
23	ZARABANDA LEJANA (véanse también B17, F23)	4'	1926 Ed. Joaquín Rodrigo

F OBRAS PARA GUITARRA
(véanse también secciones A, G y H)

1	ALBUM DE CECILIA, EL (versión por José de Azpiazu) i) María de los Reyes (Sevillanas) ii) A la jota (Jota de las palomas) iii) Canción del hada rubia iv) Canción del hada morena	10'	1948 UME

2	ARANJUEZ, MA PENSEE (versión del 2º tiempo del *Concierto de Aranjuez*)	4'	1968	Ed. Joaquín Rodrigo
3	BAJANDO DE LA MESETA	4'	1954	Ed. Joaquín Rodrigo
3 bis	DOS PIEZAS CABALLERESCAS (versión para cuatro guitarras)	6'	1945	Schott
4	DOS PRELUDIOS	6'	1977	Ed. Joaquín Rodrigo
5	ECOS DE SEFARAD	3'	1987	Ed. Joaquín Rodrigo
6	ELOGIO DE LA GUITARRA	10'	1971	Berben
7	FANDANGO DEL VENTORRILLO (2 guitarras) (véase también E11)	2'	1965	Ed. Joaquín Rodrigo
8	INVOCACION Y DANZA	9'	1962	Ed. Joaquín Rodrigo
9	JUNTO AL GENERALIFE	6'	1959	Bote & Bock
10	PAJAROS DE PRIMAVERA	3'	1972	UME
11	PASTORAL (véase también E14)	2'	1965	Ed. Joaquín Rodrigo
12	POR LOS CAMPOS DE ESPAÑA i) En los trigales ii) Entre olivares	8'	1939/42	Ed. Joaquín Rodrigo
13	POR TIERRAS DE JEREZ	4'	1960	Ricordi (Milano)
14	¡QUE BUEN CAMINITO!	3'	1987	Ed. Joaquín Rodrigo
15	SONATA A LA ESPAÑOLA	9'	1969	Ed. Joaquín Rodrigo
16	SONATA GIOCOSA	10'	1960	Chester

17	TIENTO ANTIGUO	3'	1947
			Bote & Bock
18	TONADILLA (2 guitarras)	10'	1959
			Ricordi (Paris)
19	TRES PEQUENAS PIEZAS	6'	1963
	i) Ya se van los pastores		Ed. Joaquín Rodrigo
	ii) Por Caminos de Santiago		
	iii) Pequeña Sevillana		
20	TRES PIEZAS ESPAÑOLAS	10'	1954
	i) Passacaglia		Schott
	ii) Fandango		
	iii) Zapateado		
21	TRIPTIC PARA GUITARRA	12'	1978
	i) Preludio		Schott
	ii) Nocturno		
	iii) Schercino		
22	UN TIEMPO FUE ITALICA FAMOSA	5'	1981
			Schott
23	ZARABANDA LEJANA	4'	1926
	(véanse también B17, E23)		Ed. Joaquín Rodrigo

G	OTRAS OBRAS INSTRUMENTALES		
1	ARIA ANTIGUA (flauta y piano)	4'	1960
			UME
1*A*	*ARIA ANTIGUA* (flauta y guitarra)		
2	CAPRICCIO (violín solo)	7'	1944
			Ed. Joaquín Rodrigo
			Schott
3	COMO UNA FANTASIA (violonchelo solo)	8'	1979
			Schott
4	DOS ESBOZOS (violín y piano)	5'	1923
	i) La enamorada junto al surtidor		Ed. Joaquín Rodrigo
	ii) Pequeña ronda		Schott
5	IMPROMPTU (arpa)	3'	1959
			UME

6 MOTO PERPETUO (bandoneón) 4' 1960
Schott

7 PRELUDIO Y RITORNELLO (clavicémbalo) 6' 1978
Ed. Joaquín Rodrigo

8 RINCONES DE ESPAÑA (armónica) 10' 1957
Ed. Joaquín Rodrigo

8*A* *RINCONES DE ESPAÑA* (guitarra y orquesta)
(véase B13 bis)

9 RUMANIANA (violín y piano) 8' 1943
UME

10 SERENATA AL ALBA DEL DIA 7' 1982
(flauta o violín y guitarra) Schott

11 SET CANÇONS VALENCIANES (violín y piano) 17' 1982
Schott

12 SICILIANA (violonchelo y piano) 5' 1929
Ed. Joaquín Rodrigo

13 SONATA A LA BREVE (violonchelo y piano) 10' 1977
Schott

14 SONATA PIMPANTE (violín y piano) 17' 1965
Ed. Joaquín Rodrigo

H CANCIONES CON PIANO
(*CON GUITARRA) (**texto)
(véanse también secciones C y J)

1 ARANJUEZ, MA PENSEE 4' 1988
** Victoria Kamhi
(versión del 2º tiempo del *Concierto de Aranjuez*)
Ed. Joaquín Rodrigo

2 ARANJUEZ MON AMOUR 4' 1967
** Guy Bontempelli
(versión del 2o tiempo del *Concierto de Aranjuez*)
Ed. Joaquín Rodrigo

3 ARBOL 2' 1987
** Fina de Calderón Ed. Joaquín Rodrigo

4 BARCAROLA 3' 1938
** Victoria Kamhi Schott

5	CANCION DEL CUCU ** Victoria Kamhi	3'	1937 Schott
6	CANCION DEL GRUMETE ** Anónimo	2'	1938 Schott
7	CANCION DE MI VIDA, LA ** Castell-Vilaseca (de *EL DUENDE AZUL*, véase J6)	3'	1946 UME
8	CANÇO DEL TEULADI ** Teodoro Llorente (véase también C4)	2'	1934 Schott
9	CANTICEL ** Josep Carner (véase también C4)	3'	1938 Schott
10	CANTICO DE LA ESPOSA ** San Juan de la Cruz (véase C1 bis)	4'	1934 Schott
11	CANTIGA ** Gil Vicente	3'	1925 Ed. Joaquín Rodrigo Schott
12	CON ANTONIO MACHADO (ciclo de 10 canciones) i) Preludio ii) Mi corazón te aguarda iii) Tu voz y tu mano iv) Mañana de abril v) Los sueños vi) Cantaban los niños vii) ¿Recuerdas? viii) Fiesta en el prado ix) Abril galán x) Canción del Duero	25'	1972 UME
13	COPLAS DEL PASTOR ENAMORADO ** Lope de Vega	3'	1935 Schott
13*A*	*COPLAS DEL PASTOR ENAMORADO**		
14	CUATRO CANCIONES SEFARDIES ** Anónimo i) Respondemos ii) Una pastora yo amí iii) Canción de cuna iv) Morena me llaman	8'	1967 Ed. Joaquín Rodrigo

15 CUATRO MADRIGALES AMATORIOS 10' 1947
** Anónimo
(véase también C5) Chester
i) ¿Con qué la lavaré?
ii) Vos me matasteis
iii) ¿De dónde venís, amore?
iv) De los álamos vengo, madre

16 DESPEDIDA Y SOLEDAD
** Anónimo
(de *LIRICAS CASTELLANAS*, véase C7) Schott

17 DOCE CANCIONES ESPAÑOLAS 15' 1951
** Popular
(véase también H40) Schott
i) Viva la novia y el novio
ii) De ronda
iii) Una palomita blanca
iv) Canción de baile con pandero
v) Porque toco el pandero
vi) Tararán
vii) En las montañas de Asturias
viii) Estando yo en mi majada
ix) Adela
x) En Jerez de la Frontera
xi) San José y María
xii) Canción de cuna

18 DOS CANCIONES PARA CANTAR A LOS NIÑOS 5' 1973
** Anónimo
i) Corderito blanco UME
ii) Quedito

19 DOS POEMAS DE JUAN RAMON JIMENEZ 5' 1965
(con flauta o violín)
i) Verde verderol
ii) Pájaro del agua

20 DUERMETE, NIÑO (soprano y bajo) 3' 1952
(de *VILLANCICOS Y CANCIONES DE* Schott
NAVIDAD, véase C13)

21 EN ARANJUEZ, CON TU AMOR 4' 1988
** Alfredo García Segura
(versión del 2º tiempo del *Concierto de Aranjuez*)
Ed. Joaquín Rodrigo

22 ESPERA, LA 3' 1952
(de *VILLANCICOS Y CANCIONES DE* Schott
NAVIDAD, véase C13)

23	ESPERA DEL AMADO ** Anónimo (de *LIRICAS CASTELLANAS*, véase C7)		Schott
24	ESTA NIÑA SE LLEVA LA FLOR ** Francisco de Figueroa	3'	1934 Schott
25	ESTRIBILLO ** S. J. Polo de Medina	2'	1934 Schott
26	FINO CRISTAL ** C. Rodríguez Pinto	3'	1935 Schott
27	FOLIAS CANARIAS ** Anónimo	3'	1948 Schott
27A	*FOLIAS CANARIAS**		
28	GROTTE, LA ** Louis Emié	3'	1962 Ed. Joaquín Rodrigo
29	MAR ME LLAMA, EL ** Castell-Vilaseca (de *EL DUENDE AZUL*, véase J6)	3'	1946 UME
30	¿POR QUE TE LLAMARE? ** Fina de Calderón	2'	1987 Ed. Joaquín Rodrigo
31	ROMANCE DE DURANDARTE* ** Anónimo	3'	1955 UME
32	ROMANCE DE LA INFANTINA DE FRANCIA ** Anónimo	5'	1928 Ed. Joaquín Rodrigo Schott
33	ROMANCE DEL COMENDADOR DE OCANA (véase también C9)	5'	1948 UME
34	ROMANCILLO ** Anónimo	3'	1954 Schott
35	SAN JUAN Y PASCUA ** Anónimo (de *LIRICAS CASTELLANAS*, véase C7)		Schott
36	SEIS ARIAS DE *EL HIJO FINGIDO* ** Lope de Vega (véase J10) i) Coplillas del Alférez ii) Cavaletta de Leonardo	18'	1963 Ed. Joaquín Rodrigo

iii) Arietta de Angela
iv) Canción de Angela
v) Romanza de Angela
vi) «Vivo y es mucho deciros»

37	SERRANILLA (véase C10 bis)	3'	1928 Ed. Joaquín Rodrigo Schott
38	SOBRE EL CUPEY ** L. Hernández Aquino	3'	1965 Schott
39	SONETO ** J. Bautista de Mesa	3'	1950 Schott
40	TRES CANCIONES ESPAÑOLAS* (véase H17) i) En Jerez de la Frontera ii) Adela iii) De ronda	6'	1951 Schott
41	TRES VILLANCICOS i) Pastorcito santo ii) Coplillas de Belén iii) Aire y donaire (véase C11)	7'	1952 Schott
41*A*	*TRES VILLANCICOS**	7'	1952 Schott
42	¡UN HOME, SAN ANTONIO! ** Rosalía de Castro	3'	1951 Schott

J MUSICA PARA TEATRO Y CINE

1	AZUCENA DE QUITO, LA (Cantata) Despedida de Azucena: Aria para soprano, oboe, corno inglés y celesta	8'	1960 Ed. Joaquín Rodrigo
2	BELLA DURMIENTE, LA (Tchaikowsky/Rodrigo (Teatro) 1 1 2 1 2 1 0 0 Str	3'	1962 Ed. Joaquín Rodrigo
3	CYRANO DE BERGERAC (Teatro) 1(fltn) 0 0 0 0 1 0 0 P Str	5'	1955 Schott
4	DESDEN CON EL DESDEN, EL (Teatro) flauta guitarra violín viola alto coro de mujeres	2'	1951 Ed. Joaquín Rodrigo

5 DESTRUCCION DE SAGUNTO, LA (Teatro) 30' 1954
1(fltn) 3 2 CA 2 0 4 3 3 1 P Hp soprano coro
Ed. Joaquín Rodrigo
- i) Danza de los tristes augurios
- ii) Homenaje a Sagunto

6 DUENDE AZUL, EL 6' 1946
(Opereta de Moreno Torroba y Rodrigo)
(véanse H7, H29) UME
- i) Canción de mi vida, La (Rodrigo)
- ii) Mar me llama, El (Rodrigo)

7 EDIPO (Teatro) 4' 1956
1 1 0 0 0 1 0 0 P Schott

8 GUERRA DE DIOS, LA (Cine) 1953
Ed. Joaquín Rodrigo

9 HEREJE, EL (Cine) 1956
Ed. Joaquín Rodrigo

10 HIJO FINGIDO, EL (Zarzuela) 80' 1960
1(1) 1 1 1 2 1 0 0 Hp T P Str Ed. Joaquín Rodrigo

10*A* SEIS ARIAS DE *EL HIJO FINGIDO*
(véase H36)

11 JUANA Y LOS CALDEREROS (Ballet) 20' 1956
Reducción para piano Ed. Joaquín Rodrigo

12 MUSICA PARA UN JARDIN (Cine) 12' 1957
(véase B9) Schott

13 PAVANA REAL (Ballet) 30' 1954
2 2 2 2 4 2 2 1 P Gtr/Hp Str tenor solo Schott
- i) El Deseo (Ricercare a modo de diana)
- ii) Danza de Damas y Caballeros
- iii) Zarabanda de amor
- iv) Escena y danza de los bufones
- iv bis) Cantiga de pastor
- v) Introducción y danza de cazadores
- vi) Escena de cetrería
- vii) Romance
- vii bis) Jornada III
- viii) Fiesta de Mayo
- ix) Danza del Heraldo y Cupido
- x) Danza del buen desear
- xi) Pavana de la Reina
- xii) Danza Final

14	SONNICA, LA CORTESANA (Teatro) 2(1) 2 2 2 4 3 3 1 P Hp	20' 1975 Ed. Joaquín Rodrigo
15	SOR INTREPIDA (Cine)	1952 Ed. Joaquín Rodrigo
16	TIESTES (Teatro) 2(1) 1 1 0 4 2 3 1 P Hp Piano	10' 1956 Ed. Joaquín Rodrigo
17	VIDA ES SUEÑO, LA (Teatro) 1 1 1 0 4 3 3 0 P Hp Str	10' 1950 Ed. Joaquín Rodrigo

INDICE DE OBRAS POR ORDEN ALFABETICO

HONORS HELD BY JOAQUIN RODRIGO

1939	Collaborator, Music Dept, Spanish National Radio. Chief of the Music Section of ONCE (Spanish National Organization for the Blind) Music Critic *Pueblo; Marca; Madrid.*
1942	National Music Award for *Concierto Heroico.*
1945	Alfonso X el Sabio Fellowship.
1947	Creator and Professor of the Manuel de Falla Chair, Faculty of Philosophy and Letters of the Complutense University, Madrid.
1948	Cervantes Prize.
1950	Numerary Member of the Royal Academy of Fine Arts of San Fernando of Madrid.
1953	Grand Cross of Alfonso X el Sabio.
1954	Elected Vice-President of SIMC (International Society of Contemporary Music).
1960	Order of *Officier des Arts et Lettres*, awarded by the French government.
1961	*Coupe de la guitare* Prize (France) awarded for *Invocación y Danza.*
1963	Order of *Chevalier de La Légion d'Honneur* awarded by the French government.
1964	*Doctor Honoris Causa* awarded by the University of Salamanca.
1966	Grand Cross of Civil Merit. Gold Medal for Meritorious Work.
1968	Member of the *Société Européenne de la Culture.* Member of the *Académie du Monde Latin.* Honorary Member of the San Carlos Academy, Valencia.

1976 Honorary Fellow of the Madrid *Ateneo*.
President of the Spanish National Committee for Music, CIM (International Music Council), UNESCO.

1979 Member of the Académie Royale des Sciences, des Lettres et des Beaux-Arts of Belgium.

1980 Gold Medal for Merit in Fine Arts.

1982 National Music Prize.
Doctor Honoris Causa, University of Southern California.

1987 Gold Medal of the Valencia Generalitat.
Honorary Member of the Valencia Generalitat.

1988 *Doctor Honoris Causa*, Polytechnic University of Valencia.
Director of the Royal Academy of Fine Arts of San Fernando de Madrid.

1989 Gold Medal, Complutense University of Madrid.
Honorary Advisor, SGAE (General Society of Spanish Authors).
Doctor Honoris Causa, University of Alicante.
Doctor Honoris Causa, Complutense University of Madrid.
Medal of Artistic Merit, City of Madrid.

1990 *Doctor Honoris Causa*, University of Exeter.
Gold Medal, Madrid.

1991 Conservatory of Valencia renamed in honor of Joaquín Rodrigo.
Recipient of the Silver Seal of the Valencia Council.
Fundación Guerrero Prize.
Title of Marqués de los Jardines de Aranjuez, conferred by King Juan Carlos of Spain.

HONORS AWARDED TO VICTORIA KAMHI

1977 Awarded the Alfonso X the Wise medal.

1981 Received the Gold Medal of Mexico City, Mexico, for having saved her husband's life during a hotel fire in the María Isabel Sheraton Hotel of Mexico City.

1981 Gold Medal of the Red Cross of Spain.

1982 Named an adoptive daughter of the city of Sagunto.

1991 Awarded the Noblelady's "Ribbon of Queen Isabella."